Linda S. Brunauer Karen J. Weichelman

# INSTRUCTOR'S RESOURCE MANUAL

# CHEMISTRY

## THE CENTRAL SCIENCE

Ninth Edition

Brown LeMay Bursten

Upper Saddle River, NJ 07458

Project Manager: Kristen Kaiser
Acquisitions Editor: Nicole Folchetti
Editor in Chief: John Challice
Executive Managing Editor: Kathleen Schiaparelli
Assistant Managing Editor: Dinah Thong
Production Editor: Natasha Wolfe
Supplement Cover Management/Design: Paul Gourhan
Manufacturing Buyer: Ilene Kahn
*Cover Image Credit: Ken Eward/Biografx*

Pearson Education, Inc.
Upper Saddle River, NJ 07458



The author and publisher of this book have used their best efforts in preparing this book. These efforts include the development, research, and testing of the theories and programs to determine their effectiveness. The author and publisher make no warranty of any kind, expressed or implied, with regard to these programs or the documentation contained in this book. The author and publisher shall not be liable in any event for incidental or consequential damages in connection with, or arising out of, the furnishing, performance, or use of these programs.

Printed in the United States of America

10 9 8 7 6 5 4 3 2 1

ISBN 0-13-009802-7

Pearson Education Ltd., *London*
Pearson Education Australia Pty. Ltd., *Sydney*
Pearson Education Singapore, Pte. Ltd.
Pearson Education North Asia Ltd., *Hong Kong*
Pearson Education Canada, Inc., *Toronto*
Pearson Educacíon de Mexico, S.A. de C.V.
Pearson Education—Japan, *Tokyo*
Pearson Education Malaysia, Pte. Ltd.
Pearson Education, *Upper Saddle River, New Jersey*

# A Note to the Instructor

Our chapter sequence provides a fairly standard organization, but we recognize that not everyone teaches all of the topics in exactly the order we have chosen. We have therefore made sure that instructors can make common changes in teaching sequence with no loss in student comprehension. In particular, many instructors prefer to introduce gases (Chapter 10) after stoichiometry (Chapter 3) or after thermochemistry (Chapter 5) rather than with states of matter. The chapter on gases has been written to permit this change with *no* disruption in the flow of material. It is also possible to treat the balancing of redox equations (Sections 20.1 and 20.2) earlier, after the introduction of redox reactions in Section 4.4. Finally, thermodynamics (Chapters 5 and 19) can be taught as a single unit, either early or late in the book. The following summary describes these possible changes in greater detail and gives some suggested considerations:

**Common alternative chapter sequences in using BLB9:**

If you wish to cover *gases* earlier in the course than Chapter 10, there are several available options:

- Chapter 10 (Gases) – can be used with no disruption anywhere after Chapter 3. One of the authors has successfully covered Sections 10.1 – 10.6 (dealing with the gas laws and their applications) before thermochemistry (Chapter 5), and then treated Sections 10.7-10.9 (dealing with the kinetic-molecular theory and its applications) before Chapter 11 (Intermolecular Forces, Liquids, and Solids).

If you wish to cover *balancing redox equations* as part of the discussion of solution reactions in Chapter 4:

- Sections 20.1 and 20.2 (Redox Equations) can be seamlessly moved to be covered immediately after Section 4.4.

If you wish to cover *thermodyanmics* (Chapters 5 and 19) together, you have two options:

- If you wish to delay coverage of Chapter 5, you should cover Section 5.1 before Chapter 6 to assure that students grasp the general concept of energy and are familiar with the units in which it is expressed. That allows treatment of energy-related discussions associated with electronic structure and bonding (such as ionization energy) to be discussed with no difficulty. The rest of Chapter 5 can then be taught with Chapter 19.

- If you wish to cover Chapter 19 earlier, the discussion of entropy and the second law of thermodynamics (Sections 19.1-19.4) can be taught with Chapter 5. The discussion of free energy, however, brings in the concept of equilibrium (especially Section 19.7), and much of that topic flows more naturally after Chapter 15. If you wish to discuss free energy earlier, you must consider whether you want to introduce the idea of chemical equilibrium and the equilibrium constant as part of that discussion.

## ACKNOWLEDGEMENT

We would like to thank our families, friends and colleagues for their advice, encouragement and support throughout the often hectic process of preparing this resource manual.

# Table of Contents


CHAPTER 1. INTRODUCTION: MATTER AND MEASUREMENT ..... 1

CHAPTER 2. ATOMS, MOLECULES, AND IONS ..... 14

CHAPTER 3. STOICHIOMETRY: CALCULATIONS WITH CHEMICAL FORMULAS AND EQUATIONS ..... 27

CHAPTER 4. AQUEOUS REACTIONS AND SOLUTION STOICHIOMETRY ..... 40

CHAPTER 5. THERMOCHEMISTRY ..... 55

CHAPTER 6. ELECTRONIC STRUCTURE OF ATOMS ..... 66

CHAPTER 7. PERIODIC PROPERTIES OF THE ELEMENTS ..... 78

CHAPTER 8. BASIC CONCEPTS OF CHEMICAL BONDING ..... 89

CHAPTER 9. MOLECULAR GEOMETRY AND BONDING THEORIES ..... 101

CHAPTER 10. GASES ..... 116

CHAPTER 11. INTERMOLECULAR FORCES, LIQUIDS, AND SOLIDS ..... 129

CHAPTER 12. MODERN MATERIALS ..... 146

CHAPTER 13. PROPERTIES OF SOLUTIONS ..... 159

CHAPTER 14. CHEMICAL KINETICS ..... 175

CHAPTER 15. CHEMICAL EQUILIBRIUM ..... 193

CHAPTER 16. ACID-BASE EQUILIBRIA ..... 204

CHAPTER 17. ADDITIONAL ASPECTS OF AQUEOUS EQUILIBRIA ..... 218

CHAPTER 18. CHEMISTRY OF THE ENVIRONMENT ..... 231

CHAPTER 19. CHEMICAL THERMODYNAMICS ..... 243

CHAPTER 20. ELECTROCHEMISTRY ..... 253

CHAPTER 21. NUCLEAR CHEMISTRY ..... 267

CHAPTER 22. CHEMISTRY OF THE NONMETALS ..... 279

CHAPTER 23. METALS AND METALLURGY ..... 298

CHAPTER 24. CHEMISTRY OF COORDINATION COMPOUNDS .................................................. 309

CHAPTER 25. THE CHEMISTRY OF LIFE: ORGANIC AND BIOLOGICAL CHEMISTRY .......... 321

# Chapter 1. Introduction: Matter and Measurement

## Media Resources

### Figures and Tables

| **In Transparency Pack and on MediaPortfolio:** | **Section:** |
|---|---|
| Figure 1.5 Elements, Compounds and Mixtures | 1.2 Classifications of Matter |
| Figure 1.6 Abundance of Elements | 1.2 Classifications of Matter |
| Figure 1.9 Classification Scheme for Matter | 1.2 Classifications of Matter |
| Figure 1.13 Distillation Apparatus | 1.3 Properties of Matter |
| Figure 1.15 The Scientific Method | 1.3 Properties of Matter |
| Table 1.5 Selected Prefixes Used in the Metric System | 1.4 Units of Measurement |
| Figure 1.25 Accuracy and Precision | 1.5 Uncertainty in Measurement |

| **On MediaPortfolio:** | **Section:** |
|---|---|
| Figure 1.1 Molecular Models | 1.1 The Study of Chemistry |
| Figure 1.10 Reaction of $H_2$ With $O_2$ | 1.3 Properties of Matter |
| Table 1.4 SI Base Units | 1.4 Units of Measurement |
| Figure 1.18 Comparison of Temperature Scales | 1.4 Units of Measurement |
| Figure 1.19 Comparison of Volume Units | 1.4 Units of Measurement |
| Figure 1.20 Common Laboratory Devices | 1.4 Units of Measurement |

| **Animations:** | **Section:** |
|---|---|
| Electrolysis of Water | 1.2 Classifications of Matter |

| **Movies:** | **Section:** |
|---|---|
| Mixtures and Compounds | 1.3 Properties of Matter |
| Paper Chromatography of Ink | 1.3 Properties of Matter |
| Sodium and Potassium in Water | 1.3 Properties of Matter |

| **Activities:** | **Section:** |
|---|---|
| Phases of Matter | 1.2 Classifications of Matter |
| Classification of Matter | 1.2 Classifications of Matter |
| Distillation of Saltwater | 1.3 Properties of Matter |
| Significant Figures | 1.5 Uncertainty in Measurement |

| **3-D Models** | **Section:** |
|---|---|
| Oxygen | 1.1 The Study of Chemistry |
| Water | 1.1 The Study of Chemistry |
| Carbon Dioxide | 1.1 The Study of Chemistry |
| Ethanol | 1.1 The Study of Chemistry |
| Ethylene Glycol | 1.1 The Study of Chemistry |
| Aspirin | 1.1 The Study of Chemistry |

# Other Resources

| **Further Readings:** | **Section:** |
|---|---|
| Chemistry in the Real World | 1.1 The Study of Chemistry |
| Chemicals in Everyday Life | 1.1 The Study of Chemistry |
| A Miracle Drug | 1.1 The Study of Chemistry |
| What's the Use? | 1.2 Classifications of Matter |
| It's Elementary | 1.2 Classifications of Matter |
| Important Elements | 1.2 Classifications of Matter |
| Origin of the Names of Chemical Elements | 1.2 Classifications of Matter |
| Element 110 Makes a Very Fleeting Debut | 1.2 Classifications of Matter |
| Elementary My Dear Watson | 1.2 Classifications of Matter |
| Elementary Riddles | 1.2 Classifications of Matter |
| T-Shirt Chromatography: A Chromatogram You Can Wear | 1.3 Properties of Matter |
| Why Does Popcorn Pop? An Introduction to the Scientific Method | 1.3 Properties of Matter |
| Using History to Teach The Scientific Method: The Case of Argon | 1.3 Properties of Matter |
| Having Fun with the Metric System | 1.4 Units of Measurement |
| Le Grand K | 1.4 Units of Measurement |
| Method for Separating or Identifying Plastics | 1.4 Units of Measurement |
| Bearing Down on the Kilogram Standard | 1.4 Units of Measurement |
| Meter Sticks in the Demonstration of Error Measurements | 1.4 Units of Measurement |
| Basic Principles of Scale Reading | 1.4 Units of Measurement |
| Measuring with a Purpose. Involving Students in the Learning Process | 1.4 Units of Measurement |
| *Scientific American*, September 2001 | 1.4 Units of Measurement |
| Precision and Accuracy in Measurements: A Tale of Four Graduated Cylinders | 1.5 Uncertainty in Measurement |
| Error, Precision, and Uncertainty | 1.5 Uncertainty in Measurement |
| Significant Figures | 1.5 Uncertainty in Measurement |
| Significant Figures: A Classroom Demonstration | 1.5 Uncertainty in Measurement |
| A Joke Based on Significant Figures | 1.5 Uncertainty in Measurement |
| A Simple but Effective Demonstration for Illustrating Significant Figure Rules When Making Measurements and Doing Calculations | 1.5 Uncertainty in Measurement |
| Expanded Dimensional Analysis: A Blending of English and Math | 1.6 Dimensional Analysis |
| Appalachian Trail Problems | 1.6 Dimensional Analysis |

| **Live Demonstrations:** | **Section:** |
|---|---|
| The First Demonstration: Proof that Air is a Substance | 1.1 The Study of Chemistry |

| | |
|---|---|
| Science Demonstrations, Experiments, and Resources. A Reference List for Elementary through College Teachers Emphasizing Chemistry with Some Physics and Life Science | 1.1 The Study of Chemistry |
| Ira Remsen's Investigation of Nitric Acid | 1.3 Properties of Matter |
| An Experiment to Demonstrate the Application of the Scientific Method | 1.3. Properties of Matter |
| A Simple Demonstration for Introducing the Metric System to Introductory Chemistry Classes | 1.4 Units of Measurement |
| Sugar in a Can of Soft Drink: A Density Exercise | 1.4 Units of Measurement |
| The Mysterious Sunken Ice Cube | 1.4 Units of Measurement |
| Densities and Miscibilities of Liquids and Liquid Mixtures | 1.4 Units of Measurement |

# Chapter 1. Introduction: Matter and Measurement

## Common Student Misconceptions

- Students often confuse mass and weight.
- Students have difficulty with algebraic manipulation. Conversion of temperatures between Celsius and Fahrenheit scales is particularly problematic.
- Students tend to equate density with mass.
- Students may not be familiar with many of the commonly used metric system prefixes.
- Students often use precision and accuracy interchangeably.
- Students often cannot find exact numbers in calculations.
- Students have problems with the difference in emphasis between significant figures and decimal places in arithmetic manipulations.
- Students often either round off too soon in calculations or they report the result to as many figures as their calculators produce.
- Some students do not understand the use of a conversion factor of exactly 1.
- Many students have problems using dimensional analysis ("from physics") in chemistry. This text bases the whole of stoichiometry on dimensional analysis: students should be encouraged to embrace the concept as soon as possible.
- In dimensional analysis problems students do not see that a physical quantity is a multiplication of value and units. Therefore, they do not perform algebraic operations on both the number and units.

## Lecture Outline

### 1.1 The Study of Chemistry

- Chemistry:
  - Study of properties of materials and changes that they undergo.
  - Can be applied to all aspects of life (e.g., development of pharmaceuticals, leaf color change in fall etc.).

#### The Molecular Perspective of Chemistry[1,2,3,4,5,6,7,8]

Chemistry involves the study of the properties and behavior of matter.

- **Matter**:
  - Physical material of the universe.
  - Has mass.
  - Occupies space.
  - ~100 **Elements** constitute all matter.
- **Elements**:

---

[1] "Oxygen" 3-D Model from MediaPortfolio
[2] "Water" 3-D Model from MediaPortfolio
[3] "Carbon Dioxide" 3-D Model from MediaPortfolio
[4] "Ethanol" 3-D Model from MediaPortfolio
[5] "Ethylene Glycol" 3-D Model from MediaPortfolio
[6] "Aspirin" 3-D Model from MediaPortfolio
[7] Figure 1.1 from MediaPortfolio
[8] "The First Demonstration: Proof that Air is a Substance" from Live Demonstrations

- Made up of unique **atoms**.
- Names of the elements are derived from a wide variety of sources (e.g., Latin or Greek, mythological characters, names of people or places).

- **Molecules**:
  - Combinations of atoms held together in specific shapes.
  - Macroscopic (observable) properties of matter relate to microscopic realms of atoms.
  - Properties relate to composition (types of atoms present) and structure (arrangement of atoms) present.

### Why Study Chemistry?[9,10,11,12]

We study chemistry because:

- It has a considerable impact on society (health care, food, clothing, conservation of natural resources, environmental issues etc.).
- It is part of your curriculum! Chemistry serves biology, engineering, agriculture, geology, physics etc. **Chemistry is the *central science*.**

## 1.2 Classifications of Matter

- Matter is classified by *state* (solid, liquid or gas) or by *composition* (element, compound or mixture).

### States of Matter[13]

- Solids, liquids and gases are the three forms of matter called the **states of matter**.
- Properties described on the macroscopic level:
  - **Gas**: No fixed volume or shape, conforms to shape of container, compressible.
  - **Liquid**: Volume independent of container, no fixed shape, incompressible.
  - **Solid**: Volume and shape independent of container, rigid, incompressible.
- Properties described on the molecular level:
  - **Gas**: Molecules far apart, move at high speeds, collide often.
  - **Liquid**: Molecules closer than gas, move rapidly but can slide over each other.
  - **Solid**: Molecules packed closely in definite arrangements.

### Pure Substances

- **Pure substances**:
  - Matter with fixed composition and distinct proportions.
  - **Elements** (cannot be decomposed into simpler substances, i.e. only one kind of atom).
  - **Compounds** (consist of two or more elements).
- **Mixtures**:
  - Combination of two or more pure substances.
  - Each substance retains its own identity.

### Elements[14,15,16,17,18,19,20,21,22]

---

[9] "Chemistry in the Real World" from Further Readings
[10] "Chemicals in Everyday Life" from Further Readings
[11] "Science Demonstrations, Experiments, and Resources. A Reference List for Elementary through College Teachers Emphasizing Chemistry with some Physics and Life Science" from Live Demonstrations
[12] "A Miracle Drug" from Further Readings
[13] "Phases of Matter" Activity from MediaPortfolio
[14] Figure 1.5 from MediaPortfolio and Transparency Pack
[15] Figure 1.6 from MediaPortfolio and Transparency Pack
[16] "What's the Use" from Further Readings

- 114 known.
- Vary in abundance.
- Each is given a unique name.
- Organized in periodic table.
- Each is given a one- or two-letter symbol derived from its name.

### Compounds[23]

- **Compounds** are combinations of elements.
  Example: The compound $H_2O$ is a combination of elements H and O.
- The opposite of compound formation is decomposition.
- Compounds have different properties than their component elements (e.g., water is liquid, hydrogen and oxygen are both gases at the same temperature and pressure).
- **Law of Constant (Definite) Proportions** (Proust): A compound always consists of the same combination of elements (e.g., water is always 11% H and 89% O).

### Mixtures[24,25]

- A **mixture** is a combination of two or more pure substances.
  - Each substance retains its own identity.
  - Variable composition.
  - Heterogeneous (do not have uniform composition, properties and appearance, e.g., sand).
  - Homogeneous (uniform throughout, e.g., air). Homogenous mixtures are **solutions**.

## 1.3 Properties of Matter

- Each substance has a unique set of physical and chemical properties:
  - **Physical properties**: Measured without changing the substance (e.g., color, density, odor, melting point, etc.).
  - **Chemical properties**: Describe how substances react or change to form different substances (e.g., hydrogen burns in oxygen).
  - Properties may be categorized as intensive or extensive:
  - **Intensive properties**: Do not depend on amount of substance present (e.g., temperature, melting point etc.).
    - Intensive properties give an idea of the composition of a substance whereas extensive properties given an indication of the quantity of substance present.
  - **Extensive properties**: Depend on quantity of substance present (e.g., mass, volume etc.).

### Physical and Chemical Changes[26,27,28]

- **Physical change**: substance changes physical appearance without altering its identity (e.g., **changes of state**).

---

17 "It's Elementary" from Further Readings
18 "Important Elements" from Further Readings
19 "Origin of the Names of Chemical Elements" from Further Readings
20 "Element 110 Makes a Very Fleeting Debut" from Further Readings
21 "Elementary My Dear Watson" from Further Readings
22 "Elementary Riddles" from Further Readings
23 "Electrolysis of Water" Animation from MediaPortfolio
24 Figure 1.9 from MediaPortfolio and Transparency Pack
25 "Classification of Matter" Activity from MediaPortfolio
26 Figure 1.10 from MediaPortfolio
27 "Ira Remsen's Investigation of Nitric Acid" from Live Demonstrations
28 "Sodium and Potassium in Water" Movie from MediaPortfolio

- **Chemical changes** (or **chemical reactions**): substances transform into chemically different substances (i.e. identity changes, e.g., decomposition of water, explosion of nitrogen triiodide).

### Separation of Mixtures[29,30,31,32]

Key: Separation techniques exploit differences in properties of the *components*.

- Filtration: Remove solid from liquid.
- Distillation: Boil off one or more components of the mixture.
- Chromatography: Exploit solubility of components.

### *The Scientific Method*[33,34,35,36,37]

- **The scientific method**: Guidelines for the practice of science.
  - Collect data (observe, experiment, etc.).
  - Look for patterns, try to explain them and develop a **hypothesis**.
  - Test hypothesis, refine it.
  - Bring all information together into a **scientific law** (concise statement or equation that summarizes tested hypotheses).
  - Bring hypotheses and laws together into a theory. A **theory** should explain general principles.

## 1.4 Units of Measurement[38,39,40,41]

- Many properties of matter are quantitative: associated with numbers.
- A measured quantity must have BOTH a number and a unit.
- The units most often used for scientific measurement are those of the **metric system**.

### SI Units[42]

- 1960: All scientific units use **S**ystème **I**nternational d'Unités (**SI** Units).
- There are seven base units.
- Smaller and larger units are obtained by decimal fractions or multiples of the base units.

### Length and Mass[43,44,45,46]

- SI base unit of length = meter (1 m = 1.0936 yards).
- SI base unit of mass (not weight) = kilogram (1 kg = 2.2 pounds).

---

[29] Figure 1.13 from MediaPortfolio and Transparency Pack
[30] "Paper Chromatography of Ink" Movie from MediaPortfolio
[31] "T-Shirt Chromatography: A Chromatogram You Can Wear" from Further Readings
[32] "Mixtures and Compounds" Movie From MediaPortfolio
[33] Figure 1.15 from MediaPortfolio and Transparency Pack
[34] "An Experiment to Demonstrate the Application of the Scientific Method" from Live Demonstrations
[35] "Why Does Popcorn Pop? An Introduction to the Scientific Method" from Further Readings
[36] "Using History to Teach The Scientific Method: The Role of Errors" from Further Readings
[37] "Distillation of Seawater" Activity from MediaPortfolio
[38] "A Simple Demonstration for Introducing the Metric System to Introductory Chemistry Classes" from Live Demonstrations
[39] "Having Fun with the Metric System" from Further Readings
[40] "Measuring with a Purpose. Involving Students in the Learning Process" from Further Readings
[41] "*Scientific American*, September 2001" from Further Readings
[42] Table 1.4 from MediaPortfolio
[43] Table 1.5 from MediaPortfolio and Transparency Pack
[44] "Le Grand K" from Further Readings
[45] "Bearing Down on the Kilogram Standard" from Further Readings
[46] "Basic Principles of Scale Reading" from Further Readings

- **Mass** is a measure of the amount of material in an object.

### Temperature[47]

- Scientific studies use Celsius and Kelvin scales.
- **Celsius scale**: Water freezes at 0°C and boils at 100°C (sea level).
- **Kelvin scale** (SI Unit):
    - Water freezes at 273.15 K and boils at 373.15 K (sea level).
    - Based on properties of gases.
    - Zero is lowest possible temperature (absolute zero).
    - 0 K = –273.15°C.
- Fahrenheit (not used in science):
    - Water freezes at 32°F and boils at 212°F (sea level).
    - Conversions:

$$°F = \frac{9}{5}°C + 32$$

$$°C = \frac{5}{9}(°F - 32)$$

$$°C = K - 273.15$$

$$K = °C + 273.15$$

### Derived SI Units

- These are formed from the 7 base units.
- Example: Velocity is distance traveled per unit time, so units of velocity are units of distance (m) divided by units of time (s): m/s.

### Volume[48,49]

- Units of volume = (units of length)$^3$ = m$^3$.
- This unit is unrealistically large, so we use more reasonable units:
    - cm$^3$ (also known as mL (milliliter) or cc (cubic centimeters))
    - dm$^3$ (also known as liters, L).
- Important: The liter is not an SI unit.

### Density[50,51,52,53]

- Used to characterize substances.
- **Density** is defined as mass divided by volume.
- Units: g/cm$^3$ or g/mL (for solids and liquids); g/L (often used for gases).
- Originally based on mass (the density was defined as the mass of 1.00 g of pure water).

## 1.5 Uncertainty in Measurement

- Two types of numbers:
    - Exact numbers (known as counting or defined).

---

[47] Figure 1.18 from MediaPortfolio
[48] Figure 1.19 from MediaPortfolio
[49] Figure 1.20 from MediaPortfolio
[50] "Sugar in a Can of Soft Drink A Density Exercise" from Live Demonstrations
[51] "The Mysterious Sunken Ice Cube" from Live Demonstrations
[52] "Method for Separating or Identifying Plastics" from Further Readings
[53] "Densities and Miscibilities of Liquids and Liquid Mixtures" from Live Demonstrations

- Inexact numbers (derived from measurement).
- All measurements have some degree of uncertainty or *error* associated with them.

## Precision and Accuracy[54,55,56,57]

- **Precision**: how well measured quantities agree with each other.
- **Accuracy**: how well measured quantities agree with the "true value".
- Figure 1.25 is very helpful in making this distinction.

## Significant Figures[58,59,60,61,62]

- In a measurement it is useful to indicate the exactness of the measurement. This exactness isreflected in the number of significant figures.
- Guidelines for determining the number of significant figures in a measured quantity:
  - The number of significant figures is the number of digits known with certainty plus one uncertain digit. (Example: 2.2405 g means we are sure the mass is 2.240 g but we are uncertain about the nearest 0.0001 g.)
  - Final calculations are only as significant as the least significant measurement.
- Rules:
  1. Nonzero numbers and zeros between nonzero numbers are always significant.
  2. Zeros before the first nonzero digit are not significant. (Example: 0.0003 has one significant figure.)
  3. Zeros at the end of the number after a decimal point are significant.
     Zeros at the end of a number before a decimal point are ambiguous (e.g., 10,300 g). Exponential notation eliminates this ambiguity.
- Method:
  1. Write the number in scientific notation.
  2. The number of digits remaining is the number of significant figures.
  3. Example:
     $2.50 \times 10^2$ cm has 3 significant figures as written.
     $1.03 \times 10^4$ g has 3 significant figures.
     $1.030 \times 10^4$ g has 4 significant figures.
     $1.0300 \times 10^4$ g has 5 significant figures.

## Significant Figures in Calculations

- Multiplication and Division:
  1. Report to the least number of significant figures
     (e.g., 6.221 cm x 5.2 cm = 32 $cm^2$).
- Addition and Subtraction:
  1. Report to the least number of decimal places
     (e.g., 20.4 g – 1.322 g = 19.1 g).

---

[54] Figure 1.25 from Matter and Transparency Pack
[55] "Error, Precision and Uncertainty" from Further Readings
[56] "Precision and Accuracy in Measurements: A Tale of Four Graduated Cylinders" from Further Readings
[57] "Meter Sticks in the Demonstration of Error Measurements" from Further Readings
[58] "A Simple but Effective Demonstration for Illustrating Significant Figure Rules When Making Measurements and Doing Calculations" from Further Readings
[59] "Significant Figures" from Further Readings
[60] Significant Figures: A Classroom Demonstration" from Further Readings
[61] "A Joke Based on Significant Figures" from Further Readings
[62] "Significant Figures" Activity from MediaPortfolio

- In multiple step calculations always retain an extra significant figure until the end to prevent rounding errors.

## 1.6 Dimensional Analysis[63,64]

- **Dimensional analysis** is a method of calculation utilizing a knowledge of units.
- Given units can be multiplied and divided to give the desired units.
- Conversion factors are used to manipulate units:

  Desired unit = given unit x (conversion factor).
- The **conversion factors** are simple ratios:

  Conversion factor = (desired unit) / (given unit).

### Using Two or More Conversion Factors

- We often need to use more than one conversion factor in order to complete a problem.
- When identical units are found in the numerator and denominator of a conversion, they will cancel. The final answer MUST have the correct units.
- For example:
  - Suppose that we want to convert length in meters to length in inches. We could do this conversion with the following conversion factors:

    1 meter = 100 centimeters and 1 inch = 2.54 centimeters
- The calculation would involve both conversion factors; the units of the final answer will be inches:

  (# meters) (100 centimeters / 1 meter) (1 inch / 2.54 centimeters) = # inches

### Conversions Involving Volume

- We often will encounter conversions from one measure to a different measure.
- For example:
  - Suppose that we wish to know the mass in grams of 2.00 cubic inches of gold given that the density of the gold is 19.3 $g/cm^3$.
  - We could do this conversion with the following conversion factors:

    2.54 cm = 1 inch and 1 $cm^3$ = 19.3 g gold
  - The calculation would involve both of these factors:

    $(2.00 \text{ in.}^3)(2.54 \text{ cm / in.})^3 (19.3 \text{ g gold } / 1 \text{ cm}^3) = 633 \text{ g gold}$
  - Note that the calculation will NOT be correct unless the centimeter to inch conversion factor is cubed!! Both the units AND the number must be cubed.

### Summary of Dimensional Analysis:

- In dimensional analysis always ask three questions:
  1. What data are we given?
  2. What quantity do we need?
  3. What conversion factors are available to take us from what we are given to what we need?

---

[63] "Expanded Dimensional Analysis: A Blending of English and Math" from Further Readings

[64] "Appalachian Trail Problems" from Further Readings

## Further Readings:

1. R. Lipkin, "Element 110 Makes a Very Fleeting Debut," *Science News*, **November 26, 1994**, Vol. 146, 356.

2. Martin B. Jones and Christina R. Miller, "Chemistry in the Real World," *J. Chem. Educ.*, Vol. 78, **2001**, 484–487.

3. Milton J. Wieder, "It's Elementary," *J. Chem. Educ.*, Vol. 78, **2001**, 468–469.

4. Terry L. Heiser, "Elementary My Dear Watson," *J. Chem. Educ.*, Vol. 66, **1989**, 980. Puzzles involving element names and symbols.

5. Doris Eckey, "Elementary Riddles", *J. Chem. Educ.*, Vol. 71, **1994**, 1051. A series of riddles involving the names of the elements.

6. Raymond B. Seymour, "Chemicals in Everyday Life," *J. Chem. Educ.*, Vol. 64, **1987**, 63–68.

7. Each of the "What's the Use?" articles, written by Alton Banks, focuses on the uses of a specific element. See *J. Chem. Educ.*, Vols. 66 (**1989**), 67 (**1990**), 68 (**1991**) and 69 (**1992**)

8. Vivi Ringes, "Origin of the Names of Chemical Elements," *J. Chem. Educ.*, Vol. 66, **1989**, 731–738.

9. P. G. Nelson, , "Important Elements," *J. Chem. Educ.*, Vol. 68, **1991**, 732–737.

10. Jeanne M. Buccigros, "T-Shirt Chromatography: A Chromatogram You Can Wear," *J. Chem. Educ.*, Vol. 69, **1992**, 977–978.

11. Kenneth E. Kolb and Doris K. Kolb, "Method for Separating or Identifying Plastics," *J. Chem. Educ.*, Vol. 68, **1991**, 348. A demonstration of the concept of density.

12. Frederick C. Sauls, "Why Does Popcorn Pop? An Introduction to the Scientific Method," *J. Chem. Educ.*, Vol. 86, **1991**, 415–416.

13. Carmen J. Guinta, "Using History to Teach Scientific Method: The Case of Argon," *J. Chem. Educ.*, Vol. 75, **1998**, 1322–1325. The scientific method is introduced using a case-study approach involving the discovery of argon.

14. Mark L. Campbell, "Having Fun with the Metric System," *J. Chem. Educ.*, Vol. 68, **1991**, 1043. A word game.

15. "Bearing Down on the Kilogram Standard," *Science News*, Vol. 147, **January 28, 1995**, 63. A short article dealing with the problems of maintaining "Le Grand K," The platinum-iridium bar whose mass defines the kilogram.

16. Robert Suder, "Meter Sticks in the Demonstration of Error Measurements," *J. Chem. Educ.*, Vol. 66, **1989**, 437.

17. Gavin D. Peckhan, "Basic Principles of Scale Reading," *J. Chem. Educ.*, Vol. 71, **1994**, 423–424.

18. Patricia A. Metz and Jeffrey R. Pribyl, “Measuring with a Purpose. Involving Students in the Learning Process,” *J. Chem. Educ.*, Vol. 72, **1995**, 130–132.

19. Richard S. Treptow, “Precision and Accuracy in Measurements: a Tale of Four Graduated Cylinders,” *J. Chem. Educ.*, Vol. 75, **1998**, 992–995.

20. A special issue devoted to nanotechnology. *Scientific American*, **September 2001**.

21. Charles J. Guare, “Error, Precision, and Uncertainty,” *J. Chem. Educ.*, Vol. 68, **1991**, 649–652.

22. Kenton B. Abel and William M. Hemmerlin, “Significant Figures,” *J. Chem. Educ.*, Vol. 67, **1990**, 213.

23. H. Graden Kirksey and Paul Krause, “Significant Figures: A Classroom Demonstration,” *J. Chem. Educ.*, Vol. 69, **1992**, 497–498.

24. Ben Ruekberg, “A Joke Based on Significant Figures,” *J. Chem. Educ.*, Vol. 71, **1994**, 306.

25. Ronald DeLorenzo, "Expanded Dimensional Analysis: A Blending of English and Math," *J. Chem. Educ.*, Vol. 71, **1994**, 789–791.

26. Brian N. Akers, “Appalachian Trail Problems,” *J. Chem. Educ.*, Vol. 75, **1998**, 1571–1572. This short article provides some unit analysis problems.

27. Sophie Jourdier, “A Miracle Drug,” *Chemistry in Britain*, Vol. 35, **1999**, 33–35. An article on the history of aspirin.

## Live Demonstrations:

1. David A. Katz, “Science Demonstrations, Experiments, and Resources. A Reference List for Elementary through College Teachers Emphasizing Chemistry with Some Physics and Life Science,” *J. Chem. Educ.*, Vol. 68, **1991**, 235–244. An extensive listing of various demonstrations, experiments and resources for the science educator.

2. Lee R. Summerlin, Christie L. Borgford, and Julie B. Ealy, “Ira Remsen's Investigation of Nitric Acid,” *Chemical Demonstrations. A Sourcebook for Teachers*, Volume 2 (Washington: American Chemical Society, **1988**), pp. 4–5.

3. Irving R Tannenbaum, “An Experiment to Demonstrate the Application of the Scientific Method,” *J. Chem. Educ.*, Vol. 66, **1989**, 597. A simple experiment to heat water to boiling.

4. David A. Franz and David Speckhard, "Densities and Miscibilities of Liquids and Liquid Mixtures," *J. Chem. Educ.*, Vol. 68, **1991**, 594. Demonstrations involving densities and miscibility of liquids.

5. Lee. R. Summerlin, Christie L. Borgford, and Julie B. Ealy, “The First Demonstration: Proof That Air Is a Substance,” *Chemical Demonstrations, A Sourcebook for Teachers*, Volume 2 (Washington: American Chemical Society, **1988**), p. 3.

6. Clarke W. Earley, “A Simple Demonstration for Introducing the Metric System to Introductory Chemistry Classes,” *J. Chem. Educ.*, Vol. 76, **1999**, 1215-1216.

7. Lee. R. Summerlin, Christie L. Borgford, and Julie B. Ealy, "Sugar in a Can of Soft Drink: A Density Exercise," *Chemical Demonstrations, A Sourcebook for Teachers*, Volume 2 (Washington: American Chemical Society, 1988), p. 126-127.

8. Lee. R. Summerlin, Christie L. Borgford, and Julie B. Ealy, "The Mysterious Sunken Ice Cube," *Chemical Demonstrations, A Sourcebook for Teachers*, Volume 2 (Washington: American Chemical Society, 1988), p. 15-16.

# Chapter 2. Atoms, Molecules, and Ions

## Media Resources

### Figures and Tables

| On Transparency Pack and MediaPortfolio: | Section: |
|---|---|
| Figure 2.4 Cathode-Ray Tube | 2.2 The Discovery of Atomic Structure |
| Figure 2.5 Millikan Experiment | 2.2 The Discovery of Atomic Structure |
| Figure 2.8 Radiation in an Electric Field | 2.2 The Discovery of Atomic Structure |
| Figure 2.10 Rutherford's Experiment | 2.2 The Discovery of Atomic Structure |
| Figure 2.11 Rutherford's Model | 2.2 The Discovery of Atomic Structure |
| Figure 2.13 Diagram of Mass Spectrometer | 2.4 Atomic Weights |
| Figure 2.16 Periodic Table | 2.5 The Periodic Table |
| Figure 2.20 Models of Common Molecules | 2.6 Molecules and Molecular Compounds |
| Figure 2.22 Charges of Common Ions | 2.7 Ions and Ionic Compounds |
| Figure 2.23 Formation of Sodium and Chloride Ions | 2.7 Ions and Ionic Compounds |
| Figure 2.24 Elements Essential for Life | 2.7 Ions and Ionic Compounds |
| Figure 2.26 Naming Anions | 2.8 Naming Inorganic Compounds |
| Figure 2.27 Relationship Between Anion And Acid Names | 28. Naming Inorganic Compounds |

| On MediaPortfolio: | Section: |
|---|---|
| Figure 2.9 "Plum-Pudding" Model | 2.2 The Discovery of Atomic Structure |
| Figure 2.12 Cross-Section of an Atom | 2.3 The Modern View of Atomic Structure |
| Figure 2.14 Mass Spectrum of Cl | 2.4 Atomic Weights |
| Figure 2.15 Periodic Nature of Elements | 2.5 The Periodic Table |
| Figure 2.19 Diatomic Elements | 2.6 Molecules and Molecular Compounds |
| Figure 2.21 Representation of Molecules | 2.6 Molecules and Molecular Compounds |
| Table 2.4 Common Cations | 2.8 Naming Inorganic Compounds |
| Table 2.5 Common Anions | 2.8 Naming Inorganic Compounds |
| Table 2.6 Prefixes Used in Naming Binary Compounds | 2.8 Naming Inorganic Compounds |

| Animations: | Section: |
|---|---|
| Multiple Proportions | 2.1 The Atomic Theory of Matter |
| Millikan Oil Drop Experiment | 2.2 The Discovery of Atomic Structure |
| Separation of Alpha, Beta, and Gamma Rays | 2.2 The Discovery of Atomic Structure |
| Rutherford Experiment: Nuclear Atom | 2.2 The Discovery of Atomic Structure |

| Activities: | Section: |
|---|---|
| Postulates of Atomic Theory | 2.1 The Atomic Theory of Matter |
| Multiple Proportions | 2.1 The Atomic Theory of Matter |
| Element Symbology | 2.3 The Modern View of Atomic Structure |
| Isotopes of Hydrogen | 2.3 The Modern View of Atomic Structure |
| Isotope Symbology | 2.3 The Modern View of Atomic Structure |
| Periodic Table | 2.5 The Periodic Table |
| Naming Cations | 2.8 Naming Inorganic Compounds |
| Naming Anions | 2.8 Naming Inorganic Compounds |

| | |
|---|---|
| Naming Two Series of Two Oxyanions | 2.8 Naming Inorganic Compounds |
| Naming a Series of Four Oxyanions | 2.8 Naming Inorganic Compounds |
| Naming Polyatomic Ions | 2.8 Naming Inorganic Compounds |
| Naming Ionic Compounds | 2.8 Naming Inorganic Compounds |

## Other Resources

| **Further Readings:** | **Section:** |
|---|---|
| Analogical Demonstration | 2.1 The Atomic Theory of Matter |
| Using Games to Teach Chemistry. An Annotated Bibliography | 2.1 The Atomic Theory of Matter |
| A Millikan Oil Drop Analogy | 2.2 The Discovery of Atomic Structure |
| Marie Curie's Doctoral Thesis: Prelude to a Nobel Prize | 2.2 The Discovery of Atomic Structure |
| Bowling Balls and Beads: A Concrete Analogy to the Rutherford Experiment | 2.2 The Discovery of Atomic Structure |
| The Discovery of the Electron, Proton, and Neutron | 2.2 The Discovery of Atomic Structure |
| The Curie-Becquerel Story | 2.2 The Discovery of Atomic Structure |
| Isotope Separation | 2.3 The Modern View of Atomic Structure |
| Relative Atomic Mass and the Mole: A Concrete Analogy to Help Students Understand These Abstract Concepts | 2.4 Atomic Weights |
| Using Monetary Analogies to Teach Average Atomic Mass | 2.4 Atomic Weights |
| Pictorial Analogies IV: Relative Atomic Weights | 2.4 Atomic Weights |
| Periodic Tables of Elemental Abundance | 2.5 The Periodic Table |
| A Second Note on the Term "Chalcogen' | 2.5 The Periodic Table |
| Making New Elements | 2.6 Molecules and Molecular Compounds |
| Teaching Inorganic Nomenclature: A Systematic Approach | 2.8 Naming Inorganic Compounds |
| Flow Chart for Naming Inorganic Compounds | 2.8 Naming Inorganic Compounds |
| A Mnemonic for Oxy-Anions | 2.8 Naming Inorganic Compounds |

| **Live Demonstrations:** | **Section:** |
|---|---|
| Dramatizing Isotopes: Deuterated Ice Cubes Sink | 2.3 The Modern View of Atomic Structure |

# Chapter 2. Atoms, Molecules, and Ions

## Common Student Misconceptions

- Students have problems with the concept of amu.
- Students think that molecules are the particles described by any chemical formula.
- Beginning students often do not see the difference between empirical and molecular formulas.
- Students think that polyatomic ions can easily dissociate into smaller ions.
- Students often fail to recognize the importance of the periodic table as a tool for organizing and remembering chemical facts.
- It is critical that students learn the names and formulas of common and polyatomic ions as soon as possible. They sometimes need to be told that this information will be used throughout their careers as chemists (even if that career is only one semester).
- Students often cannot relate the charges on common ions to their position on the periodic table.

## Lecture Outline

### 2.1 The Atomic Theory of Matter[1,2,3,4,5]

- Greek Philosophers: Can matter be subdivided into fundamental particles?
- Democritus (460–370 BC): All matter can be divided into indivisible *atomos*.
- Dalton: Proposed atomic theory with the following postulates:
  - Elements are composed of atoms.
  - All atoms of an element are identical.
  - In chemical reactions atoms are not changed into different types of atoms. Atoms are neither created nor destroyed.
  - Compounds are formed when atoms of elements combine.
- **Atoms** are the building blocks of matter.
- *Law of constant composition*: The relative kinds and numbers of atoms are constant for a given compound.
- *Law of conservation of mass (matter)*: During a chemical reaction, the total mass before reaction is equal to the total mass after reaction.
  - Conservation means something can neither be created nor destroyed. Here, it applies to matter (mass). Later we will apply it to energy (Chapter 5).
- *Law of multiple proportions*: If two elements A and B combine to form more than one compound, then the mass of B which combines with the mass of A is a ratio of small whole numbers.
- Dalton's theory *predicted* the law of multiple proportions.

### 2.2 The Discovery of Atomic Structure

- By 1850 scientists knew that atoms consisted of charged particles.
- **Subatomic particles**: those particles that make up the atom.
- Recall: The law of electrostatic attraction: like charges repel and opposite charges attract.

#### Cathode Rays and Electrons[6,7,8,9,10]

---

[1] "Multiple Proportions" Animation from MediaPortfolio
[2] "Analogical Demonstration" from Further Readings
[3] "Using Games to Teach Chemistry: An Annotated Bibliography" from Further Readings
[4] "Multiple Proportions" Activity from MediaPortfolio
[5] "Postulates of Atomic Theory" Activity from MediaPortfolio

- Cathode rays first discovered in mid-1800s from studies of electrical discharge through partially evacuated tubes (cathode ray tubes or CRTs).
    - Computer terminals were once popularly referred to as CRTs (cathode-ray tubes).
    - Cathode rays = radiation produced when high voltage is applied across the tube.
- The voltage causes negative particles to move from the negative electrode (cathode) to the positive electrode (anode).
- The path of the electrons can be altered by the presence of a magnetic field.
- Consider cathode rays leaving the positive electrode through a small hole.
    - If they interact with a magnetic field perpendicular to an applied electric field, then the cathode rays can be deflected by different amounts.
    - The amount of deflection of the cathode rays depends on the applied magnetic and electric fields.
    - In turn, the amount of deflection also depends on the charge-to-mass ratio of the electron.
    - In 1897 Thomson determined the charge-to-mass ratio of an electron.
        - Charge-to-mass ratio: $1.76 \times 10^8$ C/g.
        - C is a symbol for coulomb.
            - SI unit for electric charge.
- Millikan Oil-Drop Experiment
    - Goal: Find the charge on the electron to determine its mass.
    - Oil drops are sprayed above a positively charged plate containing a small hole.
    - As the oil drops fall through the hole they acquire a negative charge.
    - Gravity forces the drops downward. The applied electric field forces the drops upward.
    - When a drop is perfectly balanced, then the weight of the drop is equal to the electrostatic force of attraction between the drop and the positive plate.
    - Millikan carried out the above experiment and determined the charges on the oil drops to be multiples of $1.60 \times 10^{-19}$ C.
    - He concluded the charge on the electron must be $1.60 \times 10^{-19}$ C.
- Knowing the charge to mass ratio of the electron, we can calculate the mass of the electron:

$$\text{Mass} = \frac{1.60 \times 10^{-19}\,\text{C}}{1.76 \times 10^{8}\,\text{C/g}} = 9.10 \times 10^{-28}\,\text{g}$$

## Radioactivity[11,12,13,14]

- **Radioactivity** is the spontaneous emission of radiation.
- Consider the following experiment:
    - A radioactive substance is placed in a lead shield containing a small hole so that a beam of radiation is emitted from the shield.
    - The radiation is passed between two electrically charged plates and detected.
    - Three spots are observed on the detector:
        1. A spot deflected in the direction of the positive plate.
        2. A spot that is not affected by the electric field.

---

[6] Figure 2.4 from MediaPortfolio and Transparency Pack
[7] Figure 2.5 from MediaPortfolio and Transparency Pack
[8] "Millikan Oil Drop Experiment" Animation from MediaPortfolio
[9] "A Millikan Oil Drop Analogy" from Further Readings
[10] "The Discovery of the Electron, Proton, and Neutron" from Further Readings
[11] "Marie Curie's Doctoral Thesis: Prelude to a Nobel Prize" from Further Readings
[12] "Separation of Alpha, Beta & Gamma Rays" Animation from MediaPortfolio
[13] "Making New Elements" from Further Readings
[14] "The Curie-Becquerel Story" from Further Readings

3. A spot deflected in the direction of the negative plate.

- A large deflection towards the positive plate corresponds to radiation that is negatively charged and of low mass. This is called β-radiation (consists of electrons).
  - No deflection corresponds to neutral radiation. This is called γ-radiation (similar to X-rays).
- A small deflection toward the negatively charged plate corresponds to high mass, positively charged radiation. This is called α-radiation (positively charged core of a helium atom).
  - X-rays and γ radiation are true electromagnetic radiation, whereas α- and β-radiation are actually streams of particles--helium nuclei and electrons, respectively.

### The Nuclear Atom[15,16,17,18,19,20,21]

- The plum pudding model: an early picture of the atom.
- The Thomson model pictures the atom as a sphere with small electrons embedded in a positively charged mass.
- Rutherford carried out the following "gold foil" experiment:
  - A source of α-particles was placed at the mouth of a circular detector.
  - The α-particles were shot through a piece of gold foil.
  - Both the gold nucleus and the α-particle are positively charged, so they repel each other.
  - Most of the α-particles went straight through the foil without deflection.
  - If the Thomson model of the atom was correct, then Rutherford's result was impossible.
- Rutherford modified Thomson's model as follows:
  - Assume the atom is spherical, but the positive charge must be located at the center with a diffuse negative charge surrounding it.
  - In order for the majority of α-particles that pass through a piece of foil to be undeflected, the majority of the atom must consist of a low mass, diffuse negative charge - the electron.
  - To account for the small number of large deflections of the α-particles, the center or **nucleus** of the atom must consist of a dense positive charge.

## 2.3 The Modern View of Atomic Structure[22]

- The atom consists of positive, negative and neutral entities (**protons**, **electrons** and **neutrons**).
- Protons and neutrons are located in the nucleus of the atom, which is small. Most of the mass of the atom is due to the nucleus.
- Electrons are located outside of the nucleus. Most of the volume of the atom is due to electrons.
- The quantity $1.602 \times 10^{-19}$ C is called the **electronic charge**. The charge on an electron is $-1.602 \times 10^{-19}$ C; the charge on a proton is $+1.602 \times 10^{-19}$ C; neutrons are uncharged.
  - Atoms have an equal number of protons and electrons thus they have no net electrical charge.
- Masses are so small that we define the **atomic mass unit**, amu.
  - 1 amu = $1.66054 \times 10^{-24}$ g.
  - The mass of a proton is 1.0073 amu, a neutron is 1.0087 amu, and an electron is $5.486 \times 10^{-4}$ amu.
- The **angstrom** is a convenient non-SI unit of length used to denote atomic dimensions.
  - Since most atoms have radii around $1 \times 10^{-10}$ m, we define 1 Å = $1 \times 10^{-10}$ m.

---

[15] Figure 2.8 from MediaPortfolio and Transparency Pack
[16] Figure 2.9 from MediaPortfolio
[17] Figure 2.10 from MediaPortfolio and Transparency Pack
[18] Figure 2.11 from MediaPortfolio and Transparency Pack
[19] "Rutherford Experiment: Nuclear Atom" Animation from MediaPortfolio
[20] "Bowling Balls and Beads: A Concrete Analogy to the Rutherford Experiment" from Further Readings
[21] "The Discovery of the Electron, Proton, and Neutron" from Further Readings
[22] Figure 2.12 from MediaPortfolio

### Isotopes, Atomic Numbers, and Mass Numbers[23,24,25,26,27]

- All atoms of a specific element have the same number of protons.
    - **Isotopes** of a specific element differ in the number of neutrons.
- **Atomic number** (Z) = number of protons in the nucleus.
- **Mass number** (A) = total number of nucleons in the nucleus (i.e. protons and neutrons).
- By convention, for element X, we write $^{A}_{Z}X$ .
    - Thus isotopes have the same Z but different A.
        - There can be a variable number of neutrons for the same number of protons. Isotopes have the same number of protons but different numbers of neutrons.
    - An atom of a specific isotope is called a **nuclide**.
        - Examples: Nuclides of hydrogen include:
          $^{1}H$ = hydrogen (protium); $^{2}H$ = deuterium, $^{3}H$ = tritium; tritium is radioactive.

## 2.4 Atomic Weights

### The Atomic Mass Scale[28]

- Consider 100 g of water:
    - Upon decomposition 11.1 g of hydrogen and 88.9 g of oxygen are produced.
    - The mass ratio of O to H in water is 88.9/11.1 = 8.
    - Therefore, the mass of O is 2 x 8 = 16 times the mass of H.
    - If H has a mass of 1 then O has a *relative mass* of 16.
    - We can measure atomic masses using a mass spectrometer.
    - We know $^{1}H$ has a mass of $1.6735 \times 10^{-24}$ g and $^{16}O$ has a mass of $2.6560 \times 10^{-23}$ g.
    - *Atomic mass units* (amu) are convenient units to use when dealing with extremely small masses of individual atoms.
- 1 amu = $1.66054 \times 10^{-24}$ g and 1 g = $6.02214 \times 10^{23}$ amu
- By definition, the mass of $^{12}C$ is exactly 12 amu.

### Average Atomic Masses[29,30]

- We average the masses of isotopes to give relative atomic masses:
- Naturally occurring C consists of 98.892% $^{12}C$ (12 amu) and 1.108% $^{13}C$ (13.00335 amu).
- The average mass of C is
    - (0.98892)(12 amu) + (0.01108)(13.00335) = 12.011 amu.
- **Atomic weight** (AW) is also known as average atomic mass (atomic weight).
- Atomic weights are listed on the periodic table.
    - A **mass spectrometer** is an instrument that allows for direct and accurate determination of atomic (and molecular) weights.

#### *The Mass Spectrometer*[31,32]

---

23 "Isotope Separation" from Further Readings
24 "Dramatizing Isotopes: Deuterated Ice Cubes Sink" from Live Demonstrations
25 "Element Symbology" Activity from MediaPortfolio
26 "Isotopes of Hydrogen" Activity from MediaPortfolio
27 "Isotope Symbology" Activity from MediaPortfolio
28 "Relative Atomic Mass and the Mole: A Concrete Analogy to Help Students Understand These Abstract Concepts" from Further Readings
29 "Using Monetary Analogies to Teach Average Atomic Mass" from Further Readings
30 "Pictorial Analogies IV: Relative Atomic Weights" from Further Readings

- Mass spectrometers are pieces of equipment designed to measure atomic and molecular masses accurately.
- The sample is charged as soon as it enters the spectrometer.
- The charged sample is accelerated using an applied voltage.
- The ions are then passed into an evacuated tube and through a magnetic field.
- The magnetic field causes the ions to be deflected by different amounts depending on their mass.
- The ions are then detected.
  - A graph of signal intensity vs. mass of the ion is called a *mass spectrum*.

## 2.5 The Periodic Table[33,34,35,36,37]

- **The periodic table** is used to organize the elements in a meaningful way.
- As a consequence of this organization, there are periodic properties associated with the periodic table.
- Columns in the periodic table are called **groups**.
  - Several numbering conventions are used (i.e., groups may be numbered from 1 to 18, or from 1A to 8A and 1B to 8B).
- Rows in the periodic table are called periods.
- Some of the groups in the periodic table are given special names.
  - These names indicate the similarities between group members.
  - Examples:
    - Group 1A: alkali metals
    - Group 7A: halogens
- **Metallic elements** are located on the left-hand side of the periodic table (most of the elements are metals).
- **Nonmetallic elements** are located in the top right-hand side of the periodic table.
- Elements with properties similar to both metals and nonmetals are called **metalloids** and are located at the interface between the metals and nonmetals.
  - These include the elements B, Si, Ge, As, Sb and Te.
- Metals tend to be malleable, ductile, and lustrous and are good thermal and electrical conductors. Nonmetals generally lack these properties; they tend to be brittle as solids, dull in appearance, and do not conduct heat or electricity well.

## 2.6 Molecules and Molecular Compounds

- A **molecule** consists of two or more atoms bound together.

### Molecules and Chemical Formulas[38,39,40]

- Each molecule has a **chemical formula**.
- The chemical formula indicates
  1. Which atoms are found in the molecule, and
  2. In what proportion they are found.

---

[31] Figure 2.13 from MediaPortfolio and Transparency Pack
[32] Figure 2.14 from MediaPortfolio
[33] "Periodic Tables of Elemental Abundance" from Further Readings
[34] Figure 2.15 from MediaPortfolio
[35] Figure 2.16 from MediaPortfolio and Transparency Pack
[36] "A Second Note on the Term 'Chalcogen'" from Further Readings
[37] "Periodic Table" Activity from MediaPortfolio
[38] Figure 2.19 from MediaPortfolio
[39] Figure 2.20 from MediaPortfolio and Transparency Pack
[40] "Making New Elements" from Further Readings

- A molecule made up of two atoms is called a **diatomic molecule.**
- Different forms of an element which have different chemical formulas are known as allotropes. Allotropes differ in their chemical and physical properties. See Chapter 7 for more information on allotropes of common elements.
- Compounds composed of molecules are **molecular compounds**.
  - These contain at least two types of atoms.
  - Most molecular substances contain only nonmetals.

### Molecular and Empirical Formulas

- **Molecular formulas**
  - Give the actual numbers and types of atoms in a molecule.
  - Examples: $H_2O$, $CO_2$, $CO$, $CH_4$, $H_2O_2$, $O_2$, $O_3$, and $C_2H_4$.
- **Empirical formulas**
  - Give the relative numbers and types of atoms in a molecule (they give the lowest whole-number ratio of atoms in a molecule).
  - Examples: $H_2O$, $CO_2$, $CO$, $CH_4$, $HO$, $CH_2$.

### Picturing Molecules[41,42]

- Molecules occupy three-dimensional space.
- However, we often represent them in two dimensions.
- The **structural formula** gives the connectivity between individual atoms in the molecule.
- The structural formula may or may not be used to show the three-dimensional shape of the molecule.
- If the structural formula does show the shape of the molecule then either a perspective drawing, ball-and-stick model or space-filling model is used.
  - *Perspective drawings* use dashed lines and wedges to represent bonds receding and emerging from the plane of the paper.
  - *Ball-and-stick models* show atoms as contracted spheres and the bonds as sticks.
    - The angles in the ball-and-stick model are accurate.
  - *Space-filling models* give an accurate representation of the relative sizes of the atoms and the 3D shape of the molecule.

## 2.7 Ions and Ionic Compounds

- If electrons are added to or removed from a neutral atom, an **ion** is formed.
- When an atom or molecule loses electrons it becomes positively charged.
  - Positively charged ions are called **cations**.
- When an atom or molecule gains electrons it becomes negatively charged.
  - Negatively charged ions are called **anions**.
- In general, metal atoms tend to lose electrons and nonmetal atoms gain electrons.
- When molecules lose electrons, **polyatomic ions** are formed (e.g. $SO_4^{2-}$, $NO_3^-$).

### Predicting Ionic Charges[43]

- An atom or molecule can lose more than one electron.
- Many atoms gain or lose enough electrons to have the same number of electrons as the nearest noble gas (group 8A).
- The number of electrons an atom loses is related to its position on the periodic table.

### Ionic Compounds[44]

---

[41] "Representing Substances" Animation from MediaPortfolio
[42] Figure 2.21 from MediaPortfolio
[43] Figure 2.22 from MediaPortfolio and Transparency Pack

- A great deal of chemistry involves the transfer of electrons between species.
- Example:
  - To form NaCl, the neutral sodium atom, Na, must lose an electron to become a cation: $Na^+$.
  - The electron cannot be lost entirely, so it is transferred to a chlorine atom, Cl, which then becomes an anion: $Cl^-$.
  - The $Na^+$ and $Cl^-$ ions are attracted to form an ionic NaCl lattice which crystallizes.
- NaCl is an example of an **ionic compound**--consisting of positively charged cations and negatively charged anions.
  - Important: Note that there are no easily identified NaCl molecules in the ionic lattice. Therefore, we cannot use molecular formulas to describe ionic substances.
- In general, ionic compounds are combinations of metals and nonmetals, whereas molecular compounds are composed of nonmetals only.
- Writing empirical formulas for ionic compounds:
  - You need to know the ions of which it is composed.
  - The formula must reflect the electrical neutrality of the compound.
  - You must combine cations and anions in a ratio so that the total positive charge is equal to the total negative charge.
  - Example: Consider the formation of $Mg_3N_2$:
    - Mg loses two electrons to become $Mg^{2+}$
    - Nitrogen gains three electrons to become $N^{3-}$.
    - For a neutral species, the number of electrons lost and gained must be equal.
    - However, Mg can only lose electrons in twos and N can only accept electrons in threes.
    - Therefore, Mg needs to lose six electrons (2x3) and N gains those six electrons (3x2).
    - That is, 3Mg atoms need to form $3Mg^{2+}$ ions (total 3x2 positive charges) and 2N atoms need to form $2N^{3-}$ ions (total 2x3 negative charges).
    - Therefore, the formula is $Mg_3N_2$.

### *Chemistry and Life: Elements Required by Living Organisms*[45]

- Of the 114 elements known, only about 26 are required for life.
- Water accounts for more than 70% of the mass of the cell.
- Carbon is the most common solid constituent of cells.
- The most important elements for life are H, C, N, O, P and S (red).
- The next most important ions are $Na^+$, $Mg^{2+}$, $K^+$, $Ca^{2+}$, and $Cl^-$ (blue).
- The other 15 elements are only needed in trace amounts (green).

## 2.8 Naming Inorganic Compounds

- Chemical nomenclature: the naming of substances.
- Common names: traditional names for substances (e.g., water, ammonia).
- Systematic names: naming based on a systematic set of rules.
  - Divided into organic compounds (those containing C, usually in combination with H, O, N, or S) and inorganic compounds (all other compounds).

### Names and Formulas of Ionic Compounds[46,47,48,49]

**1. Positive Ions (Cations)**[50]

---

[44] Figure 2.23 from MediaPortfolio and Transparency Pack
[45] Figure 2.24 from MediaPortfolio and Transparency Pack
[46] "Teaching Inorganic Nomenclature: A Systematic Approach" from Further Readings
[47] "Flow Chart for Naming Inorganic Compounds" from Further Readings
[48] "Naming Cations" Activity from MediaPortfolio
[49] "Naming Anions" Activity from MediaPortfolio

- Cations formed from a metal have the same name as the metal.
  - Example: $Na^+$ = sodium ion.
  - Ions formed from a single atom are called *monoatomic ions*.
- Many transition metals exhibit variable charge.
  - If the metal can form more than one cation, then the charge is indicated in parentheses in the name.
    - Examples: $Cu^+$ = copper(I) ion; $Cu^{2+}$ = copper(II) ion.
  - An alternative nomenclature method uses the endings *-ous* and *-ic* to represent the lower and higher charged ions, respectively.
    - Examples: $Cu^+$ = cuprous ion; $Cu^{2+}$ = cupric ion.
- Cations formed from non-metals end in **-ium**.
  - Examples: $NH_4^+$ ammonium ion; $H_3O^+$ hydronium ion.

**2. Negative Ions (Anions)**[51,52,53,54,55,56]

- Monoatomic anions (with only one atom) use the ending **-ide**.
  - Example: $Cl^-$ is the chloride ion.
- Some polyatomic anions also use the -ide ending:
  - Examples: hydroxide, cyanide and peroxide ions.
- Polyatomic anions (with many atoms) containing oxygen are called **oxyanions**.
  - Their names end in **-ate** or **-ite**. (The one with more oxygen is called **-ate.**)
  - Examples: $NO_3^-$ is nitr**ate**, $NO_2^-$ is nitr**ite**.
- Polyatomic anions containing oxygen with more than two members in the series are named as follows (in order of **decreasing oxygen**):
  - **per-….-ate** example: $ClO_4^-$ **per**chlor**ate**
  - **-ate** $ClO_3^-$ chlor**ate**
  - **-ite** $ClO_2^-$ chlor**ite**
  - **hypo-….-ite** $ClO^-$ **hypo**chlor**ite**
- Polyatomic anions containing oxygen with additional hydrogens are named by adding hydrogen or bi- (one H), dihydrogen (two H) etc. to the name as follows:
  - $CO_3^{2-}$ is the carbon**ate** anion
  - $HCO_3^-$ is the hydrogen carbonate (or **bi**carbonate) anion.
  - $H_2PO_4^-$ is the **dihydrogen** phosphate anion.

**3. Ionic Compounds**[57]

- These are named cation then anion.
- Example: $BaBr_2$ = barium bromide.

## Names and Formulas of Acids

- Acids: Substances that yield hydrogen ions when dissolved in water (Arrhenius definition).
  - The names of acids are related to the names of anions:
  - **-ide** becomes **hydro-….-ic** acid; example: HCl **hydro**chlor**ic** acid
  - **-ate** becomes **-ic** acid; $HClO_4$ perchlor**ic** acid

---

[50] Table 2.4 from MediaPortfolio
[51] "A Mnemonic for Oxy-Anions" from Further Readings
[52] Figure 2.26 from MediaPortfolio and Transparency Pack
[53] "Naming Two Series of Two Oxyanions" Activity from MediaPortfolio
[54] "Naming a Series of Four Oxyanions" Activity from MediaPortfolio
[55] "Naming Polyatomic Ions" Activity from MediaPortfolio
[56] Table 2.5 from MediaPortfolio
[57] "Naming Ionic Compounds" Activity from MediaPortfolio

- **-ite** becomes **-ous** acid. HClO hypochlor**ous** acid

### Names and Formulas for Binary Molecular Compounds[58,59]

- Binary molecular compounds have two elements.
- The most metallic element (i.e. the one to the farthest left on the periodic table) is usually written first. Exception: $NH_3$.
- If both elements are in the same group, the lower one is written first.
- Greek prefixes are used to indicate the number of atoms (e.g., mono, di, tri).
  - The prefix mono is never used with the first element (i.e., carbon monoxide, CO).
- Examples:
  - $Cl_2O$ is **di**chlorine *mono*xide.
  - $N_2O_4$ is **di**nitrogen *tetr*oxide.
  - $NF_3$ is nitrogen *tri*fluoride.
  - $P_4S_{10}$ is **tetra**phosphorus *deca*sulfide.

## 2.9 Some Simple Organic Compounds

- **Organic chemistry** is the study of carbon-containing compounds.
  - *Organic compounds* are those that contain carbon and hydrogen, often in combination with other elements.

### Alkanes

- Compounds containing only carbon and hydrogen are called **hydrocarbons**.
- In **alkanes** each carbon atom is bonded to four other atoms.
- The names of alkanes end in *-ane*.
  - Examples: methane, ethane, propane, butane.

### Some Derivatives of Alkanes

- When *functional groups*, specific groups of atoms, are used to replace hydrogen atoms on alkanes, new classes of organic compounds are obtained.
  - **Alcohols** are obtained by replacing a hydrogen atom of an alkane with an –OH group.
  - Alcohol names derive from the name of the alkane and have an *-ol* ending.
    - Examples: methane becomes methanol; ethane becomes ethanol.
  - Carbon atoms often form compounds with long chains of carbon atoms.
    - Properties of alkanes and derivatives change with changes in chain length.
    - *Polyethylene*, a material used to make many plastic products, is an alkane with thousands of carbons.
    - It is an example of a *polymer*.
- Carbon may form *multiple bonds* to itself or other atoms.
  - Examples include:
    - *Unsaturated hydrocarbons* (e.g., ethylene): contain carbon-carbon multiple bonds.
    - *Carboxylic acids* (e.g., acetic acid).
    - *Ketones* (e.g., acetone).

---

[58] Figure 2.27 from MediaPortfolio and Transparency Pack
[59] Table 2.6 from MediaPortfolio

## Further Readings:

1. John J. Fortman, "Analogical Demonstration," *J. Chem. Educ.*, Vol. 69, **1992**, 323–324. This reference includes demonstrations of the concepts of the conservation of mass in chemical reactions, the Law of Multiple Proportions, etc.

2. Doris Eckey, "A Millikan Oil Drop Analogy," *J. Chem. Educ.*, Vol. 73, **1996**, 237–238.

3. Mary V. Lorenz, "Bowling Balls and Beads: A Concrete Analogy to the Rutherford Experiment," *J. Chem. Educ.*, Vol. 65, **1988**, 1082.

4. Barrie M. Peake, "The Discovery of the Electron, Proton, and Neutron," *J. Chem. Educ.*, Vol. 66, **1989**, 738.

5. Peter Armbruster and Fritz Peter Hessberger, "Making New Elements," *Scientific American*, **September, 1998**, 72–77.

6. Robert L. Wolke, "Marie Curie's Doctoral Thesis: Prelude to a Nobel Prize," *J. Chem. Educ.*, Vol. 65, **1988**, 561–573.

7. Harold F. Walton, "The Curie-Becquerel Story," *J. Chem. Educ.*, Vol. 69, **1992**, 10–15.

8. William Spindel and Takanobu Ishida, "Isotope Separation," *J. Chem. Educ.*, Vol. 68, **1991**, 312–318. An article describing methods used to isolate important isotopes.

9. Steven I. Dutch, "Periodic Tables of Elemental Abundance," *J. Chem. Educ.*, Vol. 76, **1999**, 356–358.

10. Josefina Arce de Sanabia, "Relative Atomic Mass and the Mole: A Concrete Analogy to Help Students Understand These Abstract Concepts," *J. Chem. Educ*. Vol. 70, **1993**, 233–234.

11. Arthur M. Last and Michael J. Webb, "Using Monetary Analogies to Teach Average Atomic Mass," *J. Chem. Educ*. Vol. 70, **1993**, 234–235.

12. John H. Fortman, "Pictorial Analogies IV: Relative Atomic Weights," *J. Chem. Educ*. Vol. 70, **1993**, 235–236.

13. Gerhard Lind, "Teaching Inorganic Nomenclature: A Systematic Approach," *J. Chem. Educ.*, Vol. 69, **1992**, 613–614.

14. Werner Fishcher, "A Second Note on the Term 'Chalcogen'," *J. Chem. Educ.,* Vol. 78, **2001**, 1333.

15. David Robson, "Flow Chart for Naming Inorganic Compounds," J. Chem. Educ., Vol. 60, **1983**, 131–132.

16. Steven J. Hawkes, "A Mnemonic for Oxy-Anions," *J. Chem. Educ.*, Vol. 67, **1990**, 149.

17. Jeanne V. Russel, "Using Games to Teach Chemistry. An Annotated Bibliography," *J. Chem. Educ.*, Vol. 76, **1999**, 481–484. This is the first article in a special issue that contains many articles describing games and puzzles that may be used to teach chemistry.

## Live Demonstrations:

1. Arthur B. Ellis, Edward A Adler, and Frederick H. Juergens, "Dramatizing Isotopes: Deuterated Ice Cubes Sink," *J. Chem. Educ.*, Vol. 67, **1990**, 159–160. Differences in density of $H_2O(l)$ and $D_2O(s)$ are used to demonstrate the effects of isotopic substitution.

# Chapter 3. Stoichiometry: Calculations with Chemical Formulas and Equations

## Media Resources

### Figures and Tables

| In Transparency Pack and on MediaPortfolio: | Section: |
|---|---|
| Figure 3.3 Difference Between Subscripts and Coefficients | 3.1 Chemical Equations |
| Figure 3.4 Combustion of Methane | 3.1 Chemical Equations |
| Figure 3.5 Formation of MgO | 3.2 Some Simple Patterns of Chemical Reactivity |
| Figure 3.8 Mass of a Molecule and a Mole of $H_2O$ | 3.4 The Mole |
| Figure 3.10 Procedure for Mass to Formula Unit Conversion | 3.4 The Mole |
| Figure 3.11 Procedure to Calculate Empirical Formula | 3.5 Empirical Formulas from Analysis |
| Figure 3.13 Procedure for Stoichiometric Calculations | 3.6 Quantitative Information from Balanced Equations |
| Figure 3.15 Illustration of Limiting Reagent | 3.7 Limiting Reactants |

| On MediaPortfolio: | Section: |
|---|---|
| Figure 3.12 Apparatus Used to Determine %C and %H | 3.5 Empirical Formulas from Analysis |

| Animations: | Section: |
|---|---|
| Limiting Reactant | 3.7 Limiting Reactants |

| Movies: | Section: |
|---|---|
| Sodium and Potassium in Water | 3.1 Chemical Equations |
| Reactions with Oxygen | 3.2 Some Simple Patterns of Chemical Reactivity |
| Formation of Water | 3.2 Some Simple Patterns of Chemical Reactivity |
| Reduction of CuO | 3.5 Empirical Formulas from Analysis |

| Activities: | Section: |
|---|---|
| Reading a Chemical Equation | 3.1 Chemical Equations |
| Reading a Balanced Chemical Equation | 3.1 Chemical Equations |
| Counting Atoms | 3.1 Chemical Equations |
| Balancing Equations | 3.1 Chemical Equations |
| Molecular Weight and Weight Percent | 3.3 Formula Weights |
| Molecular Formula Determination: $C_2H_6O$ | 3.5 Empirical Formulas from Analyses |
| Stoichiometry Calculation | 3.6 Quantitative Information from Balanced Equations |
| Limiting Reagents | 3.7 Limiting Reactants |

# Other Resources

| Further Readings: | Section: |
|---|---|
| More Chemistry in a Soda Bottle: A Conservation of Mass Activity | 3.1 Chemical Equations |
| Antoine Lavoisier and the Conservation of Matter | 3.1 Chemical Equations |
| Chemical Wastes and the Law of Conservation of Matter | 3.1 Chemical Equations |
| Balancing Chemical Equations by Inspection | 3.1 Chemical Equations |
| A New Inspection Method for Balancing Redox Equations | 3.1 Chemical Equations |
| On Balancing Chemical Equations: Past and Present (A Critical Review and Annotated Bibliography) | 3.1 Chemical Equations |
| How to Say How Much: Amounts and Stoichiometry | 3.1 Chemical Equations |
| The Fruit Basket Analogy | 3.1 Chemical Equations |
| Lime | 3.2 Some Simple Patterns of Chemical Reactivity |
| Percentage Composition and Empirical Formula—A New View | 3.3 Formula Weights |
| Using Monetary Analogies to Teach Average Atomic Mass | 3.3 Formula Weights |
| Pictorial Analogies IV: Relative Atomic Weights | 3.3 Formula Weights |
| Relative Atomic Mass and the Mole: A Concrete Analogy to Help Students Understand These Abstract Concepts | 3.4. The Mole |
| Developing an Intuitive Approach to Moles | 3.4 The Mole |
| The Mole, the Periodic Table, and Quantum Numbers: An Introductory Trio | 3.4 The Mole |
| The Size of a Mole | 3.4 The Mole |
| What's a Mole For? | 3.4 The Mole |
| The Mole Concept: Developing an Instrument to Assess Conceptual Understanding | 3.4 The Mole |
| Moles, Pennies, and Nickels | 3.4 The Mole |
| A Mole Mnemonic | 3.4 The Mole |
| A Mole of M&M's | 3.4 The Mole |
| How to Visualize Avogadro's Number | 3.4 The Mole |
| Analogies for Avogadro's Number | 3.4 The Mole |
| Demonstrations of the Enormity of Avogadro's Number | 3.4 The Mole |
| Analogies that Indicate the Size of Atoms and Molecules and the Magnitude of Avogadro's Number | 3.4 The Mole |
| Gram Formula Weights and Fruit Salad | 3.4 The Mole |
| A Known-to-Unknown Approach to Teach About Empirical and Molecular Formulas | 3.5 Empirical Formulas from Analysis |
| Making Assumptions Explicit: How the Law of Conservation of Matter Can Explain Empirical Formula Problems | 3.5 Empirical Formulas from Analysis |
| A Simple Rhyme for a Simple Formula | 3.5 Empirical Formulas from Analysis |
| Amounts Tables as a Diagnostic Tool for Flawed Stoichiometric Reasoning | 3.6 Quantitative Information from Balanced Equations |

| | |
|---|---|
| Stoogiometry: A Cognitive Approach to Teaching Stoichiometry | 3.6 Quantitative Information from Balanced Equations |
| Teaching Stoichiometry: A Two-Cycle Approach | 3.6 Quantitative Information from Balanced Equations |
| A Recipe for Teaching Stoichiometry | 3.6 Quantitative Information from Balanced Equations |
| Pictorial Analogies XII: Stoichiometric Calculations | 3.6 Quantitative Information from Balanced Equations |
| Limiting and Excess Reagents, Theoretical Yield | 3.7 Limiting Reactants |
| Limiting Reactant: An Alternative Analogy | 3.7 Limiting Reactants |
| Limiting Reagent Problems Made Simple for Students | 3.7 Limiting Reactants |
| Coffee, Coins, and Limiting Reagents | 3.7 Limiting Reactants |
| Electron Results and Reaction Yields | 3.7 Limiting Reactants |

| **Live Demonstrations:** | **Section:** |
|---|---|
| Measuring Avogadro's Number on the Overhead Projector | 3.4 The Mole |
| Demonstrations for Nonscience Majors: Using Common Objects to Illustrate Abstract Concepts | 3.4 The Mole |
| Copper Sulfate: Blue to White | 3.5 Empirical Formulas from Analysis |
| Combustion of Hydrocarbons: A Stoichiometry Demonstration | 3.5 Empirical Formulas from Analysis |

# Chapter 3. Stoichiometry: Calculations with Chemical Formulas and Equations

## Common Student Misconceptions

- Students who have good high school backgrounds find this chapter quite easy. Those who have poor high school backgrounds find this chapter extremely difficult. Very few students have heard the term *stoichiometry* and can be intimidated by the language of chemistry.
- Students have a problem with differentiating between the subscript in a chemical formula and the coefficient of the formula.
- Balancing equations requires some trial and error. Algorithm loving students find this uncomfortable.
- Many students will be unfamiliar with "National Mole Day" (i.e., that 6:02 AM on October 23 is the start of National Mole Day).
- Some students cannot distinguish between the number of moles actually manipulated in the laboratory versus the number of moles required by stoichiometry.
- Students do not appreciate that the coefficients in an empirical formula are not exact whole numbers because of experimental or round-off errors. In general, students have problems with the existence of experimental error.
- The concept of limiting reagents is one of the most difficult for beginning students. Part of the problem is that students do not understand the difference between the amount of material present in the laboratory (or given in the problem) and the number of moles required by stoichiometry.
- Students do not understand that the reagent that gives the smallest amount of product is the limiting reagent. They need much numerical practice at this concept. The use of analogies is often quite helpful.
- Students are often quite happy with a percent yield in excess of 100%.

## Lecture Outline

### 3.1 Chemical Equations[1,2,3,4,5,6,7,8,9,10,11,12,13,14,15]

- The quantitative nature of chemical formulas and reactions is called **stoichiometry**.
- Lavoisier observed that mass is conserved in a chemical reaction.
  - This observation is known as the **law of conservation of mass**.

---

[1] "More Chemistry in a Soda Bottle: A Conservation of Mass Activity" from Further Readings
[2] "Antoine Lavoisier and the Conservation of Matter" from Further Readings
[3] "Chemical Wastes and the Law of Conservation of Matter" from Further Readings
[4] Figure 3.3 from MediaPortfolio and Transparency Pack
[5] Figure 3.4 from MediaPortfolio and Transparency Pack
[6] "Sodium and Potassium in Water" Movie from MediaPortfolio
[7] "Balancing Chemical Equations by Inspection" from Further Readings
[8] "A New Inspection Method for Balancing Redox Equations" from Further Readings
[9] "On Balancing Chemical Equations: Past and Present (A Critical Review and Annotated Bibliography)" from Further Readings
[10] "How to Say How Much: Amounts and Stoichiometry" from Further Readings
[11] "The Fruit Basket Analogy" from Further Readings
[12] "Reading a Chemical Equation" Activity from MediaPortfolio
[13] "Reading a Balanced Chemical Equation" Activity from MediaPortfolio
[14] "Counting Atoms" Activity from MediaPortfolio
[15] "Balancing Equations" Activity from MediaPortfolio

- **Chemical equations** give a description of a chemical reaction.
- There are two parts to any equation:
  - **Reactants** (written to the left of the arrow) and
  - **Products** (written to the right of the arrow):

$$2H_2 + O_2 \rightarrow 2H_2O$$

- There are two sets of numbers in a chemical equation:
- Numbers in front of the chemical formulas (called stoichiometric *coefficients*) and
- Numbers in the formulas (they appear as subscripts).
- Stoichiometric coefficients give the *ratio* in which the reactants and products exist.
- The subscripts give the ratio in which the atoms are found in the molecule.
  - Example:
    - $H_2O$ means there are two H atoms for each one molecule of water.
    - **$2H_2O$** means that there are two water molecules present.
- Note: in $2H_2O$ there are *four* hydrogen atoms present (two for each water molecule).
- Matter cannot be lost in any chemical reactions.
  - Therefore, the products of a chemical reaction have to account for all the atoms present in the reactants--we must *balance* the chemical equation.
  - When balancing a chemical equation we adjust the stoichiometric coefficients in front of chemical formulas.
    - Subscripts in a formula are *never* changed when balancing an equation.
- Example: The reaction of methane with oxygen:

$$CH_4 + O_2 \rightarrow CO_2 + H_2O$$

  - Counting *atoms* in the reactants:
    - 1 C;
    - 4 H; and
    - 2 O.
  - In the products:
    - 1 C;
    - 2 H; and
    - 3 O.
  - It appears as though H has been lost and O has been created.
  - To balance the equation, we adjust the stoichiometric coefficients:

$$CH_4 + \mathbf{2}O_2 \rightarrow CO_2 + \mathbf{2}H_2O$$

- The physical state of each reactant and product may be added to the equation:

$$CH_4(g) + \mathbf{2}O_2(g) \rightarrow CO_2(g) + \mathbf{2}H_2O(g)$$

- Reaction conditions occasionally appear above or below the reaction arrow (e.g., "Δ" often is used to indicate the addition of heat).

## 3.2 Some Simple Patterns of Chemical Reactivity

### Combination and Decomposition Reactions[16,17,18,19]

- In **combination reactions** two or more substances react to form one product.
- Combination reactions have more reactants than products.
  - Consider the reaction:

$$2Mg(s) + O_2(g) \rightarrow 2MgO(s)$$

[16] "Reactions with Oxygen" Movie from MediaPortfolio
[17] "Lime" from Further Readings
[18] Figure 3.5 from MediaPortfolio and Transparency Pack
[19] "Formation of Water" Movie from MediaPortfolio

- Since there are fewer products than reactants, the Mg has combined with $O_2$ to form MgO.
- Note that the structure of the reactants has changed:
- Mg consists of closely packed atoms and $O_2$ consists of dispersed molecules.
- MgO consists of a lattice of $Mg^{2+}$ and $O^{2-}$ ions.

- In **decomposition reactions** one substance undergoes a reaction to produce two or more other substances.
- Decomposition reactions have more products than reactants.
  - Consider the reaction that occurs in an automobile air bag:

$$2NaN_3(s) \rightarrow 2Na(s) + 3N_2(g)$$

    - Since there are more products than reactants, the sodium azide has decomposed into sodium metal and nitrogen gas.

### Combustion in Air

- **Combustion reactions** are rapid reactions that produce a flame.
  - Most combustion reactions involve reaction of $O_2(g)$ from air.
  - Example: Combustion of a hydrocarbon (propane) to produce carbon dioxide and water.

$$C_3H_8(g) + 5O_2(g) \rightarrow 3CO_2(g) + 4H_2O(l)$$

## 3.3 Formula Weights

### Formula and Molecular Weights[20,21]

- **Formula weight** (FW) is the sum of atomic weights for the atoms shown in the chemical formula.
  - Example: FW ($H_2SO_4$)
    - = 2AW(H) + AW(S) + 4AW(O)
    - = 2(1.0 amu) + 32.0 amu + 4(16.0 amu)
    - = 98.0 amu.
- **Molecular weight** (MW) is the sum of the atomic weights of the atoms in a molecule as shown in the molecular formula.
  - Example: MW ($C_6H_{12}O_6$)
    - = 6(12.0 amu) + 12 (1.0 amu) + 6 (16.0 amu)
    - = 180.0 amu.
- Formula weight of the repeating unit (*formula unit*) is used for ionic substances.
  - Example: FW (NaCl)
    - = 23.0 amu + 35.5 amu
    - = 58.5 amu.

### Percentage Composition from Formulas[22,23]

- Percent composition is obtained by dividing the mass contributed by each element (number of atoms times AW) by the formula weight of the compound and multiplying by 100.

$$\%\ \text{element} = \frac{(\text{number of atoms of that element})(\text{atomic weight of element})(100)}{(\text{formula weight of compound})}$$

## 3.4 The Mole[24,25,26,27,28,29,30,31,32,33,34,35,36,37,38]

---

[20] "Using Monetary Analogies to Teach Average Atomic Mass" from Further Readings
[21] "Pictorial Analogies IV: Relative Atomic Weights" from Further Readings
[22] "Percentage Composition and Empirical Formula – A New View" from Further Readings
[23] "Molecular Weight and Weight Percent" Activity from MediaPortfolio

- The **mole** (abbreviated "mol") is a convenient measure of chemical quantities.
- 1 mole of something = $6.0221421 \times 10^{23}$ of that thing.
    - This number is called **Avogadro's number**.
    - Thus, 1 mole of carbon atoms = $6.0221421 \times 10^{23}$ carbon atoms.
- Experimentally, 1 mole of $^{12}C$ has a mass of 12 g.

### Molar Mass[39,40]

- The mass in grams of 1 mole of substance is said to be the **molar mass** of that substance. Molar mass has units of g/mol (also written $g{\cdot}mol^{-1}$).
- The mass of 1 mole of $^{12}C$ = 12 g.
- The molar mass of a molecule is the sum of the molar masses of the atoms:
    - Example: The molar mass of $N_2$ = 2 x (molar mass of N).
- Molar masses for elements are found on the periodic table.
- The formula weight is numerically equal to the molar mass.

### Interconverting Masses, Moles, and Number of Particles[41]

- Look at units:
    - Mass: g
    - Moles: mol
    - Molar mass: g/mol
    - Number of particles: $6.022 \times 10^{23}$ $mol^{-1}$ (Avogadro's number).
    - Note: g/mol x mol = g (i.e. molar mass x moles = mass), and
    - mol x $mol^{-1}$ = a number (i.e. moles x Avogadro's number = molecules).
- To convert between grams and moles, we use the molar mass.
- To convert between moles and molecules we use Avogadro's number.

## 3.5 Empirical Formulas from Analyses[42,43]

---

[24] "Relative Atomic Mass and the Mole: A Concrete Analogy to Help Students Understand These Abstract Concepts" from Further Readings
[25] "Developing an Intuitive Approach to Moles" from Further Readings
[26] "The Mole, the Periodic Table, and Quantum Numbers: An Introductory Trio" from Further Readings
[27] "The Size of a Mole" from Further Readings
[28] "What's a Mole For?" from Further Readings
[29] "The Mole Concept: Developing An Instrument to Assess Conceptual Understanding" from Further Readings
[30] "Moles, Pennies, and Nickels" from Further Readings
[31] "A Mole of M&M's" from Further Readings
[32] "A Mole Mnemonic" from Further Readings
[33] "How to Visualize Avogadro's Number" from Further Readings
[34] "Demonstrations of the Enormity of Avogadro's Number" from Further Readings
[35] "Analogies for Avogadro's Number" from Further Readings
[36] "Analogies that Indicate the Size of Atoms and Molecules and the Magnitude of Avogadro's Number" from Further Readings
[37] "Measuring Avogadro's Number on the Overhead Projector" from Live Demonstrations
[38] "Demonstrations for Nonscience Majors: Using Common Objects to Illustrate Abstract Concepts" from Live Demonstrations
[39] Figure 3.8 from MediaPortfolio and Transparency Pack
[40] "Gram Formula Weights and Fruit Salad" from Further Readings
[41] Figure 3.10 from MediaPortfolio and Transparency Pack

- Recall that the empirical formula gives the *relative* number of atoms in the molecule.
- Finding empirical formula from mass percent data:
  - We start with the mass percent of elements (i.e. empirical data) and calculate a formula.
  - Assume we start with 100 g of sample.
  - The mass percent then translates as the number of grams of each element in 100 g of sample.
  - From these masses, the number of moles can be calculated (using the atomic weights from the periodic table).
  - The lowest whole-number ratio of moles is the empirical formula.
- Finding the empirical mass percent of elements from the empirical formula.
  - If we have the empirical formula, we know how many moles of each element is present in one mole of same.
  - Then we use molar masses (or atomic weights) to convert to grams of each element.
  - We divide the number of grams of element by grams of 1 mole of sample to get the fraction of each element in 1 mole of sample.
  - Multiply each fraction by 100 to convert to a percent.

### Molecular Formula from Empirical Formula[44,45,46,47]

- The empirical formula (relative ratio of elements in the molecule) may not be the molecular formula (actual ratio of elements in the molecule).
- Example: ascorbic acid (vitamin C) has empirical formula $C_3H_4O_3$.
  - The molecular formula is $C_6H_8O_6$.
  - To get the molecular formula from the empirical formula, we need to know the molecular weight, MW.
  - The ratio of molecular weight (MW) to formula weight (FW) of the empirical formula must be a whole number.

### Combustion Analysis[48,49,50]

- Empirical formulas are routinely determined by combustion analysis.
- A sample containing C, H and O is combusted in excess oxygen to produce $CO_2$ and $H_2O$.
- The amount of $CO_2$ gives the amount of C originally present in the sample.
- The amount of $H_2O$ gives the amount of H originally present in the sample.
  - Watch stoichiometry: 1 mol $H_2O$ contains 2 mol H.
- The amount of O originally present in the sample is given by the difference between the amount of sample and the amount of C and H accounted for.
- More complicated methods can be used to quantify the amounts of other elements present, but they rely on analogous methods.

## 3.6 Quantitative Information from Balanced Equations[51,52,53,54,55,56,57]

---

42 "A Known-to-Unknown Approach to Teach About Empirical and Molecular Formulas" from Further Readings
43 "Making Assumptions Explicit: How the Law of Conservation of Matter Can Explain Empirical Formula Problems" from Further Readings
44 "A Simple Rhyme for a Simple Formula" from Further Readings
45 Figure 3.11 from MediaPortfolio and Transparency Pack
46 "Copper Sulfate: Blue to White" from Live Demonstrations
47 "Molecular Formula Determination: $C_2H_6O$" Activity from MediaPortfolio
48 Figure 3.12 from MediaPortfolio
49 "Reduction of CuO" Movie from MediaPortfolio
50 "Combustion of Hydrocarbons: A Stoichiometry Demonstration" from Live Demonstrations
51 "Amounts Tables as a Diagnostic Tool for Flawed Stoichiometric Reasoning" from Further Readings

- The coefficients in a balanced chemical equation give the relative numbers of molecules (or formula units) involved in the reaction.
- The stoichiometric coefficients in the balanced equation may be interpreted as:
  - The relative numbers of molecules or formula units involved in the reaction or
  - The relative numbers of moles involved in the reaction.
- The molar quantities indicated by the coefficients in a balanced equation are called *stoichiometrically equivalent quantities*.
- Stoichiometric relations or ratios may be used to convert between quantities of reactants and products in a reaction.
- It is important to realize that the stoichiometric ratios are the ideal proportions in which reactants are needed to form products.
- The number of grams of reactant cannot be *directly* related to the number of grams of product.
  - To get grams of product from grams of reactant:
    - Convert grams of reactant to moles of reactant (use molar mass),
    - Convert moles of one reactant to moles of other reactants and products (use the stoichiometric ratio from the balanced chemical equation),
    - Convert moles back into grams for desired product (use molar mass).

## 3.7 Limiting Reactants[58,59,60,61,62,63]

- It is not necessary to have all reactants present in stoichiometric amounts.
- Often, one or more reactants is present in excess.
- Therefore, at the end of reaction, those reactants present in excess will still be in the reaction mixture.
- The one or more reactants which are completely consumed are called the **limiting reactants or limiting reagents**.
  - Reactants present in excess are called *excess reactants* or *excess reagents*.
- Consider 10 $H_2$ molecules mixed with 7 $O_2$ molecules to form water.
  - The balanced chemical equation tells us that the stoichiometric ratio of $H_2$ to $O_2$ is 2 to 1:

$$2H_2(g) + O_2(g) \rightarrow 2H_2O(l)$$

  - This means that our 10 $H_2$ molecules require 5 $O_2$ molecules (2:1).
  - Since we have 7 $O_2$ molecules, our reaction is *limited* by the amount of $H_2$ we have (the $O_2$ is present in excess).
  - So, all 10 $H_2$ molecules can (and do) react with 5 of the $O_2$ molecules producing 10 $H_2O$ molecules.
  - At the end of the reaction, 2 $O_2$ molecules remain unreacted.

### Theoretical Yields[64,65]

---

52 "Stoogiometry: A Cognitive Approach to Teaching Stoichiometry" from Further Readings
53 "Teaching Stoichiometry: A Two-Cycle Approach" from Further Readings
54 "Pictorial Analogies XII: Stoichiometric Calculations" from Further Readings
55 "A Recipe for Teaching Stoichiometry" from Further Readings
56 Figure 3.13 from MediaPortfolio and Transparency Pack
57 "Stoichiometry Calculation" Activity from MediaPortfolio
58 "Limiting Reactant" Animation from MediaPortfolio
59 "Limiting Reactant: An Alternative Analogy" from Further Readings
60 "Limiting Reagents" Activity from MediaPortfolio
61 "Limiting Reagent Problems Made Simple for Students" from Further Readings
62 "Coffee, Coins, and Limiting Reagents" From Further Readings
63 Figure 3.15 from MediaPortfolio and Transparency Pack
64 "Limiting and Excess Reagents, Theoretical Yield" from Further Readings

- The amount of product predicted from stoichiometry taking into account limiting reagents is called the **theoretical yield**.
  - This is often different from the *actual yield* - the amount of product actually obtained in the reaction.
- The **percent yield** relates the actual yield (amount of material recovered in the laboratory) to the theoretical yield:

$$\text{Percent yield} = \frac{\text{actual yield}}{\text{theoretical yield}} \times 100$$

[65] "Electron Results and Reaction Yields" from Further Readings

## Further Readings:

1. Frederic L. Holmes, "Antoine Lavoisier and The Conservation of Matter," *Chemical and Engineering News*, **September 12, 1994**, 38–45.

2. John W. Hill, "Chemical Wastes and the Law of Conservation of Matter," *J. Chem. Educ.*, Vol. 58, **1981**, 996.

3. Daniel Q. Duffy, Stephanie A. Shaw, William D. Bare and Kenneth A. Goldsby, "More Chemistry in a Soda Bottle: A Conservation of Mass Activity," *J. Chem. Educ.*, Vol. 72, **1995**, 734–736.

4. William C. Herndon, "On Balancing Chemical Equations: Past and Present (A Critical Review and Annotated Bibliography)," *J. Chem. Educ.*, Vol. 74, **1997**, 1359–1362.

5. Zoltan Toth, "Balancing Chemical Equations by Inspection," *J. Chem. Educ.*, Vol. 74, **1997**, 1363–1364.

6. William Bleam, Jr., "The Fruit Basket Analogy," *J. Chem. Educ.*, Vol. 58, **1981**, 184. An analogy to help students master balancing equations.

7. Chunshi Guo, "A New Inspection Method for Balancing Redox Equations," *J. Chem. Educ.*, Vol. 74, **1997**, 1365–1366.

8. Kenneth W. Watkins, "Lime," J. *Chem. Educ.*, Vol. 60, **1983**, 60–63. An article on a some of the uses of quicklime (CaO) and hydrated lime ($Ca(OH)_2$).

9. Arthur M. Last and Michael J. Webb, "Using Monetary Analogies to Teach Average Atomic Mass," *J. Chem. Educ.*, Vol. 70, **1993**, 234–235.

10. John H. Fortman, "Pictorial Analogies IV: Relative Atomic Weights," *J. Chem. Educ.*, Vol. 70, **1993**, 235–236.

11. Josefina Arce de Sanabia, "Relative Atomic Mass and the Mole: A Concrete Analogy to Help Students Understand These Abstract Concepts," *J. Chem. Educ.*, Vol. 70, **1993**, 233–234.

12. George L. Gilbert, "Percentage Composition and Empirical Formula-A New View," *J. Chem. Educ.*, Vol. 75, **1998**, 851.

13. Dawn M. Wakeley and Hans de Grys, "Developing an Intuitive Approach to Moles," *J. Chem. Educ.*, Vol. 77, **2000**, 1007–1009.

14. Mali Yin and Raymond S. Ochs, "The Mole, the Periodic Table, and Quantum Numbers: An Introductory Trio," *J. Chem. Educ.*, Vol. 78, **2001**, 1345–1347.

15. Miriam Toloudis, "The Size of a Mole," *J. Chem. Educ.*, Vol. 73, **1996**, 348.

16. Sheryl Dominic, "What's a Mole For?", *J. Chem. Educ.*, Vol. 73, **1996**, 309.

17. Shanthi R. Krishnan and Ann C. Howe, "The Mole Concept: Developing An Instrument to Assess Conceptual Understanding," *J. Chem. Educ.*, Vol. 71, **1994**, 653–655.

18. R. Thomas Myers, "Moles, Pennies, and Nickels," *J. Chem. Educ*., Vol. 66, **1898**, 249.

19. Bernard S. Brown, "A Mole Mnemonic," *J. Chem. Educ*., Vol. 68, **1991**, 1039.

20. Carmela Merlo and Kathleen E. Turner, "A Mole of M&M's," *J. Chem. Educ*., Vol. 70, **1993**, 453.

21. Henk van Lubeck, "How to Visualize Avogadro's Number," *J. Chem. Educ*., Vol. 66, **1989**, 762.

22. Paul S. Poskozim, James W. Wazorick, Permsook Tiempetpaisal and Joyce Albin Poskozim, "Analogies for Avogadro's Number," *J. Chem. Educ*., Vol. 63, **1986**, 125–126.

23. Damon Diemente, "Demonstrations of the Enormity of Avogadro's Number," *J. Chem. Educ*., Vol. 75, **1998**, 1565–1566.

24. M. Dale Alexander, Gordon J. Ewing, and Floyd T. Abbott, "Analogies that Indicate the Size of Atoms and Molecules and the Magnitude of Avogadro's Number," *J. Chem. Educ*., Vol. 61, **1984**, 591.

25. Wayne L. Felty, "Gram Formula Weights and Fruit Salad," *J. Chem. Educ*., Vol. 62, **1985**, 61.

26. P. K. Thamburaj, "A Known-to-Unknown Approach to Teach About Empirical and Molecular Formulas," *J. Chem. Educ*., Vol. 78, **2001**, 915–916.

27. Stephen DeMeo, "Making Assumptions Explicit: How the Law of Conservation of Matter Can Explain Empirical Formula Problems," *J. Chem. Educ*., Vol. 78, **2001**, 1050–1052.

28. Joel S. Thompson, "A Simple Rhyme for a Simple Formula," *J. Chem. Educ*., Vol. 65, **1988**, 704. An easy way to remember the strategy for converting percentage composition to an empirical formula. "Percent to mass, Mass to mol, Divide by small, Multiply 'til whole".

29. John Olmsted III, "Amounts Tables as a Diagnostic Tool for Flawed Stoichiometric Reasoning," *J. Chem. Educ*., Vol. 76, **1999**, 52–54.

30. Carla R. Krieger, "Stoogiometry: A Cognitive Approach to Teaching Stoichiometry," *J. Chem. Educ*., Vol. 74, **1997**, 306–309.

31. Richard L. Poole, "Teaching Stoichiometry: A Two-Cycle Approach," *J. Chem. Educ*., Vol. 66, **1989**, 57.

32. Jean B. Umland, "A Recipe for Teaching Stoichiometry," *J. Chem. Educ*., Vol. 61, **1984**, 1036–1037.

33. Addison Ault, "How to Say How Much: Amounts and Stoichiometry," *J. Chem. Educ*., Vol. 78, **2001**, 1347–1348.

34. John J. Fortman, "Pictorial Analogies XII: Stoichiometric Calculations," *J. Chem. Educ*., Vol. 71, **1994**, 571–572.

35. Ernest F. Silversmith, "Limiting and Excess Reagents, Theoretical Yield," *J. Chem. Educ*., Vol. 62, **1985**, 61.

36. Zoltan Toth, "Limiting Reactant: An Alternative Analogy," *J. Chem. Educ*., Vol. 76, **1999**, 934.

37. A. H. Kalantar, "Limiting Reagent Problems Made Simple for Students," *J. Chem. Educ.*, Vol. 62, **1985**, 106.

38. Dennis McMinn, "Coffee, Coins, and Limiting Reagents," *J. Chem. Educ.*, Vol. 61, **1984**, 591.

39. Romeu C. Rocha-Filho, "Electron Results and Reaction Yields," *J. Chem. Educ.*, Vol. 64, **1987**, 248.

## Live Demonstrations:

1. M. Dale Alexander and Wayne C. Wolsey, "Combustion of Hydrocarbons: A Stoichiometry Demonstration," J. Chem. Educ. Vol. 70, **1993**, 327–328. The combustion of methane, propane, and butane are compared in this simple demonstration of stoichiometry.

2. Sally Solomon and Chinhyu Hur, "Measuring Avogadro's Number on the Overhead Projector," *J. Chem. Educ.*, Vol. 70, **1993**, 252–253. A monolayer of stearic acid on water is used to estimate Avogadro's number.

3. William Laurita, "Demonstrations for Nonscience Majors: Using Common Objects to Illustrate Abstract Concepts," *J. Chem. Educ*. Vol. 67, **1990**, 60–61. This reference includes a demonstration of the measurement of Avogadro's number.

4. Lee. R. Summerlin,, Christie L. Borgford, and Julie B. Ealy, "Copper Sulfate: Blue to White," *Chemical Demonstrations, A Sourcebook for Teachers*, Volume 2 (Washington: American Chemical Society, **1988**), pp. 69–70. An exploration of color change associated with the dehydration of copper sulfate.

# Chapter 4. Aqueous Reactions and Solution Stoichiometry

## Media Resources

### Figures and Tables

| In Transparency Pack and on MediaPortfolio: | Section: |
| --- | --- |
| Table 4.1 Solubility Guidelines for Common Ionic Compounds in Water | 4.2 Precipitation Reactions |
| Table 4.3 Summary of the Electrolytic Behavior Of Common Soluble Ionic and Molecular Compounds | 4.3 Acid-Base Reactions |
| Table 4.5 Activity Series of Metals in Aqueous Solutions | 4.4 Oxidation-Reduction Reactions |
| Figure 4.18 Procedure for Solving Stoichiometry Problems | 4.6 Solution Stoichiometry and Chemical Analysis |
| Figure 4.20 Titrating an Acid | 4.6 Solution Stoichiometry and Chemical Analysis |

| On MediaPortfolio: | Section: |
| --- | --- |
| Figure 4.3 Dissolution of Ionic and Molecular Compounds | 4.1 General Properties of Aqueous Solutions |
| Figure 4.4 Formation of $PbI_2$ | 4.2 Precipitation Reactions |
| Figure 4.6 Formation of $NH_4OH$ | 4.3 Acid-Base Reactions |
| Table 4.2 Common Strong Acids and Bases | 4.3 Acid-Base Reactions |
| Figure 4.12 Oxidation and Reduction | 4.4 Oxidation-Reduction Reactions |

| Animations: | Section: |
| --- | --- |
| Electrolytes and Nonelectrolytes | 4.1 General Properties of Aqueous Solutions |
| Dissolution of NaCl in Water | 4.1 General Properties of Aqueous Solutions |
| Introduction to Aqueous Acids | 4.3 Acid-Base Reactions |
| Introduction to Aqueous Bases | 4.3 Acid-Base Reactions |
| Oxidation-Reduction Reactions: Part I | 4.4 Oxidation-Reduction Reactions |
| Oxidation-Reduction Reactions: Part II | 4.4 Oxidation-Reduction Reactions |
| Solution Formation from a Solid | 4.5 Concentrations of Solutions |
| Dissolution of $KMnO_4$ | 4.5 Concentrations of Solutions |
| Solution Formation by Dilution | 4.5 Concentrations of Solutions |
| Acid-Base Titration | 4.6 Solution Stoichiometry and Chemical Analysis |

| Movies: | Section: |
| --- | --- |
| Strong and Weak Electrolytes | 4.1 General Properties of Aqueous Solutions |
| Precipitation Reactions | 4.2 Precipitation Reactions |
| Oxidation-Reduction Chemistry of Tin and Zinc | 4.4 Oxidation-Reduction Reactions |
| Formation of Silver Crystals | 4.4 Oxidation-Reduction Reactions |

| Activities: | Section: |
| --- | --- |
| Writing a Net Ionic Equation | 4.2 Precipitation Reactions |
| Strong Acids | 4.3 Acid-Base Reactions |
| Oxidation Numbers | 4.4 Oxidation-Reduction Reactions |

| | |
|---|---|
| Precipitation, Redox and Neutralization Reactions | 4.4 Oxidation-Reduction Reactions |
| Acid-Base Titration | 4.6 Solution Stoichiometry and Chemical Analysis |

| **3-D Models:** | **Section:** |
|---|---|
| Sodium Chloride | 4.1 General Properties of Aqueous Solutions |
| Sucrose | 4.1 General Properties of Aqueous Solutions |
| Ethanol | 4.1 General Properties of Aqueous Solutions |
| HCl | 4.1 General Properties of Aqueous Solutions |
| Acetic Acid | 4.1 General Properties of Aqueous Solutions |

## Other Resources

| **Further Readings:** | **Section:** |
|---|---|
| An Analogy for Solubility: Marbles and Magnets | 4.2 Precipitation Reactions |
| Reinforcing Net Ionic Equation Writing | 4.2 Precipitation Reactions |
| Significance, Concentration Calculations, Weak and Strong Acids | 4.3 Acid-Base Reactions |
| When Is a Strong Electrolyte Strong? | 4.3 Acid-Base Reactions |
| Pictorial Analogies X: Solutions of Electrolytes | 4.3 Acid-Base Reactions |
| Reinforcing Net Ionic Equation Writing | 4.3 Acid-Base Reactions |
| Oxidation and Reduction | 4.4 Oxidation-Reduction Reactions |
| Oxidation Numbers | 4.4 Oxidation-Reduction Reactions |
| Simple Method for Determination of Oxidation Numbers of Atoms in Compounds | 4.4 Oxidation-Reduction Reactions |
| What Makes Gold Such a Noble Metal? | 4.4 Oxidation-Reduction Reactions |
| A Cyclist's Guide to Ionic Concentration | 4.5 Concentrations of Solutions |
| Teaching Dilutions | 4.5 Concentrations of Solutions |
| On the Use of Intravenous Solutions to Teach Some Principles of Solution Chemistry | 4.5 Concentrations of Solutions |
| Acid-Base Indicators: a New Look at an Old Topic | 4.6 Solution Stoichiometry and Chemical Analysis |

| **Live Demonstrations:** | **Section:** |
|---|---|
| Conductivity and Extent of Dissociation of Acids in Aqueous Solution. | 4.1 General Properties of Aqueous Solutions |
| Name That Precipitate | 4.2 Precipitation Reactions |
| Solubility of Some Silver Compounds | 4.2 Precipitation Reactions |
| Food is Usually Acidic, Cleaners are Usually Basic | 4.3 Acid-Base Reactions |
| Fizzing and Foaming: Reactions of Acids with Carbonates | 4.3 Acid-Base Reactions |
| Determination of Neutralizing Capacity of Antacids | 4.3 Acid-Base Reactions |
| Milk of Magnesia versus Acid | 4.3 Acid-Base Reactions |
| Alka Seltzer Poppers: An Interactive Exploration | 4.3 Acid-Base Reactions |
| Demonstrations with Red Cabbage Indicator | 4.3 Acid-Base Reactions |
| A Hand-Held Reaction: Production of Ammonia Gas | 4.3 Acid-Base Reactions |
| Oxidation States of Manganese: $Mn^{7+}$, $Mn^{6+}$, $Mn^{4+}$, and $Mn^{2+}$ | 4.4 Oxidation-Reduction Reactions |
| Producing Hydrogen Gas from Calcium Metal | 4.4 Oxidation-Reduction Reactions |
| Activity Series for Some Metals | 4.4 Oxidation-Reduction Reactions |
| Making Hydrogen Gas from an Acid and a Base | 4.4 Oxidation-Reduction Reactions |

| | |
|---|---|
| An Activity Series: Zinc, Copper, and Silver Half Cells | 4.4 Oxidation-Reduction Reactions |
| Floating Pennies | 4.4 Oxidation-Reduction Reactions |
| Colorful Acid-Base Indicators | 4.6 Solution Stoichiometry and Chemical Analysis |
| Rainbow Colors with Mixed Acid-Base Indicators | 4.6 Solution Stoichiometry and Chemical Analysis |
| Acid-Base Indicators Extracted from Plants | 4.6 Solution Stoichiometry and Chemical Analysis |
| Teas as Natural Indicators | 4.6 Solution Stoichiometry and Chemical Analysis |

# Chapter 4. Aqueous Reactions and Solution Stoichiometry

## Common Student Misconceptions

- Molarity is moles of solute per *liter of solution* not per liter of solvent.
- Students sometimes use moles instead of molarity in $M_{initial}V_{initial} = M_{final}V_{final}$.
- Students sometimes think that water is a good conductor.
- Students sometimes have a problem with the arbitrary difference between strong and weak electrolytes.
- The symbols $\leftrightharpoons$ (equilibrium) and $\leftrightarrow$ (resonance) are often confused.
- Students often do not see that the net ionic equation for the reaction between strong acids and strong bases is always $H^+(aq) + OH^-(aq) \rightarrow H_2O(l)$.
- Students try to split polyatomic ions into smaller ions when they write net ionic equations.
- Students do not appreciate the difference between equivalence point and end point.

## Lecture Outline

### 4.1 General Properties of Aqueous Solutions

- A solution is a homogeneous mixture of two or more substances.
- A solution is made when one substance (the **solute**) is dissolved in another (the **solvent**).
- The solute is the substance that is present in smallest amount.
- Solutions in which water is the solvent are called **aqueous solutions**.

#### Electrolytic Properties[1,2,3]

- All aqueous solutions can be classified in terms of whether or not they conduct electricity.
- If a substance forms ions in solution, then the substance is an **electrolyte**, and the solution conducts electricity. Example: NaCl.
- If a substance does not form ions in solution, then the substance is a **nonelectrolyte**, and the solution does not conduct electricity. Example: sucrose.

#### Ionic Compounds in Water[4,5]

- When an ionic compound dissolves in water, the ions are said to *dissociate*.
  - This means that in solution, the solid no longer exists as a well-ordered arrangement of ions in contact with one another.
  - Instead, each ion is surrounded by a shell of water molecules.
  - This tends to stabilize the ions in solution and prevent cations and anions from recombining.
  - The positive ions have the surrounding oxygen atoms of water pointing towards the ion, negative ions have the surrounding hydrogen atoms of water pointing towards the ion.
  - The transport of ions through the solution causes electric current to flow through the solution.

#### Molecular Compounds in Water[6]

- When a molecular compound (e.g. $CH_3OH$ ) dissolves in water, there are no ions formed.

---

1 "Electrolytes and Nonelectrolytes" Animation from MediaPortfolio
2 "Sodium Chloride" 3-D Model from MediaPortfolio
3 "Sucrose" 3-D Model from MediaPortfolio
4 Figure 4.3 from MediaPortfolio
5 "Dissolution of NaCl in Water" Animation from MediaPortfolio
6 "Ethanol" 3-D Model from MediaPortfolio

- Therefore, there is nothing in the solution to transport electric charge and the solution does not conduct electricity.
- There are some important exceptions.
  - For example, $NH_3(g)$ reacts with water to form $NH_4^+(aq)$ and $OH^-(aq)$.
  - For example, $HCl(g)$ in water *ionizes* to form $H^+(aq)$ and $Cl^-(aq)$.

### Strong and Weak Electrolytes[7,8,9,10]

- Compounds whose aqueous solutions conduct electricity well are called **strong electrolytes.**
  - These substances exist only as ions in solution.
  - Example NaCl:

$$NaCl(aq) \rightarrow Na^+(aq) + Cl^-(aq)$$

  - The single arrow indicates that the $Na^+$ and $Cl^-$ ions have no tendency to recombine to form NaCl molecules.
  - In general, soluble ionic compounds are strong electrolytes.
- Compounds whose aqueous solutions conduct electricity poorly are called **weak electrolytes**
  - These substances exist as a mixture of ions and un-ionized molecules in solution.
    - The predominant form of the solute is the un-ionized molecule.
  - Example: acetic acid, $HC_2H_3O_2$.

$$HC_2H_3O_2(aq) \rightleftharpoons H^+(aq) + C_2H_3O_2^-(aq)$$

  - The double arrow means that the reaction is significant in both directions.
  - It indicates that there is a balance between the forward and reverse reactions.
  - This balance produces a state of chemical equilibrium.

## 4.2 Precipitation Reactions[11,12,13,14]

- Reactions that result in the formation of an insoluble product are known as precipitation reactions.
- A precipitate is an insoluble solid formed by a reaction in solution.
  - Example: $Pb(NO_3)_2(aq) + 2KI(aq) \rightarrow PbI_2(s) + 2KNO_3(aq)$

### Solubility Guidelines for Ionic Compounds[15,16]

- The solubility of a substance is the amount of that substance that can be dissolved in a given quantity of solvent.
- A substance with a solubility of less than 0.01 mol/L is regarded as being *insoluble*.
- Experimental observations have led to empirical guidelines for predicting the solubility.
- Solubility guidelines for common ionic compounds in water:
  - Compounds containing alkali metal ions or ammonium ion are soluble.
  - Compounds containing $NO_3^-$ or $C_2H_3O_2^-$ are soluble.
  - Compounds containing $Cl^-$, $Br^-$ or $I^-$ are soluble.
    - Exceptions: Compounds of $Ag^+$, $Hg_2^{2+}$, and $Pb^{2+}$.
    - Compounds containing $SO_4^{2-}$ are soluble.

---

[7] "Strong and Weak Electrolytes" Movie from MediaPortfolio
[8] "Conductivity and Extent of Dissociation of Acids in Aqueous Solution" from Live Demonstrations
[9] "HCl" 3-D Model from MediaPortfolio
[10] "Acetic Acid" 3-D Model from MediaPortfolio
[11] "Name That Precipitate" from Live Demonstrations
[12] "An Analogy for Solubility: Marbles and Magnets" from Further Readings
[13] "Precipitation Reactions" Movie from MediaPortfolio
[14] Figure 4.4 from MediaPortfolio
[15] Table 4.1 from MediaPortfolio and Transparency Pack
[16] "Solubility of Some Silver Compounds" from Live Demonstrations

- Exceptions: Compounds of $Sr^{2+}$, $Ba^{2+}$, $Hg_2^{2+}$, and $Pb^{2+}$
- Compounds containing $S^{2-}$ are insoluble.
  - Exceptions: Compounds of $NH_4^+$, the alkali metal cations, and $Ca^{2+}$, $Sr^{2+}$, and $Ba^{2+}$.
- Compounds of $CO_3^{2-}$ or $PO_4^{3-}$ are insoluble.
  - Exceptions: Compounds of $NH_4^+$ and the alkali metal cations.
- Compounds of $OH^-$ are insoluble.
  - Exceptions: Compounds of the alkali metal cations, and $Ca^{2+}$, $Sr^{2+}$, and $Ba^{2+}$.

### Exchange (Metathesis) Reactions

- **Exchange reactions** or **metathesis reactions** involve swapping ions in solution:

$$AX + BY \rightarrow AY + BX.$$

- Many precipitation and acid-base reactions exhibit this pattern.

### Ionic Equations[17,18]

- Consider $2KI(aq) + Pb(NO_3)_2(aq) \rightarrow PbI_2(s) + 2KNO_3(aq)$.
- Both $KI(aq) + Pb(NO_3)_2(aq)$ are colorless solutions. When mixed, they form a bright yellow precipitate of $PbI_2$ and a solution of $KNO_3$.
- The final product of the reaction contains solid $PbI_2$, aqueous $K^+$ and aqueous $NO_3^-$ ions.
- Sometimes we want to highlight the reaction between ions.
- The **molecular equation** lists all species in their molecular forms:

$$Pb(NO_3)_2(aq) + 2KI(aq) \rightarrow PbI_2(s) + 2KNO_3(aq)$$

- The **complete ionic equation** lists all strong soluble electrolytes in the reaction as ions:

$$Pb^{2+}(aq) + 2NO_3^-(aq) + 2K^+(aq) + 2I^-(aq) \rightarrow PbI_2(s) + 2K^+(aq) + 2NO_3^-(aq)$$

  - Only strong electrolytes dissolved in aqueous solution are written in ionic form.
  - Weak electrolytes and nonelectrolytes are written in their molecular form.
- The **net ionic equation** lists only those ions which are not common on both sides of the reaction:

$$Pb^{2+}(aq) + 2I^-(aq) \rightarrow PbI_2(s)$$

  - Note that **spectator ions**, ions that are present in the solution but play no direct role in the reaction, are omitted in the net ionic equation.

## 4.3 Acid-Base Reactions

### Acids[19,20]

- **Acids** are substances that are able to ionize in aqueous solution to form $H^+$.
  - Ionization occurs when a neutral substance forms ions in solution.
    Example: $HC_2H_3O_2$ (acetic acid).
- Since $H^+$ is a naked proton, we refer to acids as proton donors and bases as proton acceptors.
- Common acids are HCl, $HNO_3$, vinegar and vitamin C.
- Acids that ionize to form *one* $H^+$ ion are called *monoprotic* acids.
- Acids that ionize to form *two* $H^+$ ions are called *diprotic acids*.

### Bases[21,22]

- **Bases** are substances that accept or react with the $H^+$ ions formed by acids.
- Hydroxide ions, $OH^-$, react with the $H^+$ ions to form water:

---

[17] "Reinforcing Net Ionic Equation Writing" from Further Readings
[18] "Writing a Net Ionic Equation" Activity from MediaPortfolio
[19] "Introduction to Aqueous Acids" Animation from MediaPortfolio
[20] Table 4.2 from MediaPortfolio
[21] "Introduction to Aqueous Bases" Animation from MediaPortfolio
[22] Figure 4.6 from MediaPortfolio

$$H^+(aq) + OH^-(aq) \rightarrow H_2O(l)$$

- Common bases are $NH_3$ (ammonia), Draino, milk of magnesia.
- Compounds that do not contain $OH^-$ ions can also be bases.
  - Proton transfer between $NH_3$ (a weak base) and water (a weak acid) is an example of an acid-base reaction.
  - Since there is a mixture of $NH_3$, $H_2O$, $NH_4^+$, and $OH^-$ in solution, we write

$$NH_3(aq) + H_2O(l) \leftrightharpoons NH_4^+(aq) + OH^-(aq)$$

## Strong and Weak Acids and Bases[23]

- **Strong acids** and **strong bases** are strong electrolytes.
  - They are completely ionized in solution.
  - Strong bases include: Group 1A metal hydroxides, $Ca(OH)_2$, $Ba(OH)_2$, and $Sr(OH)_2$.
  - Strong acids include: HCl, HBr, HI, $HClO_3$, $HClO_4$, $H_2SO_4$, and $HNO_3$.
  - We write the ionization of HCl as:

$$HCl \rightarrow H^+ + Cl^-$$

- **Weak acids** and **weak bases** are weak electrolytes.
  - Therefore, they are partially ionized in solution.
- HF(*aq*) is a weak acid; most acids are weak acids.
- We write the ionization of HF as:

$$HF \leftrightharpoons H^+ + F^-$$

## Identifying Strong and Weak Electrolytes[24,25,26,27,28]

- Compounds can be classified as strong electrolytes, weak electrolytes or nonelectrolytes by looking at their solubility.
- Strong electrolytes:
  - If a compound is water soluble and ionic, then it is probably a strong electrolyte.
  - If a compound is water soluble and not ionic, and is a strong acid, then it is a strong electrolyte.
  - Similarly, if a compound is water soluble and not ionic, but is a strong base, then it is a strong electrolyte.
- Weak electrolytes:
  - If a compound is water soluble and not ionic, and is a weak acid or weak base, then it is a weak electrolyte.
- Nonelectrolytes:
  - Otherwise, the compound is probably a nonelectrolyte.

## Neutralization Reactions and Salts[29,30,31,32,33]

- A **neutralization reaction** occurs when an acid and a base react:
  - $HCl(aq) + NaOH(aq) \rightarrow H_2O(l) + NaCl(aq)$
  - (acid) + (base) → (water) + (salt)

---

23 "Significance, Concentration Calculations, Weak and Strong Acids" from Further Readings
24 "When is a Strong Electrolyte Strong?" from Further Readings
25 "Pictorial Analogies X: Solutions of Electrolytes" from Further Readings
26 "Food is Usually Acidic, Cleaners are Usually Basic" from Live Demonstrations
27 Table 4.3 from MediaPortfolio and Transparency Pack
28 "Strong Acids" Activity from MediaPortfolio
29 "Demonstrations with Red Cabbage Indicator" from Live Demonstrations
30 "Determination of Neutralizing Capacity of Antacids" from Live Demonstrations
31 "Milk of Magnesia versus Acid" from Live Demonstrations
32 "Alka Seltzer Poppers: An Interactive Exploration" from Live Demonstrations
33 "Reinforcing Net Ionic Equation Writing" from Further Readings

- In general an acid and base react to form a **salt**.
- A salt is any ionic compound whose cation comes from a base and anion from an acid.
- The other product, $H_2O$, is a common weak electrolyte.
- Typical examples of neutralization reactions:
  - Reaction between an acid and a metal hydroxide:
    - $Mg(OH)_2$ (milk of magnesia) is a suspension.
    - As HCl is added, the magnesium hydroxide dissolves, and a clear solution containing $Mg^{2+}$ and $Cl^-$ ions is formed.
    - Molecular equation:
$$Mg(OH)_2(s) + 2HCl(aq) \rightarrow MgCl_2(aq) + 2H_2O(l)$$
    - Net ionic equation:
$$Mg(OH)_2(s) + 2H^+(aq) \rightarrow Mg^{2+}(aq) + 2H_2O(l)$$
      - Note that the magnesium hydroxide is an insoluble solid; it appears in the net ionic equation.

### Acid-Base Reactions with Gas Formation[34,35]

- There are many bases besides $OH^-$ that react with $H^+$ to form molecular compounds.
  - Reaction of sulfides with acid gives rise to $H_2S(g)$.
    - Sodium sulfide ($Na_2S$) reacts with HCl to form $H_2S(g)$:
    - Molecular equation:
$$Na_2S(aq) + 2HCl(aq) \rightarrow H_2S(g) + 2NaCl(aq)$$
    - Net ionic equation:
$$2H^+(aq) + S^{2-}(aq) \rightarrow H_2S(g)$$
  - Carbonates and hydrogen carbonates (or bicarbonates) will form $CO_2(g)$ when treated with an acid.
    - Sodium hydrogen carbonate ($NaHCO_3$; baking soda) reacts with HCl to form bubbles of $CO_2(g)$:
    - Molecular equation:
$$NaHCO_3(s) + HCl(aq) \rightarrow NaCl(aq) + H_2CO_3(aq) \rightarrow H_2O(l) + CO_2(g) + NaCl(aq)$$
    - Net ionic equation:
$$H^+(aq) + HCO_3^-(aq) \rightarrow H_2O(l) + CO_2(g)$$

## 4.4 Oxidation-Reduction Reactions

### Oxidation and Reduction[36,37,38,39,40]

- **Oxidation-reduction** or *redox* reactions involve transfer of electrons between reactants.
- When a substances loses electrons, it undergoes **oxidation**:
$$Ca(s) + 2H^+(aq) \rightarrow Ca^{2+}(aq) + H_2(g)$$
  - The neutral Ca has lost two electrons to $2H^+$ to become $Ca^{2+}$.
  - We say Ca has been oxidized to $Ca^{2+}$.
- When a substance gains electrons, it undergoes **reduction**:
$$2Ca(s) + O_2(g) \rightarrow 2CaO(s).$$
  - In this reaction the neutral $O_2$ has gained electrons from the Ca to become $O^{2-}$ in CaO.

---

[34] "Fizzing and Foaming Reactions of Acids with Carbonates" from Live Demonstrations
[35] "A Hand-Held Reaction: Production of Ammonia Gas" from Live Demonstrations
[36] "Gain and Loss of Electrons" Animation from MediaPortfolio
[37] "Oxidation-Reduction Reactions: Part I" Animation from MediaPortfolio
[38] "Oxidation-Reduction Reactions: Part II" Animation from MediaPortfolio
[39] "Oxidation and Reduction" from Further Readings
[40] Figure 4.12 from MediaPortfolio

- We say $O_2$ has been reduced to $O^{2-}$.
- In all redox reactions, one species is reduced at the same time as another is oxidized.

## Oxidation Numbers[41,42,43,44]

- Electrons are not explicitly shown in chemical equations.
- **Oxidation numbers** (or *oxidation states*) help up keep track of electrons during chemical reactions.
- Oxidation numbers are assigned to atoms using specific rules.
  - For an atom in its *elemental form*, the oxidation number is always zero.
  - For any *monatomic ion*, the oxidation number equals the charge on the ion.
  - *Nonmetals* usually have negative oxidation numbers.
    - The oxidation number of *oxygen* is usually –2.
      - The major exception is in peroxides (containing the $O_2^{2-}$ ion).
  - The oxidation number of *hydrogen* is +1 when bonded to nonmetals and –1 when bonded to metals.
  - The oxidation number of *fluorine* is –1 in all compounds. The other *halogens* have an oxidation number of –1 in most binary compounds.
  - *The sum of the oxidation numbers* of all atoms in a neutral compound is zero.
  - The sum of the oxidation numbers in a polyatomic ion equals the charge of the ion.
- The oxidation of an element is evidenced by its increase in oxidation number; reduction is accompanied by a decrease in oxidation number.

## Oxidation of Metals by Acids and Salts[45]

- The reaction of a metal with either an acid or a metal salt is called a **displacement reaction.**
- General pattern:

$$A + \mathbf{BX} \rightarrow \mathbf{AX} + B$$

  - Example: It is common for metals to produce hydrogen gas when they react with acids. Consider the reaction between Mg and HCl:

$$Mg(s) + 2HCl(aq) \rightarrow MgCl_2(aq) + H_2(g)$$

    - In the process the metal is oxidized and the $H^+$ is reduced.
  - Example: It is possible for metals to be oxidized in the presence of a salt:

$$Fe(s) + Ni(NO_3)_2(aq) \rightarrow Fe(NO_3)_2(aq) + Ni(s)$$

    - The net ionic equation shows the redox chemistry well:

$$Fe(s) + Ni^{2+}(aq) \rightarrow Fe^{2+}(aq) + Ni(s)$$

    - In this reaction iron has been oxidized to $Fe^{2+}$ while the $Ni^{2+}$ has been reduced to Ni.
- Always keep in mind that whenever one substance is oxidized, some other substance *must* be reduced.

## The Activity Series[46,47,48,49,50,51,52,53,54]

---

41 "Oxidation Numbers" from Further Readings
42 "Simple Method for Determination of Oxidation Numbers of Atoms in Compounds" from Further Readings
43 "Oxidation States of Manganese: $Mn^{7+}$, $Mn^{6+}$, $Mn^{4+}$, and $Mn^{2+}$" from Live Demonstrations
44 "Oxidation Numbers" Activity from MediaPortfolio
45 "Producing Hydrogen Gas from Calcium Metal" from Live Demonstrations
46 Table 4.5 from MediaPortfolio and Transparency Pack
47 "Formation of Silver Crystals" Movie from MediaPortfolio
48 "Activity Series for Some Metals" from Live Demonstrations
49 "Making Hydrogen Gas from an Acid and a Base" from Live Demonstrations
50 "An Activity Series: Zinc, Copper, and Silver Half Cells" from Live Demonstrations
51 "Floating Pennies" from Live Demonstrations
52 "What Makes Gold Such a Noble Metal?" from Further Readings

- We can list metals in order of decreasing ease of oxidation.
  - This list is an **activity series.**
- The metals at the top of the activity series are called *active metals.*
- The metals at the bottom of the activity series are called *noble metals.*
- A metal in the activity series can only be oxidized by a metal ion below it.
- If we place Cu into a solution of $Ag^+$ ions, then $Cu^{2+}$ ions can be formed because Cu is above Ag in the activity series:

$$Cu(s) + 2AgNO_3(aq) \rightarrow Cu(NO_3)_2(aq) + 2Ag(s)$$

or

$$Cu(s) + 2Ag^+(aq) \rightarrow Cu^{2+}(aq) + 2Ag(s)$$

## 4.5 Concentrations of Solutions

- The term **concentration** is used to indicate the amount of solute dissolved in a given quantity of solvent or solution.

### Molarity[55,56]

- Solutions can be prepared with different concentrations by adding different amounts of solute to solvent.
- The amount (moles) of solute per liter of solution is the **molarity** (symbol *M*) of the solution:

$$\text{Molarity} = \frac{\text{moles solute}}{\text{liters of solution}}$$

- By knowing the molarity of a quantity of liters of solution, we can easily calculate the number of moles (and, by using molar mass, the mass) of solute.
- Consider weighed copper sulfate, $CuSO_4$ (39.9 g, 0.250 mol) placed in a 250 ml volumetric flask. A little water is added and the flask swirled to ensure the copper sulfate dissolves. When all the copper sulfate has dissolved, the flask is filled to the mark with water.
  - The molarity of the solution is 0.250 mol $CuSO_4$ / 0.250 L solution = 1.00 *M.*

### Expressing the Concentration of an Electrolyte[57]

- When an ionic compound dissolves, the relative concentrations of the ions in the solution depend on the chemical formula of the compound.
  - Example: For a 1.0 *M* solution of NaCl:
    - The solution is 1.0 *M* in $Na^+$ ions and 1.0 *M* in $Cl^-$ ions.
  - Example: For a 1.0 *M* solution of $Na_2SO_4$:
    - The solution is 2.0 *M* in $Na^+$ ions and 1.0 *M* in $SO_4^{2-}$ ions.

### Interconverting Molarity, Moles, and Volume

- The definition of molarity contains three quantities: molarity, moles of solute, and liters of solution.
  - If we know any two of these, we can calculate the third.
  - Dimensional analysis is very helpful in these calculations.

### Dilution[58,59,60]

---

53 "Oxidation-Reduction Chemistry of Tin and Zinc" Movie from MediaPortfolio
54 "Precipitation, Redox, and Neutralization Reactions" Activity from MediaPortfolio
55 "Solution Formation from a Solid" Animation from MediaPortfolio
56 "Dissolution of $KMnO_4$" Animation from MediaPortfolio
57 "A Cyclist's Guide to Ionic Concentration" from Further Readings
58 "Solution Formation by Dilution" Animation from MediaPortfolio
59 "Teaching Dilutions" from Further Readings

- A solution in concentrated form (*stock solution*) is mixed with solvent to obtain a solution of lower solute concentration.
    - This process is called **dilution**.
- An alternate way of making a solution is to take a solution of known molarity and dilute it with more solvent.
- Since the number of moles of solute remains the same in the concentrated and dilute forms of the solution, we can show:

$$M_{\text{initial}}V_{\text{initial}} = M_{\text{final}}V_{\text{final}}.$$

- An alternate form of this equation is:

$$M_{\text{concentrated}}V_{\text{concentrated}} = M_{\text{dilute}}V_{\text{dilute}}$$

## 4.6 Solution Stoichiometry and Chemical Analysis[61]

- In approaching stoichiometry problems:
    - Recognize that there are two different types of units:
        - Laboratory units (the macroscopic units that we measure in lab) and
        - Chemical units (the microscopic units that relate to moles).
    - Always convert the laboratory units into chemical units first.
        - Convert grams to moles using molar mass.
        - Convert volume or molarity into moles using $M$ = mol/L.
    - Use the stoichiometric coefficients to move between reactants and products.
        - ***This step requires the balanced chemical equation.***
    - Convert the laboratory units back into the required units.
        - Convert moles to grams using molar mass.
        - Convert moles to molarity or volume using $M$ = mol/L.

### Titrations[62,63,64,65,66,67,68,69]

- A common way to determine the concentration of a solution is via **titration**.
- We determine the concentration of one substance by allowing it to undergo a specific chemical reaction, of known stoichiometry, with another substance whose concentration is known (**standard solution**).
- Example: Suppose we know the molarity of an NaOH solution and we want to find the molarity of an HCl solution.
    - What do we know?
        - Molarity of NaOH, volume of HCl.
    - What do we want?
        - Molarity of HCl.
    - What do we do?

---

60 "On the Use of Intravenous Solutions to Teach Some Principles of Solution Chemistry" from Further Readings
61 Figure 4.18 from MediaPortfolio and Transparency Pack
62 Figure 4.20 from MediaPortfolio and Transparency Pack
63 "Acid-Base Titration" Animation from MediaPortfolio
64 "Acid-Base Titration" Activity from MediaPortfolio
65 "Colorful Acid-Base Indicators" from Live Demonstrations
66 "Rainbow Colors with Mixed Acid-Base Indicators" from Live Demonstrations
67 "Acid-Base Indicators Extracted from Plants" from Live Demonstrations
68 "Teas as Natural Indicators" from Live Demonstrations
69 "Acid-Base Indicators: a New Look at an Old Topic" from Further Readings

- Take a known volume of the HCl solution (i.e., 20.00 mL) and measure the number of milliliters of NaOH required to react completely with the HCl solution.
- The point at which stoichiometrically equivalent quantities of NaOH and HCl are brought together is known as the **equivalence point** of the titration.
- In a titration we often use an acid-base **indicator** to allow us to determine when the equivalence point of the titration has been reached.
  - Acid-base indicators change color at the *end point* of the titration.
  - The indicator is chosen so that the end point corresponds to the equivalence point of the titration.
- What do we get?
  - Volume of NaOH. Since we already have the molarity of the NaOH, we can calculate moles of NaOH.
- Next step?
  - We also know HCl + NaOH → NaCl + $H_2O$.
  - Therefore, we know moles of HCl.
- Can we finish?
  - Knowing mol (HCl) and volume of HCl, we can calculate the molarity.

## Further Readings:

1. Richard A. Kjonaas, "An Analogy for Solubility: Marbles and Magnets," *J. Chem. Educ.*, Vol. 61, **1984**, 765.

2. H. van Lubeck, "Significance, Concentration Calculations, Weak and Strong Acids," *J. Chem. Educ.*, Vol. 60, **1983**, 189.

3. Albert Kowalak, "When is a Strong Electrolyte Strong?" *J. Chem. Educ.*, Vol. 65, **1988**, 607.

4. John J. Fortman, "Pictorial Analogies X: Solutions of Electrolytes," *J. Chem. Educ.*, Vol. 71, **1994**, 27–28.

5. Betty J. Wruck, "Reinforcing Net Ionic Equation Writing," *J. Chem. Educ.*, Vol. 73, **1996**, 149–150.

6. Marten J. ten Hoor and Aletta Jacobsscholengemeenschap, "Oxidation and Reduction," *J. Chem. Educ.*, Vol. 60, **1983**, 132. An analogy for remembering oxidation and reduction.

7. Gian Calzaferri, "Oxidation Numbers," *J. Chem. Educ.*, Vol. 76, **1999**, 362–363.

8. Joel M. Kauffman, "Simple Method for Determination of Oxidation Numbers of Atoms in Compounds," *J. Chem. Educ.*, Vol. 63, **1986**, 474–475.

7. R. Lipkin, "What Makes Gold Such a Noble Metal?" *Science News*, July 22, **1995**, 62.

8. Arthur M. Last, "A Cyclist's Guide to Ionic Concentration," *J. Chem. Educ.*, Vol. 75, **1998**, 1433.

9. Lloyd J. McElroy, "Teaching Dilutions," *J. Chem. Educ.*, Vol. 73, **1996**, 765–766.

10. Irwin L. Shaprio, "On the Use of Intravenous Solutions to Teach Some Principles of Solution Chemistry," *J. Chem. Educ.*, Vol. 59, **1982**, 725.

11. Ara S. Kooser, Judith L. Jenkins, and Lawrence E. Welch, "Acid-Base Indicators: a New Look at an Old Topic," *J. Chem. Educ.*, Vol. 78, **2001**, 1504–1506

## Live Demonstrations:

1. Bassam Z. Shakhashiri, "Conductivity and Extent of Dissociation of Acids in Aqueous Solution," *Chemical Demonstrations: A Handbook for Teachers of Chemistry*, Volume 3 (Madison: The University of Wisconsin Press, **1989**), pp. 140–145. Universal indicator and a conductivity probe are used to explore the relative acidity and conductivity of a series of aqueous acids.

2. A. M. Sarquis and L. M. Woodward, "Alka Seltzer Poppers: an Interactive Exploration," *J. Chem. Educ.*, Vol. 76, **1999**, 386–386. An interactive exercise involving the addition of water to Alka Seltzer®; this demonstration may be used to introduce a variety of concepts such as acid-base chemistry, kinetics, and solubility.

3. Lee R. Summerlin, Christie L. Borgford, and Julie B. Ealy, "Name That Precipitate," *Chemical Demonstrations, A Sourcebook for Teachers*, *Volume 2* (Washington: American Chemical Society, **1988**), pp. 121–123. Students explore a variety of ionic reactions that result in the formation of colored precipitates.

4. Lee. R. Summerlin, Christie L. Borgford, and Julie B. Ealy, "Solubility of Some Silver Compounds," *Chemical Demonstrations, A Sourcebook for Teachers*, *Volume 2* (Washington: American Chemical Society, **1988**), pp. 83–85. The solubility of a series of silver salts and complexes is explored in this colorful demonstration.

5. Bassam Z. Shakhashiri, "Food is Usually Acidic, Cleaners Are Usually Basic," *Chemical Demonstrations: A Handbook for Teachers of Chemistry, Volume 3* (Madison: The University of Wisconsin Press, **1989**), pp. 65–69. The pH of a variety of household chemicals is determined using indicators and pH meters.

6. Bassam Z. Shakhashiri, "Fizzing and Foaming: Reactions of Acids with Carbonates," *Chemical Demonstrations: A Handbook for Teachers of Chemistry, Volume 3* (Madison: The University of Wisconsin Press, **1989**), pp. 96–99.

7. Bassam Z. Shakhashiri, "Determination of Neutralizing Capacity of Antacids", *Chemical Demonstrations: A Handbook for Teachers of Chemistry, Volume 3* (Madison: The University of Wisconsin Press, **1989**), pp. 162–166.

8. Lee. R. Summerlin, Christie L. Borgford, and Julie B. Ealy, "Milk of Magnesia versus Acid," *Chemical Demonstrations, A Sourcebook for Teachers*, *Volume 2* (Washington: American Chemical Society, **1988**), p. 173. An antacid, milk of magnesia, is mixed with acid in this demonstration.

9. John J. Fortman and Katherine M. Stubbs, "Demonstrations with Red Cabbage Indicator," *J. Chem. Educ.*, Vol. 69, **1992**, 66–67. The acidic or basic nature of solutions of gases is investigated.

10. Lee R. Summerlin, Christie L. Borgford, and Julie B. Ealy, "A Hand-Held Reaction: Production of Ammonia Gas," *Chemical Demonstrations, A Sourcebook for Teachers, Volume 2* (Washington: American Chemical Society, **1988**), p. 38. An example of a reaction involving two solids ($NH_4Cl(s)$ and $Ca(OH)_2$) is demonstrated.

11. Lee. R. Summerlin, and James. L. Ealy, Jr., "Oxidation States of Manganese: $Mn^{7+}$, $Mn^{6+}$, $Mn^{4+}$, and $Mn^{2+}$," *Chemical Demonstrations, A Sourcebook for Teachers*, *Volume 1* (Washington: American Chemical Society, 1988), p.133–134 .

12. Lee. R. Summerlin, Christie L. Borgford, and Julie B. Ealy, " Producing Hydrogen Gas from Calcium Metal," *Chemical Demonstrations, A Sourcebook for Teachers*, *Volume 2* (Washington: American Chemical Society, **1988**), pp. 51–52.

13. Lee. R. Summerlin, and James. L. Ealy, Jr., "Activity Series for Some Metals," *Chemical Demonstrations, A Sourcebook for Teachers*, *Volume 1* (Washington: American Chemical Society, **1988**), p. 150. An overhead projector demonstration employing hydrogen gas formation.

14. Lee. R. Summerlin, Christie L. Borgford, and Julie B. Ealy, " Making Hydrogen Gas from an Acid and a Base," *Chemical Demonstrations, A Sourcebook for Teachers*, *Volume 2* (Washington: American Chemical Society, **1988**), pp. 33–34. Hydrogen gas is collected as a product of the reaction of aluminum with either HCl or NaOH.

15. Bassam Z. Shakhashiri, "An Activity Series: Zinc, Copper, and Silver Half Cells," *Chemical Demonstrations: A Handbook for Teachers of Chemistry, Volume 4* (Madison: The University of Wisconsin Press, **1992**), pp. 101–106.

16. Lee. R. Summerlin, Christie L. Borgford, and Julie B. Ealy, "Floating Pennies," *Chemical Demonstrations, A Sourcebook for Teachers*, *Volume 2* (Washington: American Chemical Society, **1988**), p. 63. The zinc core of copper-coated pennies reacts with acid to form pennies that float in this demonstration.

17. Dianne N. Epp, "Teas as Natural Indicators," *J. Chem. Educ*., Vol. 70, **1993**, 326. Infusions from a series of herbal teas provide a source of natural pH indicators in this simple demonstration.

18. Bassam Z. Shakhashiri, "Colorful Acid-Base Indicators," *Chemical Demonstrations: A Handbook for Teachers of Chemistry, Volume 3* (Madison: The University of Wisconsin Press, **1989**), pp. 33–40.

19. Bassam Z. Shakhashiri, "Rainbow Colors with Mixed Acid-Base Indicators," *Chemical Demonstrations: A Handbook for Teachers of Chemistry, Volume 3* (Madison: The University of Wisconsin Press, **1989**), pp. 41–46.

20. Bassam Z. Shakhashiri, "Acid-Base Indicators Extracted from Plants," *Chemical Demonstrations: A Handbook for Teachers of Chemistry, Volume 3* (Madison: The University of Wisconsin Press, **1989**), pp. 50–57.

# Chapter 5. Thermochemistry

## Media Resources

### Figures and Tables

| In Transparency Pack and on MediaPortfolio: | Section: |
|---|---|
| Figure 5.5 Energy Interconversions | 5.1 The Nature of Energy |
| Figure 5.10 Discharging a Battery | 5.2 The First Law of Thermodynamics |
| Figure 5.13 Work Done by a Moving Piston | 5.3 Enthalpy |
| Figure 5.19 Bomb Calorimeter | 5.5 Calorimetry |
| Figure 5.21 Enthalpy Diagram for the Combustion of $CH_4$ | 5.6 Hess's Law |
| Table 5.3 Standard Enthalpies of Formation at 298 K | 5.7 Enthalpies of Formation |
| Figure 5.22 Enthalpy Diagram for the Combustion of Propane | 5.7 Enthalpies of Formation |
| Figure 5.24 Sources of Energy Consumed in The U.S. | 5.8 Fuels and Foods |

| On MediaPortfolio: | Section: |
|---|---|
| Figure 5.6 Internal Energy of $H_2$, $O_2$ and $H_2O$ | 5.2 The First Law of Thermodynamics |
| Figure 5.7 Heat and Work | 5.2 The First Law of Thermodynamics |
| Table 5.1 Sign Conventions Used and the Relationship Among $q$, $w$, and $\Delta E$ | 5.2 The First Law of Thermodynamics |
| Figure 5.9 A State Function | 5.2 The First Law of Thermodynamics |
| Figure 5.11 Work Done by Hydrogen Gas | 5.3 Enthalpy |
| Figure 5.12 Enthalpy Changes | 5.3 Enthalpy |
| Figure 5.16 Enthalpy of a Reverse Reaction | 5.4 Enthalpies of Reaction |
| Figure 5.18 Coffee-Cup Calorimeter | 5.5 Calorimetry |

| Animations: | Section: |
|---|---|
| Work of Gas Expansion | 5.3 Enthalpy |
| Changes of State | 5.3 Enthalpy |

| Movies: | Section: |
|---|---|
| Formation of Water | 5.2 The First Law of Thermodynamics |
| Thermite | 5.2 The First Law of Thermodynamics |
| Nitrogen Triiodide | 5.6 Hess's Law |
| Thermite | 5.6 Hess's Law |
| Formation of Aluminum Bromide | 5.7 Enthalpies of Formation |

| Activities: | Section: |
|---|---|
| Dissolution of Ammonium Nitrate | 5.2 The First Law of Thermodynamics |
| Enthalpy of Solution | 5.4 Enthalpies of Reaction |
| Calorimetry | 5.5 Calorimetry |

# Other Resources

| **Further Readings:** | **Section:** |
|---|---|
| Weight-Loss Diets and the Law of Conservation of Energy | 5.2 The First Law of Thermodynamics |
| Pictorial Analogies III: Heat Flow, Thermodynamics, and Entropy | 5.3 Enthalpy |
| Analogical Demonstrations | 5.3 Enthalpy |
| Heat Flow vs. Cash Flow: A Banking Analogy | 5.3 Enthalpy |
| A Specific Heat Analogy | 5.5 Calorimetry |
| Heat Capacity, Body Temperature, and Hypothermia | 5.5 Calorimetry |
| The Conversion of Chemical Energy. Part 1. Technological Examples | 5.8 Foods and Fuels |
| The Geochemistry of Coal. Part II: The Components of Coal | 5.8 Foods and Fuels |
| *Scientific American,* **September 1990** | 5.8 Foods and Fuels |
| Beware—Fertilizer Can EXPLODE! | 5.8 Foods and Fuels |
| The Discovery of Nitroglycerine: Its Preparation And Therapeutic Utility | 5.8 Foods and Fuels |
| Hydrogen: The Ultimate Fuel and Energy Carrier | 5.8 Foods and Fuels |
| Chemical Fuels from the Sun | 5.8 Foods and Fuels |
| The Ice that Burns. Can Methane Hydrates Fuel the 21st Century? | 5.8 Foods and Fuels |

| **Live Demonstrations:** | **Section:** |
|---|---|
| Evaporation as an Endothermic Process | 5.2 The First Law of Thermodynamics |
| Flaming Cotton | 5.4 Enthalpies of Reaction |
| Endothermic Reaction: Ammonium Nitrate | 5.4 Enthalpies of Reaction |
| Heat of Neutralization | 5.4 Enthalpies of Reaction |
| Chemical Cold Pack | 5.4 Enthalpies of Reaction |
| A Chemical Hand Warmer | 5.4 Enthalpies of Reaction |
| Boiling Water in a Paper Cup: Heat Capacity of Water | 5.5 Calorimetry |
| Making Canned Heat | 5.8 Foods and Fuels |

# Chapter 5. Thermochemistry

## Common Student Misconceptions

- Students confuse power and energy.
- Students fail to note that the first law of thermodynamics *is* the law of conservation of energy.
- Students have difficulty in determining what constitutes the system and surroundings.
- Sign conventions in thermodynamics are always problematic.
- Students do not realize that a chemical reaction carried out in an open container occurs at constant pressure.
- Students do not realize that Hess's law is a consequence of the fact that enthalpy is a state function.
- Students should be directed to Appendix C of the text for a list of standard enthalpy values. (They are unlikely to find this information on their own!).

## Lecture Outline

### 5.1 The Nature of Energy

- **Thermodynamics** is the study of energy and its transformations.
- **Thermochemistry** is the study of the relationships between chemical reactions and energy changes involving heat.

#### Kinetic Energy and Potential Energy

- **Kinetic energy** is the energy of motion:

$$E_k = \frac{1}{2}mv^2$$

- **Potential energy** is the energy an object possesses by virtue of its position or composition.
  - Electrostatic energy is an example
    - It arises from interactions between charged particles.

$$Eel = \frac{kQ_1Q_2}{r^2}$$

  - Potential energy can be converted into kinetic energy.
    - Example: A ball of clay dropped off a building.

#### Units of Energy

- SI unit is the **joule**, J.
- From $E_k = \frac{1}{2}mv^2$, $1\text{J} = 1\text{kg x}\frac{\text{m}^2}{\text{s}^2}$
- Traditionally, we use the **calorie** as a unit of energy.
  - 1 cal = 4.184 J (exactly)
- The nutritional Calorie, Cal = 1,000 cal.

#### System and Surroundings

- A **system** is the part of the universe we are interested in studying.
- **Surroundings** are the rest of the universe (i.e., the surroundings are the portions of the universe not involved in the system).
- Example: If we are interested in the interaction between hydrogen and oxygen in a cylinder, then the $H_2$ and $O_2$ in the cylinder form a system.

### Transferring Energy: Work and Heat[1]

- From physics:
  - **Force** is a push or pull on an object.
  - **Work** is the energy used to move an object against a force.

$$w = F \times d$$

  - **Heat** is the energy transferred from a hotter object to a colder one.
  - **Energy** is the capacity to do work or to transfer heat.

## 5.2 The First Law of Thermodynamics[2]

- **The first law of thermodynamics** states that energy cannot be created or destroyed.
- The first law of thermodynamics is the law of conservation of energy.
  - That is, the energy of (system + surroundings) is constant.
  - Thus any energy transferred from a system must be transferred to the surroundings (and vice versa).

### Internal Energy[3]

- The total energy of a system is called the **internal energy**.
  - It is the sum of all the kinetic and potential energies of all components of the system.
- Absolute internal energy cannot be measured, only changes in internal energy.
- Change in internal energy, $\Delta E = E_{\text{final}} - E_{\text{initial}}$.
- Example: A mixture of $H_2(g)$ and $O_2(g)$ has a higher internal energy than $H_2O(g)$.
- Going from $H_2(g)$ and $O_2(g)$ to $H_2O(g)$ results in a negative change in internal energy, indicating that the system has lost energy to the surroundings:

$$H_2(g) + O_2(g) \rightarrow 2H_2O(g) \qquad \Delta E < 0$$

- Going from $H_2O(g)$ to $H_2(g)$ and $O_2(g)$ results in a positive change in internal energy, indicating that the system has gained energy from the surroundings:

$$2H_2O \rightarrow H_2(g) + O_2(g) \qquad \Delta E > 0$$

### Relating $\Delta E$ to Heat and Work[4,5,6]

- From the first law of thermodynamics:
  - When a system undergoes a physical or chemical change, the change in internal energy is given by the heat added to or liberated from the system plus the work done on or by the system:

$$\Delta E = q + w$$

- Heat flowing from the surroundings to the system is positive, $q > 0$.
- Work done by the surroundings on the system is positive, $w > 0$.

### Endothermic and Exothermic Processes[7,8]

- An **endothermic** process is one that *absorbs* heat from the surroundings.
  - An endothermic reaction feels cold.
- An **exothermic** process is one that *transfers* heat to the surroundings.
  - An exothermic reaction feels hot.

---

[1] Figure 5.5 from MediaPortfolio and Transparency Pack
[2] "Weight-Loss Diets and the Law of Conservation of Energy" from Further Readings
[3] Figure 5.6 from MediaPortfolio
[4] Figure 5.7 from MediaPortfolio
[5] "Formation of Water" Movie from MediaPortfolio
[6] Table 5.1 from MediaPortfolio
[7] "Thermite" Movie from MediaPortfolio
[8] "Dissolution of Ammonium Nitrate" Activity from MediaPortfolio

### State Functions[9,10,11]

- A **state function** depends only on the initial and final states of a system.
  - Example: The altitude difference between Denver and Chicago does not depend on whether you fly or drive, only on the elevation of the two cities above sea level.
  - Similarly, the internal energy of 50 g of $H_2O(l)$ at 25°C does not depend on whether we cool 50 g of $H_2O(l)$ from 100°C to 25°C or heat 50 g of $H_2O(l)$ at 0°C to 25°C.
- A state function does not depend on how the internal energy is used.
  - Example: A battery in a flashlight can be discharged by producing heat and light. The same battery in a toy car is used to produce heat and work. The change in internal energy of the battery is the same in both cases.,

## 5.3 Enthalpy[12,13,14,15,16,17,18]

- Chemical changes may involve release or absorption of heat.
- Many also involve work done on or by the system.
  - Work is often either electrical or mechanical work.
  - Mechanical work done by a system involving expanding gases is called **pressure-volume work** or *P-V* work.
- The heat transferred between the system and surroundings during a chemical reaction carried out under constant pressure is called **enthalpy**, *H*.
- Again, we can only measure the change in enthalpy, $\Delta H$.
- Mathematically,

$$\Delta H = H_{\text{final}} - H_{\text{initial}} = \Delta E + P\Delta V$$
$$w = -P\Delta V;\ \Delta E = q + w$$
$$\Delta H = \Delta E + P\Delta V = q_{\text{p}} + w - w = q_{\text{p}}$$

  - For most reactions $P\Delta V$ is small thus $\Delta H = \Delta E$
- Heat transferred from surroundings to the system has a positive enthalpy (i.e., $\Delta H > 0$ for an endothermic reaction).
- Heat transferred from the system to the surroundings has a negative enthalpy (i.e., $\Delta H < 0$ for an exothermic reaction).
- Enthalpy is a state function.

### *A Closer Look at Energy, Enthalpy, and P-V Work*[19]

- Consider:
  - A cylinder of cross-sectional area *A*,
  - A piston exerting a pressure, $P = F/A$, on a gas inside the cylinder,
  - The volume of gas expanding through $\Delta V$ while the piston moves a height $\Delta h = h_{\text{f}} - h_{\text{i}}$.
  - The magnitude of work done = $F \times \Delta h = P \times A \times \Delta h = P \times \Delta V$.
  - Since work is being done by the system on the surroundings,

---

[9] Figure 5.9 from MediaPortfolio
[10] Figure 5.10 from MediaPortfolio and Transparency Pack
[11] "Evaporation as an Endothermic Process" from Live Demonstrations
[12] "Pictorial Analogies III: Heat Flow, Thermodynamics and Entropy" from Further Readings
[13] "Analogical Demonstrations" from Further Readings
[14] Figure 5.11 from MediaPortfolio
[15] Figure 5.12 from MediaPortfolio
[16] "Heat Flow vs. Cash Flow: A Banking Analogy" from Further Readings
[17] Figure 5.13 from MediaPortfolio and Transparency Pack
[18] "Changes of State" Animation from MediaPortfolio
[19] "Work of Gas Expansion" Animation from MediaPortfolio

  - $w = -P\Delta V$.
- Using the first law of thermodynamics,
  - $\Delta E = q - P\Delta V$.
- If the reaction is carried out under constant volume,
  - $\Delta V = 0$ and $\Delta E = q_v$.
- If the reaction is carried out under constant pressure,
  - $\Delta E = q_p - P\Delta V$, or
  - $q_p = \Delta H = \Delta E + P\Delta V$
  - and $\Delta E = \Delta H - P\Delta V$

## 5.4 Enthalpies of Reaction[20,21,22,23,24,25,26]

- For a reaction, $\Delta H_{rxn} = H(\text{products}) - H(\text{reactants})$.
- The enthalpy change that accompanies a reaction is called the **enthalpy of reaction** or *heat of reaction* ($\Delta H_{rxn}$).
- Consider the thermochemical equation for the production of water:

  $2H_2(g) + O_2(g) \rightarrow 2H_2O(g)$ $\quad \Delta H = -483.6$ kJ
  - The equation tells us that 483.6 kJ of energy are released to the surroundings when water is formed.
  - $\Delta H$ noted at the end of the balanced equation depends on the number of moles of reactants and products associated with the $\Delta H$ value.
  - These equations are called *thermochemical equations*.
- Enthalpy diagrams are used to represent enthalpy changes associated with a reaction.
- In the enthalpy diagram for the combustion of $H_2(g)$, the reactants, $2H_2(g) + O_2(g)$, have a higher enthalpy than the products $2H_2O(g)$; this reaction is exothermic.
- Enthalpy is an extensive property.
  - Therefore, the *magnitude* of enthalpy is directly proportional to the amount of reactant consumed.
  - Example: If one mol of $CH_4$ is burned in oxygen to produce $CO_2$ and water, 890 kJ of heat is released to the surroundings. If two mol of $CH_4$ is burned, then 1780 kJ of heat is released.
- The sign of $\Delta H$ depends on the direction of the reaction.
  - The enthalpy change for a reaction is equal in magnitude but opposite in sign to $\Delta H$ for the reverse reaction.
  - Example: $CH_4(g) + 2O_2(g) \rightarrow CO_2(g) + 2H_2O(l)$ $\quad \Delta H = -890$ kJ,
  - But $CO_2(g) + 2H_2O(l) \rightarrow CH_4(g) + 2O_2(g)$ $\quad \Delta H = +890$ kJ.
- Enthalpy change depends on state.
  - $2H_2O(g) \rightarrow 2H_2O(l)$ $\quad \Delta H = -88$ kJ

## 5.5 Calorimetry

- **Calorimetry** is a measurement of heat flow.
- **Calorimeter** is an apparatus that measures heat flow.

### Heat Capacity and Specific Heat[27,28,29]

---

[20] "Flaming Cotton" from Live Demonstrations
[21] "Enthalpy of Solution" Activity from MediaPortfolio
[22] "Heat of Neutralization" from Live Demonstrations
[23] "Chemical Cold Pack" from Live Demonstrations
[24] "A Chemical Hand Warmer" from Live Demonstrations
[25] "Endothermic Reaction: Ammonium Nitrate" from Live Demonstrations
[26] Figure 5.16 from MediaPortfolio
[27] "Boiling Water in a Paper Cup: Heat Capacity of Water" from Live Demonstrations

- **Heat capacity** is the amount of energy required to raise the temperature of an object by 1°C.
    - **Molar heat capacity** is the heat capacity of 1 mol of a substance.
    - **Specific heat**, or specific heat capacity is the heat capacity of 1 g of a substance.
- Heat, $q$ = (specific heat) x (grams of substance) x $\Delta T$.
- Be careful of the sign of $q$.

### Constant-Pressure Calorimetry[30]

- Most common technique: use atmospheric pressure as the constant pressure.
- Recall $\Delta H = q_P$.
- Easiest method: use a coffee cup calorimeter.

$$q_{soln} = \text{(specific heat of solution) x (grams of solution) x } \Delta T = -q_{rxn}$$

- For dilute aqueous solutions, the specific heat of the solution will be close to that of pure water.

### Bomb Calorimetry (Constant-Volume Calorimetry)[31,32]

- Reactions can be carried out under conditions of constant volume instead of constant pressure.
- Constant volume calorimetry is carried out in a **bomb calorimeter.**
- The most common type of reaction studied under these conditions is combustion.
- If we know the heat capacity of the calorimeter, $C_{calorimeter}$, then the heat of reaction,

$$q_{rxn} = -C_{calorimeter} \text{ x } \Delta T.$$

- Since the reaction is carried out under constant volume, $q$ relates to $\Delta E$.

## 5.6 Hess's Law[33,34,35]

- **Hess's Law**: If a reaction is carried out in a series of steps, $\Delta H$ for the reaction is the sum of $\Delta H$ for each of the steps.
- The total change in enthalpy is independent of the number of steps.
- Total $\Delta H$ is also independent of the nature of the path.

$$CH_4(g) + 2O_2(g) \rightarrow CO_2(g) + 2H_2O(g) \qquad \Delta H = -802 \text{ kJ}$$
$$2H_2O(g) \rightarrow 2H_2O(l) \qquad \Delta H = -88 \text{ kJ}$$

---

$$CH_4(g) + 2O_2(g) \rightarrow CO_2(g) + 2H_2O(l) \qquad \Delta H = -890 \text{ kJ}$$

- Therefore, for the reaction $CH_4(g) + 2O_2(g) \rightarrow CO_2(g) + 2H_2O(l)$, $\Delta H = -890$ kJ.
- Note that $\Delta H$ is sensitive to the states of the reactants and products.
- Hess's law allows us to calculate enthalpy data for reactions which are difficult to carry out directly: $C(s) + O_2(g)$ produces a *mixture* of $CO(g)$ and $CO_2(g)$.

## 5.7 Enthalpies of Formation[36,37]

- Hess's law states that if a reaction is carried out in a number of steps, $\Delta H$ for the overall reaction is the sum of the $\Delta H$s for each of the individual steps.

---

28 "A Specific Heat Analogy" from Further Readings
29 "Heat Capacity, Body Temperature and Hypothermia" from Further Readings
30 Figure 5.18 from MediaPortfolio
31 Figure 5.19 from MediaPortfolio and Transparency Pack
32 "Calorimetry" Activity from MediaPortfolio
33 Figure 5.21 from MediaPortfolio and Transparency Pack
34 "Nitrogen Triiodide" Movie from MediaPortfolio
35 "Thermite" Movie from MediaPortfolio
36 Table 5.3 from MediaPortfolio and Transparency Pack
37 "Formation of Aluminum Bromide" Movie from MediaPortfolio

- Consider the formation of $CO_2(g)$ and $2H_2O(l)$ from $CH_4(g)$ and $2O_2(g)$.
  - If the reaction proceeds in one step:
  $$CH_4(g) + 2O_2(g) \rightarrow CO_2(g) + 2H_2O(l),$$
  then $\Delta H_1 = -890$ kJ.
  - However, if the reaction proceeds through a CO intermediate:
  $$CH_4(g) + 2O_2(g) \rightarrow CO(g) + 2H_2O(l) + \tfrac{1}{2}O_2(g) \qquad \Delta H_2 = -607 \text{ kJ}$$
  $$CO(g) + 2H_2O(l) + \tfrac{1}{2}O_2(g) \rightarrow CO_2(g) + 2H_2O(l) \qquad \Delta H_3 = -283 \text{ kJ},$$
  Then $\Delta H$ for the overall reaction is:
  $$\Delta H_2 + \Delta H_3 = -607 \text{ kJ} - 283 \text{ kJ} = -890 \text{ kJ} = \Delta H_1$$
- If a compound is formed from its constituent elements, then the enthalpy change for the reaction is called the **enthalpy of formation**, $\Delta H_f$.
- *Standard state* (standard conditions) refer to the substance at:
  - 1 atm and 25°C (298 K).
- **Standard enthalpy**, $\Delta H°$, is the enthalpy measured when everything is in its standard state.
- **Standard enthalpy of formation** of a compound, $\Delta H°_f$, is the enthalpy change for the formation of 1 mol of compound with all substances in their standard states.
- If there is more than one state for a substance under standard conditions, the more stable one is used. Example: When dealing with carbon we use graphite because graphite is more stable than diamond or $C_{60}$.
- The standard enthalpy of formation of the most stable form of an element is zero.

### Using Enthalpies of Formation to Calculate Enthalpies of Reaction[38]

- Use Hess's law!
- Example: Calculate $\Delta H$ for
$$C_3H_8(g) + 5O_2(g) \rightarrow 3CO_2(g) + 4H_2O(l)$$
- We start with the reactants, decompose them into elements, then rearrange the elements to form products. The overall enthalpy change is the sum of the enthalpy changes for each step.
  - Decomposing into elements (note $O_2$ is already elemental, so we concern ourselves with $C_3H_8$):
  $$C_3H_8(g) \rightarrow 3C(s) + 4H_2(g) \qquad \Delta H_1 = -\Delta H°_f[C_3H_8(g)]$$
  - Next we form $CO_2$ and $H_2O$ from their elements:
  $$3C(s) + 3O_2(g) \rightarrow 3CO_2(g) \qquad \Delta H_2 = 3\Delta H°_f[CO_2(g)]$$
  $$4H_2(g) + 2O_2(g) \rightarrow 4H_2O(l) \qquad \Delta H_3 = 4\Delta H°_f[H_2O(l)]$$
  - We look up the values and add:
  $$\Delta H°_{rxn} = -1(-103.85 \text{ kJ}) + 3(-393.5 \text{ kJ}) + 4(-285.8 \text{ kJ}) = -2220 \text{ kJ}$$
- In general:
$$\Delta H°_{rxn} = \Sigma n\Delta H°_f(\text{products}) - \Sigma m\Delta H°_f(\text{reactants})$$
  - Where $n$ and $m$ are the stoichiometric coefficients.

## 5.8 Foods and Fuels

- **Fuel value** is the energy released when 1 g of substance is burned.
- The fuel value of any food or fuel is a positive value that must be measured by calorimetry.

### Foods

- Fuel value is usually measured in Calories (1 nutritional Calorie, 1 Cal = 1000 cal).
- Most energy in our bodies comes from the oxidation of carbohydrates and fats.
- In the intestines carbohydrates are converted into glucose, $C_6H_{12}O_6$, or blood sugar.
  - In the cells glucose reacts with $O_2$ in a series of steps which ultimately produce $CO_2$, $H_2O$, and energy.

---

[38] Figure 5.22 from MediaPortfolio and Transparency Pack

$$C_6H_{12}O_6(s) + 6O_2(g) \rightarrow 6CO_2(g) + 6H_2O(l) \qquad \Delta H^\circ = -2803 \text{ kJ}$$

- Fats, for example tristearin, react with $O_2$ as follows:

$$2C_{57}H_{110}O_6(s) + 163O_2(g) \rightarrow 114CO_2(g) + 110H_2O(l) \qquad \Delta H^\circ = -75{,}250 \text{ kJ.}$$

- Fats contain more energy than carbohydrates. Fats are not water soluble. Therefore, fats are good for energy storage.

## Fuels[39,40,41,42]

- In the United States we use about $1.03 \times 10^{17}$ kJ/year ($1.0 \times 10^6$ kJ of fuel per person per day).
- Most of this energy comes from petroleum and natural gas.
- The remainder of the energy comes from coal, nuclear and hydroelectric sources.
- Coal, petroleum and natural gas are **fossil fuels**. They are not renewable.
- **Natural gas** consists largely of carbon and hydrogen. Compounds such as $CH_4$, $C_2H_6$, $C_3H_8$ and $C_4H_{10}$ are typical constituents.
- **Petroleum** is a liquid consisting of hundreds of compounds. Impurities include S, N and O compounds.
- **Coal** contains high molecular weight compounds of C and H. In addition compounds containing S, O and N are present as impurities that form air pollutants when burned in air.
- *Syngas* (synthesis gas): a gaseous mixture of hydrocarbons produced from coal by *coal gasification*.

## Other Energy Sources[43,44,45,46,47,48]

- Nuclear energy: energy released in splitting or fusion of nuclei of atoms
- Fossil fuels and nuclear energy are *nonrenewable* sources of energy
- **Renewable energy** sources include:
  - Solar energy
  - Wind energy
  - Geothermal energy
  - Hydroelectric energy
  - Biomass energy
  - These are virtually inexhaustible and will be come increasingly important as fossil fuels are depleted.

---

[39] "The Conversion of Chemical Energy. Part 1. Technological Examples" from Further Readings
[40] "Making Canned Heat" from Live Demonstrations
[41] "The Geochemistry of Coal, Part II: The Components of Coal" from Further Readings
[42] Figure 5.24 from MediaPortfolio and Transparency Pack
[43] *Scientific American*, **September 1990** from Further Readings
[44] "Hydrogen: The Ultimate Fuel and Energy Carrier" from Further Readings
[45] "Chemical Fuels from the Sun" from Further Readings
[46] "The Ice that Burns. Can Methane Hydrates Fuel the 21st Century?" from Further Readings
[47] "Beware—Fertilizer Can Explode" from Further Readings
[48] "The Discovery of Nitroglycerine: It's Preparation and Therapeutic Utility" from Further Readings

## Further Readings:

1. John J. Fortman, "Pictorial Analogies III: Heat Flow, Thermodynamics, and Entropy," *J. Chem. Educ.*, Vol. 70, **1993**, 102–103.

2. John W. Hill, "Weight-Loss Diets and the Law of Conservation of Energy," *J. Chem. Educ.*, Vol. 58, **1981**, 996.

3. John J. Fortman, "Analogical Demonstrations," *J. Chem. Educ.*, Vol. 69, **1992**, 323–324. This reference contains a quick analogical demonstration on heat transfer.

4. Charles M. Wynn, Sr., "Heat Flow vs. Cash Flow: A Banking Analogy," *J. Chem. Educ.*, Vol. 74, **1997**, 3978.

5. Brother Thomas McCullogh CSC, "A Specific Heat Analogy," *J. Chem. Educ.*, Vol. 57, **1980**, **896**.

6. Doris R. Kimbrough, "Heat Capacity, Body Temperature, and Hypothermia," *J. Chem. Educ.*, Vol. 75, **1998**, 48–49.

7. Donald J. Wink, "The Conversion of Chemical Energy. Part 1. Technological Examples," *J. Chem. Educ.*, Vol. 69, **1992**, 108–111.

8. Harold H. Schobert, "The Geochemistry of Coal. Part II: The Components of Coal," *J. Chem. Educ.*, Vol. 66, **1989**, 290–293.

9. *Scientific American*, **September 1990**, Volume 263. This is a special issue devoted to uses of energy in our society.

10. Michael Laing, "Beware-Fertilizer Can EXPLODE!" *J. Chem. Educ.*, Vol. 70, **1990**, 392–394.

11. Gustav P. Dinga, "Hydrogen: The Ultimate Fuel and Energy Carrier," *J. Chem. Educ.*, Vol. 65, **1988**, 688–691.

12. Israel Dostrovsky, "Chemical Fuels from the Sun," *Scientific American*, Vol. 265, **1991**, 102–107.

13. Richard Monastersky, "The Ice that Burns. Can Methane Hydrates Fuel the 21st Century?" *Science News*, Vol. 154, **1998**, 312–313. This article explores a potential new source of natural gas.

14. Natalie I. Foster and Ned D. Heindel, "The Discovery of Nitroglycerine: Its Preparation and Therapeutic Utility," *J. Chem. Educ.*, Vol 58, **1981**, 364–365.

## Live Demonstrations:

1. Lee R. Summerlin, Christie L. Borgford, and Julie B Ealy, "Flaming Cotton," *Chemical Demonstrations, A Sourcebook for Teachers, Volume* 2 (Washington: American Chemical Society, **1988**), p. 104. A cotton ball sprinkled with sodium peroxide bursts into flame upon addition of water.

2. Lee R. Summerlin and James L. Ealy, Jr. , "Endothermic Reaction: Ammonium Nitrate," *Chemical Demonstrations, A Sourcebook for Teachers,* (Washington: American Chemical Society, **1988**), p. 65. Temperature changes that accompany dissolution of ammonium nitrate in water are measured.

3. Bassam Z. Shakhashiri, "Evaporation as an Endothermic Process," *Chemical Demonstrations: A Handbook for Teachers of Chemistry, Volume 3* (Madison: The University of Wisconsin Press, **1989**), pp. 249–251.

4. Bassam Z. Shakhashiri, "Heat of Neutralization," *Chemical Demonstrations: A Handbook for Teachers of Chemistry, Volume 1* (Madison: The University of Wisconsin Press, **1983**), pp. 15–16.

5. Bassam Z. Shakhashiri, "Chemical Cold Pack," *Chemical Demonstrations: A Handbook for Teachers of Chemistry, Volume 1* (Madison: The University of Wisconsin Press, **1983**), pp. 8–9.

6. Lee. R. Summerlin,, Christie L. Borgford, and Julie B. Ealy, "A Chemical Hand Warmer," *Chemical Demonstrations, A Sourcebook for Teachers, Volume 2* (Washington: American Chemical Society, **1988**), pp.101–102. Oxidation of iron in a plastic baggie us used to prepare a hand-warmer.

7. Bassam Z. Shakhashiri, "Boiling Water in a Paper Cup: Heat Capacity of Water," *Chemical Demonstrations: A Handbook for Teachers of Chemistry, Volume 3* (Madison: The University of Wisconsin Press, **1989**), pp. 239–241.

8. Lee. R. Summerlin,, Christie L. Borgford, and Julie B. Ealy, "Making Canned Heat," *Chemical Demonstrations, A Sourcebook for Teachers, Volume 2* (Washington: American Chemical Society, **1988**), pp. 111–112. Saponification of stearic acid in the presence of alcohol is used to prepare a solid fuel--canned heat.

# Chapter 6. Electronic Structure of Atoms

## Media Resources

### Figures and Tables

| In Transparency Pack and on MediaPortfolio: | Section: |
|---|---|
| Figure 6.3 Wave Characteristics of Electromagnetic Waves | 6.1 The Wave Nature of Light |
| Figure 6.4 Electromagnetic Spectrum | 6.1 The Wave Nature of Light |
| Table 6.1 Common Wavelength Units for Electromagnetic Radiation | 6.1 The Wave Nature of Light |
| Figure 6.7 Photoelectric Effect | 6.2 Quantized Energy and Photons |
| Figure 6.10 Continuous Visible Spectrum | 6.3 Line Spectra and the Bohr Model |
| Figure 6.12 Line Spectra of Na and H | 6.3 Line Spectra and the Bohr Model |
| Figure 6.13 Energy Levels in the H Atom From The Bohr Model | 6.3 Line Spectra and the Bohr Model |
| Figure 6.16 Electron-Density Distribution in H | 6.5 Quantum Mechanics and Atomic Orbitals |
| Table 6.2 Relationship Among Values of $n$, $l$, and $m_l$ through $n = 4$ | 6.5 Quantum Mechanics and Atomic Orbitals |
| Figure 6.17 Bohr Model of H | 6.5 Quantum Mechanics and Atomic Orbitals |
| Figure 6.18 Electron-Density Distribution of *s* Orbitals | 6.6 Representations of Orbitals |
| Figure 6.20 Electron-Density Distribution of *p* Orbitals | 6.6 Representations of Orbitals |
| Figure 6.21 *d* Orbitals | 6.6 Representations of Orbitals |
| Figure 6.22 Energy-Level Diagrams of Many-Electron Atoms | 6.7 Many-Electron Atoms |
| Table 6.3 Electron Configurations of Several Lighter Elements | 6.8 Electron Configurations |
| Figure 6.27 Periodic Electron Configurations | 6.9 Electron Configurations and the Periodic Table |
| Figure 6.28 Outer-Shell Ground-State Electron Configurations | 6.9 Electron Configurations and the Periodic Table |

| On MediaPortfolio: | Section: |
|---|---|
| Figure 6.2 Characteristics of Water Waves | 6.1 The Wave Nature of Light |
| Figure 6.19 Coutour Representations of *s* Orbitals | 6.6 Representations of Orbitals |
| Figure 6.23 Electron Spin | 6.7 Many-Electron Atoms |
| Figure 6.24 Stern-Gerlach Experiment | 6.7 Many-Electron Atoms |
| Figure 6.25 Nuclear Spin | 6.7 Many-Electron Atoms |

| Animations: | Section: |
|---|---|
| Photoelectric Effect | 6.2 Quantized Energy and Photons |
| Radial Electron Distribution | 6.6 Representations of Orbitals |
| Electron Configurations | 6.8 Electron Configurations |

| Movies: | Section: |
|---|---|
| Flame Tests for Metals | 6.3 Line Spectra and the Bohr Model |

| **Activities:** | **Section:** |
|---|---|
| Quantum Numbers | 6.5 Quantum Mechanics and Atomic Orbitals |
| Line Spectrum of Sodium | 6.7 Many-Electron Atoms |

## Other Resources

| **Further Readings:** | **Section:** |
|---|---|
| Put Body to Them! | 6.2 Quantized Energy and Photons |
| Presenting the Bohr Atom | 6.3 Line Spectra and the Bohr Model |
| Suitable Light Sources and Spectroscopes for Student Observation of Emission Spectra in Lecture Halls | 6.3 Line Spectra and the Bohr Model |
| Niels Bohr | 6.3 Line Spectra and the Bohr Model |
| 100 Years of Quantum Mysteries | 6.3 Line Spectra and the Bohr Model |
| Perspectives on the Uncertainty Principle and Quantum Reality | 6.4 The Wave Behavior of Matter |
| Introducing the Uncertainty Principle Using Diffraction of Light Waves | 6.4 The Wave Behavior of Matter |
| On a Relation Between the Heisenberg and deBroglie Principles | 6.4 The Wave Behavior of Matter |
| A Student's Travels, Close Dancing, Bathtubs, and the Shopping Mall: More Analogies in Teaching Introductory Chemistry | 6.5 Quantum Mechanics and Atomic Orbitals |
| The Mole, the Periodic Table, and Quantum Numbers: An Introductory Trio | 6.5 Quantum Mechanics and Atomic Orbitals |
| Electron Densities: Pictorial Analogies for Apparent Ambiguities in Probability Calculations | 6.6 Representations of Orbitals |
| Magnetic Whispers: Chemistry and Medicine Finally Tune Into Controversial Molecular Chatter | 6.7 Many-Electron Atoms |
| *Chemistry in Britain*, Vol. 32, **June 1996** | 6.7 Many-Electron Atoms |
| Demystifying Introductory Chemistry; Part 1. Electron Configurations from Experiment | 6.8 Electron Configurations |
| Quantum Analogies on Campus | 6.8 Electron Configurations |
| Housing Electrons: Relating Quantum Numbers, Energy Levels, and Electron Configurations | 6.8 Electron Configurations |
| Pictorial Analogies VII: Quantum Numbers and Orbitals | 6.8 Electron Configurations |
| The Quantum Shoe Store and Electron Structure | 6.8 Electron Configurations |
| "New" Schemes for Applying the Aufbau Principle | 6.8 Electron Configurations |
| A Low-Cost Classroom Demonstration of the Aufbau Principle | 6.8 Electron Configurations |
| Some Analogies for Teaching Atomic Structure at the High School Level | 6.8 Electron Configurations |
| Ionization Enerties, Parallel Spins, and the Stability Of Half-Filled Shells | 6.8 Electron Configurations |
| The Periodic Table and Electron Configurations | 6.9 Electron Configurations and the Periodic Table |

**Live Demonstrations:**
Simple and Inexpensive Classroom Demonstration Of Nuclear Magnetic Resonance and Magnetic Resonance Imaging

**Section:**
6.7 Electronic Structure of Atoms

# Chapter 6. Electronic Structure of Atoms

## Common Student Misconceptions

- This is often students first glimpse at the realm of quantum theory. They need to understand that the model has been built up to rationalize experimental data. They also need to know that elements of one theory are maintained in the subsequent theory.
- Using the unit $s^{-1}$ for frequency makes the units cancel more easily.
- Some students will have difficulty in converting between angstroms, nanometers, etc.

## Lecture Outline

### 6.1 The Wave Nature of Light[1,2,3,4]

- The **electronic structure** of an atom refers to the arrangement of electrons.
- Visible light is a form of **electromagnetic radiation** or *radiant energy*.
- Radiation carries energy through space.
- Electromagnetic radiation is characterized by its wave nature.
- All waves have a characteristic **wavelength**, $\lambda$ (lambda), and amplitude, $A$.
- The **frequency**, $\nu$ (nu), of a wave is the number of cycles which pass a point in one second.
    - The units of $\nu$ are Hertz ($1 \text{ Hz} = 1 \text{ s}^{-1}$).
- The speed of a wave is given by its frequency multiplied by its wavelength.
    - For light, speed, $c = \lambda\nu$,
    - Electromagnetic radiation moves through a vacuum with a speed of approximately $3.00 \times 10^{-8}$ m/s.
- Electromagnetic waves have characteristic wavelengths and frequencies.
- The *electromagnetic spectrum* is a display of the various types of electromagnetic radiation arranged in order of increasing wavelength.
    - Example: visible radiation has wavelengths between 400 nm (violet) and 750 nm (red).

### 6.2 Quantized Energy and Photons

- Some phenomena can't be explained using a wave model of light:
    - *Blackbody radiation*: emission of light from hot objects.
    - The *photoelectric effect*: emission of electrons from metal surfaces on which light shines.
    - *Emission spectra*: emission of light from electronically excited gas atoms.

#### Hot Objects and the Quantization of Energy

- Heated solids emit radiation (black body radiation)
    - The wavelength distribution depends on the temperature (i.e., "red hot" objects are cooler than "white hot" objects).
- Planck investigated black body radiation.
    - He proposed that energy can only be absorbed or released from atoms in certain amounts.
    - These amounts are called quanta.

---

[1] Figure 6.2 from MediaPortfolio
[2] Figure 6.3 from MediaPortfolio and Transparency Pack
[3] Figure 6.4 from MediaPortfolio and Transparency Pack
[4] Table 6.1 from MediaPortfolio and Transparency Pack

- A **quantum** is the smallest amount of energy that can be emitted or absorbed as electromagnetic radiation.
- The relationship between energy and frequency is:

$$E = h\nu$$

  - where $h$ is **Planck's constant** ($6.63 \times 10^{-34}$ J·s).
- To understand quantization consider the notes produced by a violin (continuous) and a piano (quantized):
  - A violin can produce any note when the fingers are placed at an appropriate spot on the bridge.
  - A piano can only produce notes corresponding to the keys on the keyboard.

### The Photoelectric Effect and Photons[5,6,7]

- The photoelectric effect provides evidence for the particle nature of light.
  - It also provides evidence for quantization.
- Einstein assumed that light traveled in energy packets called **photons**.
  - The energy of one photon, $E = h\nu$.
- Light shining on the surface of a metal can cause electrons to be ejected from the metal.
  - The electrons will only be ejected if the photons have sufficient energy:
    - Below the threshold frequency no electrons are ejected.
    - Above the threshold frequency, the excess energy appears as the kinetic energy of the ejected electrons.
- Light has wave-like AND particle-like properties.

## 6.3 Line Spectra and the Bohr Model

### Line Spectra[8,9,10]

- Radiation composed of only one wavelength is called *monochromatic*.
- Radiation that spans a whole array of different wavelengths is called *continuous*.
- When radiation from a light source such as a light bulb is separated into its different wavelength components, a **spectrum** is produced.
  - White light can be separated into a **continuous spectrum** of colors.
    - A rainbow is a continuous spectrum of light produced by dispersal of sunlight by raindrops or mist.
  - Note that there are no dark spots on the continuous spectrum which would correspond to different lines.
- Not all radiation is continuous.
  - A gas placed in a partially evacuated tube and subjected to a high voltage produces single colors of light.
  - The spectrum that we see contains radiation of only specific wavelengths; this is called a **line spectrum**.

### Bohr's Model[11]

- Rutherford assumed the electrons orbited the nucleus analogous to planets around the sun.
  - However, a charged particle moving in a circular path should lose energy.

---

5 "Photoelectric Effect" Animation from MediaPortfolio
6 Figure 6.7 from MediaPortfolio and Transparency Pack
7 "Put Body to Them!" from Further Readings
8 Figure 6.10 from MediaPortfolio and Transparency Pack
9 Figure 6.12 from MediaPortfolio and Transparency Pack
10 "Flame Tests for Metals" Movie from MediaPortfolio
11 "Presenting the Bohr Atom" from Further Readings

- This means that the atom should be unstable according to Rutherford's theory.
- Bohr noted the line spectra of certain elements and assumed the electrons were confined to specific energy states. These were called orbits.
- Bohr model is based on three postulates:
  - Only orbits of specific radii, corresponding to certain definite energies, are permitted for electrons in an atom.
  - An electron in a permitted orbit has a specific energy and is an "allowed" energy state.
  - Energy is only emitted or absorbed by an electron as it moves from one allowed energy state to another.
    - The energy is gained or lost as a photon.

## The Energy States of the Hydrogen Atom[12,13,14]

- Colors from excited gases arise because electrons move between energy states in the atom.
- Since the energy states are quantized, the light emitted from excited atoms must be quantized and appear as line spectra.
- Bohr showed mathematically that

$$E_n = -R_H\left(\frac{1}{n^2}\right)$$

  - where $n$ is the *principal quantum number* (i.e., $n = 1, 2, 3, \ldots \infty$), and $R_H$ is the Rydberg constant $= 2.18 \times 10^{-18}$ J.
- The first orbit in the Bohr model has $n = 1$ and is closest to the nucleus.
- The furthest orbit in the Bohr model has $n \rightarrow \infty$ and corresponds to $E = 0$.
- Electrons in the Bohr model can only move between orbits by absorbing and emitting energy in quanta ($E = h\nu$).
  - The **ground state** = the lowest energy state.
  - An electron in a higher energy state is said to be in an **excited state.**
- The amount of energy absorbed or emitted on moving between states is given by

$$\Delta E = E_f - E_i = h\nu = R_H\left\{\frac{1}{n_i^2} - \frac{1}{n_f^2}\right\}$$

- When $n_i > n_f$ energy is emitted and when $n_f > n_i$ energy is absorbed.

## Limitations of the Bohr Model[15]

- The Bohr Model has several limitations:
  - It cannot explain the spectra of atoms other than hydrogen.
  - Electrons do not move about the nucleus in circular orbits.
- However the model introduces two important ideas:
  - The energy of an electron is quantized: electrons exist only in certain energy levels described by quantum numbers.
  - Energy gain or loss is involved in moving an electron from one energy level to another.

# 6.4 The Wave Behavior of Matter

- Knowing that light has a particle nature, it seems reasonable to ask whether matter has a wave nature.

---

[12] Figure 6.13 from MediaPortfolio and Transparency Pack

[13] "Suitable Light Sources and Spectroscopes for Student Observation of Emission Spectra in Lecture Halls" from Further Readings

[14] "Neils Bohr" from Further Readings

[15] "100 Years of Quantum Mysteries" from Further Readings

- This question was answered by Louis deBroglie.
- Using Einstein's and Planck's equations, deBroglie derived:

$$\lambda = h/mv$$

- The **momentum**, $mv$, is a particle property, whereas $\lambda$ is a wave property.
  - **Matter waves** is the term used to describe wave characteristics of material particles.
  - Therefore, in one equation de Broglie summarized the concepts of waves and particles as they apply to low-mass, high-speed objects.
  - As a consequence of deBroglie's discovery, we now have techniques such as X-ray diffraction and electron microscopy to study small objects.

### The Uncertainty Principle[16,17,18]

- **Heisenberg's uncertainty principle**: We cannot determine the *exact* position, direction of motion, and speed of subatomic particles simultaneously.
- For electrons: We cannot determine their momentum and position simultaneously.

## 6.5 Quantum Mechanics and Atomic Orbitals[19]

- Schrödinger proposed an equation containing both wave and particle terms.
- Solving the equation leads to **wave functions**, $\psi$.
- The wave function gives the shape of the electron's orbital.
  - The square of the wave function, $\psi^2$, gives the probability of finding the electron.
  - That is, $\psi^2$ gives the electron density for the atom.
    - $\psi^2$ is called the **probability density**.
- **Electron density** is another way of expressing probability.
  - A region of high electron density is one where there is a high probability of finding an electron.

### Orbitals and Quantum Numbers[20,21,22,23,24]

- If we solve the Schrödinger equation we get wave functions and energies for the wave functions.
- We call $\psi$ **orbitals**.
- Schrödinger's equation requires three quantum numbers:
- *Principal quantum number, n*. This is the same as Bohr's $n$.
  - As $n$ becomes larger, the atom becomes larger and the electron is further from the nucleus.
- *Azimuthal quantum number, l*. This quantum number depends on the value of $n$.
  - The values of $l$ begin at 0 and increase to $n - 1$.
  - We usually use letters for $l$ ($s$, $p$, $d$ and $f$ for $l = 0, 1, 2,$ and 3). Usually we refer to the $s$, $p$, $d$ and $f$ orbitals.
  - This quantum number defines the shape of the orbital.
- Magnetic quantum number, $m_l$.
  - This quantum number depends on $l$.
  - The magnetic quantum number has integer values between $-l$ and $+l$.

---

[16] "Introducing the Uncertainty Principle Using Diffraction of Light Waves" from Further Readings
[17] "Perspectives on the Uncertainty Principle and Quantum Reality" from Further Readings
[18] "On a Relation between the Heisenberg and deBroglie Principles" from Further Readings
[19] "A Student's Travels, Close Dancing, Bathtubs, and the Shopping Mall: More Analogies in Teaching Introductory Chemistry" from Further Readings
[20] Figure 6.16 from MediaPortfolio and Transparency Pack
[21] "The Mole, the Periodic Table, and Quantum Numbers: An Introductory Trio" from Further Readings
[22] Table 6.2 from MediaPortfolio and Transparency Pack
[23] "Quantum Numbers" Activity from MediaPortfolio
[24] Figure 6.17 from MediaPortfolio and Transparency Pack

- Magnetic quantum numbers give the three-dimensional orientation of each orbital.
- A collection of orbitals with the same value of $n$ is called an **electron shell**.
  - A set of orbitals with the same $n$ and $l$ is called a **subshell**.
    - Each subshell is designated by a number and a letter.
    - For example, $3p$ orbitals have $n = 3$ and $l = 1$.
- Orbitals can be ranked in terms of energy to yield an Aufbau diagram.
  - Note that this Aufbau diagram is for a single electron system.
- As $n$ increases note that the spacing between energy levels becomes smaller.

## 6.6 Representation of Orbitals

### The s Orbitals[25,26,27,28]

- All *s* orbitals are spherical.
- As $n$ increases, the *s* orbitals get larger.
- As $n$ increases, the number of **nodes** increases.
  - A node is a region in space where the probability of finding an electron is zero.
    - $\psi^2 = 0$ at a node.
  - For an *s* orbital the number of nodes is given by $n - 1$.

### The *p* Orbitals[29]

- There are three *p* orbitals: $p_x$, $p_y$ and $p_z$.
  - The three *p* orbitals lie along the *x*-, *y*-, and *z*-axes of a Cartesian system.
  - The letters correspond to allowed values of $m_l$ of $-1$, 0, and $+1$.
- The orbitals are dumb-bell shaped; each has two *lobes*.
- As $n$ increases, the *p* orbitals get larger.
- All *p* orbitals have a node at the nucleus.

### The *d* and *f* Orbitals[30]

- There are five *d* and seven f orbitals.
  - Three of the *d* orbitals lie in a plane bisecting the *x*-, *y*-, and *z*-axes.
  - Two of the *d* orbitals lie in a plane aligned along the *x*-, *y*-, and *z*-axes.
  - Four of the *d* orbitals have four lobes each.
  - One *d* orbital has two lobes and a collar.

## 6.7 Many-Electron Atoms

### Orbitals and Their Energies[31]

- In a many-electron atom, for a given value of $n$,
  - The energy of an orbital increases with increasing value of $l$.
- Orbitals of the same energy are said to be **degenerate**.
- For $n \geq 2$, the *s* and *p* orbitals are no longer degenerate.
- Therefore, the Aufbau diagram looks slightly different for many-electron systems.

---

[25] "Electron Densities: Pictorial Analogies for Apparent Ambiguities in Probability Calculations" from Further Readings
[26] Figure 6.18 from MediaPortfolio and Transparency Pack
[27] Figure 6.19 from MediaPortfolio
[28] "Radial Electron Distribution" Animation from MediaPortfolio
[29] Figure 6.20 from MediaPortfolio and Transparency Pack
[30] Figure 6.21 from MediaPortfolio and Transparency Pack
[31] Figure 6.22 from MediaPortfolio and Transparency Pack

### Electron Spin and the Pauli Exclusion Principle[32,33,34,35,36,37,38]

- Line spectra of many electron atoms show each line as a closely spaced pair of lines.
- Stern and Gerlach designed an experiment to determine why.
  - A beam of atoms was passed through a slit and into a magnetic field and the atoms were then detected.
  - Two spots were found: one with the electrons spinning in one direction and one with the electrons spinning in the opposite direction.
- Since **electron spin** (electron as a tiny sphere spinning on its own axis) is quantized,
  - We define $m_s$ = **spin magnetic quantum number** = ± ½.
- **Pauli's exclusion principle** states that no two electrons can have the same set of 4 quantum numbers.
  - Therefore, two electrons in the same orbital must have opposite spins.

## 6.8 Electron Configurations[39,40,41,42,43,44,45]

- **Electron configurations** tell us how the electrons are distributed among the various orbitals of an atom.
- The most stable configuration or ground state is that in which the electrons are in the lowest possible energy state.
- When writing ground-state electronic configurations:
  - Electrons fill orbitals in order of increasing energy with no more than two electrons per orbital.
  - No two electrons can fill one orbital with the same spin (Pauli).
  - For degenerate orbitals, electrons fill each orbital singly before any orbital gets a second electron.
  - How do we show spin?
    - An arrow pointing upwards has $m_s$ = + ½ (spin up).
    - An arrow pointing downwards has $m_s$ = – ½ (spin down).

### Hund's Rule[46,47,48,49]

---

[32] Figure 6.23 from MediaPortfolio
[33] Figure 6.24 from MediaPortfolio
[34] Figure 6.25 from MediaPortfolio
[35] "Magnetic Whispers: Chemistry and Medicine Finally Tune Into Controversial Molecular Chatter" from Further Readings
[36] "*Chemistry in Britain*, June 1996" from Further Readings
[37] "Simple and Inexpensive Classroom Demonstration of Nuclear Magnetic Resonance and Magnetic Resonance Imaging" from Live Demonstrations
[38] "Line Spectrum of Sodium" Activity from MediaPortfolio
[39] "Demystifying Introductory Chemistry; Part I. Electron Configurations from Experiment" from Further Readings
[40] "Quantum Analogies on Campus" from Further Readings
[41] "Housing Electrons: Relating Quantum Numbers, Energy Levels, and Electron Configurations" from Further Readings
[42] "Pictorial Analogies VII: Quantum Numbers and Orbitals" from Further Readings
[43] "The Quantum Shoe Store and Electron Structure" from Further Readings
[44] "New Schemes for Applying the Aufbau Principle" from Further Readings
[45] "A Low-Cost Classroom Demonstration of the Aufbau Principle" from Further Readings
[46] "Some Analogies for Teaching Atomic Structure at the High School Level" from Further Readings
[47] Table 6.3 from MediaPortfolio and Transparency Pack
[48] "Ionization Energies, Parallel Spins, and the Stability of Half-Filled Shells" from Further Readings
[49] "Electron Configurations" Animation from MediaPortfolio

- **Hund's rule**: For degenerate orbitals, the lowest energy is attained when the number of electrons with the same spin is maximized.
  - Thus electrons fill each orbital singly with their spins parallel before any orbital gets a second electron.
  - By placing electrons in different orbitals, electron-electron repulsions are minimized.

### Condensed Electron Configurations

- Electron configurations may be written using a shorthand notation (*condensed electron configuration*):
  - Write the **valence electrons** explicitly.
    - **Valence electrons**: electrons in the outer shell.
      - These electrons are gained and lost in reactions.
  - Write the **core electrons** corresponding to the filled noble gas in square brackets.
    - Core electrons: electrons in the inner shells.
      - These are generally not involved in bonding.
  - Example:
    - P: $\mathbf{1s^2 2s^2 2p^6} 3s^2 3p^3$,
    - but **Ne** is $\mathbf{1s^2 2s^2 2p^6}$.
    - Therefore, P: **[Ne]**$3s^2 3p^3$.

### Transition Metals

- After Ar the *d* orbitals begin to fill.
- After the 3*d* orbitals are full the 4*p* orbitals begin to fill.
- The ten elements between Ti and Zn are called the **transition metals** or **transition elements**.
- The 4*f* orbitals begin to fill with Ce.
  - Note: The electron configuration of La is [Xe]$6s^2 5d^1 4f^0$
- The 4*f* orbitals are filled for the elements Ce – Lu which are called **lanthanide elements** (or rare earth elements).
- The 5*f* orbitals are filled for the elements Th – Lr which are called **actinide elements**.
  - Most actinides are not found in nature.

## 6.9 Electron Configurations and the Periodic Table[50,51,52]

- The periodic table can be used as a guide for electron configurations.
- The period number is the value of *n*.
- Groups 1A and 2A have their *s* orbitals being filled.
- Groups 3A – 8A have their *p* orbitals being filled.
- The *s*-block and *p*-block of the periodic table contain the representative or main-group elements.
- Groups 3B – 2B have their *d* orbitals being filled.
- The lanthanides and actinides have their *f* orbitals being filled.
  - The actinides and lanthanide elements are collectively referred to as the ***f*-block metals**.
- Note that the 3*d* orbitals fill after the 4*s* orbital. Similarly, the 4*f* orbitals fill after the 5*d* orbitals.

---

[50] "The Periodic Table and Electron Configurations" from Further Readings
[51] Figure 6.27 from MediaPortfolio and Transparency Pack
[52] Figure 6.28 from MediaPortfolio and Transparency Pack

## Further Readings:

1. Robert R. Perkins, "Put Body to Them!" *J. Chem. Educ*., Vol. 72, **1995**, 151–152. This reference includes analogies for quantized states.

2. Bianca L. Haendler, "Presenting the Bohr Atom," *J. Chem. Educ*., Vol. 59, **1982**, 372–376. Presenting the role of the Bohr theory within the framework of the development of quantum mechanics.

3. Elvin Hughes, Jr., and Arnold George, "Suitable Light Sources and Spectroscopes for Student Observation of Emission Spectra in Lecture Halls," *J. Chem. Educ*., Vol. 61, **1984**, 908–909.

4. Max Tegmark and John Archibald Wheeler, "100 Years of Quantum Mysteries," *Scientific American*, February 2001, 68–75.

5. Dennis R. Sievers, "Niels Bohr," *J. Chem. Educ*., Vol. 59, **1982**, 303–304. A short biography of Niels Bohr.

6. Pedro L. Muino, "Introducing the Uncertainty Principle Using Diffraction of Light Waves," *J. Chem. Educ*., Vol. 77, **2000**, 1025–1027.

7. Lawrence S. Bartell, "Perspectives on the Uncertainty Principle and Quantum Reality," *J. Chem. Educ*., Vol. 62, **1985**, 192–196. This reading contains some practical applications of the uncertainty principle.

8. Oliver G. Ludwig, "On a Relation between the Heisenberg and deBroglie Principles," *J. Chem. Educ*., Vol. 70, **1993**, 28.

9. Goeff Rayner-Canham, "A Student's Travels, Close Dancing, Bathtubs, and the Shopping Mall: More Analogies in Teaching Introductory Chemistry," *J. Chem. Educ*., Vol. 71, **1994**, 943–944. This reference includes an analogy dealing with the probability model of the atom.

10. Mali Yin and Raymond S. Ochs, "The Mole, the Periodic Table, and Quantum Numbers: An Introductory Trio," *J. Chem. Educ*., Vol. 78, **2001**, 1345–1347.

11. Ronald J. Gillespie, James N. Spencer and Richard S. Moog, "Demystifying Introductory Chemistry; Part 1. Electron Configurations from Experiment," *J. Chem. Educ*., Vol. 73, **1996**, 617–622. The use of experimental data to investigate electron configurations is presented in this reference.

12. Ngai Ling Ma, "Quantum Analogies on Campus," *J. Chem. Educ*., Vol. 73, **1996**, 1016–1017.

13. Maria Gabriela Lagorio, "Electron Densities: Pictorial Analogies for Apparent Ambiguities in Probability Calculations," *J. Chem. Educ*., Vol. 77, **2000**, 1444–1445.

14. Peter Weiss, "Magnetic Whispers: Chemistry and Medicine Finally Tune Into Controversial Molecular Chatter," *Science News*, Vol. 159, **2001**, 42–44.

15. Anthony Garofalo, "Housing Electrons: Relating Quantum Numbers, Energy Levels, and Electron Configurations," *J. Chem. Educ*., Vol. 74, **1997**, 709–719.

16. John J. Fortman, "Pictorial Analogies VII: Quantum Numbers and Orbitals," *J. Chem. Educ*., Vol. 70, **1993**, 649–650.

17. M. Bonneau, "The Quantum Shoe Store and Electron Structure," *J. Chem. Educ*., Vol. 68, **1991**, 837.

18. Robert D. Freeman, ""New" Schemes for Applying the Aufbau Principle," *J. Chem. Educ*., Vol. 67, **1990**, 576.

19. James R. Hanley, III, and James R. Hanley, Jr., "A Low-Cost Classroom Demonstration of the Aufbau Principle," *J. Chem. Educ*., Vol. 56, **1979**, 747.

20. Peter Cann, "Ionization Energies, Parallel Spins, and the Stability of Half-Filled Shells," *J. Chem. Educ.*, Vol. 77, **2000**, 1056–1061.

21. *Chemistry in Britain*, Vol. 32, **June, 1996**. This issue contains several articles on the uses of NMR--its developments and its uses in medicine.

22. Ngoh Khang Goh, Lian Sai Chia, and Daniel Tan, "Some Analogies for Teaching Atomic Structure at the High School Level," *J. Chem. Educ*., Vol. 71, **1994**, 733–734. Analogies for orbitals, Hund's Rule, and the 4 quantum numbers are included in this reference.

23. Judith A. Strong, "The Periodic Table and Electron Configurations," *J. Chem. Educ*., Vol. 63, **1986**, 834.

## Literature Demonstration

1. Joel A. Olson, Karen J. Nordell, Marla A. Chesnik, Clark R. Landis, Arthur B. Ellis, M.S. Rzchowski, S. Michael Condren, George C. Lisensky, and James W. Long, "Simple and Inexpensive Classroom Demonstration of Nuclear Magnetic Resonance and Magnetic Resonance Imaging," *J. Chem. Educ*., Vol. 77, **2000**, 882–889.

# Chapter 7. Periodic Properties of the Elements

## Media Resources

### Figures and Tables

| In Transparency Pack and on MediaPortfolio: | Section: |
|---|---|
| Figure 7.3 Effective Nuclear Charge for Mg | 7.2 Effective Nuclear Charge |
| Figure 7.5 Bonding Atomic Radii of Some Elements | 7.3 Sizes of Atoms and Ions |
| Figure 7.6 Comparison of Atomic and Ionic Radii | 7.3 Sizes of Atoms and Ions |
| Table 7.2 Successive Values of Ionization Energies, *I*, for the Elements | 7.4 Ionization Energy |
| Figure 7.9 Graph of First Ionization Energy Versus Atomic Number | 7.4 Ionization Energy |
| Figure 7.10 First Ionization Energy Chart | 7.4 Ionization Energy |
| Figure 7.11 Electron Affinities | 7.5 Electron Affinities |
| Figure 7.12 Periodic Table Showing Trends in Metallic Character | 7.6 Metals, Nonmetals, and Metalloids |
| Figure 7.14 Charges of Common Ions | 7.6 Metals, Nonmetals, and Metalloids |
| Table 7.4 Some Properties of the Alkali Metals | 7.7 Group Trends for the Active Metals |
| Table 7.5 Some Properties of the Alkaline Earth Metals | 7.7 Group Trends for the Active Metals |
| Table 7.6 Some Properties of the Group 6A Elements | 7.8 Group Trends for Selected Nonmetals |
| Table 7.7 Some Properties of the Halogens | 7.8 Group Trends for Selected Nonmetals |
| Table 7.8 Some Properties of the Noble Gases | 7.8 Group Trends for Selected Nonmetals |

| On MediaPortfolio: | Section: |
|---|---|
| Figure 7.4 Bonding and Nonbonding Atomic Radii | 7.3 Sizes of Atoms and Ions |

| Animations: | Section: |
|---|---|
| Effective Nuclear Charge | 7.2 Effective Nuclear Charge |
| Periodic Trends: Atomic Radii | 7.3 Sizes of Atoms and Ions |
| Gain and Loss of Electrons | 7.4 Ionization Energy |
| Ionization Energy | 7.4 Ionization Energy |
| Periodic Trends: Ionization Energies | 7.4 Ionization Energy |
| Electron Affinities | 7.5 Electron Affinities |
| Periodic Trends: Electron Affinity | 7.5 Electron Affinities |
| Periodic Trends: Acid-Base Behavior of Oxides | 7.6 Metals, Nonmetals, and Metalloids |

| Movies: | Section: |
|---|---|
| Sodium and Potassium in Water | 7.7 Group Trends for the Active Metals |
| Physical Properties of the Halogens | 7.8 Group Trends for Selected Nonmetals |

| Activities: | Section: |
|---|---|
| Periodic Table | 7.1 Development of the Periodic Table |
| Ionization Energy | 7.4 Ionization Energy |
| First Ionization Energies | 7.4 Ionization Energy |

## Other Resources

| **Further Readings:** | **Section:** |
|---|---|
| Using the Learning Cycle to Introduce Periodicity | 7.1 Development of the Periodic Table |
| The Nuts and Bolts of Chemistry | 7.1 Development of the Periodic Table |
| Mendeleev and Moseley: The Principal Discoverers of the Periodic Law | 7.1 Development of the Periodic Table |
| Mendeleev's Other Prediction | 7.1 Development of the Periodic Table |
| Atomic Number before Moseley | 7.1 Development of the Periodic Table |
| D. I. Mendeleev and the English Chemists | 7.1 Development of the Periodic Table |
| The Evolution of the Periodic System | 7.1 Development of the Periodic Table |
| Periodic Tables of Elemental Abundance | 7.1 Development of the Periodic Table |
| A Different Approach to a 3-D Periodic System Including Stable Isotopes | 7.1 Development of the Periodic Table |
| Screen Percentages Based on Slater Effective Nuclear Charge as a Versatile Tool for Teaching Periodic Trends | 7.2 Effective Nuclear Charge |
| Pictorial Analogies VI: Radial and Angular Wave Function Plots | 7.3 Sizes of Atoms and Ions |
| Using Balls from Different Sports to Model the Variation of Atomic Sizes | 7.3. Sizes of Atoms and Ions |
| Periodic Contractions Among the Elements; Or, On Being the Right Size | 7.3 Sizes of Atoms and Ions |
| Periodicity in the Acid-Base Behavior of Oxides and Hydroxides | 7.6 Metals, Nonmetals, and Metalloids |
| Metalloids | 7.6 Metals, Nonmetals, and Metalloids |
| The Legend of Dr. Pepper/Seven-Up | 7.7 Group Trends for the Active Metals |
| A Little Lithium May Be Just What the Doctor Ordered | 7.7 Group Trends for the Active Metals |
| A Variation on the Demonstration of the Properties of the Alkali Metals | 7.7 Group Trends for the Active Metals |
| Update on Intake: Calcium Consumption Low | 7.7 Group Trends for the Active Metals |
| A Second Note on the Term 'Chalcogen' | 7.8 Group Trends for Selected Nonmetals |
| Allotropes and Polymorphs | 7.8 Group Trends for Selected Nonmetals |
| Aqueous Hydrogen Peroxide: Its Household Uses and Concentration Units | 7.8 Group Trends for Selected Nonmetals |

| **Live Demonstrations:** | **Section:** |
|---|---|
| Halogens Compete for Electrons | 7.5 Electron Affinities |
| Acidic and Basic Properties of Oxides | 7.6 Metals, Nonmetals, and Metalloids |
| Disappearing Ink | 7.6 Metals, Nonmetals, and Metalloids |
| A Dramatic Flame Test Demonstration | 7.7 Group Trends for the Active Metals |
| Producing Hydrogen Gas from Calcium Metal | 7.7 Group Trends for the Active Metals |
| Preparation and Properties of Oxygen | 7.8 Group Trends for Selected Nonmetals |
| Plastic Sulfur | 7.8 Group Trends for Selected Nonmetals |

# Chapter 7. Periodic Properties of the Elements

## Common Student Misconceptions

- Students need to be shown how position on the periodic table and electron configurations can be used to highlight periodic properties.
- Emphasize the periodic table as an organizational tool; it will help students recall chemical facts.
- Students find the descriptive chemistry/group trends a bit overwhelming at first.
- Live demonstrations or CD videos are very helpful in stimulating student interest in the group trends.
- Students often have problems with the sign convention for electron affinities.

## Lecture Outline

### 7.1 Development of the Periodic Table[1,2,3,4,5,6,7,8,9,10]

- The periodic table is the most significant tool that chemists use for organizing and recalling chemical facts.
- Elements in the same column contain the same number of outer-shell electrons or **valence electrons**.
- The majority of the elements were discovered between 1735 and 1843.
  - Discovery of new elements is an ongoing process.
- How do we organize the different elements in a meaningful way that will allow us to make predictions about undiscovered elements?
  - Arrange elements to reflect the trends in chemical and physical properties.
- The periodic table arises from the periodic patterns in the electronic configurations of the elements.
  - Elements in the same column contain the same number of valence electrons.
  - The trends within a row or column form patterns that help us make predictions about chemical properties and reactivity.
- In the first attempt Mendeleev and Meyer arranged the elements in order of increasing atomic weight.
  - Certain elements were missing from this scheme.
  - Example: In 1871 Mendeleev noted that As properly belonged underneath P and not Si, which left a missing element underneath Si. He predicted a number of properties for this element.
    - In 1886 Ge was discovered; the properties of Ge match Mendeleev's predictions well.
- Modern periodic table: Elements are arranged in order of *increasing atomic number.*

### 7.2 Effective Nuclear Charge[11,12,13]

---

1 "Periodic Table" Activity from MediaPortfolio
2 "The Evolution of the Periodic System" from Further Readings
3 "Using the Learning Cycle to Introduce Periodicity" from Further Readings
4 "The Nuts and Bolts of Chemistry" from Further Readings
5 "Mendeleev and Moseley: The Principal Discoverers of the Periodic Table" from Further Readings
6 "Mendeleev's Other Prediction" from Further Readings
7 "Atomic Number before Moseley" from Further Readings
8 "D. I. Mendeleev and the English Chemists" from Further Readings
9 "Periodic Tables of Elemental Abundance" from Further Readings
10 "A Different Approach to a 3-D Periodic System Including Stable Isotopes" from Further Readings
11 "Effective Nuclear Charge" Animation from MediaPortfolio
12 Figure 7.3 from MediaPortfolio and Transparency Pack
13 "Screen Percentages Based on Slater Effective Nuclear Charge as a Versatile Tool for Teaching Periodic Trends" from Further Readings

- **Effective nuclear charge** is the net positive charge experienced by an electron on a many-electron atom.
- The effective nuclear charge is not the same as the charge on the nucleus because of the effect of the inner electrons.
- The electron is attracted to the nucleus, but repelled by the inner-shell electrons that shield or screen it from the full nuclear charge.
  - This shielding is called the screening effect.
- The nuclear charge experienced by an electron depends on its distance from the nucleus and the number of electrons in the spherical volume out to the electron in question.
- As the average number of screening electrons ($S$) increases, the effective nuclear charge ($Z_{eff}$) decreases.

$$Z_{eff} = Z - S$$

- As the distance from the nucleus increases, $S$ increases and $Z_{eff}$ decreases.

## 7.3 Sizes of Atoms and Ions[14,15]

- Consider a collection of argon atoms in the gas phase.
  - When they undergo collisions, they ricochet apart because electron clouds cannot penetrate each other to a significant extent.
  - The *apparent* radius is determined by the closest distances separating the nuclei during such collisions.
  - This radius is the *nonbonding radius*.
- Now consider a simple diatomic molecule.
  - The distance between the two nuclei is called the **bonding atomic radius**.
    - It is shorter than the nonbonding radius.
  - If the two atoms which make up the molecule are the same, then half the bond distance is called the covalent radius of the atom.

### Periodic Trends in Atomic Radii[16,17]

- Atomic size varies consistently through the periodic table.
  - As we move down a group the atoms become larger.
  - As we move across a period atoms become smaller.
  - There are two factors at work:
    - The principal quantum number, $n$, and
    - The effective nuclear charge, $Z_{eff}$.
  - As the principal quantum number increases (i.e., we move down a group), the distance of the outermost electron from the nucleus becomes larger. Hence the atomic radius increases.
  - As we move across the periodic table, the number of core electrons remains constant, however, the nuclear charge increases. Therefore, there is an increased attraction between the nucleus and the outermost electrons. This attraction causes the atomic radius to decrease.

### Trends in the Sizes of Ions[18,19,20]

- Ionic size is important:
  - In predicting lattice energy.

---

[14] Figure 7.4 from MediaPortfolio
[15] "Pictorial Analogies VI: Radial and Angular Wave Function Plots" from Further Readings
[16] "Periodic Trends: Atomic Radii" Animation from MediaPortfolio
[17] Figure 7.5 from MediaPortfolio and Transparency Pack
[18] Figure 7.6 from MediaPortfolio and Transparency Pack
[19] "Using Balls from Different Sports to Model the Variation of Atomic Sizes" from Further Readings
[20] "Periodic Contractions Among the Elements; Or, On Being the Right Size" from Further Readings

- In determining the way in which ions pack in a solid.
- Just as atomic size is periodic, ionic size is also periodic.
- In general:
  - Cations are smaller than their parent atoms.
    - Electrons have been removed from the most spatially extended orbital.
    - The effective nuclear charge has increased.
    - Therefore, the cation is smaller than the parent atom.
  - Anions are larger than their parent atoms.
    - Electrons have been added to the most spatially extended orbital.
    - This means total electron-electron repulsion has increased.
    - Therefore, anions are larger than their parent atoms.
- For ions with the same charge, ionic size increases down a group.
- All the members of an **isoelectronic series** have the same number of electrons.
  - As nuclear charge increases in an isoelectronic series the ions become smaller:

$$O^{2-} > F^{-} > Na^{+} > Mg^{2+} > Al^{3+}$$

## 7.4 Ionization Energy[21,22,23,24]

- The **ionization energy** of an atom or ion is the minimum energy required to remove an electron from the ground state of the isolated gaseous atom or ion.
- The first ionization energy, $I_1$, is the amount of energy required to remove an electron from a gaseous atom:

$$Na(g) \rightarrow Na^{+}(g) + e^{-}$$

- The second ionization energy, $I_2$, is the energy required to remove the second electron from a gaseous ion:

$$Na^{+}(g) \rightarrow Na^{2+}(g) + e^{-}$$

- The larger the ionization energy, the more difficult it is to remove the electron.
- There is a sharp increase in ionization energy when a core electron is removed.

### Variations in Successive Ionization Energies[25]

- Ionization energies for an element increase in magnitude as successive electrons are removed.
  - As each successive electron is removed, more energy is required to pull an electron away from an increasingly more positive ion.
- A sharp increase in ionization energy occurs when an inner-shell electron is removed.

### Periodic Trends in First Ionization Energies[26,27,28]

- Ionization energy decreases down a group.
  - This means that the outermost electron is more readily removed as we go down a group.
  - As the atom gets bigger, it becomes easier to remove an electron form the most spatially extended orbital.
    - Example: For the noble gases the ionization energies follow the order He > Ne > Ar > Kr > Xe.
- Ionization energy generally increases across a period.

---

[21] "Gain and Loss of Electrons" Animation from MediaPortfolio
[22] "Ionization Energy" Animation from MediaPortfolio
[23] "Periodic Trends: Ionization Energies" Animation from MediaPortfolio
[24] "Ionization Energy" Activity from MediaPortfolio
[25] Table 7.2 from MediaPortfolio and Transparency Pack
[26] Figure 7.9 from MediaPortfolio and Transparency Pack
[27] "First Ionization Energies" Activity from MediaPortfolio
[28] Figure 7.10 from MediaPortfolio and Transparency Pack

- As we move across a period, $Z_{eff}$ increases, making it more difficult to remove an electron.
- Two exceptions: removing the first *p* electron and removing the fourth *p* electron.
    - The *s* electrons are more effective at shielding than *p* electrons. So, forming the $s^2p^0$ configuration is more favorable.
    - When a second electron is placed in a *p* orbital, the electron-electron repulsion increases. When this electron is removed, the resulting $s^2p^3$ configuration is more stable than the starting $s^2p^4$ configuration. Therefore, there is a decrease in ionization energy.

### Electron Configurations of Ions

- These are derived from the electron configurations of elements with the required number of electrons added or removed from the most accessible orbital.
    - Li: $[He]2s^1$ becomes $Li^+$: [He]
    - F: $[He]2s^22p^5$ becomes $F^-$: $[He]2s^22p^6 = [Ar]$
- Transition metals tend to lose the valence shell electrons first and then as many *d* electrons as are required to reach the desired charge on the ion.
    - Thus electrons are removed from 4*s* **before** the 3*d*, etc.

## 7.5 Electron Affinities[29,30,31,32]

- **Electron affinity** is the energy change when a gaseous atom gains an electron to form a gaseous ion:
    - Electron affinity: $Cl(g) + e^- \rightarrow Cl^-(g)$ $\Delta E = -349$ kJ/mol
    - Ionization energy: $Cl(g) \rightarrow Cl^+(g) + e^-$ $\Delta E = 1251$ kJ/mol
- Electron affinity can either be exothermic (as the above example) or endothermic:

$$Ar(g) + e^- \rightarrow Ar^-(g) \qquad \Delta E > 0$$

- Look at electron configurations to determine whether electron affinity is positive or negative.
    - The extra electron in Ar needs to be placed in the 4*s* orbital which is significantly higher in energy than the 3*p* orbital.
    - The added electron in Cl is placed in the 3*p* orbital to form the stable $3p^6$ electron configuration.
    - Electron affinities do not change greatly as we move down in a group.

## 7.6 Metal, Nonmetals and Metalloids[33]

- **Metallic character** refers to the extent to which the element exhibits the physical and chemical properties of metals.
    - Metallic character increases down a group.
    - Metallic character decreases from left to right across a period.

### Metals[34,35,36,37,38]

- Metals are shiny and lustrous, malleable and ductile.
- Metals are solids at room temperature (exception: mercury is liquid at room temperature; gallium and cesium melt just above room temperature) and have very high melting temperatures.

---

29 "Electron Affinities" Animation from MediaPortfolio
30 "Periodic Trends: Electron Affinity" Animation from MediaPortfolio
31 Figure 7.11 from MediaPortfolio and Transparency Pack
32 "Halogens Compete for Electrons" from Live Demonstrations
33 Figure 7.12 from MediaPortfolio and Transparency Pack
34 Figure 7.14 from MediaPortfolio and Transparency Pack
35 "Periodic Trends: Acid-Base Behavior of Oxides" Animation from MediaPortfolio
36 "Periodicity in the Acid-Base Behavior of Oxides and Hydroxides" from Further Readings
37 "Acidic and Basic Properties of Oxides" from Live Demonstrations
38 "Disappearing Ink" from Live Demonstrations

- Metals tend to have low ionization energies and tend to form cations easily.
- Metals tend to be oxidized when they react.
- Compounds of metals with nonmetals tend to be ionic substances.
- Metal oxides form basic ionic solids.
  - Most metal oxides are basic:

$$\text{Metal oxide + water} \rightarrow \text{metal hydroxide}$$
$$Na_2O(s) + H_2O(l) \rightarrow 2NaOH(aq)$$

  - Metal oxides are able to react with acids to form salts and water:

$$\text{Metal oxide + acid} \rightarrow \text{salt + water}$$
$$MgO(s) + 2HCl(aq) \rightarrow MgCl_2(aq) + H_2O(l)$$

### Nonmetals

- Nonmetals are more diverse in their behavior than metals.
- In general, nonmetals are nonlustrous, are poor conductors of heat and electricity, and exhibit lower melting points than metals.
- Seven nonmetallic elements exist as diatomic molecules under ordinary conditions:
  - $H_2(g)$, $N_2(g)$, $O_2(g)$, $F_2(g)$, $Cl_2(g)$, $Br_2(l)$, $I_2(s)$
- When nonmetals react with metals, nonmetals tend to gain electrons:

$$\text{Metal + nonmetal} \rightarrow \text{salt}$$
$$2Al(s) + 3Br_2(l) \rightarrow 2AlBr_3(s)$$

- Compounds composed entirely of nonmetals are molecular substances.
- Most nonmetal oxides are acidic:

$$\text{Nonmetal oxide + water} \rightarrow \text{acid}$$
$$P_4O_{10}(s) + 6H_2O(l) \rightarrow 4H_3PO_4(aq)$$
$$CO_2(g) + H_2O(l) \rightarrow H_2CO_3(aq)$$

- Nonmetal oxides react with bases to form salts and water:

$$\text{Nonmetal oxide + base} \rightarrow \text{salt + water}$$
$$CO_2(g) + 2NaOH(aq) \rightarrow Na_2CO_3(aq) + H_2O(l)$$

### Metalloids[39]

- Metalloids have properties that are intermediate between those of metals and nonmetals.
  - Example: Si has a metallic luster but it is brittle.
- Metalloids have found fame in the semiconductor industry.

## 7.7 Group Trends for the Active Metals

- The **alkali metals** (group 1A) and the **alkaline earth metals** (group 2A) are often called the active metals.

### Group 1A: The Alkali Metals[40,41,42,43,44,45]

- The alkali metals are in Group 1A.
- Alkali metals are all soft.
- Their chemistry is dominated by the loss of their single *s* electron:

$$M \rightarrow M^+ + e^-$$

---

[39] "Metalloids" from Further Readings
[40] Table 7.4 From MediaPortfolio and Transparency Pack
[41] "Sodium and Potassium in Water" Movie from MediaPortfolio
[42] "A Dramatic Flame Test Demonstration" from Live Demonstrations
[43] "The Legend of Dr. Pepper/Seven-Up" from Further Readings
[44] "A Little Lithium May Be Just What the Doctor Ordered" from Further Readings
[45] "A Variation on the Demonstration of the Properties of the Alkali Metals" from Further Readings

- Reactivity increases as we move down the group.
- Alkali metals react with hydrogen to form hydrides.
  - In hydrides, the hydrogen is present as $H^-$, called the **hydride ion.**

$$2M(s) + H_2(g) \rightarrow 2MH(s)$$

- Alkali metals react with water to form MOH and hydrogen gas:

$$2M(s) + 2H_2O(l) \rightarrow 2MOH(aq) + H_2(g)$$

- Alkali metals produce different oxides when reacting with $O_2$:
  - $4Li(s) + O_2(g) \rightarrow 2Li_2O(s)$ *(oxide)*
  - $2Na(s) + O_2(g) \rightarrow Na_2O_2(s)$ *(peroxide)*
  - $K(s) + O_2(g) \rightarrow KO_2(s)$ *(superoxide)*
- Alkali metals emit characteristic colors when placed in a high-temperature flame.
  - The *s* electron is excited by the flame and emits energy when it returns to the ground state.
  - The Na line occurs at 589 nm (yellow), characteristic of the $3p \rightarrow 3s$ transition.
  - The Li line is crimson red ($2p \rightarrow 2s$ transition).
  - The K line is lilac ($4p \rightarrow 4s$ transition).

### Group 2A: The Alkaline Earth Metals[46,47,48]

- Alkaline earth metals are harder and denser than the alkali metals.
- Their chemistry is dominated by the loss of two *s* electrons:

$$M \rightarrow M^{2+} + 2e^-$$

$$Mg(s) + Cl_2(g) \rightarrow MgCl_2(s)$$

$$2Mg(s) + O_2(g) \rightarrow 2MgO(s)$$

- Reactivity increases down the group.
  - Be does not react with water.
  - Mg will only react with steam.
  - Ca and the elements below it react with water at room temperature as follows:

$$Ca(s) + 2H_2O(l) \rightarrow Ca(OH)_2(aq) + H_2(g)$$

## 7.8 Group Trends for Selected Nonmetals

### Hydrogen

- Hydrogen is a unique element.
- It most often occurs as a colorless diatomic gas, $H_2$.
- It can either gain another electron to form the hydride ion, $H^-$, or lose its electron to become $H^+$:

$$2Na(s) + H_2(g) \rightarrow 2NaH(s)$$

$$2H_2(g) + O_2(g) \rightarrow 2H_2O(l)$$

- $H^+$ is a proton.
- The aqueous chemistry of hydrogen is dominated by $H^+(aq)$.

### Group 6A: The Oxygen Group[49,50,51,52,53,54]

- As we move down the group the metallic character increases.

---

[46] "Producing Hydrogen Gas from Calcium Metal" from Live Demonstrations
[47] Table 7.5 from MediaPortfolio and Transparency Pack
[48] "An Update on Intake: Calcium Consumption Low" from Further Readings
[49] Table 7.6 from MediaPortfolio and Transparency Pack
[50] "A Second Note on the Term 'Chalcogen'" from Further Readings
[51] "Preparation and Properties of Oxygen" from Live Demonstrations
[52] "Aqueous Hydrogen Peroxide: Its Household Uses and Concentration Units" from Further Readings
[53] "Plastic Sulfur" from Live Demonstrations
[54] "Allotropes and Polymorphs" from Further Readings

- $O_2$ is a gas, Te is a metalloid, Po is a metal.
- There are two important forms of oxygen: $O_2$ and **ozone,** $O_3$.
  - $O_2$ and $O_3$ are allotropes.
    - Allotropes are different forms of the same element in the same state (in this case, gaseous).
    - Ozone can be prepared from oxygen:

$$3O_2(g) \rightarrow 2O_3(g) \qquad \Delta H = +284.6 \text{ kJ}$$

  - Ozone is pungent and toxic.
  - Oxygen (or dioxygen, $O_2$) is a potent oxidizing agent since the $O^{2-}$ ion has a noble gas configuration.
- There are two oxidation states for oxygen: –2 (e.g., $H_2O$) and –1 (e.g., $H_2O_2$).
- Sulfur is another important member of this group.
  - The most common form of sulfur is yellow $S_8$.
  - Sulfur tends to form $S^{2-}$ in compounds (sulfides).

## Group 7A: The Halogens[55,56]

- Group 7A elements are known as the **halogens** ("salt formers").
- The chemistry of the halogens is dominated by gaining an electron to form an anion:

$$X_2 + 2e^- \rightarrow 2X^-$$

- Fluorine is one of the most reactive substances known:

$$2F_2(g) + 2H_2O(l) \rightarrow 4HF(aq) + O_2(g) \qquad \Delta H = -758.9 \text{ kJ}$$

- All halogens consist of diatomic molecules, $X_2$.
- Chlorine is the most industrially useful halogen.
  - The reaction between chorine and water produces hypochlorous acid (HOCl), which is used to disinfect swimming pool water:

$$Cl_2(g) + H_2O(l) \rightarrow HCl(aq) + HOCl(aq)$$

- Halogens react with hydrogen to form gaseous hydrogen halide compounds:

$$H_2(g) + X_2 \rightarrow 2HX(g)$$

- Hydrogen compounds of the halogens are all strong acids with the exception of HF.

## Group 8A: The Noble Gases[57]

- The group 8A elements are known as the **noble gases**.
  - These are all nonmetals and monoatomic.
  - They are notoriously unreactive because they have completely filled *s* and *p* subshells.
- In 1962 the first compounds of the noble gases were prepared: $XeF_2$, $XeF_4$, and $XeF_6$.

---

[55] Table 7.7 from MediaPortfolio and Transparency Pack
[56] "Physical Properties of the Halogens" Movie from MediaPortfolio
[57] Table 7.8 from MediaPortfolio and Transparency Pack

## Further Readings:

1. N. K. Goh and L. S. Chia, "Using the Learning Cycle to Introduce Periodicity," *J. Chem. Educ.*, Vol. 66, **1989**, 747.

2. Mark J. Volkmann, "The Nuts and Bolts of Chemistry," *The Science Teacher*, Vol. 63, **1996**, 37–40. An activity to introduce the periodic table.

3. George Gorin, "Mendeleev and Moseley: The Principal Discoverers of the Periodic Law," *J. Chem. Educ.*, Vol. 73, **1996**, 490–493. An article summarizing some contributions of Mendeleev and Moseley.

4. Kimberley A. Waldron, Eric M. Fehringer, Amy E. Streeb, Jennifer E. Trosky, and Joshua J. Pearson, "Screen Percentages Based on Slater Effective Nuclear Charge as a Versatile Tool for Teaching Periodic Trends," *J. Chem. Educ.*, Vol. 78, **2001**, 635–639.

5. Eric R. Scerri, "The Evolution of the Periodic System," *Scientific American*, **September 1998,** 78–83.

6. Steven I. Dutch, "Periodic Tables of Elemental Abundance," *J. Chem. Educ.*, Vol. 76, **1999**, 356–358.

7. Alexandru T. Balaban, "A Different Approach to a 3–D Periodic System Including Stable Isotopes," *J. Chem. Educ.*, Vol. 76, **1999**, 359.

8. John J. Fortman, "Pictorial Analogies VI: Radial and Angular Wave Function Plots," *J. Chem. Educ.*, Vol. 70, **1993**, 549–550. Analogies for explaining probability distributions are presented.

9. Gabriel Pinto, "Using Balls from Different Sports to Model the Variation of Atomic Sizes," *J. Chem. Educ.*, Vol. 75, **1998**, 725–726. This reference involves analogies to investigate atomic and ionic radii.

10. Joan Mason, "Periodic Contractions Among the Elements; Or, On Being the Right Size," *J. Chem. Educ.*, Vol. 65, **1988**, 17–20. The importance of the size of atoms and ions is discussed.

11. Ronald L. Rich, "Periodicity in the Acid-Base Behavior of Oxides and Hydroxides," *J. Chem. Educ.*, Vol. 62, **1985**, 44. This article provides further information on the solubility of various oxides and hydroxides.

12. Robert H. Goldsmith, "Metalloids," *J. Chem. Educ.*, Vol. 59, **1982**, 526–527. A brief "thumbnail sketch" on metalloids.

13. Werner Fischer, "A Second Note on the Term 'Chalcogen'," *J. Chem. Educ.*, Vol. 78, **2001**, 1333.

14. Jeffrey L. Rodengen, "The Legend of Dr. Pepper/Seven-Up," (Write Stuff Syndicate: Ft. Lauderdale), **1995**.

15. B. D. Sharma, "Allotropes and Polymorphs," *J. Chem. Educ.*, Vol. 64, **1987**, 404–407. Differences of polymorphs and allotropes are explored.

16. Harold Goldwhite, "Mendeleev's Other Prediction," *J. Chem. Educ.*, Vol. 56, **1979**, 35–36.

17. Jan W. van Spronsen, "Atomic Number before Moseley," *J. Chem. Educ.*, Vol. 56, **1979**, 106.

18. Yu. I. Solov'ev, "D. I. Mendeleev and the English Chemists," *J. Chem. Educ.*, Vol. 61, **1984**, 1069–1071.

19. Joseph D. Ciparick and Richard F. Jones, "A Variation on the Demonstration of the Properties of the Alkali Metals," *J. Chem. Educ.*, Vol. 66, **1988**, 438.

20. Michael W. Miller, "A Little Lithium May Be Just What the Doctor Ordered," *Wall Street Journal*, **September 23, 1994**.

21. G. Marino, "Update on Intake: Calcium Consumption Low," *Science News*, **June 18, 1994**, p. 390.

22. Michael J. Webb, "Aqueous Hydrogen Peroxide: Its Household Uses and Concentration Units," *J. Chem. Educ.*, Vol. 62, **1985**, 152. This reference gives some examples of the uses of hydrogen peroxide.

## Live Demonstrations:

1. Lee R. Summerlin, Christie L. Borgford, and Julie B. Ealy, "Halogens Compete for Electrons," *Chemical Demonstrations, A Sourcebook for Teachers, Volume 2* (Washington: American Chemical Society, **1988**), pp. 60–61. The relative tendency of halogens to gain (or lose) electrons is explored by observation of color changes.

2. Bassam Z. Shakhashiri, "Preparation and Properties of Oxygen," *Chemical Demonstrations: A Handbook for Teachers of Chemistry, Volume 2* (Madison : The University of Wisconsin Press, **1985**), pp. 137–141. Oxygen gas, prepared from $H_2O_2$, is used to support combustion reactions.

3. Bassam Z. Shakhashiri, "Acidic and Basic Properties of Oxides," *Chemical Demonstrations: A Handbook for Teachers of Chemistry, Volume 3* (Madison: The University of Wisconsin Press, **1989**), pp. 109–113.

4. Lee. R. Summerlin, Christie L. Borgford, and Julie B. Ealy, "Disappearing Ink," *Chemical Demonstrations, A Sourcebook for Teachers, Volume 2* (Washington: American Chemical Society, **1988**), p. 176. "Disappearing ink" is made from thymolphthalein indicator and dilute sodium hydroxide.

5. Kristin A. Johnson, Rodney Schreiner, and Jon Loring, "A Dramatic Flame Test Demonstration," *J. Chem. Educ.*, Vol. 78, **2001**, 640–641.

6. Lee. R. Summerlin, Christie L. Borgford, and Julie B. Ealy, "Producing Hydrogen Gas from Calcium Metal," *Chemical Demonstrations, A Sourcebook for Teachers, Volume 2* (Washington: American Chemical Society, **1988**), pp. 51–52.

7. Lee. R. Summerlin, Christie L. Borgford, and Julie B. Ealy, "Plastic Sulfur," *Chemical Demonstrations, A Sourcebook for Teachers, Volume 2* (Washington: American Chemical Society, **1988**), p. 53. A flexible brown polymer is formed by pouring heated yellow sulfur into a beaker of water.

# Chapter 8. Basic Concepts of Chemical Bonding

## Media Resources

### Figures and Tables

| **In Transparency Pack and on MediaPortfolio:** | **Section:** |
|---|---|
| Figure 8.3 Crystal Structure of NaCl | 8.2 Ionic Bonding |
| Table 8.2 Lattice Energies for Some Ionic Compounds | 8.2 Ionic Bonding |
| Figure 8.4 Born-Haber Cycle for NaCl | 8.2 Ionic Bonding |
| Figure 8.6 Electronegativities of the Elements | 8.4 Bond Polarity and Electronegativity |
| Figure 8.7 Calculated Electron Distributions in $F_2$, HF and LiF | 8.4 Bond Polarity and Electronegativity |
| Table 8.4 Average Bond Enthalpies | 8.8 Strengths of Covalent Bonds |
| Table 8.5 Average Bond Lengths for Some Single, Double, and Triple Bonds | 8.8 Strengths of Covalent Bonds |

| **On MediaPortfolio:** | **Section:** |
|---|---|
| Table 8.1 Lewis Symbols | 8.1 Chemical Bonds, Lewis Symbols, and the Octet Rule |
| Figure 8.8 Dipole Moment | 8.4 Bond Polarity and Electronegativity |
| Figure 8.9 Oxidation Numbers, Formal Charges and Electon Distribution of HCl | 8.5 Drawing Lewis Structures |
| Figure 8.10 Molecular Structure of Ozone | 8.6 Resonance Structures |
| Figure 8.11 Paint Analogy | 8.6 Resonance Structures |
| Figure 8.12 Benzene Structure | 8.6 Resonance Structures |
| Figure 8.13 Calculation of Enthalpy of Reaction Using Average Bond Enthalpies | 8.8 Strengths of Covalent Bonds |

| **Animations:** | **Section:** |
|---|---|
| Gain and Loss of Electrons | 8.2 Ionic Bonding |
| Born-Haber Cycle | 8.2 Ionic Bonding |
| Periodic Trends: Electronegativity | 8.4 Bond Polarity and Electronegativity |
| Formal Charges | 8.5 Drawing Lewis Structures |
| Periodic Trends: Common Oxidation States | 8.5 Drawing Lewis Structures |

| **Movies:** | **Section:** |
|---|---|
| Formation of Sodium Chloride | 8.2 Ionic Bonding |

## Other Resources

| **Further Readings:** | **Section:** |
|---|---|
| The Chemical Bond as an Atomic Tug-of-War | 8.1 Chemical Bonds, Lewis Symbols, and the Octet Rule |
| Gilbert Newton Lewis and the Amazing Electron Dots | 8.1 Chemical Bonds, Lewis Symbols, and the Octet Rule |
| The Chemical Bond | 8.3 Covalent Bonding |
| Grade-12 Students' Misconceptions of Covalent Bonding and Structure | 8.3 Covalent Bonding |

| | |
|---|---|
| The Role of Lewis Structures in Teaching Covalent Bonding | 8.3 Covalent Bonding |
| Reflections on the Electron Theory of the Chemical Bond: 1900–1925 | 8.3 Covalent Bonding |
| Abegg, Lewis, Langmuir, and the Octet Rule | 8.3 Covalent Bonding |
| G. N. Lewis and the Chemical Bond | 8.3 Covalent Bonding |
| Electronegativity and Bond Type: Predicting Bond Type | 8.4 Bond Polarity and Electronegativity |
| Electronegativity from Avogadro to Pauling, Part I: Origins of the Electronegativity Concept | 8.4 Bond Polarity and Electronegativity |
| Demystifying Introductory Chemistry: Part 3. Ionization Energies, Electronegativity, Polar Bonds, and Partial Charges | 8.4 Bond Polarity and Electronegativity |
| Drawing Lewis Structures from Lewis Symbols: A Direct Electron Pairing Approach | 8.5 Drawing Lewis Structures |
| Lewis Structures Are Models for Predicting Molecular Structure, *Not* Electronic Structure | 8.5 Drawing Lewis Structures |
| Teaching a Model for Writing Lewis Structures | 8.5 Drawing Lewis Structures |
| Drawing Lewis Structures without Anticipating Octets | 8.5 Drawing Lewis Structures |
| The '6*N* + 2 Rule' for Writing Lewis Octet Structures | 8.5 Drawing Lewis Structures |
| Another Procedure for Writing Lewis Structures | 8.5 Drawing Lewis Structures |
| Using Formal Charges in Teaching Descriptive Inorganic Chemistry | 8.5 Drawing Lewis Structures |
| Lewis Structures, Formal Charge, and Oxidation Numbers: A More User-Friendly Approach | 8.5 Drawing Lewis Structures |
| Oxidation Numbers and Their Limitations | 8.5 Drawing Lewis Structures |
| Simple Method for Determination of Oxidation Numbers of Atoms in Compounds | 8.5 Drawing Lewis Structures |
| Electron Densities, Atomic Charges, And Ionic, Covalent, And Polar Bonds | |
| Explaining Resonance—A Colorful Approach | 8.6 Resonance Structures |
| A Visual Aid for Teaching the Resonance Concept | 8.6 Resonance Structures |
| Nitric Oxide—Some Old and New Perspectives | 8.7 Exceptions to the Octet Rule |
| Biological Roles of Nitric Oxide | 8.7 Exceptions to the Octet Rule |
| Nobel Prize in Medicine Goes for Research in NO | 8.7 Exceptions to the Octet Rule |
| Bioinorganic Reactions of Nitric Oxide Underlie Diverse Roles in Living Systems | 8.7 Exceptions to the Octet Rule |

| **Live Demonstrations:** | **Section** |
|---|---|
| Bending a Stream of Water | 8.4 Bond Polarity and Electronegativity |

# Chapter 8. Basic Concepts of Chemical Bonding

## Common Student Misconceptions

- Students think that a triple bond is three times as strong as a single bond. The fact that the second and third bonds ($\pi$ bonds) are weaker than the first ($\sigma$ bond) needs to be emphasized.
- Students need to be able to count the number of valence electrons in order to get the correct Lewis structure.
- Students need to be told that formal charge does not represent real charge on atoms.
- The only place the $\leftrightarrow$ arrow is used is for resonance; students often want to use this to indicate equilibrium.
- Students do not appreciate that the exceptions to the octet rule are almost as common as the examples of substances that obey it.

## Lecture Outlines

## 8.1 Chemical Bonds, Lewis Symbols, and the Octet Rule[1,2]

- The properties of many materials can be understood in terms of their microscopic properties.
- Microscopic properties of molecules include:
  - The connectivity between atoms and
  - The 3D shape of the molecule.
- When atoms or ions are strongly attracted to one another, we say that there is a **chemical bond** between them.
  - In chemical bonds, electrons are shared or transferred between atoms.
- Types of chemical bonds include:
  - **Ionic bonds** (electrostatic forces that hold ions together, e.g., NaCl);
  - **Covalent bonds** (result from sharing electrons between atoms, e.g., $Cl_2$);
  - **Metallic bonds** (refers to metal nuclei floating in a sea of electrons, e.g., Na).

### Lewis Symbols[3,4]

- The electrons involved in bonding are called *valence electrons*.
  - Valence electrons are found in the incomplete, outermost shell of an atom.
- As a pictorial understanding of where the electrons are in an atom, we represent the electrons as dots around the symbol for the element.
  - The number of valence electrons available for bonding are indicated by unpaired dots.
  - These symbols are called **Lewis symbols** or Lewis electron-dot symbols.
  - We generally place the electrons on four sides of a square around the element's symbol.

### The Octet Rule[5]

- Atoms tend to gain, lose or share electrons until they are surrounded by eight valence electrons; this is known as the **octet rule**.
  - An octet consists of full *s* and *p* subshells.
  - We know that $s^2p^6$ is a noble gas configuration.
  - We assume that an atom is stable when surrounded by eight electrons (four electron pairs).

---

[1] "The Chemical Bond as an Atomic Tug-of-War" from Further Readings
[2] "Gilbert Newton Lewis and the Amazing Electron Dots" from Further Readings
[3] Table 8.1 from MediaPortfolio
[4] "Lewis Dot Symbols" Activity from MediaPortfolio
[5] "Octet Rule" Activity from MediaPortfolio

## 8.2 Ionic Bonding[6,7,8]

- Consider the reaction between sodium and chlorine:

  $Na(s) + \frac{1}{2}Cl_2(g) \rightarrow NaCl(s)$   $\Delta H^\circ_f = -410.9$ kJ/mol

  - The reaction is violently exothermic.
  - We infer that the NaCl is more stable than its constituent elements.
    - Sodium has lost an electron to become $Na^+$ and chlorine has gained the electron to become $Cl^-$.
    - Note $Na^+$ has an Ne electron configuration and $Cl^-$ has an Ar configuration.
    - That is, both $Na^+$ and $Cl^-$ have an octet of electrons.
- NaCl forms a very regular structure in which each $Na^+$ ion is surrounded by six $Cl^-$ ions.
  - Similarly each $Cl^-$ ion is surrounded by six $Na^+$ ions.
  - There is a regular arrangement of $Na^+$ and $Cl^-$ in three dimensions.
  - Note that the ions are packed as closely as possible.
  - Note that it is not easy to find a molecular formula to describe the ionic lattice.

### Energetics of Ionic Bond Formation[9,10]

- The heat of formation of NaCl(*s*) is exothermic:

  $Na(s) + \frac{1}{2}Cl_2(g) \rightarrow NaCl(s)$   $\Delta H^\circ_f = -410.9$ kJ/mol

- Separation of the NaCl into sodium and chloride ions is endothermic:

  $NaCl(s) \rightarrow Na^+(g) + Cl^-(g)$   $\Delta H = +788$ kJ/mol

  - The energy required to separate one mole of a solid ionic compound into gaseous ions is called the **lattice energy**, $\Delta H_{lattice}$.
  - Lattice energy depends on the charge on the ions and the size of the ions.
  - The stability of the ionic compound comes from the attraction between ions of unlike charge.
  - The specific relationship is given by Coulomb's equation:

$$E = k\frac{Q_1 Q_2}{d}$$

  - Where $Q_1$ and $Q_2$ are the charges on the particles, $d$ is the distance between their centers, and $k$ is a constant.
    - As $Q_1$ and $Q_2$ increase, $E$ increases, and as $d$ increases, $E$ decreases.

### *Calculation of Lattice Energies: The Born-Haber Cycle*[11]

- The **Born-Haber cycle** is a thermodynamic cycle that analyzes lattice energy precisely.
- Consider a Born-Haber cycle for the formation of NaCl(*s*) from Na(*s*) and $Cl_2(g)$.
- The direct route is:

  $Na(s) + \frac{1}{2}Cl_2(g) \rightarrow NaCl(s)$   $\Delta H^\circ_f = -410.9$ kJ

- Alternatively, we can form:
  - Sodium gas (108 kJ; *endothermic*), then
  - Chlorine atoms (122 kJ; *endothermic*), then
  - Sodium ions (ionization energy for Na, 496 kJ; *endothermic*), then
  - Chloride ions (electron affinity for Cl, –349 kJ; *exothermic*), then
  - Form the ionic lattice (*exothermic*).
- The sum of the above enthalpies is –410.9 kJ.

---

6 "Formation of Sodium Chloride" Movie from MediaPortfolio
7 "Sodium Chloride" 3-D Model from MediaPortfolio
8 Figure 8.3 from MediaPortfolio and Transparency Pack
9 "Coulomb's Law" Activity from MediaPortfolio
10 Table 8.2 from MediaPortfolio and Transparency Pack
11 Figure 8.4 from MediaPortfolio and Transparency Pack

- The lattice energy is +788 kJ.

### Electron Configuration of Ions of the Representative Elements

- These are derived from the electron configuration of elements with the required number of electrons added or removed from the most accessible orbital.
- Electron configuration of ions can predict stable ion formation:
  - Na: [Ne]$3s^1$
  - $Na^+$: [Ne]
  - Cl: [Ne]$3s^2 3p^5$
  - $Cl^-$: [Ne]$3s^2 3p^6$ = [Ar]

### Transition-Metal Ions

- Lattice energies compensate for the loss of up to three electrons.
- We often encounter cations with charges of 1+, 2+ or 3+ in ionic compounds.
- However, transition metals can't attain a noble gas conformation (>3 electrons beyond a noble gas core).
  - Transition metals tend to lose the valence shell electrons first and then as many *d* electrons as are required to reach the desired charge on the ion.
  - Thus electrons are removed from 4*s* **before** the 3*d*, etc.

### Polyatomic Ions

- Polyatomic ions are formed when there is an overall charge on a compound containing covalent bonds.
  - Examples: $SO_4^{2-}$, $NO_3^-$
- In polyatomic ions, two or more atoms are bound together by predominantly covalent bonds.
  - The stable grouping carries a charge.

## 8.3 Covalent Bonding[12,13,14,15]

- The majority of chemical substances do not have characteristics of ionic compounds.
- We need a different model for bonding between atoms.
- A chemical bond formed by sharing a pair of electrons is called a *covalent* bond.
- Both atoms acquire noble-gas electronic configurations.
- This is the "glue" to bind atoms together.

### Lewis Structures[16,17,18,19]

- Formation of covalent bonds can be represented using Lewis symbols.
  - The structures are called **Lewis structures**.
  - We usually show each electron pair shared between atoms as a line and show unshared electron pairs as dots.
  - Each pair of shared electrons constitutes one chemical bond.
  - Example: H· + H· → H:H has electrons on a line connecting the two H nuclei; H–H.

### Multiple Bonds

---

[12] "The Chemical Bond" from Further Readings
[13] "Grade-12 Students' Misconceptions of Covalent Bonding and Structure" from Further Readings
[14] "$H_2$ Bond Formation" Animation from MediaPortfolio
[15] Figure 8.5 from MediaPortfolio
[16] "The Role of Lewis Structures in Teaching Covalent Bonding" from Further Readings
[17] "Reflections on the Electron Theory of the Chemical Bond" from Further Readings
[18] "Abegg, Lewis, Langmuir and the Octet Rule" from Further Readings
[19] "G.N. Lewis and the Chemical Bond" from Further Readings

- It is possible for more than one pair of electrons to be shared between two atoms (e.g., **multiple bonding**):
- One shared pair of electrons is a **single bond** (e.g., $H_2$);
- Two shared pairs of electrons is a **double bond** (e.g., $O_2$);
- Three shared pairs of electrons is a **triple bond** (e.g., $N_2$).
- Generally, bond distances decrease as we move from single through double to triple bonds.

## 8.4 Bond Polarity and Electronegativity

- The electron pairs shared between two different atoms are usually unequally shared.
- **Bond polarity** describes the sharing of the electrons in a covalent bond.
  - Two extremes:
    - In a **nonpolar covalent bond** the electrons are shared equally.
      - Example: Bonding between identical atoms (example: $Cl_2$).
    - In a **polar covalent bond**, one of the atoms exerts a greater attraction for bonding electrons than the other (example: HCl)
  - If the difference is large enough, an ionic bond forms (example: NaCl).

### Electronegativity[20,21,22]

- The ability of an atom *in a molecule* to attract electrons to itself is its **electronegativity**.
- The electronegativity of an element is related to its ionization energy and electron affinity.
- Pauling electronegativity scale: from 0.7 (Cs) to 4.0 (F).
- Electronegativity increases across a period and decreases down a group.

### Electronegativity and Bond Polarity[23,24,25,26,27]

- Electronegativity differences close to zero result in nonpolar covalent bonds.
  - The electrons are equally or almost equally shared.
- The greater the difference in electronegativity between two atoms, the more polar the bond (polar covalent bonds)
- There is no sharp distinction between bonding types.

### Dipole Moments[28,29]

- Molecules like HF have centers of positive and negative charge that do not coincide.
- These are **polar molecules**.
- We indicate the polarity of molecules in two ways:
  - The positive end (or pole) in a polar bond may be represented with a "δ+" and the negative pole with a "δ–".
- We can also place an arrow over the line representing the bond.

---

[20] "Periodic Trends: Electronegativity" Animation from MediaPortfolio
[21] "Electronegativity and Bond Type: Predicting Bond Type" from Further Readings
[22] Figure 8.6 from MediaPortfolio and Transparency Pack
[23] "Electronegativity from Avogadro to Pauling, Part I: Origins of the Electronegativity Concept" from Further Readings
[24] Figure 8.7 from MediaPortfolio and Transparency Pack
[25] "Demystifying Introductory Chemistry: Part 3. Ionization Energies, Electronegativity, Polar Bonds and Partial Charges" from Further Readings
[26] "Bending a Stream of Water" from Live Demonstrations
[27] "Electron Densities, Atomic Charges, And Ionic, Covalent, And Polar Bonds" from Further Readings
[28] Figure 8.8 from MediaPortfolio
[29] "Molecular Polarity" Activity from MediaPortfolio

- The arrow points toward the more electronegative element and shows the shift in electron density toward that atom.
- We can quantify the polarity of the molecule.
  - When charges are separated by a distance, a **dipole** is produced.
  - The **dipole moment** is the quantitative measure of the magnitude of the dipole ($\mu$)

$$\mu = Q r$$

    - The magnitude of the dipole moment is given in Debyes.

### Bond Types and Nomenclature

- Previously we used two different approaches to naming binary compounds
  - One for ionic compounds and another for molecular compounds
  - In both systems the less electronegative element is given first.
    - The other element follows with the ending *-ide*.
- Both approaches are sometimes used with the same substance!
  - Metals with higher oxidation numbers tend to be molecular rather than ionic.
  - For example: $TiO_2$
    - The names titanium(IV) oxide and titanium dioxide are used but titanium dioxide is more commonly used.

## 8.5 Drawing Lewis Structures[30,31,32,33,34,35,36,37]

- Some simple guidelines for drawing Lewis structures:
  - Add up all of the valence electrons on all atoms.
    - For an anion, add electrons equal to the negative charge.
    - For a cation, subtract electrons equal to the positive charge.
  - Identify the central atom.
    - When a central atom has other atoms bound to it, the central atom is usually written first.
      - Example: In $CO_3^{2-}$ the central atom is carbon.
  - Place the central atom in the center of the molecule and add all other atoms around it.
  - Place one bond (two electrons) between each pair of atoms.
  - Complete the octets for all atoms connected to the central atom (exception: hydrogen can only have two electrons).
  - Complete the octet for the central atom; use multiple bonds if necessary.

### Formal Charge[38,39,40,41,42,43,44,45]

---

30 "Drawing Lewis Structures from Lewis Symbols: A Direct Electron Pairing Approach" from Further Readings

31 "Lewis Structures Are Models for Predicting Molecular Structure, *Not* Electronic Structure" from Further Readings

32 "Teaching a Model for Writing Lewis Structures" from Further Readings

33 "Drawing Lewis Structures without Anticipating Octets" from Further Readings

34 "Another Procedure for Writing Lewis Structures" from Further Readings

35 "The '$6N + 2$ Rule' for Writing Lewis Octet Structures" from Further Readings

36 "Lewis Dot Structures" Activity from MediaPortfolio

37 "Electron Dot Structures II" Activity from MediaPortfolio

38 "Using Formal Charges in Teaching Descriptive Inorganic Chemistry" from Further Readings

39 "Formal Charges" Animation from MediaPortfolio

40 "Lewis Structures, Formal Charge and Oxidation Numbers: A More User-Friendly Approach" from Further Readings

41 "Periodic Trends: Common Oxidation States" Animation from MediaPortfolio

42 "Oxidation Numbers and Their Limitations" from Further Readings

- Sometimes it is possible to draw more than one Lewis structure with the octet rule obeyed for all the atoms.
- To determine which structure is most reasonable, we use formal charge.
- The **formal charge** of an atom is the charge that an atom (in a molecule) would have if all of the atoms had the same electronegativity.
- To calculate formal charge, electrons are assigned as follows:
  - All nonbonding (unshared) electrons are assigned to the atom on which they are found.
  - Half of the bonding electrons are assigned to each atom in a bond.
  - Formal charge is the number of valence electrons in the isolated atom, minus the number of electrons assigned to the atom in the Lewis structure.
- For example: consider $CN^-$ (cyanide ion):
  - For carbon:
    - There are four valence electrons (from periodic table).
    - In the Lewis structure there are two nonbonding electrons and three electrons from the triple bond.
    - There are five electrons from the Lewis structure.
    - Formal charge: $4 - 5 = -1$.
  - For nitrogen:
    - There are five valence electrons.
    - In the Lewis structure there are two nonbonding electrons and three from the triple bond.
    - There are five electrons from the Lewis structure.
    - Formal charge $= 5 - 5 = 0$.
- Using formal charge calculations to distinguish between alternative Lewis structures:
  - The most stable structure has the smallest formal charge on each atom and
  - The most negative formal charge on the most electronegative atoms.
- It is important to keep in mind that formal charges do NOT represent REAL charges on atoms!

## 8.6 Resonance Structures[46,47,48,49,50]

- Some molecules are not well described by a single Lewis structure.
  - Typically, structures with multiple bonds can have similar structures with the multiple bonds between different pairs of atoms.
    - Example: Experimentally, ozone has two identical bonds whereas the Lewis structure requires one single (longer) and one double bond (shorter).
- **Resonance structures** are attempts to represent a real structure that is a mix between several extreme possibilities.
  - Resonance structures are Lewis structures that differ only with respect to placement of the electrons.
  - The "true" arrangement is a blend or hybrid of the resonance structures.
  - Example: In ozone the extreme possibilities have one double and one single bond.
    - The resonance structure has two identical bonds of intermediate character.

---

[43] "Simple Method for Determination of Oxidation Numbers of Atoms in Compounds" from Further Readings
[44] "Formal Charges" Activity from MediaPortfolio
[45] Figure 8.9 from MediaPortfolio
[46] Figure 8.10 from MediaPortfolio
[47] Figure 8.11 from MediaPortfolio
[48] "Explaining Resonance—A Colorful Approach" from Further Readings
[49] "A Visual Aid for Teaching the Resonance Concept" from Further Readings
[50] "Resonance Structures" Activity from MediaPortfolio

- We use a double headed arrows (↔) to indicate resonance.
- Common examples: $O_3$, $NO_3^-$, $SO_3$, $NO_2$, and benzene.

### Resonance in Benzene[51]

- Benzene belongs to an important category of organic molecules called *aromatic* compounds.
- Benzene ($C_6H_6$) is a cyclic structure.
  - It consists of six carbon atoms in a hexagon.
  - Each carbon atom is attached to two other carbon atoms and one hydrogen atom.
  - There are alternating double and single bonds between the carbon atoms.
  - Experimentally, the C–C bonds in benzene are all the same length.
  - Experimentally, benzene is planar.
- To emphasize the resonance between the two Lewis structures (hexagons with alternating single and double bonds), we often represent benzene as a hexagon with a circle in it.

## 8.7 Exceptions to the Octet Rule[52]

- There are three classes of exceptions to the octet rule:
  - Molecules with an odd number of electrons.
  - Molecules in which one atom has less than an octet.
  - Molecules in which one atom has more than an octet.

### Odd Number of Electrons[53,54,55,56]

- Most molecules have an even number of electrons and complete pairing of electrons occurs although some molecules have an odd number of electrons.
  - Examples: $ClO_2$, NO, and $NO_2$.

### Less than an Octet[57,58]

- Molecules with less than an octet are also relatively rare.
- Most often encountered in compounds of boron or beryllium.
  - A typical example is $BF_3$.

### More than an Octet

- This is the largest class of exceptions.
- Atoms from the third period on can accommodate more than an octet.
  - Examples: $PCl_5$, $SF_4$, $AsF_6^-$, and $ICl_4^-$.
- Elements from the third period and beyond have unfilled *d* orbitals that can be used to accommodate the additional electrons.
- Size also plays a role.
  - The larger the central atom, the larger the number of atoms that can surround it.
  - The size of the surrounding atoms is also important.
  - Expanded octets occur often when the atoms bound to the central atom are the smallest and most electronegative (e.g., F, Cl, O).

---

[51] Figure 8.12 from MediaPortfolio
[52] "Exceptions to the Octet Rule" Activity from MediaPortfolio
[53] "Nitric Oxide—Some Old and New Perspectives" from Further Readings
[54] "Biological Roles of Nitric Oxide" from Further Readings
[55] "Nobel Prize in Medicine Goes for Research in NO" from Further Readings
[56] "Bioinorganic Reactions of Nitric Oxide Underlie Diverse Roles in Living Systems" from Further Readings
[57] "$BF_3$" 3-D Model from MediaPortfolio
[58] "$NH_3BF_3$" 3-D Model from MediaPortfolio

## 8.8 Strengths of Covalent Bonds[59,60]

- The energy required to break a covalent bond is called the **bond enthalpy**, *D*.
  - That is, for the $Cl_2$ molecule, $D(Cl–Cl)$ is given by $\Delta H$ for the reaction:
    $$Cl_2(g) \rightarrow 2Cl(g).$$
- When more than one bond is broken:
  $$CH_4(g) \rightarrow C(g) + 4H(g) \qquad \Delta H = 1660 \text{ kJ}$$
  - The bond enthalpy is a fraction of $\Delta H$ for the atomization reaction:
    $$D(C–H) = \tfrac{1}{4}\,\Delta H = \tfrac{1}{4}(1660 \text{ kJ}) = 415 \text{ kJ}.$$
- Bond enthalpy is always a positive quantity.

### Bond Enthalpies and the Enthalpies of Reactions[61]

- We can use bond enthalpies to calculate the enthalpy for a chemical reaction.
- We recognize that in any chemical reaction bonds need to be broken and then new bonds form.
- The enthalpy of the reaction is given by:
  - The sum of bond enthalpies for bonds broken less the sum of bond enthalpies for bonds formed.
- Where $\Delta H_{rxn}$ is the enthalpy for a reaction,
  $$\Delta H_{rxn} = \Sigma D(\text{bonds broken}) - \Sigma D(\text{bonds formed})$$
- We illustrate the concept with the reaction between methane, $CH_4$, and chlorine:
  $$CH_4(g) + Cl_2(g) \rightarrow CH_3Cl(g) + HCl(g)$$
  - In this reaction one C–H bond and one Cl–Cl bond are broken while one C–Cl bond and one H–Cl bond are formed.
  - So $\Delta H_{rxn} = [D(C–H) + D(Cl–Cl)] - [D(C–Cl) + D(H–Cl)] = -104$ kJ.
  - The overall reaction is exothermic which means than the bonds formed are stronger than the bonds broken.
  - The above result is consistent with Hess's law.

### Bond Enthalpy and Bond Length[62]

- The distance between the nuclei of the atoms involved in a bond is called the **bond length**.
- Multiple bonds are shorter than single bonds.
  - We can show that multiple bonds are stronger than single bonds.
  - As the number of bonds between atoms increases, the atoms are held closer and more tightly together.

---

[59] Table 8.4 from MediaPortfolio and Transparency Pack
[60] "Bond Enthalpy" Activity from MediaPortfolio
[61] Figure 8.13 from MediaPortfolio
[62] Table 8.5 from MediaPortfolio and Transparency Pack

## Further Readings:

1. Georgios R. Tsaparlis, "The Chemical Bond as an Atomic Tug-of-War," *J. Chem. Educ.*, Vol. 61, **1984**, 677. An analogy between a covalent bond and a game of tug-and-war is suggested in this reference.

2. Natalie Foote Tiernan, "Gilbert Newton Lewis and the Amazing Electron Dots," *J. Chem. Educ.*, Vol. 62, **1985**, 569–570.

3. Roger L. DeKock, "The Chemical Bond," *J. Chem. Educ.*, Vol. 64, **1987**, 934–941. Chemical bonds and their properties are reviewed in this article.

4. Raymond F. Peterson and David F. Treagust, "Grade-12 Students' Misconceptions of Covalent Bonding and Structure," *J. Chem. Educ.*, Vol. 66, **1989**, 459–460. Common weaknesses in student comprehension of covalent bonding are explored in this article.

5. S. R. Logan, "The Role of Lewis Structures in Teaching Covalent Bonding," *J. Chem. Educ.*, Vol. 78, **2001**, 1457–1458.

6. Anthony N. Stranges, "Reflections on the Electron Theory of the Chemical Bond: 1900-1925," *J. Chem. Educ.*, Vol. 61, **1984**, 185–190.

7. William B. Jensen, "Abegg, Lewis, Langmuir, and the Octet Rule," *J. Chem. Educ.*, Vol. 61, **1984**, 191–200.

8. Linus Pauling, "G. N. Lewis and the Chemical Bond," *J. Chem. Educ.*, Vol. 61, **1984**, 201–203.

9. Gordon Sproul, "Electronegativity and Bond Type: Predicting Bond Type," *J. Chem. Educ.*, Vol. 78, **2001**, 387–390.

10. William B. Jensen, "Electronegativity from Avogadro to Pauling, Part I: Origins of the Electronegativity Concept," *J. Chem. Educ.*, Vol. 73, **1996**, 11–20. The January 1996 edition of the Journal of Chemical Education is a special tribute to Linus Pauling and contains many interesting articles.

11. James N. Spencer, Richard S. Moog, and Ronald J. Gillespie, "Demystifying Introductory Chemistry: Part 3. Ionization energies, Electronegativity, Polar Bonds and Partial Charges," *J. Chem. Educ.*, Vol. 73, **1996**, 627–631.

12. Wan-Yaacob Ahmad and Mat B. Zakaria, "Drawing Lewis Structures from Lewis Symbols: A Direct Electron Pairing Approach," *J. Chem. Educ.*, Vol. 76, **1999**, 329–331.

13. Gordon H. Purser, "Lewis Structures Are Models for Predicting Molecular Structure, *Not* Electronic Structure," *J. Chem. Educ.*, Vol. 76, **1999**, 1013–1017.

14. Juan Quilez Pardo, "Teaching a Model for Writing Lewis Structures," *J. Chem. Educ.*, Vol. 66, **1989**, 456–458.

15. James Allen Carroll, "Drawing Lewis Structures Without Anticipating Octets," *J. Chem. Educ.*, Vol. 63. **1986**, 28–31.

16. Melvin E. Zandler and Erach R. Talty, "The '6N + 2 Rule' for Writing Lewis Octet Structures," *J. Chem. Educ.*, Vol. 61, **1984**, 124–127.

17. Thomas J. Clark, "Another Procedure for Writing Lewis Structures," *J. Chem. Educ.*, Vol. 61, **1984**, 100.

18. David G. DeWit, "Using Formal Charges in Teaching Descriptive Inorganic Chemistry," *J. Chem. Educ.*, Vol. 71, **1994**, 750–755.

19. John E. Packer and Shiela D. Woodgate, "Lewis Structures, Formal Charge, and Oxidation Numbers: A More User-Friendly Approach," *J. Chem. Educ.*, Vol. **68**, **1991**, 456–458. Simple rules for writing Lewis structures are discussed.

20. R. J. Gillespie, "Electron Densities, Atomic Charges, And Ionic, Covalent, And Polar Bonds," *J. Chem. Educ.*, Vol. 78, **2001**, 1688–1691.

21. Kenton B. Abel and William M Hemmerlin, "Explaining Resonance–A Colorful Approach," *J. Chem. Educ.*, Vol. 68, **1991**, 834.

22. Francis Delvigne, "A Visual Aid for Teaching the Resonance Concept," *J. Chem. Educ.*, Vol. 66, **1989**, 461–462.

23. Eric W. Ainscough and Andrew M. Brodie, "Nitric Oxide–Some Old and New Perspectives," *J. Chem. Educ.*, Vol. 72, **1995**, 686–692.

24. Solomon H. Snyder and David S. Bredt, "Biological Roles of Nitric Oxide," *Scientific American*, May 1992, 68–77.

25. Rebecca Rawls, "Nobel Prize in Medicine Goes for Research in NO," *Chemical and Engineering News*, **October 19, 1998**, 13.

26. Rebecca Rawls, "Bioinorganic Reactions of Nitric Oxide Underlie Diverse Roles in Living Systems," *Chemical and Engineering News*, **May 6, 1996**, 38–42.

27. A. A. Woolf, "Oxidation Numbers and Their Limitations," *J. Chem. Educ.*, Vol. 65, **1988**, 45–46.

28. Joel M. Kauffman, "Simple Method for Determination of Oxidation Numbers of Atoms in Compounds," *J. Chem. Educ.*, Vol. 63, **1986**, 474–475.

## Literature Demonstrations:

1. Lee. R. Summerlin,, Christie L. Borgford, and Julie B. Ealy, "Bending a Stream of Water," *Chemical Demonstrations, A Sourcebook for Teachers, Volume 2* (Washington: American Chemical Society, 1988), p. 91. The polarity of water and cyclohexane are compared in this demonstration.

# Chapter 9. Molecular Geometry and Bonding Theories

## Media Resources

### Figures and Tables

| **In Transparency Pack and on MediaPortfolio:** | **Section:** |
|---|---|
| Figure 9.2 Shapes of Some $AB_2$ and $AB_3$ Molecules | 9.1 Molecular Shapes |
| Figure 9.3 Molecular Shapes of $AB_n$ Molecules | 9.1 Molecular Shapes |
| Table 9.1 Electron-Domain Geometries as a Function of the Number of Electron Domains | 9.2 VSEPR Model |
| Table 9.2 Electron-Pair Geometries and Molecular Shapes for Molecules with Two, Three, and Four Electron Domains About the Central Atom | 9.2 VSEPR Model |
| Table 9.3 Electron-Domain Geometries and Molecular Shapes for Molecules with Five and Six Electron Domains About the Central Atom | 9.2 VSEPR Model |
| Figure 9.15 Potential Energy Diagram | 9.5 Hybrid Orbitals |
| Figure 9.16 Formation of *sp* Hybrid Orbitals | 9.5 Hybrid Orbitals |
| Figure 9.18 Formation of $sp^2$ Hybrid Orbitals | 9.5 Hybrid Orbitals |
| Figure 9.19 Formation of $sp^3$ Hybrid Orbitals | 9.5 Hybrid Orbitals |
| Table 9.4 Geometric Arrangements Characteristic of Hybrid Orbital Sets | 9.5 Hybrid Orbitals |
| Figure 9.24 Hybridization of Carbon Orbitals in Ethylene | 9.6 Multiple Bonds |
| Figure 9.25 Formation of a $\pi$ Bond in Ethylene | 9.6 Multiple Bonds |
| Figure 9.28 Bonding in Benzene | 9.6 Multiple Bonds |
| Figure 9.33 Formation of $H_2$ Molecular Orbitals | 9.7 Molecular Orbitals |
| Figure 9.37 Molecular Orbitals Formed by the 2*p* Orbitals on Two Atoms | 9.8 Second-Row Diatomic Molecules |
| Figure 9.41 Molecular Orbital Electron Configurations | 9.8 Second-Row Diatomic Molecules |

| **On MediaPortfolio:** | **Section:** |
|---|---|
| Figure 9.1 Representations of Tetrahedral Molecules | 9.1 Molecular Shapes |
| Figure 9.4 Tetrahedral, Trigonal Pyramidal and Bent Geometries | 9.1 Molecular Shapes |
| Figure 9.6 Molecular Geometry of $NH_3$ | 9.2 VSEPR Model |
| Figure 9.7 Bonding and Nonbonding Electron Pairs | 9.2 VSEPR Model |
| Figure 9.8 Trigonal Bipyramid | 9.2 VSEPR Model |
| Figure 9.9 Octahedron | 9.2 VSEPR Model |
| Figure 9.10 Representations of Acetic Acid | 9.2 VSEPR Model |
| Figure 9.11 Dipole Moment of $CO_2$ | 9.3 Molecular Shape and Molecular Polarity |
| Figure 9.12 Dipole Moment of $O_2$ | 9.3 Molecular Shape and Molecular Polarity |
| Figure 9.13 Molecules with Polar Bonds | 9.3 Molecular Shape and Molecular Polarity |
| Figure 9.14 Overlap of Orbitals | 9.4 Covalent Bonding and Orbital Overlap |
| Figure 9.20 Bonding in $H_2O$ | 9.5 Hybrid Orbitals |
| Figure 9.21 Predicting the Hybrid Orbitals in $NH_3$ | 9.5 Hybrid Orbitals |

| | |
|---|---|
| Figure 9.22 Formation of a $\pi$ Bond | 9.6 Multiple Bonds |
| Figure 9.26 Formation of Two $\pi$ Bonds in Acetylene | 9.6 Multiple Bonds |
| Figure 9.27 Formation of $\sigma$ and $\pi$ Bonds in Formaldehyde | 9.6 Multiple Bonds |
| Figure 9.31 Rotation Around a Carbon-Carbon Double Bond | 9.6 Multiple Bonds |
| Figure 9.34 Energy-Level Diagrams for $H_2$ and $He_2$ | 9.7 Molecular Orbitals |
| Figure 9.36 Energy-Level Diagram for $Li_2$ | 9.8 Second-Row Diatomic Molecules |
| Figure 9.39 Energy-Level Diagram for Overlap Between 2*s* and 2*p* Orbitals | 9.8 Second-Row Diatomic Molecules |
| Figure 9.42 Measuring Magnetic Properties | 9.8 Second-Row Diatomic Molecules |

| **Animations:** | **Section:** |
|---|---|
| VSEPR | 9.1 Molecular Shapes |
| Hybridization | 9.5 Hybrid Orbitals |

| **Activities:** | **Section:** |
|---|---|
| Molecular Polarity | 9.3 Molecular Shape and Molecular Polarity |
| Promotion of Electron and Hybridization of Orbitals | 9.5 Hybrid Orbitals |
| Promotion of Electron and Hybridization of Orbitals II | 9.5 Hybrid Orbitals |
| Promotion of Electron and Hybridization of Orbitals III | 9.5 Hybrid Orbitals |

| **3-D Models:** | **Section:** |
|---|---|
| Carbon Tetrachloride | 9.1 Molecular Shapes |
| VSEPR–Basic Molecular Configurations | 9.2 VSEPR Model |

## Other Resources

| **Further Readings:** | **Section:** |
|---|---|
| Teaching VSEPR: The Plastic Egg Model | 9.2 VSEPR Model |
| Multiple Bonds and the VSEPR Model | 9.2 VSEPR Model |
| Molecular Geometry | 9.2 VSEPR Model |
| The Use of Molecular Modeling and VSEPR Theory in the Undergraduate Curriculum to Predict the Three-Dimensional Structure of Molecules | 9.2 VSEPR Model |
| Lewis Structures Are Models for Predicting Molecular Structure, *Not* Electronic Structure | 9.2 VSEPR Model |
| The Ropes: A Molecular Polarity Activity | 9.3 Molecular Shape and Molecular Polarity |
| Identifying Polar and Nonpolar Molecules | 9.3 Molecular Shape and Molecular Polarity |
| The Significance of the Bond Angle in Sulfur Dioxide | 9.3 Molecular Shape and Molecular Polarity |
| Put the Body to Them! | 9.3 Molecular Shape and Molecular Polarity |
| Difficulties with the Geometry and Polarity of Molecules: Beyond Misconceptions | 9.3 Molecular Shape and Molecular Polarity |
| Demystifying Introductory Chemistry Part 2. Bonding and Molecular Geometry without Orbitals—The Electron-Domain Model | 9.4 Covalent Bonding and Orbital Overlap |

| | |
|---|---|
| Grade-12 Students' Misconceptions of Covalent Bonding and Structure | 9.4 Covalent Bonding and Orbital Overlap |
| A Colorful Demonstration to Simulate Orbital Hybridization | 9.5 Hybrid Orbitals |
| Resonance Analogy Using Cartoon Characters | 9.6 Multiple Bonds |
| Explaining Resonance—A Colorful Approach | 9.6 Multiple Bonds |
| A Visual Aid for Teaching the Resonance Concept | 9.6 Multiple Bonds |
| The Eye's Photochemistry: A Quick Snap | 9.6 Multiple Bonds |
| The Molecules of Visual Excitation | 9.6 Multiple Bonds |
| Delocalization: The Key Concept of Covalent Bonding | 9.6 Multiple Bonds |
| The 'Big Dog–Puppy Dog' Analogy for Resonance | 9.6 Multiple Bonds |
| Molecular Orbital Theory of Bond Order and Valency | 9.7 Molecular Orbitals |
| Orbital Bartending | 9.7 Molecular Orbitals |
| The Relative Energies of Molecular Orbitals for Second-Row Homonuclear Diatomic Molecules: The Effect of *s-p* Mixing | 9.8 Second-Row Diatomic Molecules |

| **Live Demonstrations:** | **Section:** |
|---|---|
| Bending a Stream of Water | 9.3 Molecular Shape and Molecular Polarity |

# Chapter 9. Molecular Geometry and Bonding Theories

## Common Student Misconceptions

- Students find it difficult to think in three dimensions. Often, they believe that a square planar arrangement is the best arrangement for least repulsion of four points.
- Students often confuse the electron pair geometry and the molecular geometry.
- Students need to realize that in order to determine whether a molecule is polar, they need to establish the correct molecular geometry.
- Students don't realize that hybridization is determined by the electron pair geometry, not by the molecular geometry.
- Students need to realize that in wave mechanics bonding orbitals result from constructive interference and antibonding orbitals form destructive interference.

## Lecture Outline

### 9.1 Molecular Shapes[1,2,3,4,5,6]

- Lewis structures give atomic connectivity: they tell us which atoms are physically connected to which.
- The shape of a molecule is determined by its **bond angles**.
  - The angles made by the lines joining the nuclei of the atoms in a molecule are the bond angles.
- Consider $CCl_4$:
  - Experimentally we find all Cl–C–Cl bond angles are 109.5°.
  - Therefore, the molecule cannot be planar.
  - All Cl atoms are located at the vertices of a tetrahedron with the C at its center.
- In order to predict molecular shape, we assume that the valence electrons repel each other.
  - Therefore, the molecule adopts the three-dimensional geometry that minimizes this repulsion.
  - We call this model the **V**alence **S**hell **E**lectron **P**air **R**epulsion (**VSEPR**) model.

### 9.2 The VSEPR Model[7,8,9,10,11,12]

- A covalent bond forms between two atoms when a pair of electrons occupies the space between the atom.
  - This is a **bonding pair** of electrons.
  - Such a region is an **electron domain**.
- A **nonbonding pair** or *lone pair* of electrons defines an electron domain located principally on one atom.

---

[1] Figure 9.1 from MediaPortfolio
[2] Figure 9.2 from MediaPortfolio and Transparency Pack
[3] Figure 9.3 from MediaPortfolio and Transparency Pack
[4] Figure 9.4 from MediaPortfolio
[5] "Carbon Tetrachloride" 3-D Model from MediaPortfolio
[6] "VSEPR" Animation from MediaPortfolio
[7] Table 9.1 from MediaPortfolio and Transparency Pack
[8] Figure 9.6 from MediaPortfolio
[9] "Teaching VSEPR: The Plastic Egg Model" from Further Readings
[10] Table 9.2 from MediaPortfolio and Transparency Pack
[11] "Molecular Geometry" from Further Readings
[12] "VSEPR–Basic Molecular Configurations" 3-D Model from MediaPortfolio

- Example: $NH_3$ has three bonding pairs and one lone pair.
- VSEPR predicts that the best arrangement of electron domains is the one that minimizes the repulsions among them.
  - The arrangement of electron domains about the central atom of an $AB_n$ molecule is its **electron-domain geometry**.
  - There are five different electron-domain geometries:
    - Linear (two electron domains), trigonal planar (three domains), tetrahedral (four domains), trigonal bipyramidal (five domains) and octahedral (six domains).
- The **molecular geometry** is the arrangement of the atoms in space.
  - To determine the shape of a molecule we distinguish between lone pairs and bonding pairs.
  - We use the electron domain geometry to help us predict the molecular geometry.
    - Draw the Lewis structure.
    - Count the total number of electron pairs around the central atom.
    - Arrange the electron pairs in one of the above geometries to minimize electron-electron repulsion.
  - Next, determine the three-dimensional structure of the molecule:
    - We ignore lone pairs in the molecular geometry.
    - Describe the molecular geometry in terms of the angular arrangement of the bonded atoms.
    - Multiple bonds are counted as one electron domain.

## The Effect of Nonbonding Electrons and Multiple Bonds on Bond Angles[13,14]

- We refine VSEPR to predict and explain slight distortions from "ideal" geometries.
- Consider three molecules with tetrahedral electron domain geometries:
  - $CH_4$, $NH_3$, and $H_2O$.
  - By experiment, the H–X–H bond angle decreases from C (109.5° in $CH_4$) to N (107° in $NH_3$) to O (104.5° in $H_2O$).
  - A bonding pair of electrons is attracted by two nuclei. They do not repel as much as lone pairs which are primarily attracted by only one nucleus.
  - Electron domains for nonbonding electron pairs thus exert greater repulsive forces on adjacent electron domains.
    - They tend to compress the bond angles.
    - The bond angle decreases as the number of nonbonding pairs increases.
  - Similarly, electrons in multiple bonds repel more than electrons in single bonds. (e.g. in $Cl_2CO$ the O–C–Cl angle is 124.3°, and the Cl–C–Cl bond angle is 111.4°).
- We will encounter 11 basic molecular shapes:
  - Three atoms ($AB_2$)
    - Linear
    - Bent
  - Four atoms ($AB_3$):
    - Trigonal planar
    - Trigonal pyramidal
    - T-shaped
  - Five atoms ($AB_4$):
    - Tetrahedral
    - Square planar
    - See-saw
  - Six atoms ($AB_5$):

---

[13] Figure 9.7 from MediaPortfolio

[14] "Multiple Bonds and the VSEPR Model" from Further Readings

    - Trigonal bipyramidal
    - Square pyramidal
  - Seven atoms ($AB_6$):
    - Octahedral

### Molecules with Expanded Valence Shells[15,16,17,18,19,20]

- Atoms that have expanded octets have $AB_5$ (trigonal bipyramidal) or $AB_6$ (octahedral) electron domain geometries.
  - Trigonal bipyramidal structures have a plane containing three electron pairs.
    - The fourth and fifth electron pairs are located above and below this plane.
    - In this structure two trigonal pyramids share a base.
  - For octahedral structures, there is a plane containing four electron pairs.
    - Similarly, the fifth and sixth electron pairs are located above and below this plane.
    - Two square pyramids share a base.
- Consider a trigonal bipyramid:
  - The three electron pairs in the plane are called *equatorial*;
  - The two electron pairs above and below this plane are called *axial*;
  - The axial electron pairs are 180° apart and 90° to the equatorial electrons;
  - The equatorial electron pairs are 120° apart;
  - To minimize electron–electron repulsion, nonbonding pairs are always placed in equatorial positions and bonding pairs in either axial or equatorial positions.
- Consider an octahedron:
  - The four electron pairs in the plane are at 90° to each other;
  - The two axial electron pairs are 180° apart and at 90° to the electrons in the plane.
  - Because of the symmetry of the system, each position is equivalent.
  - If we have five bonding pairs and one lone pair, it doesn't matter where the lone pair is placed.
    - The molecular geometry is square pyramidal.
  - If two lone pairs are present, the repulsions are minimized by pointing them toward opposite sides of the octahedron.
    - The molecular geometry is square planar.

### Shapes of Larger Molecules

- In acetic acid, $CH_3COOH$, there are three interior atoms: two C and one O.
- We assign the molecular (and electron-domain) geometry about each interior atom separately:
  - The geometry around the first C is tetrahedral;
  - The geometry around the second C is trigonal planar; and
  - The geometry around the O is bent (tetrahedral).

## 9.3 Molecular Shape and Molecular Polarity[21,22,23,24,25,26,27,28,29,30,31]

---

15 "The Use of Molecular Modeling and VSEPR Theory in the Undergraduate Curriculum to Predict the Three-Dimensional Structure of Molecules" from Further Readings
16 Table 9.3 from MediaPortfolio and Transparency Pack
17 "Lewis Structures Are Models for Predicting Molecular Structure *Not* Electronic Structure" from Further Readings
18 Figure 9.8 from MediaPortfolio
19 Figure 9.9 from MediaPortfolio
20 Figure 9.10 from MediaPortfolio
21 Figure 9.11 from MediaPortfolio
22 Figure 9.12 from MediaPortfolio
23 "Bending a Stream of Water" from Live Demonstrations

- Polar molecules interact with electric fields.
- We previously saw that binary compounds are polar if their centers of negative and positive charge do not coincide.
  - If two charges, equal in magnitude and opposite in sign, are separated by a distance *d*, then a *dipole* is established.
  - The dipole moment, μ, is given by

$$\mu = Qr$$

    - Where *Q* is the magnitude of the charge.
- We can extend this to polyatomic molecules.
  - For each bond in a polyatomic molecule, we can consider the **bond dipole**.
    - The dipole moment due only to the two atoms in the bond is the bond dipole.
  - Because bond dipoles and dipole moments are *vector quantities*, the orientation of these individual dipole moments determines whether the molecule has an overall dipole moment.
  - Examples:
    - In $CO_2$ each $^{\delta+}C\text{–}O^{\delta-}$ dipole is canceled because the molecule is linear.
    - In $H_2O$, the $^{\delta+}H\text{–}O^{\delta-}$ dipoles do not cancel because the molecule is bent.
- It is possible for a molecule with polar bonds to be either polar or nonpolar.
  - Example:
    - For diatomic molecules:
      - Polar bonds always result in an overall dipole moment.
    - For triatomic molecules:
    - If the molecular geometry is bent, there is an overall dipole moment;
    - If the molecular geometry is linear, and the B atoms are the same, there is no overall dipole moment;
    - If the molecular geometry is linear and the B atoms are different, there is an overall dipole moment.
    - For molecules with four atoms:
    - If the molecular geometry is trigonal pyramidal, there is an overall dipole moment;
    - If the molecular geometry is trigonal planar, and the B atoms are identical, there is no overall dipole moment;
    - If the molecular geometry is trigonal planar and the B atoms are different, there is an overall dipole moment.

## 9.4 Covalent Bonding and Orbital Overlap[32,33,34]

- Lewis structures and VSEPR theory give us the shape and location of electrons in a molecule.
- They do not explain why a chemical bond forms.

---

[24] "Molecular Polarity" Activity from MediaPortfolio
[25] Figure 9.13 from MediaPortfolio
[26] "Difficulties with the Geometry and Polarity of Molecules: Beyond Misconceptions" from Further Readings
[27] "The Ropes: A Molecular Polarity Activity" from Further Readings
[28] "Identifying Polar and Nonpolar Molecules" from Further Readings
[29] "The Significance of the Bond Angle in Sulfur Dioxide" from Further Readings
[30] "Put the Body to Them!" from Further Readings
[31] "Demystifying Introductory Chemistry Part 2. Bonding and Molecular Geometry Without Orbitals–The Electron Domain Model" from Further Readings
[32] Figure 9.14 from MediaPortfolio
[33] Figure 9.15 from MediaPortfolio and Transparency Pack
[34] "Grade-12 Students' Misconceptions of Covalent Bonding and Structure" from Further Readings

- How can quantum mechanics be used to account for molecular shape? What are the orbitals that are involved in bonding?
- We use **valence-bond theory**:
  - A covalent bond forms when the orbitals on two atoms **overlap**.
    - The shared region of space between the orbitals is called the orbital overlap.
    - There are two electrons (usually one from each atom) of opposite spin in the orbital overlap.
  - As two nuclei approach each other their atomic orbitals overlap.
  - As the amount of overlap increases, the energy of the interaction decreases.
  - At some distance the minimum energy is reached.
    - The minimum energy corresponds to the bonding distance (or bond length).
  - As the two atoms get closer, their nuclei begin to repel and the energy increases.
  - At the bonding distance, the attractive forces between nuclei and electrons just balance the repulsive forces (nucleus-nucleus, electron-electron).

## 9.5 Hybrid Orbitals[35]

- We can apply the idea of orbital overlap and valence-bond theory to polyatomic molecules.

### *sp* Hybrid Orbitals[36,37]

- Consider the $BeF_2$ molecule:
  - Be has a $1s^22s^2$ electron configuration.
  - There is no unpaired electron available for bonding.
  - We conclude that the atomic orbitals are not adequate to describe orbitals in molecules.
- We know that the F–Be–F bond angle is 180° (VSEPR theory).
- We also know that one electron from Be is shared with each one of the unpaired electrons from F.
- We assume that the Be orbitals in the Be–F bond are 180° apart.
- We could promote an electron from the 2*s* orbital on Be to the 2*p* orbital to get two unpaired electrons for bonding.
  - BUT the geometry is still not explained.
- We can solve the problem by allowing the 2*s* and one 2*p* orbital on Be to mix or form two new **hybrid orbitals** (a process called **hybridization**).
  - The two equivalent hybrid orbitals that result from mixing an *s* and a *p* orbital and are called *sp* hybrid orbitals.
  - The two lobes of an *sp* hybrid orbital are 180° apart.
  - According to the valence-bond model, a linear arrangement of electron domains implies *sp* hybridization.
  - Since only one of 2*p* orbitals of Be has been used in hybridization, there are two unhybridized *p* orbitals remaining on Be.
  - The electrons in the *sp* hybrid orbitals form shared electron bonds with the two fluorine atoms.

### $sp^2$ and $sp^3$ Hybrid Orbitals[38,39,40,41]

- Important: When we mix *n* atomic orbitals we must get *n* hybrid orbitals.
- Three $sp^2$ hybrid orbitals are formed from hybridization of one *s* and *two p* orbitals.
  - Thus, there is one unhybridized *p* orbital remaining.

---

35 "A Colorful Demonstration to Simulate Orbital Hybridization" from Further Readings
36 Figure 9.16 from MediaPortfolio and Transparency Pack
37 "Promotion of Electron and Hybridization of Orbitals" Activity from MediaPortfolio
38 Figure 9.18 from MediaPortfolio and Transparency Pack
39 "Promotion of Electron and Hybridization of Orbitals II" Activity from MediaPortfolio
40 Figure 9.19 from MediaPortfolio and Transparency Pack
41 Figure 9.20 from MediaPortfolio

- The large lobes of the $sp^2$ hybrids lie in a trigonal plane.
- Molecules with trigonal planar electron-pair geometries have $sp^2$ orbitals on the central atom.
- Four $sp^3$ hybrid orbitals are formed from hybridization of one *s* and three *p* orbitals.
  - Therefore, there are four large lobes.
  - Each lobe points towards the vertex of a tetrahedron.
  - The angle between the large lobes is 109.5°.
  - Molecules with tetrahedral electron pair geometries are $sp^3$ hybridized.

### Hybridization Involving *d* Orbitals[42,43]

- Since there are only three *p* orbitals, trigonal bipyramidal and octahedral electron-pair geometries must involve *d* orbitals.
- Trigonal bipyramidal electron pair geometries require $sp^3d$ hybridization.
- Octahedral electron pair geometries require $sp^3d^2$ hybridization.
- Note that the electron pair VSEPR geometry corresponds well with the hybridization.
  - Use of *d* orbitals in making hybrid orbitals corresponds well with the idea of an expanded octet.

### Summary[44,45]

- We need to know the electron-domain geometry before we can assign hybridization.
- To assign hybridization:
  - Draw a Lewis structure.
  - Assign the electron-domain geometry using VSEPR theory.
  - Specify the hybridization required to accommodate the electron pairs based on their geometric arrangement.
  - Name the geometry by the positions of the atoms.

## 9.6 Multiple Bonds[46,47,48,49,50]

- In the covalent bonds we have seen so far the electron density has been concentrated symmetrically about the *internuclear axis*.
- **Sigma (σ) bonds**: electron density lies on the axis between the nuclei.
  - All single bonds are σ bonds.
- What about overlap in multiple bonds?
  - **Pi (π) bonds**: electron density lies above and below the plane of the nuclei.
    - A double bond consists of one σ bond and one π bond.
    - A triple bond has one σ bond and two π bonds.
- Often, the *p* orbitals involved in π bonding come from unhybridized orbitals.
- For example: ethylene, $C_2H_4$, has:
  - One σ and one π bond.
  - Both C atoms $sp^2$ hybridized.
  - Both C atoms with trigonal planar electron-pair and molecular geometries.
- For example: acetylene, $C_2H_2$:
  - The electron-domain geometry of each C is linear.

---

[42] "Hybridization" Animation from MediaPortfolio
[43] "Promotion of Electron and Hybridization of Orbitals III" Activity from MediaPortfolio
[44] Table 9.4 from MediaPortfolio and Transparency Pack
[45] Figure 9.21 from MediaPortfolio
[46] Figure 9.22 from MediaPortfolio
[47] Figure 9.24 from MediaPortfolio and Transparency Pack
[48] Figure 9.25 from MediaPortfolio and Transparency Pack
[49] Figure 9.26 from MediaPortfolio
[50] Figure 9.27 from MediaPortfolio

- Therefore, the C atoms are *sp* hybridized.
- The *sp* hybrid orbitals form the C–C and C–H $\sigma$ bonds.
- There are *two* unhybridized *p* orbitals on each C atom.
- *Both* unhybridized *p* orbitals form the *two* $\pi$ bonds;
  - One $\pi$ bond is above and below the plane of the nuclei;
  - One $\pi$ bond is in front and behind the plane of the nuclei.
- When triple bonds form (e.g., $N_2$), one $\pi$ bond is always above and below and the other is in front and behind the plane of the nuclei.

### Delocalized $\pi$ Bonding[51,52,53,54,55,56,57,58,59]

- So far all the bonds we have encountered are localized between two nuclei.
- In the case of benzene:
  - There are six C–C $\sigma$ bonds and six C–H $\sigma$ bonds
  - Each C atom is $sp^2$ hybridized.
  - There is one unhybridized *p* orbital on each carbon atom, resulting in six unhybridized carbon *p* orbitals in a ring.
- In benzene there are two options for the three $\pi$ bonds:
  - Localized between carbon atoms or
  - **Delocalized** over the entire ring (i.e., the $\pi$ electrons are shared by all six carbon atoms).
- Experimentally, all C–C bonds are the same length in benzene.
  - Therefore, all C–C bonds are of the same type (recall single bonds are longer than double bonds).

### General Conclusions[60]

- Every pair of bonded atoms shares one or more pairs of electrons.
- Two electrons shared between atoms on the same axis as the nuclei are $\sigma$ bonds.
- $\sigma$ Bonds are always localized in the region between two bonded atoms.
- If two atoms share more than one pair of electrons, the additional pairs form $\pi$ bonds.
- When resonance structures are possible, delocalization is also possible.

## 9.7 Molecular Orbitals[61]

- Some aspects of bonding are not explained by Lewis structures, VSEPR theory and hybridization.
  - For example:
    - Why does $O_2$ interact with a magnetic field?
    - Why are some molecules colored?
- For these molecules, we use **molecular orbital** (MO) **theory**.
- Just as electrons in atoms are found in atomic orbitals, electrons in molecules are found in **molecular orbitals**.
- Molecular orbitals:
  - Some characteristics are similar to those of atomic orbitals:

---

51 "The 'Big Dog–Puppy Dog' Analogy for Resonance" from Further Readings
52 "Resonance Analogy Using Cartoon Characters" from Further Readings
53 "Explaining Resonance–A Colorful Approach" from Further Readings
54 "A Visual Aid for Teaching the Resonance Concept" from Further Readings
55 Figure 9.28 from MediaPortfolio and Transparency Pack
56 Figure 9.31 from MediaPortfolio
57 "The Eye's Photochemistry: A Quick Snap" From Further Readings
58 "The Molecules of Visual Excitation" from Further Readings
59 "Delocalization: The Key Concept of Covalent Bonding" from Further Readings
60 "Orbital Bartending" from Further Readings
61 "Molecular Orbital Theory of Bond Order and Valency" from Further Readings

    - Each contains a maximum of two electrons with opposite spins.
    - Each has a definite energy.
    - Electron density distribution can be visualized with contour diagrams.
  - However, unlike atomic orbitals, molecular orbitals are associated with an *entire molecule*.

### The Hydrogen Molecule[62,63]

- When two AOs overlap two MOs form.
- Therefore, 1*s* (H) + 1*s* (H) must result in two MOs for $H_2$:
  - One has electron density between the nuclei (**bonding MO**);
  - One has little electron density between the nuclei (**antibonding MO**).
- **Sigma ($\sigma$) MOs** have electron density in both molecular orbitals centered about the internuclear axis.
- The $\sigma$ bonding MO is lower in energy than the $\sigma^*$ (antibonding) MO.
- **The energy level diagram** or **MO diagram** shows the energies of the orbitals in a molecule.
  - The total number of electrons in all atoms are placed in the MOs starting from lowest energy ($\sigma_{1s}$) and ending when all electrons have been accommodated.
  - Note that electrons in MOs have opposite spins.

### Bond Order

- Define **bond order** = ½ (bonding electrons – antibonding electrons).
  - Bond order = 1 for single bond.
  - Bond order = 2 for double bond.
  - Bond order = 3 for triple bond.
    - Fractional bond orders are possible.
- For example, consider the molecule $H_2$.
  - $H_2$ has two bonding electrons.
  - Bond order for $H_2$ is:

    ½ (bonding electrons - antibonding electrons) = ½ (2 – 0) = 1.
  - Therefore, $H_2$ has a single bond.
- For example, consider the species $He_2$.
  - $He_2$ has two bonding electrons and two antibonding electrons.
  - Bond order for $He_2$ is:

    ½ (bonding electrons – antibonding electrons) = ½ (2 – 2) = 0.
  - Therefore $He_2$ is *not* a stable molecule.
- MO theory correctly predicts that hydrogen forms a diatomic molecule but that helium does not!

## 9.8 Second-Row Diatomic Molecules[64]

- We look at homonuclear diatomic molecules (e.g., $Li_2$, $Be_2$, $B_2$ etc.).
- AOs combine according to the following rules:
  - The number of MOs = number of AOs.
  - AOs of similar energy combine (e.g., 1*s* + 1*s* rather than 1*s* + 2*s*).
  - As overlap increases, the energy of the bonding MO decreases and the energy of the antibonding MO increases.
  - Pauli: Each MO has at most two electrons, with spins paired.
  - Hund: For degenerate orbitals, each MO is first occupied singly before spin pairing occurs.

### Molecular Orbitals for $Li_2$ and $Be_2$[65]

---

[62] Figure 9.33 from MediaPortfolio and Transparency Pack
[63] Figure 9.34 from MediaPortfolio
[64] "The Relative Energies of Molecular Orbitals for Second-Row Homonuclear Diatomic Molecules: The Effect of *s-p* Mixing" from Further Readings

- Each $1s$ orbital combines with another $1s$ orbital to give one $\sigma_{1s}$ and one $\sigma^*_{1s}$ orbital, both of which are occupied (since Li and Be have $1s^2$ electron configurations).
- Each $2s$ orbital combines with another $2s$ orbital two give one $\sigma_{2s}$ and one $\sigma^*_{2s}$ orbital.
- The energies of the $1s$ and $2s$ orbitals are sufficiently different so that there is no cross mixing of orbitals (i.e., we do not get $1s + 2s$).
- Consider the bonding in $Li_2$.
  - There are a total of six electrons in $Li_2$:
    - 2 electrons in $\sigma_{1s}$.
    - 2 electrons in $\sigma^*_{1s}$.
    - 2 electrons in $\sigma_{2s}$.
    - 0 electrons in $\sigma^*_{2s}$.
    - Therefore the bond order is ½ (4 – 2) = 1.
- Since the $1s$ AOs are completely filled, the $\sigma_{1s}$ *and* $\sigma^*_{1s}$ are filled.
  - We generally ignore core electrons in MO diagrams.
  - Core electrons usually don't contribute significantly to bonding in molecule formation.
- Consider bonding in $Be_2$.
  - There are a total of eight electrons in $Be_2$:
    - 2 electrons in $\sigma_{1s}$.
    - 2 electrons in $\sigma^*_{1s}$.
    - 2 electrons in $\sigma_{2s}$.
    - 2 electrons in $\sigma^*_{2s}$.
    - Therefore the bond order is ½ (4 – 4) = 0.
  - $Be_2$ does not exist.

## Molecular Orbitals from 2*p* Atomic Orbitals[66]

- There are two ways in which two $p$ orbitals can overlap:
  - End on so that the resulting MO has electron density on the axis between nuclei (i.e., $\sigma$ type orbital);
  - Sideways, so that the resulting MO has electron density above and below the axis between nuclei.
    - These are called **pi ($\pi$) molecular orbitals.**
- The six $p$-orbitals (two sets of three) must give rise to six MOs:
  - $\sigma$, $\sigma^*$, $\pi$, $\pi^*$, $\pi$ and $\pi^*$.
  - Therefore there are a maximum of two $\pi$ bonds which can come from $p$ orbitals.
  - The relative energies of these six orbitals can change.

## Electron Configurations for $B_2$ Through $Ne_2$[67,68]

- Features of the energy-level diagrams for these elements:
  - $2s$ Orbitals are lower in energy than $2p$ orbitals so both $\sigma_{2s}$ orbitals ($\sigma_{2s}$ and $\sigma^*_{2s}$) are lower in energy than the lowest energy MO derived from the $2p$ AOs.
  - There is greater overlap between $2p_z$ orbitals.
    - They point directly towards one another, so the $\sigma_{2p}$ MO is lower in energy than the $\pi_{2p}$ orbitals.
    - The $\sigma^*_{2p}$ MO is higher in energy than the $\pi^*_{2p}$ orbitals.
  - The $\pi_{2p}$ and $\pi^*_{2p}$ orbitals are doubly degenerate.
  - As the atomic number decreases, it becomes more likely that a $2s$ orbital on one atom can interact with the $2p$ orbital on the other.

---

[65] Figure 9.36 from MediaPortfolio
[66] Figure 9.37 from MediaPortfolio and Transparency Pack
[67] Figure 9.39 from MediaPortfolio
[68] Figure 9.41 from MediaPortfolio and Transparency Pack

- As the 2*s*–2*p* interaction increases, the $\sigma_{2s}$ MO lowers in energy and the $\sigma_{2p}$ orbital increases in energy.
    - For $B_2$, $C_2$ and $N_2$ the $\sigma_{2p}$ orbital is higher in energy than the $\pi_{2p}$.
    - For $O_2$, $F_2$ and $Ne_2$ the $\sigma_{2p}$ orbital is lower in energy than the $\pi_{2p}$.
- Once we know the relative orbital energies, we add the required number of electrons to the MOs, taking into account Pauli's exclusion principle and Hund's rule.
- As bond order increases,
    - Bond length decreases.
    - Bond energy increases.

### Electron Configurations and Molecular Properties[69]

- Two types of magnetic behavior:
    - **Paramagnetism** (unpaired electrons in molecule).
        - Strong attraction between magnetic field and molecule.
    - **Diamagnetism** (no unpaired electrons in molecule).
        - Weak repulsion between magnetic field and molecule.
- Magnetic behavior is detected by determining the mass of a sample in the presence and absence of a magnetic field:
    - A large increase in mass indicates paramagnetism.
    - A small decrease in mass indicates diamagnetism.
- Experimentally $O_2$ is paramagnetic.
    - The Lewis structure for $O_2$ shows no unpaired electrons.
    - The MO diagram for $O_2$ shows 2 unpaired electrons in the $\pi^*_{2p}$ orbital.
    - Experimentally, $O_2$ has a short bond length (1.21 Å) and high bond dissociation energy (495 kJ/mol).
        - This suggests a double bond.
        - The MO diagram for $O_2$ predicts both paramagnetism and the double bond (bond order = 2).

### Heteronuclear Diatomic Molecules

- Heteronuclear diatomic molecules contain 2 different elements.
- If both atoms do not differ greatly in electronegativity, the description of their MOs will be similar to those for homonuclear diatomic molecules.

[69] Figure 9.42 from MediaPortfolio

## Further Readings:

1. James P. Birk and Soraya Abbassian, "Teaching VSEPR: The Plastic Egg Model," *J. Chem. Educ.*, Vol. 73, **1996**, 636–637. The use of inexpensive models for teaching VSEPR is covered in this short article.

2. Ronald J. Gillespie, "Multiple Bonds and the VSEPR Model," *J. Chem. Educ.*, Vol. 69, **1992**, 116–121.

3. Brian W. Pfennig and Richard L. Frock, "The Use of Molecular Modeling and VSEPR Theory in the Undergraduate Curriculum to Predict the Three-Dimensional Structure of Molecules," *J. Chem. Educ.*, Vol. 76, **1999**, 1018–1022.

4. Gordon H. Purser, "Lewis Structures Are Models for Predicting Molecular Structure, *Not* Electronic Structure," *J. Chem. Educ.*, Vol. 76, **1999**, 1013–1017.

5. Carlos Furio and Ma. Luisa Calatayud, "Difficulties with the Geometry and Polarity of Molecules: Beyond Misconceptions," *J. Chem. Educ.*, Vol. 73, **1996**, 36–41.

6. Thomas H. Bindel and Timothy C. Smiley, "The Ropes: A Molecular Polarity Activity," *J. Chem. Educ.*, Vol. 71, **1994**, 945.

7. R. J. Tykodi, "Identifying Polar and Nonpolar Molecules," *J. Chem. Educ.*, Vol. 66, **1989**, 1007–1011.

8. Gordon H. Purser, "The Significance of the Bond Angle in Sulfur Dioxide," *J. Chem. Educ.*, Vol. 66, **1989**, 710–713.

9. Robert R. Perkins, "Put the Body to Them!," *J. Chem. Educ.*, Vol. 72, **1995**, 151–152. This reference includes an analogical demonstration of the concept of molecular polarity.

10. Ronald J. Gillespie, James N. Spencer and Richard S. Moog, "Demystifying Introductory Chemistry Part 2. Bonding and Molecular Geometry Without Orbitals -- The Electron Domain Model," *J. Chem. Educ.*, Vol. 73, **1996**, 622–627.

11. Raymond F. Peterson and David F. Treagust, "Grade-12 Students' Misconceptions of Covalent Bonding and Structure," *J. Chem. Educ.*, Vol. 66, **1989**, 459–460.

12. D. W. Emerson, "A Colorful Demonstration to Simulate Orbital Hybridization," *J. Chem. Educ.*, Vol. 65, **1988**, 454.

13. Ronald Starkey, "Resonance Analogy Using Cartoon Characters," *J. Chem. Educ.*, Vol. 72, **1995**, 542.

14. Kenton B. Abel and William M. Hemmerlin, "Explaining Resonance-A Colorful Approach," *J. Chem. Educ.*, Vol. 8, **1991**, 834.

15. Francis Delvigne, "A Visual Aid for Teaching the Resonance Concept," *J. Chem. Educ.*, Vol. 66, **1989**, 461–462.

16. A. B. Sannigrahi and Tapas Kar, "Molecular Orbital Theory of Bond Order and Valency," *J. Chem. Educ.*, Vol. 65, **1988**, 674–676.

17. John Barbaro, "Orbital Bartending," *J. Chem. Educ.*, Vol. 71, **1994**, 1012. An analogy for orbital hybridization is suggested in this short article.

18. Albert Haim, "The Relative Energies of Molecular Orbitals for Second-Row Homonuclear Diatomic Molecules; The Effect of *s-p* Mixing," *J. Chem. Educ.*, Vol. 68, **1991**, 737–738.

19. H. O. Desseyn, M. A. Herman, and J. Mullens, "Molecular Geometry," *J. Chem. Educ.*, Vol. 62, **1985**, 220–222.

20. R. Lipkin, "The Eye's Photochemistry: A Quick Snap," *Science News*, **October 29, 1994**, p.279.

21. Lubert Stryer, "The Molecules of Visual Excitation," *Scientific American*, Vol. 255 (7), **1987**, 42–50.

22. Sture Nordholm, "Delocalization- The Key Concept of Covalent Bonding," *J. Chem. Educ.*, Vol. 65, **1988**, 581–584.

23. Todd P. Silverstein, "The 'Big Dog-Puppy Dog' Analogy for Resonance," *J. Chem. Educ.*, Vol. 76, **1999**, 206–208.

## Live Demonstrations:

1. Lee. R. Summerlin, Christie L. Borgford, and Julie B. Ealy, "Bending a Stream of Water," *Chemical Demonstrations, A Sourcebook for Teachers*, *Volume 2* (Washington: American Chemical Society, **1988**), p. 91. The polarity of water and cyclohexane are compared in this demonstration.

# Chapter 10. Gases

## Media Resources

### Figures and Tables

| In Transparency Pack and on MediaPortfolio: | Section: |
|---|---|
| Figure 10.1 Pressure of Earth's Atmosphere | 10.2 Pressure |
| Figure 10.2 Mercury Barometer | 10.2 Pressure |
| Figure 10.3 Manometer | 10.2 Pressure |
| Figure 10.7 Graph of *V* versus *P* Illustrating Boyle's Law | 10.3 The Gas Laws |
| Figure 10.18 Distribution of Molecular Speeds for Nitrogen | 10.7 Kinetic-Molecular Theory |
| Figure 10.19 Distribution of Molecular Speeds for Several Gases | 10.8 Molecular Effusion and Diffusion |
| Figure 10.23 Graph of *PV/RT* versus *P* for Several Gases | 10.9 Real Gases: Deviations from Ideal Behavior |
| Figure 10.24 Graph of *PV/RT* versus *P* for $N_2$ at Different Temperatures | 10.9 Real Gases: Deviations from Ideal Behavior |

| On MediaPortfolio: | Section: |
|---|---|
| Table 10.1 Some Common Compounds That Are Gases | 10.1 Characteristics of Gases |
| Figure 10.6 Illustration of Boyle's Experiment | 10.3 The Gas Laws |
| Figure 10.9 Graph of *V* versus *T* Illustrating Charles's Law | 10.3 The Gas Laws |
| Figure 10.10 Law of Combining Volumes | 10.3 The Gas Laws |
| Figure 10.11 Avagadro's Hypothesis | 10.3 The Gas Laws |
| Table 10.2 Numerical Values of the Gas Constant, *R*, in Various Units | 10.4 The Ideal Gas Equation |
| Figure 10.16 Collection of a Gas Over Water | 10.6 Gas Mixtures and Partial Pressures |
| Figure 10.17 Pressure of a Gas | 10.7 Kinetic-Molecular Theory |
| Figure 10.20 Effusion of a Gas | 10.8 Molecular Effusion and Diffusion |
| Figure 10.25 Effect of Finite Volume of Gas Molecules on Properties of Real Gas | 10.9 Real Gases: Deviations from Ideal Behavior |
| Figure 10.26. Effect of Attractive Forces on *P* | 10.9 Real Gases: Deviations from Ideal Behavior |
| Table 10.3 van der Waals Constants for Gas Molecules | 10.9 Real Gases: Deviations from Ideal Behavior |

| Animations: | Section: |
|---|---|
| *P-V* Relationships | 10.3 The Gas Laws |
| Airbags | 10.5 Further Applications of the Ideal-Gas Equation |
| Kinetic Energy of Gas Molecules | 10.7 Kinetic-Molecular Theory |

| Movies: | Section: |
|---|---|
| Diffusion of Bromine Vapor | 10.8 Molecular Effusion and Diffusion |

| **Activities:** | **Section:** |
|---|---|
| Manometer | 10.2 Pressure |
| Density of Gases | 10.5 Further Applications of the Ideal-Gas Equation |
| Partial Pressures | 10.6 Gas Mixtures and Partial Pressures |
| Gas Phase: Boltzmann Distribution | 10.8 Molecular Effusion and Diffusion |
| Diffusion and Effusion | 10.8 Molecular Effusion and Diffusion |
| Real Gases | 10.9 Real Gases: Deviations from Ideal Behavior |

| **3-D Models:** | **Section:** |
|---|---|
| Hydrogen Cyanide | 10.1 Characteristics of Gases |
| Hydrogen Chloride | 10.1 Characteristics of Gases |
| Hydrogen Sulfide | 10.1 Characteristics of Gases |
| Carbon Monoxide | 10.1 Characteristics of Gases |
| Carbon Dioxide | 10.1 Characteristics of Gases |
| Methane | 10.1 Characteristics of Gases |
| Nitrous Oxide | 10.1 Characteristics of Gases |
| Nitrogen Dioxide | 10.1 Characteristics of Gases |
| Ammonia | 10.1 Characteristics of Gases |
| Sulfur Dioxide | 10.1 Characteristics of Gases |

## Other Resources

| **Further Readings:** | **Section:** |
|---|---|
| Gases and Their Behavior | 10.1 Characteristics of Gases |
| Gay-Lussac: Chemist Extraordinary | 10.3 The Gas Laws |
| Gay-Lussac after 200 Years | 10.3 The Gas Laws |
| The Chemistry Behind the Air Bag | 10.5 Further Applications of the Ideal-Gas Equation |
| Chemistry of Air Bags | 10.5 Further Applications of the Ideal-Gas Equation |
| Cinema, Flirts, Snakes, and Gases | 10.7 Kinetic-Molecular Theory |
| Toy Flying Saucers and Molecular Speeds | 10.7 Kinetic-Molecular Theory |

| **Live Demonstrations:** | **Section:** |
|---|---|
| Boiling at Reduced Pressure | 10.2 Pressure |
| Boyle's Law | 10.3 The Gas Laws |
| Boyle's Law and the Monster Marshmallow | 10.3 The Gas Laws |
| Effect of Pressure on the Size of a Balloon | 10.3 The Gas Laws |
| Boyle's Law and the Mass of a Textbook | 10.3 The Gas Laws |
| Thermal Expansion of Gases | 10.3 The Gas Laws |
| Charles' Law: The Relationship between Volume and Temperature of a Gas | 10.3 The Gas Laws |
| Charles' Law of Gases: A Simple Experimental Demonstration | 10.3 The Gas Laws |
| Thermal Expansion of Gases | 10.3 The Gas Laws |
| Collapsing Can | 10.3 The Gas Laws |
| Determining the Molecular Weight of a Gas | 10.6 Gas Mixtures and Partial Pressures |

| | |
|---|---|
| Overhead Projection of Graham's Law of Gaseous Diffusion | 10.8 Molecular Effusion and Diffusion |
| Diffusion of Gases | 10.8 Molecular Effusion and Diffusion |
| Relative Velocity of Sound Propagation: Musical Molecular Weights | 10.8 Molecular Effusion and Diffusion |

# Chapter 10. Gases

## Common Student Misconceptions

- Students need to be told to *always* use Kelvin temperatures in gas problems.
- Students should always use units (and unit factor analysis) in gas-law problems to keep track of required conversions.
- Students often confuse the standard conditions for gas behavior (STP) with the standard conditions in thermodynamics.
- Students commonly confuse effusion and diffusion.

## Lecture Outline

### 10.1 Characteristics of Gases[1,2,3,4,5,6,7,8,9,10,11,12]

- All substances have three phases: solid, liquid and gas.
- Substances that are liquids or solids under ordinary conditions may also exist as gases.
  - These are often referred to as **vapors**.
- Many of the properties of gases differ from those of solids and liquids:
  - Gases are highly compressible and occupy the full volume of their containers.
  - When a gas is subjected to pressure, its volume decreases.
  - Gases always form homogeneous mixtures with other gases.
- Gases only occupy a small fraction of the volume of their containers.
  - As a result, each molecule of gas behaves largely as though other molecules were absent.

### 10.2 Pressure

- **Pressure** is the force acting on an object per unit area:

$$P = \frac{F}{A}$$

**Atmospheric Pressure and the Barometer**[13,14,15,16,17]

---

[1] "Gases and Their Behavior" from Further Readings
[2] "Hydrogen Cyanide" 3-D Model from MediaPortfolio
[3] "Hydrogen Chloride" 3-D Model from MediaPortfolio
[4] "Hydrogen Sulfide" 3-D Model from MediaPortfolio
[5] "Carbon Monoxide" 3-D Model from MediaPortfolio
[6] "Carbon Dioxide" 3-D Model from MediaPortfolio
[7] "Methane" 3-D Model from MediaPortfolio
[8] "Nitrous Oxide" 3-D Model from MediaPortfolio
[9] "Nitrogen Dioxide" 3-D Model from MediaPortfolio
[10] "Ammonia" 3-D Model from MediaPortfolio
[11] "Sulfur Dioxide" 3-D Model from MediaPortfolio
[12] Table 10.1 from MediaPortfolio
[13] Figure 10.1 from MediaPortfolio and Transparency Pack
[14] Figure 10.2 from MediaPortfolio and Transparency Pack
[15] "Boiling at Reduced Pressure" from Live Demonstrations
[16] Figure 10.3 from MediaPortfolio and Transparency Pack
[17] "Manometer" Activity from MediaPortfolio

- SI units of pressure are **pascals**.
  - 1 Pa = 1 $N/m^2$
  - 1 N = 1 $kg{\cdot}m/s^2$
  - A related unit is the **bar,** which is equal to $10^5$ Pa.
- Gravity exerts a force on the Earth's atmosphere.
  - A column of air 1 $m^2$ in cross section extending to the top of the atmosphere exerts a force of $10^5$ N.
  - Thus, the pressure of a 1 $m^2$ column of air extending to the top of the atmosphere is 100 kPa or 1 bar.
- Atmospheric pressure is measured with a *barometer*.
  - If a tube is completely filled with mercury and then inverted into a container of mercury open to the atmosphere, the mercury will rise 760 mm up the tube.
  - **Standard atmospheric pressure** is the pressure required to support 760 mm of Hg in a column.
  - Important non-SI units used to express gas pressure include:
    - **Atmospheres** (atm)
    - ***Millimeter of mercury*** (mm Hg) or **Torr**
    - 1 atm = 760 mm Hg = 760 torr = 1.01325 x $10^5$ Pa = 101.325 kPa.

## 10.3 The Gas Laws

- The equations that express the relationships among *T* (temperature), *P* (pressure), *V* (volume), and *n* (number of moles of gas) are known as *gas laws*.

### The Pressure-Volume Relationship: Boyle's Law[18,19,20,21,22,23,24]

- Weather balloons are used as a practical application of the relationship between pressure and volume of a gas.
  - As the weather balloon ascends, the volume increases.
  - As the weather balloon gets further from Earth's surface, the atmospheric pressure decreases.
- **Boyle's law**: The volume of a fixed quantity of gas, at constant temperature, is inversely proportional to its pressure.
- Mathematically:

$$V = \text{constant} \times \frac{1}{P} \text{ or } PV = \text{constant}$$

  - A plot of *V* versus *P* is a hyperbola.
  - Similarly, a plot of *V* versus 1/*P* must be a straight line passing through the origin.
- The working of the lungs illustrates this:
  - As we breathe in, the diaphragm moves down, and the ribs expand. Therefore, the volume of the lungs increases.
  - According to Boyle's law, when the volume of the lungs increases, the pressure decreases. Therefore, the pressure inside the lungs is less than atmospheric pressure.
  - Atmospheric pressure then forces air into the lungs until the pressure once again equals atmospheric pressure.

---

[18] "Boyle's Law" from Live Demonstrations
[19] "*P-V* Relationships" Animation from MediaPortfolio
[20] "Boyle's Law and the Monster Marshmallow" from Live Demonstrations
[21] Figure 10.6 from MediaPortfolio
[22] Figure 10.7 from MediaPortfolio and Transparency Pack
[23] "Effect of Pressure on the Size of a Balloon" from Live Demonstrations
[24] "Boyle's Law and the Mass of a Textbook" from Live Demonstrations

- As we breathe out, the diaphragm moves up and the ribs contract. Therefore, the volume of the lungs decreases.
- By Boyle's law, the pressure increases and air is forced out.

### The Temperature-Volume Relationship: Charles's Law[25,26,27,28]

- We know that hot-air balloons expand when they are heated.
- **Charles's law:** The volume of a fixed quantity of gas at constant pressure is directly proportional to its absolute temperature.
- Mathematically:

$$V = \text{constant} \times T \;\; or \frac{V}{T} = \text{constant}$$

  - Note that the value of the constant depends on the pressure and number of moles of gas.
  - A plot of $V$ versus $T$ is a straight line.
  - When $T$ is measured in °C, the intercept on the temperature axis is –273.15°C.
  - We define absolute zero, 0 K = –273.15°C.

### The Quantity-Volume Relationship: Avogadro's Law[29,30,31,32,33]

- Gay-Lussac's law of combining volumes: At a given temperature and pressure the volumes of gases that react with one another are ratios of small whole numbers.
- **Avogadro's hypothesis:** Equal volumes of gases at the same temperature and pressure contain the same number of molecules.
- **Avogadro's law**: The volume of gas at a given temperature and pressure is directly proportional to the number of moles of gas.
  - Mathematically:

$$V = \text{constant x } n$$

  - We can show that 22.4 L of any gas at 0°C and 1 atmosphere contains $6.02 \times 10^{23}$ gas molecules.

## 10.4 The Ideal-Gas Equation[34]

- Summarizing the Gas Laws
  - Boyle: $V \propto 1/P$ (constant $n$, $T$)
  - Charles: $V \propto T$ (constant $n$, $P$)
  - Avogadro: $V \propto n$ (constant $P$, $T$)
  - Combined: $V \propto nT/P$
- **Ideal gas equation**: $PV = nRT$
  - An **ideal gas** is a hypothetical gas whose $P$, $V$, and $T$ behavior is completely described by the ideal-gas equation.
  - $R$ = **gas constant** = 0.08206 L·atm/mol·K
- Define **STP (standard temperature and pressure)** = 0°C, 273.15 K, 1 atm.

---

25 "Thermal Expansion of Gases" from Live Demonstrations
26 Figure 10.9 from MediaPortfolio
27 "Charles Law: The Relationship Between Volume and Temperature of a Gas" from Live Demonstrations
28 "Charles Law of Gases: A Simple Experimental Demonstration" from Live Demonstrations
29 "Gay-Lussac: Chemist Extraordinary" from Further Readings
30 Figure 10.10 from MediaPortfolio
31 Figure 10.11 from MediaPortfolio
32 "Collapsing Can" from Live Demonstrations
33 "Gay-Lussac after 200 Years" from Further Readings
34 Table 10.2 from MediaPortfolio

- The molar volume of 1 mol of an ideal gas at STP is 22.4 L.

### Relating the Ideal-Gas Equation and the Gas Laws

- If $PV = nRT$ and $n$ and $T$ are constant, then $PV$ is constant and we have Boyle's law.
  - Other laws can be generated similarly.
- In general, if we have a gas under two sets of conditions, then

$$\frac{P_1V_1}{n_1T_1} = \frac{P_2V_2}{n_2T_2}$$

- We often have a situation in which $P$, $V$ and $T$ all change for a fixed number of moles of gas.
  - For this set of circumstances,

$$\frac{PV}{T} = nR = \text{constant}$$

## 10.5 Further Applications of the Ideal-Gas Equation

### Gas Densities and Molar Masses[35]

- Density has units of mass over volume.
- Rearranging the ideal-gas equation with $M$ as molar mass we get

$$\frac{n}{V} = \frac{P}{RT}$$

$$\frac{nM}{V} = \frac{PM}{RT}$$

$$\therefore d = \frac{PM}{RT}$$

- The molar mass of a gas can be determined as follows:

$$M = \frac{dRT}{P}$$

### Volumes of Gases in Chemical Reactions[36,37,38]

- The ideal-gas equation relates $P$, $V$, and $T$ to number of moles of gas.
- The $n$ can then be used in stoichiometric calculations.

## 10.6 Gas Mixtures and Partial Pressures[39]

- Since gas molecules are so far apart, we can assume they behave independently.
- Dalton observed:
  - The total pressure of a mixture of gases equals the sum of the pressures that each would exert if present alone.
  - **Partial pressure** is the pressure exerted by a particular component of a gas mixture.

---

[35] "Density of Gases" Activity from MediaPortfolio
[36] "Airbags" Animation from MediaPortfolio
[37] "The Chemistry Behind the Air Bag" from Further Readings
[38] "Chemistry of Air Bags" from Further Readings
[39] "Partial Pressures" Activity from MediaPortfolio

- **Dalton's law of partial pressures**: In a gas mixture the total pressure is given by the sum of partial pressures of each component:

$$P_t = P_1 + P_2 + P_3 + \ldots$$

- Each gas obeys the ideal gas equation.
  - Thus,

$$P_t = (n_1 + n_2 + n_3 + \cdots)\frac{RT}{V} = n_t\frac{RT}{V}$$

### Partial Pressures and Mole Fractions

- Let $n_1$ be the number of moles of gas 1 exerting a partial pressure $P_1$, then

$$P_1 = X_1 P_t$$

  - Where $X_1$ is the **mole fraction** ($n_1/n_t$).
  - Note that a mole fraction is a dimensionless number.

### Collecting Gases over Water[40,41]

- It is common to synthesize gases and collect them by displacing a volume of water.
- To calculate the amount of gas produced, we need to correct for the partial pressure of the water:

$$P_{total} = P_{gas} + P_{water}$$

- The vapor pressure of water varies with temperature.
  - Values can be found in Appendix B.

## 10.7 Kinetic-Molecular Theory[42,43,44,45,46]

- The **kinetic molecular theory** was developed to *explain* gas behavior.
  - Theory of moving molecules.
- Summary:
  - Gases consist of a large number of molecules in constant random motion.
  - The volume of individual molecules is negligible compared with the volume of the container.
  - Intermolecular forces (forces between gas molecules) are negligible.
    - Energy can be transferred between molecules during collisions, but the average kinetic energy is constant at constant temperature.
  - The collisions are perfectly elastic.
  - The average kinetic energy of the gas molecules is proportional to the absolute temperature.
- Kinetic molecular theory gives us an *understanding* of pressure and temperature on the molecular level.
  - The pressure of a gas results from the collisions with the walls of the container.
  - The magnitude of the pressure is determined by how often and how hard the molecules strike.
- The absolute temperature of a gas is a measure of the average kinetic energy.
  - Some molecules will have less kinetic energy or more kinetic energy than the average (distribution).
    - There is a spread of individual energies of gas molecules in any sample of gas.
    - As the temperature increases, the average kinetic energy of the gas molecules increases.
- As kinetic energy increases, the velocity of the gas molecules increases.
  - **Root-mean-square (rms) speed**, *u*, is the speed of a gas molecule having average kinetic energy.

---

[40] "Determining the Molecular Weight of a Gas" from Live Demonstrations
[41] Figure 10.16 from MediaPortfolio
[42] "Kinetic Energy of Gas Molecules" Animation from MediaPortfolio
[43] "Cinema, Flirts, Snakes, and Gases" from Further Readings
[44] Figure 10.17 from MediaPortfolio
[45] "Toy Flying Saucers and Molecular Speeds" from Further Readings
[46] Figure 10.18 from MediaPortfolio and Transparency Pack

- Average kinetic energy, ε, is related to rms speed:

$$\varepsilon = \tfrac{1}{2}mu^2$$

  - Where $m$ = mass of the molecule.

### Application to the Gas-Laws

- We can understand empirical observations of gas properties within the framework of the kinetic-molecular theory.
- Effect of an increase in volume (at constant temperature):
  - As volume increases at constant temperature, the average kinetic of the gas remains constant.
  - Therefore, $u$ is constant.
  - However, volume increases, so the gas molecules have to travel further to hit the walls of the container.
  - Therefore, pressure decreases.
- Effect of an increase in temperature (at constant volume):
  - If temperature increases at constant volume, the average kinetic energy of the gas molecules increases.
  - There are more collisions with the container walls.
  - Therefore, $u$ increases.
  - The change in momentum in each collision increases (molecules strike harder).
  - Therefore, pressure increases.

## 10.8 Molecular Effusion and Diffusion[47,48,49]

- The average kinetic energy of a gas is related to its mass:

$$\epsilon = \tfrac{1}{2}mu^2$$

- Consider two gases at the same temperature: the lighter gas has a higher rms speed than the heavier gas.
  - Mathematically:

$$u = \sqrt{\frac{3RT}{M}}$$

  - The lower the molar mass, $M$, the higher the rms speed for that gas at a constant temperature.
- Two consequences of the dependence of molecular speeds on mass are:
  - **Effusion** is the escape of gas molecules through a tiny hole into an evacuated space.
  - **Diffusion** is the spread of one substance throughout a space or throughout a second substance.

### Graham's Law of Effusion[50,51,52,53]

- The rate of effusion can be quantified.
- Consider two gases with molar masses $M_1$ and $M_2$, with effusion rates, $r_1$ *and* $r_2$, respectively:
  - The relative rate of effusion is given by **Graham's law**:

$$\frac{r_1}{r_2} = \sqrt{\frac{M_2}{M_1}}$$

---

47 Figure 10.19 from MediaPortfolio and Transparency Pack
48 "Gas Phase: Boltzmann Distribution" Activity from MediaPortfolio
49 "Diffusion of Gases" from Live Demonstrations
50 "Overhead Projection of Graham's Law of Diffusion" from Live Demonstrations
51 "Relative Velocity of Sound Propagation: Musical Molecular Weights" from Live Demonstrations
52 Figure 10.20 from MediaPortfolio
53 "Diffusion and Effusion" Activity from MediaPortfolio

- Only those molecules which hit the small hole will escape through it.
- Therefore, the higher the rms speed the more likely that a gas molecule will hit the hole.
- We can show

$$\frac{r_1}{r_2} = \frac{u_1}{u_2} = \sqrt{\frac{M_2}{M_1}}$$

### Diffusion and Mean Free Path[54]

- Diffusion is faster for light gas molecules.
- Diffusion is significantly slower than the rms speed.
  - Diffusion is slowed by collisions of gas molecules with one another.
  - Consider someone opening a perfume bottle: It takes awhile to detect the odor, but the average speed of the molecules at 25°C is about 515 m/s (1150 mi/hr).
- The average distance traveled by a gas molecule between collisions is called the **mean free path**.
- At sea level, the mean free path for air molecules is about 6 x $10^{-6}$ cm.

## 10.9 Real Gases: Deviations from Ideal Behavior[55,56,57,58,59,60]

- From the ideal gas equation:

$$\frac{PV}{RT} = n$$

  - For 1 mol of an ideal gas, $PV/RT = 1$ for all pressures.
    - In a real gas, $PV/RT$ varies from 1 significantly.
    - The higher the pressure the more the deviation from ideal behavior.
  - For 1 mol of an ideal gas, $PV/RT = 1$ for all temperatures.
    - As temperature increases, the gases behave more ideally.
- The assumptions in the kinetic-molecular theory show where ideal gas behavior breaks down:
  - The molecules of a gas *have* finite volume.
  - Molecules of a gas *do* attract each other.
- As the pressure on a gas increases, the molecules are forced closer together.
  - As the molecules get closer together, the volume of the container gets smaller.
  - The smaller the container, the more of the total space the gas molecules occupy.
  - Therefore, the higher the pressure, the less the gas resembles an ideal gas.
  - As the gas molecules get closer together, the intermolecular distances decrease.
  - The smaller the distance between gas molecules, the more likely that attractive forces will develop between the molecules.
  - Therefore, the less the gas resembles an ideal gas.
- As temperature increases, the gas molecules move faster and further apart.
  - Also, higher temperatures mean more energy available to break intermolecular forces.
  - As temperature increases, the negative departure from ideal-gas behavior disappears.

### The van der Waals Equation

---

[54] "Diffusion of Bromine Vapor" Demonstration from MediaPortfolio
[55] Figure 10.23 from MediaPortfolio and Transparency Pack
[56] Figure 10.24 from MediaPortfolio and Transparency Pack
[57] Figure 10.25 from MediaPortfolio
[58] "Real Gases" Activity from MediaPortfolio
[59] Figure 10.26 from MediaPortfolio
[60] Table 10.3 from MediaPortfolio

- We add two terms to the ideal gas equation to correct for
  - The volume of molecules: $(V - nb)$
  - For molecular attractions: $\left(\frac{n^2 a}{V^2}\right)$
    - The correction terms generate the **van der Waals equation**:

$$\left(P + \frac{n^2 a}{V^2}\right)(V - nb) = nRT$$

    - Where $a$ and $b$ are empirical constants.
- To understand the effect of intermolecular forces on pressure, consider a molecule that is about to strike the wall of the container.
  - The striking molecule is attracted by neighboring molecules.
  - Therefore, the impact on the wall is lessened.

## Further Readings:

1. Joseph S. Schmuckler, "Gases and Their Behavior," *J. Chem. Educ.*, Vol. 57, **1980**, 885. A collection of gas law references from past editions of the Journal of Chemical Education.

2. R. P. Graham, "Gay-Lussac: Chemist Extraordinary," *J. Chem. Educ.*, Vol. 58, **1981**, 789.

3. Harold Goldwhite, "Gay-Lussac after 200 Years," *J. Chem. Educ.*, Vol. 55, **1978**, 366–368.

4. Andreas Madlung, "The Chemistry Behind the Air Bag," *J. Chem. Educ.*, Vol. 73, **1996**, 347–348.

5. William L. Bell, "Chemistry of Air Bags," *J. Chem. Educ.*, Vol. 67, **1990**, 61.

6. Dacio R. Hartwig and Romeu C. Rocha Filho, "Cinema, Flirts, Snakes, and Gases," *J. Chem. Educ.*, Vol. 59, **1982**, 295. The kinetic theory of gases is explored with an analogy in this short reference.

7. Reggie L. Hudson, "Toy Flying Saucers and Molecular Speeds," *J. Chem. Educ.*, Vol. 59, **1982**, 1025–1026. An analogy for molecular speed distributions features a common toy: the Frisbee®.

## Live Demonstrations:

1. Lee R. Summerlin, Christie L. Borgford and Julie B. Ealy, "Boiling at Reduced Pressure," *Chemical Demonstrations, A Sourcebook for Teachers, Volume 2* (Washington: American Chemical Society, **1988**), pp 24-25.

2. Lee R. Summerlin and James L. Ealy, Jr., "Determining the Molecular Weight of a Gas," *Chemical Demonstrations, A Sourcebook for Teachers, Volume 1, 2nd edition* (Washington: American Chemical Society, **1988**), pp. 19–20. The molar mass of butane is determined from its mass and the volume of water it displaces.

3. Lee R. Summerlin and James L. Ealy, Jr., "Diffusion of Gases," *Chemical Demonstrations, A Sourcebook for Teachers, Volume 1, 2nd edition* (Washington: American Chemical Society, **1988**), pp. 14–15. Graham's Law is checked by timing color changes in pH paper caused by HCl(g) or $NH_3$(g).

4. Dianne N. Epp. "Overhead Projection of Graham's Law of Gaseous Diffusion," *J. Chem. Educ.*, Vol. 67, **1990**, 1061. HCl(g) or $NH_3$(g) are used in this demonstration of Graham's Law.

5. Bassam Z. Shakhashiri, "Boyle's Law," *Chemical Demonstrations: A Handbook for Teachers of Chemistry, Volume 2* (Madison: The University of Wisconsin Press, **1985**), pp. 14–19. The relationship between gas pressure and volume at constant temperature is explored.

6. Rick Broniec, "Boyle's Law and the Monster Marshmallow," *J. Chem. Educ.*, Vol. 59, **1982**, 974. A quick demonstration of Boyle's law.

7. Bassam Z. Shakhashiri, "Effect of Pressure on the Size of a Balloon", *Chemical Demonstrations: A handbook for Teachers of Chemistry, Volume 2* (Madison: The University of Wisconsin Press, 1985), pp. 12–13.

8. Bassam Z. Shakhashiri, "Boyle's Law and the Mass of a Textbook," *Chemical Demonstrations: A Handbook for Teachers of Chemistry, Volume 2* (Madison: The University of Wisconsin Press, 1985), pp. 20–23.

9. Bassam Z. Shakhashiri, "Thermal Expansion of Gases," *Chemical Demonstrations: a Handbook for Teachers of Chemistry, Volume 2* (Madison: The University of Wisconsin Press, 1985), pp. 24–27.

10. Lee R. Summerlin, Christie L. Borgford, and Julie B. Ealy, "Charles' Law: The Relationship Between Volume and Temperature of a Gas," *Chemical Demonstrations, A Sourcebook for Teachers, Volume 2* (Washington: American Chemical Society, **1988**), p. 23. The volume of a gas-filled balloon is changed by immersion in an ice bath or a warm water bath in this demonstration of Charles's Law.

11. Bassam Z. Shakhashiri, "Thermal Expansion of Gases," *Chemical Demonstrations: A Handbook for Teachers of Chemistry, Volume 2* (Madison: The University of Wisconsin Press, **1985**), pp. 24–27.

12. Bassam Z. Shakhashiri, "Collapsing Can," *Chemical Demonstrations: A Handbook for Teachers of Chemistry, Volume 2* (Madison: The University of Wisconsin Press, **1985**), pp. 6–8.

13. John T. Petty, "Charles' Law of Gases: A Simple Experimental Demonstration," *J. Chem. Educ.*, Vol. 72, 1995, 257. A short demonstration of Charles's Law.

14. Bassam Z. Shakhashiri, "Relative Velocity of Sound Propagation: Musical Molecular Weights," *Chemical Demonstrations: A Handbook for Teachers of Chemistry, Volume 2* (Madison: The University of Wisconsin Press, **1985**), pp. 88–89. The relationship between the pitch of a pipe organ and the molar mass of gas passed through it is explored.

# Chapter 11. Intermolecular Forces, Liquids, and Solids

## Media Resources

**Figures and Tables**

| **In Transparency Pack and on MediaPortfolio:** | **Section:** |
|---|---|
| Figure 11.1 Molecular Level Comparison of Gases, Liquids and Solids | 11.1 A Molecular Comparison of Liquids and Solids |
| Figure 11.5 Instantaneous Dipoles | 11.2 Intermolecular Forces |
| Figure 11.7 Boiling Points of Hydrides | 11.2 Intermolecular Forces |
| Figure 11.10 Hydrogen Bonding Between Water Molecules | 11.2 Intermolecular Forces |
| Figure 11.12 Flowchart for Intermolecular Forces | 11.2 Intermolecular Forces |
| Figure 11.17 Energy Changes Associated with Phase Changes | 11.4 Phase Changes |
| Figure 11.19 Heating Curve for Water | 11.4 Phase Changes |
| Figure 11.22 Vapor Pressure as a Function of Temperature | 11.5 Vapor Pressure |
| Figure 11.24 Supercritical Fluid Extraction | 11.5 Vapor Pressure |
| Figure 11.26 General Phase Diagram | 11.6 Phase Diagrams |
| Figure 11.27 Phase Diagram of $H_2O$ and $CO_2$ | 11.6 Phase Diagrams |
| Figure 11.33 Three Types of Cubic Unit Cells | 11.7 Structures of Solids |
| Figure 11.34 Space-Filling View of Cubic Unit Cells | 11.7 Structures of Solids |
| Figure 11.37 Close Packing of Spheres | 11.7 Structures of Solids |
| Figure 11.41 Structures of Diamond and Graphite | 11.8 Bonding in Solids |
| Figure 11.42 Unit Cells of Common Crystals | 11.8 Bonding in Solids |

| **On MediaPortfolio:** | **Section:** |
|---|---|
| Table 11.1 Some Characteristic Properties of the States of Matter | 11.1 A Molecular Comparison of Liquids and Solids |
| Figure 11.2 Comparison of A Covalent Bond and An Intermolecular Attraction | 11.2 Intermolecular Forces |
| Figure 11.3 Orientation of Polar Molecules and Ions | 11.2 Intermolecular Forces |
| Figure 11.4 Electrostatic Interaction Of Polar Molecules | 11.2 Intermolecular Forces |
| Table 11.2 Molecular Masses, Dipole Moments, And Boiling Points of Several Simple Organic Substances | 11.2 Intermolecular Forces |
| Table 11.3 Boiling Points of the Halogens and the Noble Gases | 11.2 Intermolecular Forces |
| Figure 11.6 Effect of Molecular Shape on Intermolecular Attraction | 11.2 Intermolecular Forces |
| Figure 11.8 Examples of Hydrogen Bonding | 11.2 Intermolecular Forces |
| Table 11.4 Viscosities of a Series of Hydrocarbons At 20°C | 11.3 Some Properties of Liquids |
| Figure 11.14 Molecular-Level View of Surface Intermolecular Forces | 11.3 Some Properties of Liquids |
| Figure 11.18 Heats of Fusion and Vaporization | 11.4 Phase Changes |

| | |
|---|---|
| Table 11.5 Critical Temperatures and Pressures of Selected Substances | 11.4 Phase Changes |
| Figure 11.20 Equilibrium Vapor Pressure | 11.5 Vapor Pressure |
| Figure 11.21 Kinetic Energies of Surface Molecules | 11.5 Vapor Pressure |
| Figure 11.28 Phase Diagram of $H_2O$ | 11.6 Phase Diagrams |
| Table 11.6 Fraction of an Atom that Occupies a Unit Cell for Various Positions in the Unit Cell | 11.7 Structures of Solids |
| Figure 11.32 Crystal Lattice and its Unit Cell | 11.7 Structures of Solids |
| Figure 11.35 Crystal Lattice of NaCl | 11.7 Structures of Solids |
| Figure 11.36 Unit Cell of NaCl | 11.7 Structures of Solids |
| Table 11.7 Types of Crystalline Solids | 11.8 Bonding in Solids |
| Figure 11.38 X-Ray Crystallography | 11.8 Bonding in Solids |
| Figure 11.45 Cross Section of a Metal | 11.8 Bonding in Solids |

| **Animations:** | **Section:** |
|---|---|
| Changes of State | 11.1 A Molecular Comparison of Liquids and Solids |
| Vapor Pressure versus Temperature | 11.5 Vapor Pressure |

| **Activities:** | **Section:** |
|---|---|
| Intermolecular Forces | 11.2 Intermolecular Forces |
| Heating Curves | 11.4 Phase Changes |
| Equilibrium Vapor Pressure | 11.5 Vapor Pressure |
| Phase Diagram | 11.6 Phase Diagrams |
| Closest-Packed Arrangements | 11.7 Structures of Solids |

| **3-D Models:** | **Section:** |
|---|---|
| Diamond | 11.8 Bonding in Solids |
| Graphite | 11.8 Bonding in Solids |

# Other Resources

| **Further Readings:** | **Section:** |
|---|---|
| Pictorial Analogies I: States of Matter | 11.1 A Molecular Comparison of Liquids and Solids |
| Put the Body to Them! | 11.2 Intermolecular Forces |
| Students as Solids, Liquids, and Gases | 11.2 Intermolecular Forces |
| Solving the Mystery of Fading Fingerprints with London Dispersion Forces | 11.2 Intermolecular Forces |
| London Dispersion Forces and 'The Wave' | 11.2 Intermolecular Forces |
| A People-and-Velcro Model for Hydrogen Bonding | 11.2 Intermolecular Forces |
| Why Do Alcoholic Beverages Have "Legs"? | 11.3 Some Properties of Liquids |
| Past, Present, and Possible Future Applications of Supercritical Fluid Extraction Technology | 11.5 Vapor Pressure |
| Supercritical Chemistry: Synthesis with a Spanner | 11.5 Vapor Pressure |
| A Computer-Simulated Experiment on Vapor–Liquid Phase Equilibrium | 11.5 Vapor Pressure |
| Journey Around a Phase Diagram | 11.6 Phase Diagrams |
| There is No Perceptible Inflection at the Triple Point | 11.6 Phase Diagrams |
| The Importance of Understanding Structure | 11.7 Structures of Solids |

| | |
|---|---|
| Revealing the Backbone Structure of ß-DNA from Laser Optical Simulations of Its X-Ray Diffraction Diagram | 11.7 Structures of Solids |
| The Fifth Bragg Lecture: W. L. Bragg—Scientific Revolutionary | 11.7 Structures of Solids |
| The Discovery of X-Ray Diffraction by Crystals | 11.7 Structures of Solids |
| Pictorial Analogies II: Types of Solids | 11.8 Bonding in Solids |
| A Model to Illustrate the Brittleness of Ionic and Metallic Crystals | 11.8 Bonding in Solids |
| Fullerenes | 11.8 Bonding in Solids |
| Buckytubes | 11.8 Bonding in Solids |

| **Live Demonstrations:** | **Section:** |
|---|---|
| Demonstration of Surface Tension | 11.3 Some Properties of Liquids |
| Viscosity Races | 11.3 Some Properties of Liquids |
| Polarity, Miscibility, and Surface Tension of Liquids | 11.3 Some Properties of Liquids |
| Lowering the Surface Tension of Water: An Illustration of the Scientific Method | 11.3 Some Properties of Liquids |
| Surface Tension of Water: the Magic Touch | 11.3 Some Properties of Liquids |
| At the Water's Edge: Surface Spreading and Surface Tension | 11.3 Some Properties of Liquids |
| Evaporation as an Endothermic Process | 11.4 Phase Changes |
| The Effect of Pressure on Boiling Point | 11.5 Vapor Pressure |
| A Simple Experiment for Demonstration of Phase Diagram of Carbon Dioxide | 11.6 Phase Diagrams |
| Kixium Monolayers: A Simple Alternative to the Bubble Raft Model for Close-Packed Spheres | 11.7 Structures of Solids |
| Close Packing of Identical Spheres | 11.7 Structures of Solids |

# Chapter 11. Intermolecular Forces, Liquids, and Solids

## Common Student Misconceptions

- Students confuse *inter*molecular and *intra*molecular forces.
- Students have difficulty in predicting the relative strength of intermolecular forces involved in different materials.
- Students confuse cohesion and adhesion.
- Students do not realize that under the right set of conditions water also sublimes.
- The term volatile is often used incorrectly, especially in the media.

## Lecture Outline

### 11.1 A Molecular Comparison of Liquids and Solids[1,2,3,4]

- Physical properties of liquids and solids are due to **intermolecular forces**.
    - These are forces *between* molecules.
- Physical properties of substances are understood in terms of kinetic-molecular theory:
    - Gases are highly compressible and assume the shape and volume of their container.
        - Gas molecules are far apart and do not interact much with one another.
    - Liquids are almost incompressible, assume the shape but not the volume of the container.
        - Liquids molecules are held together more closely than gas molecules but not so rigidly that the molecules cannot slide past each other.
    - Solids are incompressible and have a definite shape and volume:
        - Solid molecules are packed closely together.
        - The molecules are so rigidly packed that they cannot easily slide past each other.
- Solids and liquids are *condensed phases*.
- Converting a gas into a liquid or solid requires the molecules to get closer to each other.
    - We can accomplish this by cooling or compressing the gas.
- Converting a solid into a liquid or gas requires the molecules to move further apart.
    - We can accomplish this by heating or reducing the pressure on the gas.
- The forces holding solids and liquids together are called intermolecular forces.

### 11.2 Intermolecular Forces[5,6,7]

- The attraction between molecules is an *inter*molecular force.
    - Intermolecular forces are much weaker than ionic or covalent bonds (e.g., 16 kJ/mol versus 431 kJ/mol for HCl).
- When a substance melts or boils, intermolecular forces are broken.
- When a substances condenses, intermolecular forces are formed.
    - Boiling points reflect intermolecular force strength.
        - A high boiling point indicates strong attractive forces.
- Melting points also reflect the strength of attractive forces.

---

[1] "Pictorial Analogies I: States of Matter" from Further Readings
[2] "Changes of State" Animation from MediaPortfolio
[3] Figure 11.1 from MediaPortfolio and Transparency Pack
[4] Table 11.1 from MediaPortfolio
[5] "Put the Body to Them!" from Further Readings
[6] Figure 11.2 from MediaPortfolio
[7] "Students as Solids, Liquids and Gases" from Further Readings

    - A high melting point indicates strong attractive forces.
- *van der Waals* forces are the intermolecular forces that exist between neutral molecules.
    - These include London-dispersion forces, dipole-dipole forces, and hydrogen-bonding forces.
    - Ion-dipole interactions are important in solutions.
        - These are all weak (~15% as strong as a covalent or ionic bond) electrostatic interactions.

## Ion-Dipole Forces[8]

- An **ion-dipole** force is an interaction between an ion (e.g., $Na^+$) and the partial charge on the end of a polar molecule/dipole (e.g., water).
- It is especially important for solutions of ionic substances in polar liquids.
    - Example: NaCl (*aq*)

## Dipole-Dipole Forces[9,10]

- **Dipole-dipole forces** exist between neutral polar molecules.
- Polar molecules attract each other.
    - The partially positive end of one molecule attracts the partially negative end of another.
- Polar molecules need to be close together to form strong dipole-dipole interactions.
- Dipole-dipole forces are weaker than ion-dipole forces.
- If two molecules have about the same mass and size, then dipole-dipole forces increase with increasing polarity.

## London Dispersion Forces[11,12,13,14,15]

- These are the weakest of all intermolecular forces.
- It is possible for two adjacent neutral molecules to affect each other.
    - The nucleus of one molecule (or atom) attracts the electrons of the adjacent molecule (or atom).
    - For an instant, the electron clouds become distorted.
    - In that instant a dipole is formed (called an *instantaneous* dipole).
    - One instantaneous dipole can induce another instantaneous dipole in an adjacent molecule (or atom).
    - These two temporary dipoles attract each other.
    - The attraction is called the **London dispersion force** or simply a dispersion force.
        - London dispersion forces exist between all molecules.
- What affects the strength of a dispersion force?
    - Molecules must be very close together for these attractive forces to occur.
    - **Polarizability** is the ease with which an electron cloud can be deformed.
        - The larger the molecule (the greater the number of electrons) the more polarizable it is.
    - London dispersion forces increase as molecular weight increases.
    - London dispersion forces depend on the shape of the molecule.
        - The greater the surface area available for contact, the greater the dispersion forces.
        - London dispersion forces between spherical molecules are smaller than those between more cylindrically shaped molecules.
            - Example: *n*-pentane vs. neopentane.

---

[8] Figure 11.3 from MediaPortfolio
[9] Figure 11.4 from MediaPortfolio
[10] Table 11.2 from MediaPortfolio
[11] Figure 11.5 from MediaPortfolio and Transparency Pack
[12] Table 11.3 from MediaPortfolio
[13] Figure 11.6 from MediaPortfolio
[14] "Solving the Mystery of Fading Fingerprints with London Dispersion Forces" from Further Readings
[15] "London Dispersion Forces and 'The Wave'" from Further Readings

### Hydrogen Bonding[16,17,18,19]

- Experiments show that the boiling points of compounds with H–F, H–O, and H–N bonds are abnormally high.
  - Their intermolecular forces are abnormally strong.
- Hydrogen bonding is a special type of intermolecular attraction.
  - This is a special case of dipole-dipole interactions.
  - H-bonding requires:
    - H bonded to a small electronegative element (most important for compounds of F, O, and N).
    - An unshared electron pair on a nearby small electronegative ion or atom (usually F, O, or N on another molecule).
  - Electrons in the H–X bond (X is the more electronegative element) lie much closer to X than H.
  - H has only one electron, so in the H–X bond, the $H^{\delta+}$ presents an almost bare proton to the $X^{\delta-}$.
    - Therefore, H-bonds are strong.
- Hydrogen bonds have exceedingly important biological significance.
  - They are important in stabilizing protein structure, in DNA structure and function, etc.
- An interesting consequence of H-bonding is that ice floats
  - The molecules in solids are usually more closely packed than those in liquids.
    - Therefore, solids are usually more dense than liquids.
  - Ice is ordered with an open structure to optimize H-bonding.
    - In water the H–O bond length is 1.0 Å.
      - The O···H hydrogen bond length is 1.8 Å.
    - Water molecules in ice are arranged in an open, regular hexagon.
      - Each $\delta^+$ H points towards a lone pair on O.
    - Therefore, ice is less dense than water.
  - Ice floats, so it forms an insulating layer on top of lakes, rivers, etc. Therefore, aquatic life can survive in winter.
  - Water expands on freezing.
    - Frozen water in pipes may cause them to break in cold weather.

### Comparing Intermolecular Forces[20,21]

- Dispersion forces are found in all substances.
  - Their strength depends on molecular shapes and molecular weights.
- Dipole-dipole forces add to the effect of dispersion forces.
  - They are found only in polar molecules.
- H-bonding is a special case of dipole-dipole interactions.
  - It is the strongest of the intermolecular forces involving neutral species.
  - H-bonding is most important for H compounds of N, O and F.
- If ions are involved, ion-dipole (if a dipole is present) and ionic bonding are possible.
  - Ion-dipole interactions are stronger than H-bonds..
- Keep in mind that ordinary ionic or covalent bonds are much stronger than these interactions!

## 11.3 Some Properties of Liquids

### Viscosity[22,23]

---

16 Figure 11.7 from MediaPortfolio and Transparency Pack
17 "A People-and-Velcro Model for Hydrogen Bonding" from Further Readings
18 Figure 11.8 from MediaPortfolio
19 Figure 11.10 from MediaPortfolio and Transparency Pack
20 Figure 11.12 from MediaPortfolio and Transparency Pack
21 "Intermolecular Forces" Activity from MediaPortfolio

- **Viscosity** is the resistance of a liquid to flow.
- A liquid flows by sliding molecules over one another.
- Viscosity depends on:
  - The attractive forces between molecules:
    - The stronger the intermolecular forces, the higher the viscosity.
  - The tendency of molecules to become entangled:
    - Viscosity increases as molecules become entangled with one another.
  - The temperature:
    - Viscosity usually decreases with an increase in temperature.

### Surface Tension[24,25,26,27,28,29,30]

- Bulk molecules (those in the liquid) are equally attracted to their neighbors.
- Surface molecules are only attracted inward towards the bulk molecules.
  - Therefore, surface molecules are packed more closely than bulk molecules.
  - This causes the liquid to behave as if it had a "skin".
- **Surface tension** is the amount of energy required to increase the surface area of a liquid by a unit amount.
- Stronger intermolecular forces cause higher surface tension.
  - Water has a high surface tension (H-bonding)
  - $Hg(l)$ has an even higher surface tension (there are very strong metallic bonds between Hg atoms).
- Cohesive and adhesive forces are at play:
  - *Cohesive forces* are intermolecular forces that bind molecules to one another.
  - *Adhesive forces* are intermolecular forces that bind molecules to a surface.
  - Illustrate this by looking at the meniscus in a tube filled with liquid.
    - The *meniscus* is the shape of the liquid surface.
    - If adhesive forces are greater than cohesive forces, the liquid surface is attracted to its container more than the bulk molecules. Therefore, the meniscus is U-shaped (e.g., water in glass).
    - If cohesive forces are greater than adhesive forces, the meniscus is curved downwards (e.g., $Hg(l)$ in glass).
- **Capillary action** is the rise of liquids up very narrow tubes.
  - The liquid climbs until adhesive and cohesive forces are balanced by gravity.

## 11.4 Phase Changes[31]

- **Phase changes** are changes of state.
  - Matter in one state is converted into another state.
    - *Sublimation*: solid → gas.

---

[22] "Viscosity Races" from Live Demonstrations
[23] Table 11.4 from MediaPortfolio
[24] "Demonstration of Surface Tension" from Live Demonstrations
[25] "Polarity, Miscibility and Surface Tension of Liquids" from Live Demonstrations
[26] "Lowering the Surface Tension of Water: An Illustration of the Scientific Method" from Live Demonstrations
[27] "Surface Tension of Water: The Magic Touch" from Live Demonstrations
[28] "At the Water's Edge: Surface Spreading and Surface Tension" from Live Demonstrations
[29] "Why do Alcoholic Beverages Have 'Legs'" from Further Readings
[30] Figure 11.14 from MediaPortfolio
[31] Figure 11.17 from MediaPortfolio and Transparency Pack

- *Melting* or *fusion*: solid → liquid.
- *Vaporization*: liquid → gas.
- *Deposition*: gas → solid.
- *Condensation*: gas → liquid.
- *Freezing*: liquid → solid.

### Energy Changes Accompanying Phase Changes[32,33]

- Energy changes of the system for the above processes are:
  - *Melting* or *fusion*: $\Delta H_{fus} > 0$ (endothermic).
    - The enthalpy of fusion is known as the **heat of fusion**.
  - *Vaporization*: $\Delta H_{vap} > 0$ (endothermic).
    - The enthalpy of vaporization is known as the **heat of vaporization**.
  - *Sublimation*: $\Delta H_{sub} > 0$ (endothermic).
    - The enthalpy of sublimation is called the **heat of sublimation.**
  - *Deposition*: $\Delta H_{dep} < 0$ (exothermic).
  - *Condensation*: $\Delta H_{con} < 0$ (exothermic).
  - *Freezing*: $\Delta H_{fre} < 0$ (exothermic).
- Generally the heat of fusion (enthalpy of fusion) is less than heat of vaporization:
  - It takes more energy to completely separate molecules, than to partially separate them.
- All phase changes are possible under the right conditions (e.g., water sublimes when snow disappears without forming puddles).
  - The following sequence is endothermic:

    heat solid → melt → heat liquid → boil → heat gas
  - The following sequence is exothermic:

    cool gas → condense → cool liquid → freeze → cool solid

### Heating Curves[34,35]

- Plot of temperature change versus heat added is a *heating curve*.
- During a phase change adding heat causes no temperature change.
  - The added energy is used to break intermolecular bonds rather than cause a temperature change.
  - These points are used to calculate $\Delta H_{fus}$ and $\Delta H_{vap}$.
- *Supercooling*: When a liquid is cooled below its freezing point and it still remains a liquid.

### Critical Temperature and Pressure[36]

- Gases may be liquefied by increasing the pressure at a suitable temperature.
- **Critical temperature** is the highest temperature at which a substance can exist as a liquid.
- **Critical pressure** is the pressure required for liquefaction at this critical temperature.
  - The greater the intermolecular forces, the easier it is to liquefy a substance.
    - Thus the higher the critical temperature.

## 11.5 Vapor Pressure[37]

### Explaining Vapor Pressure on the Molecular Level[38]

---

[32] Figure 11.18 from MediaPortfolio
[33] "Evaporation as an Endothermic Process" from Live Demonstrations
[34] Figure 11.19 from MediaPortfolio and Transparency Pack
[35] "Heating Curves" Activity from MediaPortfolio
[36] Table 11.5 from MediaPortfolio
[37] Figure 11.20 from MediaPortfolio
[38] Figure 11.21 from MediaPortfolio

- Some of the molecules on the surface of a liquid have enough energy to escape the attraction of the bulk liquid.
    - These molecules move into the gas phase.
- As the number of molecules in the gas phase increases, some of the gas phase molecules strike the surface and return to the liquid.
- After some time the pressure of the gas will be constant.
    - A **dynamic equilibrium** has been established:
        - Dynamic equilibrium is a condition in which two opposing processes occur simultaneously at equal rates.
        - In this case, it is the point when as many molecules escape the surface as strike the surface.
    - **Vapor pressure** is the pressure exerted when the liquid and vapor are in dynamic equilibrium.
        - The pressure of the vapor at this point is called the equilibrium vapor pressure.

### Volatility, Vapor Pressure, and Temperature[39,40,41,42,43,44,45]

- If equilibrium is never established the vapor continues to form.
    - Eventually, the liquid evaporates to dryness.
- Liquids that evaporate easily are said to be **volatile**.
    - The higher the temperature, the higher the average kinetic energy, the faster the liquid evaporates.

### Vapor Pressure and Boiling Point[46]

- Liquids boil when the external pressure at the liquid surface equals the vapor pressure.
    - The **normal boiling point** is the boiling point at 760 mm Hg (1 atm).
- The temperature of the boiling point increases as the external pressure increases.
- Two ways to get a liquid to boil:
    - Increase temperature or decrease pressure.
        - Pressure cookers operate at high pressure.
        - At high pressure the boiling point of water is higher than at 1 atm.
        - Therefore, food is cooked at a higher temperature.

## 11.6 Phase Diagrams[47,48,49,50]

- **Phase diagram**: plot of pressure vs. temperature summarizing all equilibria between phases.
- Phase diagrams tell us which phase will exist at a given temperature and pressure.
- Features of a phase diagram include:
    - Vapor-pressure curve: generally as temperature increases, vapor pressure increases.
    - *Critical point*: critical temperature and pressure for the gas.
    - **Normal melting point**: melting point at 1 atm.
    - **Triple point**: temperature and pressure at which all three phases are in equilibrium.

---

[39] "Vapor Pressure versus Temperature" Animation from MediaPortfolio
[40] Figure 11.22 from MediaPortfolio and Transparency Pack
[41] Figure 11.24 from MediaPortfolio and Transparency Pack
[42] "Past, Present, and Possible Applications of Supercritical Fluid Extraction Technology" from Further Readings
[43] "Supercritical Chemistry: Synthesis with a Spanner" from Further Readings
[44] "A Computer-Simulated Experiment on a Vapor-Liquid Phase Equilibrium" from Further Readings
[45] "Equilibrium Vapor Pressure" Activity from MediaPortfolio
[46] "The Effect of Pressure on Boiling Point" from Live Demonstrations
[47] "Journey Around a Phase Diagram" from Further Readings
[48] Figure 11.26 from MediaPortfolio and Transparency Pack
[49] "There is No Perceptible Inflection at the Triple Point" from Further Readings
[50] "Phase Diagram" Activity from MediaPortfolio

- Any temperature and pressure combination not on a curve represents a single phase.

### Phase Diagrams of $H_2O$ and $CO_2$[51,52,53]

- *Water*:
  - In general, an increase in pressure favors the more compact phase of the material.
    - This is usually the solid.
  - Water is one of the few substances whose solid form is less dense than the liquid form.
    - The melting point curve for water slopes to the left.
  - The triple point occurs at 0.0098°C and 4.58 mm Hg.
  - The normal melting (freezing) point is 0°C.
  - The normal boiling point is 100°C.
  - The critical point is 374°C and 218 atm.
- *Carbon Dioxide*:
  - The triple point occurs at –56.4°C and 5.11 atm.
  - The normal sublimation point is –78.5°C. (At 1 atm $CO_2$ sublimes, it does not melt.)
  - The critical point occurs at 31.1°C and 73 atm.
  - Freeze drying: Frozen food is placed in a low pressure (< 4.58 torr) chamber.
    - The ice sublimes.

## 11.7 Structures of Solids

- **Crystalline solid:** well-ordered, definite arrangements of molecules, atoms or ions.
  - Examples: quartz, diamond, salt, sugar.
  - The intermolecular forces are similar in strength.
    - Thus they tend to melt at specific temperatures.
- **Amorphous solid**: molecules, atoms or ions do not have an orderly arrangement.
  - Examples: rubber, glass.
  - Amorphous solids have intermolecular forces that vary in strength.
    - Thus they tend to melt over a range of temperatures.

### Unit Cells[54,55,56,57,58,59]

- Crystalline solids have an ordered, repeating structure.
- The smallest repeating unit in a crystal is a **unit cell.**
  - The unit cell is the smallest unit with all the symmetry of the entire crystal.
  - The three-dimensional stacking of unit cells is the **crystal lattice**.
- There are three types of cubic unit cell.
  - **Primitive cubic**.
    - Atoms at the corners of a simple cube with each atom shared by eight unit cells.
  - **Body-centered cubic** (bcc).

---

[51] "A Simple Experiment for Demonstration of Phase Diagram of Carbon Dioxide" from Live Demonstrations
[52] Figure 11.27 from MediaPortfolio and Transparency Pack
[53] Figure 11.28 from MediaPortfolio
[54] "The Importance of Understanding Structure" from Further Readings
[55] Figure 11.32 from MediaPortfolio
[56] Figure 11.33 from MediaPortfolio and Transparency Pack
[57] Table 11.6 from MediaPortfolio
[58] Figure 11.34 from MediaPortfolio and Transparency Pack
[59] "The Importance of Understanding Structure" from Further Readings

        - There are atoms at the corners of a cube plus one in the center of the body of the cube. The corner atoms are shared by eight unit cells, and the center atom is completely enclosed in one unit cell.
    - **Face-centered cubic** (fcc).
        - There are atoms at the corners of a cube plus one atom in the center of each face of the cube. Eight unit cells share the corner atoms and two unit cells share the face atoms.

### The Crystal Structure of Sodium Chloride[60,61]

- Face-centered cubic lattice.
- There are two equivalent ways of defining this unit cell:
    - $Cl^-$ (larger) ions at the corners of the cell, or
    - $Na^+$ (smaller) ions at the corners of the cell.
- The cation to anion ratio in a unit cell is the same for the crystal.
    - In NaCl each unit cell contains the same number of $Na^+$ and $Cl^-$ ions.
- Note that the unit cell for $CaCl_2$ needs twice as many $Cl^-$ ions as $Ca^{2+}$ ions.

### Close Packing of Spheres[62,63,64,65]

- Crystalline solids have structures that maximize the attractive forces between particles.
- Their particles can be modeled by spheres.
    - Each atom or ion is represented by a sphere.
- Molecular crystals are formed by close packing of the molecules.
- Maximum intermolecular forces in crystals are achieved by the close packing of spheres.
    - A crystal is built up by placing close packed layers of spheres on top of each other.
    - There is only one place for the second layer of spheres.
    - There are two choices for the third layer of spheres:
        - The third layer eclipses the first (ABAB arrangement).
            - This is called **hexagonal close packing** (hcp).
        - The third layer is in a different position relative to the first (ABCABC arrangement).
            - This is called **cubic close packing** (ccp).
            - Note: The unit cell of a ccp crystal is face-centered cubic.
    - In both close-packed structures, each sphere is surrounded by 12 other spheres (6 in one plane, 3 above and 3 below).
- **Coordination number:** the number of spheres directly surrounding a central sphere.
    - When spheres are packed as closely as possible, there are small spaces between adjacent spheres (interstitial holes).
    - If unequally sized spheres are used, the smaller spheres are placed in the interstitial holes.
        - For example: $Li_2O$
            - The larger $O^{2-}$ ions assume the cubic close-packed structure with the smaller $Li^+$ ions in the holes.

### X-Ray Diffraction[66,67,68,69]

---

[60] Figure 11.35 from MediaPortfolio

[61] Figure 11.36 from MediaPortfolio

[62] "Kixium Monolayers: A Simple Alternative to the Bubble Raft Model for Close-Packed Spheres" from Live Demonstrations

[63] Figure 11.37 from MediaPortfolio and Transparency Pack

[64] "Close Packing of Identical Spheres" from Live Demonstrations

[65] "Closest-Packed Arrangements" Activity from MediaPortfolio

[66] "Revealing the Backbone Structure of β-DNA from Laser Optical Simulations of Its X-ray Diffraction Diagram" from Further Readings

- When waves are passed through a narrow slit they are diffracted.
- When waves are passed through a diffraction grating (many narrow slits in parallel) they interact to form a diffraction pattern (areas of light and dark bands).
- Efficient diffraction occurs when the wavelength of light is close to the size of the slits.
- The spacing between layers in a crystal is 2 – 20 Å, which is the wavelength range for X-rays.
- X-ray diffraction (X-ray crystallography):
  - X-rays are passed through the crystal and are detected on a photographic plate.
  - The photographic plate has one bright spot at the center (incident beam) as well as a diffraction pattern.
  - Each close-packing arrangement produces a different diffraction pattern.
  - Knowing the diffraction pattern, we can calculate the positions of the atoms required to produce that pattern.
  - We calculate the crystal structure based on a knowledge of the diffraction pattern.

## 11.8 Bonding in Solids[70,71]

- The physical properties of crystalline solids depend on the:
  - Attractive forces between particles and on
  - The arrangement of the particles.

### Molecular Solids[72,73]

- **Molecular solids** consist of atoms or molecules held together by intermolecular forces.
- Weak intermolecular forces give rise to low melting points.
  - Intermolecular forces: dipole-dipole, London dispersion and H-bonds.
  - Molecular solids are usually soft.
  - They are often gases or liquids are room temperature.
- Efficient packing of molecules is important (since they are not regular spheres).
- Molecular solids show poor thermal and electrical conductivity.
- Examples: $Ar(s)$, $CH_4(s)$, $CO_2(s)$, sucrose.

### Covalent-Network Solids[74,75,76]

- **Covalent-network solids** consist of atoms held together, in large networks or chains, with covalent bonds.
- They have much higher melting points and are much harder than molecular solids.
  - This is a consequence of the strong covalent bonds that connect the atoms.
- Examples: diamond, graphite, quartz ($SiO_2$), and silicon carbide (SiC).
- In diamond:
  - Each C atom has a coordination number of 4.
  - Each C atom is tetrahedral.
  - There is a three-dimensional array of atoms.
  - Diamond is hard, and has a high melting point (3550°C).

---

[67] Figure 11.38 from MediaPortfolio
[68] "The Discovery of X-Ray Diffraction by Crystals" from Further Readings
[69] "Fifth Bragg Lecture: W. L. Bragg-Scientific Revolutionary" from Further Readings
[70] "Pictorial Analogies II: Types of Solids" from Further Readings
[71] Table 11.7 from MediaPortfolio
[72] "Fullerenes" from Further Readings
[73] "Buckytubes" from Further Readings
[74] Figure 11.41 from MediaPortfolio and Transparency Pack
[75] "Diamond" 3-D Model from MediaPortfolio
[76] "Graphite" 3-D Model from MediaPortfolio

- In graphite
  - Each C atom is arranged in a planar hexagonal ring.
  - Layers of interconnected rings are placed on top of each other.
  - The distance between adjacent C atoms in the same layer is close to that seen in benzene (1.42 Å vs. 1.395 Å in benzene).
  - Electrons move in delocalized orbitals (good conductor).
  - The distance between layers is large (3.41 Å).
  - The layers are held together by weak dispersion forces.
    - They slide easily past each other.
    - Graphite is a good lubricant.

### Ionic Solids[77,78]

- **Ionic solids** consist of ions held together by ionic bonds.
  - They are hard, brittle and have high melting points.
- Ions (spherical) are held together by electrostatic forces of attraction.
- Recall:

$$E = k\frac{Q_1Q_2}{d}$$

- The larger the charges ($Q_1$, $Q_2$) and smaller the distance ($d$) between ions, the stronger the ionic bond.
- The structure of the ionic solid depends on the charges on the ions and on the relative sizes of the atoms.
- Examples of some ionic lattice types:
  - NaCl structure
    - Each ion has a coordination number of 6.
    - Face-centered cubic lattice.
    - Cation to anion ratio is 1:1.
    - Other similar examples: LiF, KCl, AgCl and CaO.
  - CsCl structure
    - $Cs^+$ has a coordination number of 8.
    - Different from the NaCl structure ($Cs^+$ is larger than $Na^+$).
    - Cation to anion ratio is 1:1.
  - Zinc blende (ZnS) structure
    - $S^{2-}$ ions adopt a face-centered cubic arrangement.
    - $Zn^{2+}$ ions have a coordination number of 4.
    - The $S^{2-}$ ions are placed in a tetrahedron around the $Zn^{2+}$ ions.
    - Another example: CuCl.
  - Fluorite ($CaF_2$) structure.
    - $Ca^{2+}$ ions in a face-centered cubic arrangement.
    - There are twice as many $F^-$ ions as $Ca^{2+}$ ions in each unit cell.
    - Other examples: $BaCl_2$, $PbF_2$.

### Metallic Solids[79]

- **Metallic solids** consist entirely of metal atoms.
  - Metallic solids are soft or hard.
  - They have high melting points.
  - They show good electrical and thermal conductivity.

---

[77] Figure 11.42 from MediaPortfolio and Transparency Pack
[78] "A Model to Illustrate the Brittleness of Ionic and Metallic Crystals" from Further Readings
[79] Figure 11.45 from MediaPortfolio

- They are ductile and malleable.
    - Examples: all metallic elements (i.e., Al, Cu, Fe, Au)
- Metallic solids have metal atoms in hexagonal close-packed, face-centered cubic or body-centered cubic arrangements.
    - Thus the coordination number for each atom is either 8 or 12.
- Problem that needs to be explained:
    - The bonding is too strong to be explained by London dispersion forces and there are not enough electrons for covalent bonds.
- Resolution:
    - The metal nuclei float in a sea of delocalized valence electrons.
    - Metals conduct heat and electricity because the valence electrons are delocalized and are mobile.

## Further Readings:


1. John J. Fortman, "Pictorial Analogies I: States of Matter," *J. Chem. Educ*., Vol. 70, **1993**, 56–57.

2. Robert R. Perkins, "Put the Body to Them!" *J. Chem. Educ*., Vol. 72, **1995**, 151–152. The difference between an intermolecular change and an intramolecular change is explored by analogy in this short reference.

3. Ponnadurai Ramasami, "Students as Solids, Liquids, and Gases," *J. Chem. Educ*., Vol. 76, **1999**, 485.

4. Doris R. Kimbrough and Ronald DeLorenzo, "Solving the Mystery of Fading Fingerprints with London Dispersion Forces," *J. Chem. Educ*., Vol. 75, **1998**, 1300–1301. A forensic chemistry application of London dispersion forces.

5. C. Jayne Wilcox, "London Dispersion Forces and 'The Wave'", *J. Chem. Educ*., Vol. 75, **1998**, 1301. A sports analogy to introduce London Dispersion Forces.

6. John W. Hill, "A People-and-Velcro Model for Hydrogen Bonding," *J. Chem. Educ*., Vol. 67, **1990**, 223. An analogy for hydrogen bonding is presented in this very short reading.

7. Todd P. Silverstein, "Why Do Alcoholic Beverages Have 'Legs'?" *J. Chem. Educ*., Vol. 75, **1998**, 723–724. Adhesive and cohesive forces are explored in this analogy involving the behavior of liquid in an alcoholic beverage.

8. Cindy L. Phelps, Neil G. Smart, and C. M. Wai. "Past, Present, and Possible Future Applications of Supercritical Fluid Extraction Technology," *J. Chem. Educ*., Vol. 73, **1996**, 1163–1168. An in-depth look at supercritical fluid extraction.

9. Martyn Poliakoff and Steve Howdle, "Supercritical Chemistry: Synthesis with a Spanner," *Chemistry in Britain*, **February 1995**, 118–121.

9. Nicholas K Kildahl, "Journey Around a Phase Diagram," *J. Chem. Educ*., Vol. 71, **1994**, 1052–1054.

10. Stephen J. Hawkes, "There is No Perceptible Inflection at the Triple Point," *J. Chem. Educ*., Vol. 76, **1999**, 226.

11. Frank Galasso, "The Importance of Understanding Structure," *J. Chem. Educ*., Vol. 70, **1993**, 287–290. The relationship between unit cells and the structure of solids is covered in this article.

12. A. A. Lucas, Ph. Lambin, R. Mairesse and M. Mathot, "Revealing the Backbone Structure of ß-DNA from Laser Optical Simulations of Its X-ray Diffraction Diagram," *J. Chem. Educ*., Vol. 76, **1999**, 378–383.

13. John J. Fortman, "Pictorial Analogies II: Types of Solids," *J. Chem. Educ*., Vol. 70, **1993**, 57–58.

14. James P. Birk, "A Model to Illustrate the Brittleness of Ionic and Metallic Crystals," *J. Chem. Educ*., Vol. 62, **1985**, 667. Models made from magnets and plexiglass are used to illustrate some properties of crystals.

15. Robert F. Curl and Richard E. Smalley, "Fullerenes," *Scientific American*, **October 1991**, 54–63. An early review on fullerenes.

16. Norman C. Craig, Brian J. Brown, William S. Chamness, and Elaine B. Mulvey, "A Computer–Simulated Experiment on Vapor-Liquid Phase Equilibrium," *J. Chem. Educ*., Vol. 65, **1988**, 792–793.

17. Philip E. Ross, "Buckytubes," *Scientific American*, December 1991, 24.

18. Henry S. Lipson, "The Fifth Bragg Lecture: W. L. Bragg-Scientific Revolutionary," *J. Chem. Educ*., Vol. 60, **1983**, 405–407.

19. J. C. Speakman, "The Discovery of X-Ray Diffraction by Crystals," *J. Chem. Educ*., Vol. 57, **1980**, 489–490.

## Live Demonstrations:

1. Lee. R. Summerlin, and James. L. Ealy, Jr., "The Effect of Pressure on Boiling Point," *Chemical Demonstrations, A Sourcebook for Teachers, Volume 1* (Washington: American Chemical Society, **1988**), p. 21.

2. Bassam Z. Shakhashiri, "Evaporation As an Endothermic Process," *Chemical Demonstrations: A Handbook for Teachers of Chemistry, Volume 3* (Madison: The University of Wisconsin Press, **1989**), pp. 249–251. A "drinking duck" toy and a beaker of water are used to demonstrate the endothermic nature of evaporation.

3. Van T. Lieu, "A Simple Experiment for Demonstration of Phase Diagram of Carbon Dioxide," *J. Chem. Educ*., Vol. 73, **1996**, 837–838. A syringe filled with dry ice is used in this simple and quick demonstration.

4. William M. Hemmerlin and Kenton Abel, "Viscosity Races," *J. Chem. Educ*., Vol. 68, **1991**, 417. A simple demonstration to illustrate the relationship between molecular size and viscosity.

5. Todd P. Silverstein, "Polarity, Miscibility, and Surface Tension of Liquids," *J. Chem. Educ*., Vol. 70, **1993**, 253. A short demonstration exploring the properties of liquids.

6. Paul G. Jasien, Glenn Barnett, and David Speckhard, "Lowering the Surface Tension of Water: An Illustration of the Scientific Method," *J. Chem. Educ*., Vol. 70, **1993**, 251–252.

7. Andrew J. Rosenthal, "Demonstration of Surface Tension," *J. Chem. Educ.*, Vol. 78, **2001**, 332–333.

8. Lee. R. Summerlin, and James. L. Ealy, Jr., "Surface Tension of Water: The Magic Touch," *Chemical Demonstrations, A Sourcebook for Teachers, Volume 1* (Washington: American Chemical Society, **1988**), p. 45. The effect of a wetting agent on surface tension is demonstrated.

9. Bassam Z. Shakhashiri, "At the Water's Edge: Surface Spreading and Surface Tension," *Chemical Demonstrations: A Handbook for Teachers of Chemistry, Volume 3* (Madison: The University of Wisconsin Press, **1989**), pp. 301–304.

10. Keenan E. Dungey, George Lisensky, and S. Michael Condren, "Kixium Monolayers: A Simple Alternative to the Bubble Raft Model for Close-Packed Spheres," *J. Chem. Educ.*, Vol. 76, **1999**, 618–619.

11. Daryl L. Ostercamp, "Close Packing of Identical Spheres," *J. Chem. Educ*., Vol. 69, **1992**, 162. An overhead projector demonstration of close packing.

# Chapter 12. Modern Materials

## Media Resources

### Figures and Tables

| **In Transparency Pack and on MediaPortfolio:** | **Section:** |
|---|---|
| Figure 12.3 Ordering in Liquid Crystalline Phases | 12.1 Liquid Crystals |
| Figure 12.4 Structures and Liquid Crystal Temperature Intervals | 12.1 Liquid Crystals |
| Figure 12.5 Ordering in a Cholesteric Liquid Crystal | 12.1 Liquid Crystals |
| Figure 12.7 Schematic Illustration of a LCD | 12.1 Liquid Crystals |
| Table 12.1 Polymers of Commercial Importance | 12.2 Polymers |
| Figure 12.9 Segment of a Polyethylene Chain | 12.2 Polymers |
| Figure 12.13 Structure of Natural Rubber | 12.2 Polymers |
| Figure 12.18 Requirements of an Implant Device | 12.3 Biomaterials |
| Table 12.5 Superconducting Materials: Dates of Discovery and Transition Temperatures | 12.5 Superconductivity |
| Figure 12.28 Unit Cell of $YBa_2Cu_3O_7$ | 12.5 Superconductivity |

| **On MediaPortfolio:** | **Section:** |
|---|---|
| Figure 12.10 Interactions Between Polymer Chains | 12.2 Polymers |
| Equation 12.4 Synthesis of Rubber | 12.2 Polymers |
| Table 12.4 Properties of Some Ceramic and Selected Nonceramic Materials | 12.4 Ceramics |
| Figure 12.33 Schematic Illustration of a Sputtering Apparatus | 12.6 Thin Films |

| **Movies:** | **Section:** |
|---|---|
| Synthesis of Nylon 610 | 12.2 Polymers |

| **3-D Models:** | **Section:** |
|---|---|
| Silicon Carbide | 12.4 Ceramics |
| $YBa_2Cu_3O_7$ | 12.5 Superconductivity |

## Other Resources

| **Further Readings:** | **Section:** |
|---|---|
| Liquid Crystal Inquiries: Add a New Phase to Your Curriculum | 12.1 Liquid Crystals |
| Liquid Crystals Display New Potential | 12.1 Liquid Crystals |
| Preparation and Properties of Cholesteric Liquid Crystals | 12.1 Liquid Crystals |
| Polymer Literature and Samples for Classroom Use | 12.2 Polymers |
| Pictorial Analogies V: Polymers | 12.2 Polymers |
| Plastic Fantastic | 12.2 Polymers |
| Polymers Are Everywhere | 12.2 Polymers |
| Wallace Hume Carothers and Nylon, the First Completely Synthetic Fiber | 12.2 Polymers |

| | |
|---|---|
| Neoprene and Nylon Stockings: The Legacy of Wallace Hume Carothers | 12.2 Polymers |
| Polymers and Processes | 12.2 Polymers |
| Performance Polymers | 12.2 Polymers |
| Thermosetting Resins | 12.2 Polymers |
| Elastomers I: Natural Rubber | 12.2 Polymers |
| Dr. Baekland's Bakelite | 12.2 Polymers |
| Alkanes: Abundant, Pervasive, Important, and Essential | 12.2 Polymers |
| Polymer Structure—Organic Aspects (Definitions) | 12.2 Polymers |
| How to Learn and Have Fun with Poly(Vinyl Alcohol) and White Glue | 12.2 Polymers |
| Biomaterials and Biomedical Engineering | 12.3 Biomaterials |
| The Science and Applications of Biomaterials | 12.3 Biomaterials |
| The Whole Body Catalogue: Replacement to Mix and Match | 12.3 Biomaterials |
| The Chemistry of Modern Dental Filling Materials | 12.3 Biomaterials |
| Tissue Engineering 12.3 Biomaterials | |
| *Scientific American*, **April 1999** | 12.3 Biomaterials |
| Contemporary Biomaterials. Understanding Surfaces Is Key to the Design of Clinically Useful Materials | 12.3 Biomatierials |
| New Power Line Will Make Use of a Miracle of Physics | 12.4 Ceramics |
| A Multitechnique Approach for Materials Characterization. Using X-Ray Diffractometry, Visible Spectroscopy, and Atomic Absorption Analysis to Determine Thin Metal Film Thickness | 12.5 Thin Films |
| To Bead or Not to Bead? That Is the Question When Researchers Make Ultrathin Coatings | 12.5 Thin Films |
| Making a Mark | 12.5 Thin Films |
| Katharine Blodgett and Thin Films | 12.5 Thin Films |

| **Live Demonstrations:** | **Section:** |
|---|---|
| Slime: Gelation of Poly(vinyl alcohol) with Borax | 12.2 Polymers |
| The Gelation of PolyVinyl Alcohol with Borax. A Novel Class Participation Experiment Involving the Preparation and Properties of a "Slime" | 12.2 Polymers |
| Solid Foams | 12.2 Polymers |
| Polyurethane Foam | 12.2 Polymers |
| Synthesis of Nylon | 12.2 Polymers |
| The Disappearing Coffee Cup | 12.2 Polymers |

# Chapter 12. Modern Materials

## Lecture Outline

### Modern Materials

- Goal for modern chemistry and chemists: design materials with specific properties.
- Achieved by:
  - Modifying natural materials.
  - Synthesizing entirely new materials.
    - Example: Information storage is a severe problem because traditional print media take up too much physical space.
    - Solution: Decrease the size of the print to nanometer size.
      - Scanning tunneling microscopes are used to write letters 170 Å in height on a graphite tablet.

### 12.1 Liquid Crystals[1,2]

- Solids are characterized by their order.
- Liquids are characterized by almost random ordering of molecules.
- There is an intermediate phase where liquids show a limited amount of ordering:
  - **Liquid crystals** are substances that exhibit one or more ordered phases at a temperature above the melting point.
  - Example: The first systematic report of a liquid crystal was cholesteryl benzoate.
    - It melts at 145°C.
    - Between 145°C and 179°C cholesteryl benzoate is milky and liquid crystalline.
    - At 179°C the milky liquid suddenly clears.
    - Cholesteryl benzoate passes through an intermediate liquid crystalline phase.
      - It has some properties of liquids and some of solids.
    - The liquid flows (liquid properties) but has some order (crystal properties).

#### Types of Liquid-Crystalline Phases[3,4,5,6]

- Liquid crystal molecules are usually long and rodlike.
  - In normal liquid phases they are randomly oriented.
- Three types of liquid crystalline phase depend on the ordering of the molecules:
  - **Nematic liquid-crystalline phase** (least ordered).
    - Ordered along the long axis of the molecule only.
  - **Smectic liquid-crystalline phase**.
    - Ordered along the long axis of the molecule *and* in one other dimension.
  - Molecules that exhibit nematic and smectic crystals are often fairly long relative to their thickness.
  - Smectic liquid crystals often contain C=N or N=N bonds and benzene rings that add stiffness.
    - Many contain polar groups.
    - Dipole-dipole interactions promote alignment of the molecules.

---

1 "Liquid Crystal Inquiries: Add a New Phase to your Curriculum" from Further Readings
2 "Liquid Crystals Display New Potential" from Further Readings
3 Figure 12.3 from MediaPortfolio and Transparency Pack
4 "Preparation and Properties of Cholesteric Liquid Crystals" from Further Readings
5 Figure 12.4 from MediaPortfolio and Transparency Pack
6 Figure 12.5 from MediaPortfolio and Transparency Pack

- **Cholesteric liquid-crystalline phase** (most ordered).
  - Molecules are aligned along their long axis.
  - In addition, the molecules are arranged in layers.
  - Molecules in each plane are twisted slightly relative to molecules in neighboring layers.
  - Many of the molecules are derivatives of cholesterol.
    - For example, cholesteryl octanoate.
    - The molecules are long, flat, and rod-like with a flexible tail.
    - The flexible tail causes the twist between the layers.
    - The flexible tail usually contains many C–C bonds (e.g., the hydrocarbon tail in cholesteryl octanoate).
    - The rings in the cholesterol portion are not planar, but give the molecule a flat, sausage-like shape.
  - Changes in temperature and pressure cause ordering between layers to change.
    - This results in color changes.

### *Liquid Crystal Displays*[7]

- An application of liquid crystals: liquid crystal displays (LCD).
- These take advantage of the ability of applied electrical fields to change the orientation of liquid crystalline molecules.
  - This causes a change in their optical properties.
- The layers in a cholesteric liquid crystal can rotate the plane of polarized light.
  - In a liquid crystal display (LCD) the liquid crystal is sandwiched between two polarizers (one horizontal and one vertical), two electrodes, and a reflector.
- Bright display with voltage off (i.e., liquid crystal layers are undisturbed):
  - Light enters and is vertically polarized.
  - Vertically polarized light passes through the liquid crystal and gradually becomes horizontally polarized.
  - Horizontally polarized light reaches the reflector.
  - Horizontal light passes back through the horizontal polarizer.
  - The horizontally polarized light passes back through the liquid crystal and is gradually vertically polarized.
  - The vertically polarized light passes back through the vertical polarizer and back to the eye.
- Dark display with voltage on (the voltage disrupts the ordering in the liquid crystal):
  - Light is polarized by the vertical polarizer.
  - The vertically polarized light is undisturbed by the liquid crystal.
  - The vertically polarized light reaches the horizontal polarizer and is absorbed.
  - Therefore, the light never reaches the reflector and does not leave the system.
  - Therefore the display appears dark.

## 12.2 Polymers[8,9]

- **Polymers** are molecules of high molecular weight that are made by *polymerization* (joining together) of smaller molecules of low molecular mass.
- The building block small molecules for polymers are called **monomers**.
  - Examples of polymers include plastics, DNA, proteins, and rubber.

### Addition Polymerization[10,11,12,13,14,15]

---

[7] Figure 12.7 from MediaPortfolio and Transparency Pack
[8] "Pictorial Analogies V: Polymers" from Further Readings
[9] "Polymer Literature and Samples for Classroom Use" from Further Readings
[10] "Slime: Gelation of Poly(vinyl alcohol) with Borax" from Live Demonstrations

- Many synthetic polymers have a backbone of C–C bonds.
- Carbon atoms have the ability to form unusually strong, stable bonds with each other.
  - Example: ethylene $H_2C=CH_2$.
- Ethylene can polymerize by opening the C–C $\pi$ bond to form C–C $\sigma$ bonds with adjacent ethylene molecules.
  - The result is polyethylene.
- This is an example of **addition polymerization.**
  - Ethylene molecules are added to each other.

## Condensation Polymerization[16,17,18,19,20,21,22]

- In **condensation polymerization** two molecules are joined to form a larger molecule by the elimination of a small molecule (like water).
- An example of such a **condensation reaction**:
  - An amine ($R–NH_2$) condenses with a carboxylic acid (R–COOH) to form water and an amide.
  - Amino acids are linked together in this manner to form polymer chains–proteins!
  - A protein is an example of a **copolymer**–a polymer formed from different monomers.
- Another example of condensation polymerization is the formation of nylon 6,6.
  - Diamine and adipic acid are joined to form nylon 6,6.

## Types of Polymers[23]

- Some terms used to describe polymers are:
  - **Plastic**: Material that can be formed into various shapes, usually with heat and pressure.
  - **Thermoplastic**: Material that can be reshaped.
    - Recycling of polyethylene takes advantage of this property!
  - **Thermosetting plastic**: Material that is shaped via an irreversible process.
    - These are not readily reshaped.
  - **Elastomer**: Material that exhibits elastic or rubbery behavior.
    - If a moderate amount of deforming force is added, the elastomer will return to its original shape when the deforming force is removed.

## Structural and Physical Properties of Polymers[24,25,26,27,28,29]

---

[11] "The Gelation of PolyVinyl Alcohol with Borax. A Novel Class Participation Experiment Involving the Preparation and Properties of a 'Slime'" from Live Demonstrations
[12] Table 12.1 from MediaPortfolio and Transparency Pack
[13] "Polymers are Everywhere" from Further Readings
[14] "How to Learn and Have Fun with Poly(Vinyl Alcohol) and White Glue" from Further Readings
[15] "Alkanes: Abundant, Pervasive, Important, and Essential" from Further Readings
[16] "Synthesis of Nylon 610" Movie from MediaPortfolio
[17] "Synthesis of Nylon" from Live Demonstrations
[18] "Polymers and Processes" from Further Readings
[19] "Wallace Hume Carothers and Nylon, the First Completely Synthetic Fiber" from Further Readings
[20] "Neoprene and Nylon Stockings: The Legacy of Wallace Hume Carothers" from Further Readings
[21] "Dr. Baekland's Bakelite" from Further Readings
[22] "The Disappearing Coffee Cup" from Live Demonstrations
[23] "Thermosetting Resins" from Further Readings
[24] Figure 12.9 from MediaPortfolio and Transparency Pack
[25] "Polyurethane Foam" from Live Demonstrations
[26] "Performance Polymers" from Further Readings
[27] Figure 12.10 from MediaPortfolio
[28] "Polymer Structure–Organic Aspects (Definitions)" from Further Readings

- Polymer chains tend to be flexible and easily entangled or folded.
- Polymers are fairly amorphous (noncrystalline).
  - They soften over a wide range of temperatures.
  - They may show some ordering.
    - The degree of *crystallinity* reflects the extent of the order.
- Stretching or extruding a polymer can increase crystallinity.
- The degree of crystallinity is also strongly influenced by average molecular mass:
  - Low-density polyethylene (LDPE), which is used in plastic wrap, has an average molecular mass of $10^4$ amu.
  - High-density polyethylene (HDPE), which is used in milk cartons, has an average molecular mass of $10^6$ amu.
- We can modify the polymeric properties by the addition of substances with lower molecular mass.
  - Plasticizers are molecules that interfere with interactions between polymer chains.
    - These make polymers more pliable.

### Crosslinking-Polymers[30,31,32,33]

- Bonds formed between polymer chains make the polymer stiffer.
  - Forming such bonds is referred to as **cross-linking**.
  - The greater the number of cross-links, the more rigid the polymer becomes.
- Example: Natural rubber is too soft and chemically reactive to be useful.
  - **Vulcanization** of rubber involves formation of cross-links in the polymer chain.
  - Rubber is cross-linked in a process employing short chains of sulfur atoms.
  - Vulcanized rubber has more useful properties.
    - It is more elastic and less susceptible to chemical reaction than natural rubber.

## 12.3 Biomaterials[34,35]

- A **biomaterial** is any material that has a biomedical application.
  - Example: a therapeutic or diagnostic use.

### Characteristics of Biomaterials[36,37,38,39]

- Choice of biomaterial for an application is influenced by the chemical characteristics.
  - *Biocompatibility*:
    - A substance is **biocompatible** if it is readily accepted by the body without causing an inflammatory response.
    - The chemical nature and physical texture of the object are important.
  - *Physical requirements:*
    - The material must be able to withstand the physical stresses of use.
    - For example, materials used for hip-joint replacements must be wear-resistant.

---

[29] "Solid Foams" from Live Demonstrations
[30] "Elastomers I: Natural Rubber" from Further Readings
[31] Equation 12.4 from MediaPortfolio
[32] Figure 12.13 from MediaPortfolio and Transparency Pack
[33] "Plastic Fantastic" from Further Readings
[34] April 1999 issue of *Scientific American* from Further Readings
[35] "Contemporary Biomaterials: Understanding Surfaces is Key to Design of Clinically Useful Materials" from Further Readings
[36] Figure 12.18 from MediaPortfolio and Transparency Pack
[37] "Biomaterials and Biomedical Engineering" from Further Readings
[38] "The Science and Applications of Biomaterials" from Further Readings
[39] "The Whole Body Catalolgue: Replacement to Mix and Match" from Further Readings

- *Chemical requirements*:
  - Must be *medical grade*.
  - Must be innocuous over the lifetime of the application.
  - For example, polymers can not contain plasticizers or other substances that might be released and cause a problem for the patient.

### Polymeric Biomaterials[40]

- Our bodies are composed of many biopolymers.
  - Examples include proteins, polysaccharides (sugar polymers), nucleic acids (DNA, RNA).
  - These have complex structures with many polar groups along the polymer chain.
  - The repeat unit often varies along the chain.
    - For example, in proteins the monomers are amino acids.
    - There are 20 different amino acids commonly found incorporated into proteins.
- Man-made polymers are usually simpler.
  - One or two different repeat units may be used.
  - Often this contributes to the body's ability to detect these as "foreign objects."

### Examples of Biomaterial Applications[41]

- Heart replacement and repairs:
  - Aortic valve replacements have become common.
  - Mechanical valves.
    - They must be designed to avoid hemolysis (breakdown of red blood cells) and other complications that may result from roughness in the surface of the material.
    - They must be designed to become incorporated into the body's tissues (fixed in place).
- *Vascular grafts*:
  - Replacement of portions of diseased arteries.
  - Current materials still present the risk of blood clots.
- *Artificial tissue*:
  - Lab-grown skin used for tissue grafts in burn patients.
  - Grown on a polymeric support or scaffold.
- *Hip replacements*:
  - Artificial hip joints.
  - The materials must be stable under stress and resist fatigue and abrasion.
  - The materials must be biocompatible.

## 12.4 Ceramics[42,43]

- **Ceramics** are:
  - Inorganic, nonmetallic solids.
    - They are either crystalline or amorphous (e.g., glass is an amorphous material).
      - Examples: china, cement, roof tiles.
- Ceramics can have covalent-network bonding, ionic bonding or a combination of these.
  - They are hard, brittle, stable to high temperatures, less dense than metals, more elastic than metals, have very high melting points, and resist corrosion.
  - Ceramics come in a variety of forms:
  - Silicates, oxides, carbides, nitrides, aluminates.
  - Most contain metals.

---

[40] "The Chemistry of Modern Dental Filling Materials" from Further Readings
[41] "Tissue Engineering" from Further Readings
[42] Table 12.4 from MediaPortfolio
[43] "Silicon Carbide" 3-D Model from MediaPortfolio

- Typical examples: alumina ($Al_2O_3$), silicon carbide ($SiC$), zirconia ($ZrO_2$) and beryllia ($BeO$).

### Processing of Ceramics

- Ceramics are brittle.
- Small defects developed during processing make ceramics weaker.
- Sintering involves heating of very pure uniform particles ($<10^{-6}$ m in diameter) at high temperatures under pressure to force individual particles to bond together.
- **Sol-gel process**: formation of pure uniform particles.
  - A metal alkoxide is formed (e.g., $Ti(OCH_2CH_3)_4$).
    - Alkoxides contain organic groups bonded to a metal atom through oxygen atoms.
    - Formed by reaction of a metal and an alcohol.
    - Example:

$$Ti(s) + 4CH_3CH_2OH(l) \rightarrow Ti(OCH_2CH_3)_4(s) + 2H_2(g)$$

  - A sol is formed by reacting the alkoxide with water (to form $Ti(OH)_4$).
    - A sol is a suspension of extremely small particles.
  - A gel is formed by condensing the sol and eliminating water.
    - A gel is a suspension of extremely small particles that has the consistency of gelatin.
  - The gel is heated to remove water and is converted into a finely divided oxide powder.
  - The oxide powder has particles with sizes between 0.003 and 0.1 μm in diameter.
  - A ceramic object is formed from the powder.
    - It is compacted under pressure and scintered at high temperature.

### Ceramic Composites

- **Composite**: two or more materials making up a ceramic.
  - Result: a tougher ceramic.
- The most effective method is to add fibers to ceramic material.
  - Example: $SiC$ fibers added to aluminosilicate glass.
  - Fiber must have a length $\geq 100$ times its diameter.

### Applications of Ceramics

- Used in cutting tool industry.
  - Also used in abrasives (e.g., $SiC$).
- Used in electronic industry.
  - Semiconductor integrated circuits are usually mounted on a ceramic substrate such as alumina).
- Piezoelectric materials (generation of an electrical potential after mechanical stress) are used in watches and ultrasonic generators.
  - Example: quartz (crystalline $SiO_2$)
- Used to make tiles on the space shuttle.

## 12.5 Superconductivity [44,45]

- Superconductors show no resistance to flow of electricity.
  - **Superconductivity** involves "frictionless" flow of electrons.
  - Superconducting behavior starts only when cooled below the **superconducting transition temperature, $T_c$.**
  - High-temperature superconductors were discovered in 1986 ($YBa_2Cu_3O_7$, yttrium-barium-copper oxide, $T_c = 95$ K).
    - In 2001 the highest $T_c$ was 133 K for $HgBa_2Ca_2Cu_3O_{8+x}$.

---

[44] "New Power Line Will Make Use of a Miracle of Physics" from Further Readings

[45] Table 12.5 from MediaPortfolio and Transparency Pack

    - Potential use: Carry electric current without resistance in generators, motors, faster computer chips, etc.
  - Development of new high-temperature superconducting materials is an active area of research.
- Superconducting materials exhibit the Meissner effect.
  - Meissner effect: permanent magnets levitate over superconductors.
    - The superconductor excludes all magnetic field lines, so the magnet floats in space.
    - Potential application: levitated trains.

### Superconducting Ceramic Oxides[46,47]

- 1986: The first **superconducting ceramic** was discovered.
  - Ceramic oxide containing lanthanum, barium and copper.
- One of the most widely studied ceramic superconductors is $YBa_2Cu_3O_7$.

### New Superconductors

- New superconducting materials are continually being discovered:
  - $C_{60}$ reacted with an alkali metal and $MgB_2$ has been shown to exhibit a superconducting transition below approximately 40 K.

## 12.6 Thin Films[48,49,50]

- **Thin films** generally have a thickness between 0.1 μm and 300 μm.
- Useful thin films must:
  - Be chemically stable.
  - Adhere well to the surface they cover (the *substrate*).
  - Be uniform in thickness.
  - Be chemically pure or have a controlled composition.
  - Have low density of imperfections.
  - Have other special properties as required for the particular application.

### Uses of Thin Films

- Typical uses of thin films include:
  - Microelectronics (conductors, resistors and capacitors).
  - Optical coatings (reduce reflection from a lens).
  - Protective coatings for metals.
    - For example "chrome" plating, silver plating.
  - Increase the hardness of tools.
    - Example: thin films such as tungsten carbide.
  - Reduce scratching on glass.
- $SnO_2$ is the most common thin film.

### Formation of Thin Films[51,52]

---

[46] Figure 12.28 from MediaPortfolio and Transparency Pack

[47] "$YBa_2Cu_3O_7$" 3-D Model from MediaPortfolio

[48] "A Multitechnique Approach for Materials Characterization. Using X-Ray Diffractometry, Visible Spectroscopy, and Atomic Absorption Analysis to Determine Thin Metal Film Thickness" from Further Readings

[49] "Katharine Blodgett and Thin Films" from Further Readings

[50] "To Bead or Not to Bead? That is the Question When Researchers Make Ultrathin Coatings" from Further Readings

[51] "Making a Mark" from Further Readings

[52] Figure 12.33 from MediaPortfolio

- Three usual methods are vacuum deposition, sputtering, and chemical-vapor deposition.
- **Vacuum Deposition**
  - Requires a substance that can be vaporized without breaking chemical bonds.
  - The material to be deposited is placed in one chamber and the objects to be coated in another.
  - The material to be deposited is heated in a high-vacuum chamber at low pressure.
- The pressure is reduced (low pressure means low sublimation point) while the material is heated.
  - The material vaporizes and condenses on the object to be coated.
    - To ensure an even coating, the objects are often rotated.
  - Examples of material used to form the thin films: $MgF_2$, $Al_2O_3$, and $SiO_2$.
- **Sputtering**
  - Sputter coating involves the use of high voltage to remove material from a source or target.
  - The atoms from the target move through an ionized gas in a chamber and are deposited on the substrate.
  - The target is the negative electrode (cathode) and the substrate the positive electrode (anode).
  - Ar atoms (in the chamber) are ionized to $Ar^+$.
    - The $Ar^+$ ions strike the negative electrode and force an atom to be ejected from the target.
    - The target atoms have a high kinetic energy and travel in all directions.
    - Some target atoms eventually hit the substrate and form a thin film on it.
  - Widely used to form:
    - Thin films of elements such as Si, Ti, Al, Au, Ag.
    - Thin films of carbides, borides and nitrides on metal tool surfaces.
    - Thin films of soft lubricating films.
    - Energy-conserving coatings on architectural glass.
- **Chemical-Vapor Deposition**
  - Surface is coated with a volatile, stable compound at a high temperature which is below the melting point of the substrate.
  - The compound on the surface undergoes a chemical reaction to form a stable coating.
  - Examples:
    - $TiBr_4(g) + 2H_2(g) \rightarrow Ti(s) + 4HBr(g)$
    - $SiCl_4(g) + 2H_2(g) \rightarrow Si(s) + 4HCl(g)$
    - $SiCl_4(g) + 2H_2(g) + 2CO_2(g) \rightarrow SiO_2(s) + 4HCl(g) + 2CO(g)$
    - $12WF_6(g) + C_6H_6(g) + 33H_2(g) \rightarrow 6W_2C(s) + 72HF(g)$

## Further Readings:

1. Renata-Maria Marroum, "Liquid Crystal Inquiries: Add a New Phase to Your Curriculum," *The Science Teacher*, Vol. 65, **1996**, 32–35. Liquid crystals are used as tools to demonstrate phase transitions.

2. Richard Bissell and Neville Boden, "Liquid Crystals Display New Potential," *Chemistry in Britain*, Vol. 31(1), **January 1995**, 38–41.

3. Graeme Patch and Gregory A. Hope, "Preparation and Properties of Cholesteric Liquid Crystals," *J. Chem. Educ.*, Vol. 62, **1985**, 454–455. The liquid crystal properties of cholesterol compounds are studied as a function of temperature and composition. This reference includes instructions for the preparation of a number of such compounds.

4. John J. Meister, "Polymer Literature and Samples for Classroom Use," *J. Chem. Educ.*, Vol. 72, **1995**, 593–595. This reference provides a list of sources for suppliers of polymer samples as well as polymer literature references.

5. John H. Fortman, "Pictorial Analogies V: Polymers," *J. Chem. Educ.*, Vol. 70, **1993**, 403–404. Several analogies for polymer formation are featured in this reference.

6. Melissa Lee, "Polymers and Processes," *Chemistry in Britain*, Vol. 31(9), **September 1998**.

7. Alan Gray, "Performance Polymers," *Chemistry in Britain*, Vol. 34(3), **March 1998**, 44–45. A short article on innovations in engineering thermoplastics.

8. Michael Chisholm, "Plastic Fantastic," *Chemistry in Britain*, Vol. 34(4), **April 1998**, 33–36. An article looking at the uses of polymethyl methacrylate.

9. Raymond B. Seymour, "Polymers Are Everywhere," *J. Chem. Educ.*, Vol. 65, **1988**, 327–334. Uses of polymers throughout history are outlined in this reference.

10. John W. Nicholson and H. Mary Anstice, "The Chemistry of Modern Dental Filling Materials," *J. Chem. Educ.*, Vol. 76, **1999**, 1497–1501. A look at some interesting dental polymers.

11. Geoerge B. Kauffman, "Wallace Hume Carothers and Nylon, the First Completely Synthetic Fiber," *J. Chem. Educ.*, Vol. 65, **1988**, 803–808.

12. Carol Cummings, "Neoprene and Nylon Stockings: The Legacy of Wallace Hume Carothers," *J. Chem. Educ.*, Vol. 61, **1984**, 241–242.

13. W. Peng and B. Riedl, "Thermosetting Resins," *J. Chem. Educ.*, Vol. 72, **1995**, 587–592. A general description of resins or thermosets, their applications and manner of curing is featured in this reference.

14. George B. Kauffman and Raymond B. Seymour, "Elastomers I: Natural Rubber," *J. Chem. Educ.*, Vol. 67, **1990**, 422–425.

15. Miriam C. Nagel, "Dr. Baekland's Bakelite," *J. Chem. Educ.*, Vol. 57, **1980**, 811–812. A short historical article about the scientist who prepared the first commercially successful plastic.

16. Charles E. Carraher, Jr. and Raymond B. Seymour, "Polymer Structure–Organic Aspects (Definitions)," *J. Chem. Educ.*, Vol. 65, **1988**, 314–319.

17. Raymond B. Seymour, "Alkanes: Abundant, Pervasive, Important, and Essential," *J. Chem. Educ.*, Vol. 66, **1989**, 59–63.

18. V. de Zea Bermudez, P. Passos de Almeida, and J. Feria Seita, "How to Learn and Have Fun with Poly(Vinyl Alcohol) and White Glue," *J. Chem. Educ.*, Vol. 75, **1998**, 1410–1418.

19. R. Langer, "Biomaterials and Biomedical Engineering," *Chemical Engineering Science*, Vol. 50, **1995**, 4109.

20. D. F. Williams, "The Science and Applications of Biomaterials," *Int. J. of Materials and Product Technology*, Vol. 10, **1995**, 360.

21. "The Whole Body Catalogue: Replacement to Mix and Match," *New York Times*, **July 8, 1997**.

22. J. A. Hubbell and R. Langer, "Tissue Engineering," *Chemical and Engineering News*, **March 13, 1995**.

23. The **April 1999** issue of *Scientific American* is a special issue including many articles on tissue engineering.

24. A. Maureen Rouhi, "Contemporary Biomaterials. Understanding Surfaces is Key to the Design of Clinically Useful Materials," *Chemical and Engineering News*, **January 18, 1999**, 51–63.

25. "New Power Line Will Make Use of a Miracle of Physics," *New York Times*, **November 3, 1998**.

26. Alfred T. D'Agostino, "A Multitechnique Approach for Materials Characterization. Using X-Ray Diffractometry, Visible Spectroscopy, and Atomic Absorption Analysis to Determine Thin Metal Film Thickness," *J. Chem. Educ.*, Vol. 71, **1994**, 892–896.

27. Peter Weiss, "To Bead or Not to Bead? That is the Question When Researchers Make Ultrathin Coatings," *Science News*, Vol. 155, **1999**, 28–29.

28. Nina Morgan, "Making a Mark," *Chemistry in Britain*, Vol. 34(4), **April 1998**, 25–27. An interesting use of vapor deposition: detection of fingerprints!

29. Kathleen A. Davis, "Katharine Blodgett and Thin Films," *J. Chem. Educ.*, Vol. 61, **1984**, 437–439.

## Live Demonstrations:

1. E. Z. Casassa, A. M. Sarquis, and C. H. Van Dyke, "The Gelation of Polyvinyl Alcohol with Borax. A Novel Class Participation Experiment Involving the Preparation and Properties of a 'Slime'," *J. Chem. Educ.*, Vol. 63, **1986**, 57–60. A classic demonstration of polymer formation! Making SLIME!!

2. Bassam Z. Shakhashiri, "'Slime': Gelation of Poly(vinyl alcohol) with Borax," *Chemical Demonstrations: A Handbook for Teachers of Chemistry, Volume 3* (Madison: The University of Wisconsin Press, **1989**), pp. 362–363.

3. Bassam Z. Shakhashiri, “Solid Foams,” *Chemical Demonstrations: A Handbook for Teachers of Chemistry, Volume 3* (Madison: The University of Wisconsin Press, **1989**), pp. 348–350. A demonstration of the formation and destruction of solid foams.

4. Bassam Z. Shakhashiri, “Polyurethane Foam,” *Chemical Demonstrations: A Handbook for Teachers of Chemistry, Volume 1* (Madison: The University of Wisconsin Press, **1983**), pp. 216–218. Polyurethane foam is prepared in this demonstration of polymer formation.

5. Lee. R. Summerlin,, Christie L. Borgford, and Julie B. Ealy, “The Disappearing Coffee Cup,” *Chemical Demonstrations, A Sourcebook for Teachers*, Volume 2 (Washington: American Chemical Society, **1988**), pp. 96. A polystyrene coffee cup is “melted” in a pool of acetone.

6. Lee. R. Summerlin, and James. L. Ealy, Jr., “Synthesis of Nylon,” *Chemical Demonstrations, A Sourcebook for Teachers*, *Volume 1* (Washington: American Chemical Society, **1988**), pp.172–173.

# Chapter 13. Properties of Solutions

## Media Resources

### Figures and Tables

| **In Transparency Pack and on MediaPortfolio:** | **Section:** |
|---|---|
| Figure 13.1 Ionic Solid Dissolving in Water | 13.1 The Solution Process |
| Figure 13.2 Hydrated $Na^+$ and $Cl^-$ Ions | 13.1 The Solution Process |
| Figure 13.4 Enthalpy Changes Accompanying Solution Formation | 13.1 The Solution Process |
| Figure 13.13 Molecular Structures of Vitamins A and C | 13.3 Factors Affecting Solubility |
| Figure 13.17 Solubilities of Ionic Solids as a Function of Temperature | 13.3 Factors Affecting Solubility |
| Figure 13.18 Solubilities of Gases as a Function of Temperature | 13.3 Factors Affecting Solubility |
| Figure 13.19 Calculation of Molality and Molarity | 13.4 Ways of Expressing Concentration |
| Figure 13.20 Vapor Pressure Over a Solution | 13.5 Colligative Properties |
| Figure 13.22 Phase Diagrams for a Solvent and a Solution | 13.5 Colligative Properties |
| Figure 13.24 Osmotic Pressure | 13.5 Colligative Properties |
| Figure 13.26 Ion Pairs in a NaCl Solution | 13.5 Colligative Properties |

| **On MediaPortfolio:** | **Section:** |
|---|---|
| Table 13.1 Examples of Solutions | 13.1 The Solution Process |
| Figure 13.3 Enthalpic Contributions to the Overall Heat of Solution of a Solute | 13.1 The Solution Process |
| Figure 13.6 Formation of a Homogeneous Solution | 13.1 The Solution Process |
| Figure 13.9 A Saturated Solution | 13.2 Saturated Solutions and Solubility |
| Table 13.3 Solubilities of Some Alcohols in Water and in Hexane | 13.3 Factors Affecting Solubility |
| Figure 13.14 Effect of Pressure on the Solubility of a Gas | 13.3 Factors Affecting Solubility |
| Table 13.4 Molal Boiling-Point-Elevation and Freezing-Point Depression Constants | 13.5 Colligative Properites |
| Figure 13.23 Osmosis | 13.5 Colligative Properties |
| Figure 13.25 Osmosis Through a Red Blood Cell Membrane | 13.5 Colligative Properties |
| Table 13.6 Types of Colloids | 13.6 Colloids |
| Figure 13.29 Hydrophilic Groups on the Surface of a Macromolecule | 13.6 Colloids |
| Figure 13.30 Stabilization of a Hydrophobic Colloid | 13.6 Colloids |
| Figure 13.31 Stabilization of an Emulsion of Oil | 13.6 Colloids |

| **Animations:** | **Section:** |
|---|---|
| Dissolution of NaCl in Water | 13.1 The Solution Process |
| Henry's Law | 13.3 Factors Affecting Solubility |

| Activities: | Section: |
|---|---|
| Enthalpy of Solution | 13.1 The Solution Process |
| Molarity Calculation | 13.4 Ways of Expressing Concentration |
| Boiling Point Elevation and Freezing Point Depression | 13.5 Colligative Properties |
| Determination of Molar Mass | 13.5 Colligative Properties |

| 3-D Models: | Section: |
|---|---|
| Sodium Stearate | 13.6 Colloids |

## Other Resources

| Further Readings: | Section: |
|---|---|
| Crystallization from a Supersaturated Solution of Sodium Acetate | 13.2 Saturated Solutions and Solubility |
| Polarity, Miscibility, and Surface Tension | 13.3 Factors Affecting Solubility |
| An Analogy to Illustrate Miscibility of Liquids | 13.3 Factors Affecting Solubility |
| Using Computer-Based Visualization Strategies to Improve Students' Understanding of Molecular Polarity and Miscibility | 13.3 Factors Affecting Solubility |
| Henry's Law and Noisy Knuckles | 13.3 Factors Affecting Solubility |
| Soft Drink Bubbles | 13.3 Factors Affecting Solubility |
| Candy Sprinkles to Illustrate One Part Per Million | 13.4 Ways of Expressing Concentration |
| An Alternative Introduction to the Mole Fraction | 13.4 Ways of Expressing Concentration |
| Mole Fraction Analogies | 13.4 Ways of Expressing Concentration |
| Antifreeze Solutions: The Colligative Properties of Antifreeze | 13.5 Colligative Properties |
| Freeze-Proof Bugs | 13.5 Colligative Properties |
| Salts Are Mostly NOT Ionized | 13.5 Colligative Properties |
| J. H. van't Hoff | 13.5 Colligative Properties |
| Seawater Gets Fresh | 13.5 Colligative Properties |
| Colloidal Systems | 13.6 Colloids |
| Clearly Cleaner | 13.6 Colloids |
| Chemistry and Physics in the Kitchen | 13.6 Colloids |
| Put the Brakes on Wastewater Emulsions | 13.6 Colloids |
| Blood-Chemistry Tutorials: Teaching Biological Applications of General Chemistry Material | 13.6 Colloids |

| Live Demonstrations: | Section: |
|---|---|
| Copper Sulfate: Blue to White | 13.1 The Solution Process |
| Supersaturation | 13.2 Saturated Solutions and Solubility |
| Crystallization from Supersaturated Solutions of Sodium Acetate | 13.3 Factors Affecting Solubility |
| Nonadditivity of Volumes | 13.3 Factors Affecting Solubility |
| Solubility of Alcohols | 13.3 Factors Affecting Solubility |
| Why Don't Water and Oil Mix? | 13.3 Factors Affecting Solubility |
| Effect of Temperature and Pressure on the Solubility of Gases in Liquids | 13.3 Factors Affecting Solubility |
| A Simple Demonstration Model of Osmosis | 13.5 Colligative Properties |
| Osmotic Pressure of a Sugar Solution | 13.5 Colligative Properties |
| Osmosis Through the Membrane of an Egg | 13.5 Colligative Properties |

| | |
|---|---|
| **Osmosis and the Egg Membrane** | 13.5 Colligative Properites |
| **Color of the Sunset: The Tyndall Effect** | 13.6 Colloids |
| **Illustrating the Properties of Magic Sand** | 13.6 Colloids |

# Chapter 13. Properties of Solutions

## Common Student Misconceptions

- Students often confuse dilute and concentrated, and weak and strong are often confused.
- Students do not realize that crystallization is the reverse of dissolution.
- Students often forget that calculations of molality require the mass of *solvent*, not *solution*.

## Lecture Outline

### 13.1 The Solution Process[1,2,3,4]

- A solution is a homogeneous mixture of solute and solvent.
- Solutions may be gases, liquids, or solids,
- Each substance present is a component of the solution.
  - The solvent is the component present in the largest amount.
  - The other components are the solutes.
- Intermolecular forces become rearranged in the process of making solutions with condensed phases.
- Consider NaCl (solute) dissolving in water (solvent):
  - Water molecules orient themselves on the NaCl crystals.
  - H-bonds between the water molecules have to be broken.
  - NaCl dissociates into $Na^+$ and $Cl^-$.
  - Ion-dipole forces form between the $Na^+$ and the negative end of the water dipole.
    - Similar ion-dipole interactions form between the $Cl^-$ and the positive end of the water dipole.
  - Such an interaction between solvent and solute is called **solvation**.
    - If water is the solvent, the interaction is called **hydration**.

#### Energy Changes and Solution Formation[5,6,7]

- There are three steps involving energy in the formation of a solution:
  - Separation of solute molecules ($\Delta H_1$),
  - Separation of solvent molecules ($\Delta H_2$), and
  - Formation of solute-solvent interactions ($\Delta H_3$).
- We define the enthalpy change in the solution process as:

$$\Delta H_{soln} = \Delta H_1 + \Delta H_2 + \Delta H_3$$

- $\Delta H_{soln}$ can either be positive or negative depending on the intermolecular forces.
  - To determine whether $\Delta H_{soln}$ is positive or negative, we consider the strengths of all solute-solute, solvent-solvent and solute-solvent interactions:
  - Breaking attractive intermolecular forces is always endothermic.
    - $\Delta H_1$ and $\Delta H_2$ are both positive.
  - Forming attractive intermolecular forces is always exothermic.
    - $\Delta H_3$ is always negative.
- It is possible to have either $\Delta H_3 > (\Delta H_1 + \Delta H_2)$ or $\Delta H_3 < (\Delta H_1 + \Delta H_2)$.

---

[1] Table 13.1 from MediaPortfolio
[2] "Dissolution of NaCl in Water" Animation from MediaPortfolio
[3] Figure 13.1 from MediaPortfolio and Transparency Pack
[4] Figure 13.2 from MediaPortfolio and Transparency Pack
[5] Figure 13.3 from MediaPortfolio
[6] Figure 13.4 from MediaPortfolio and Transparency Pack
[7] "Enthalpy of Solution" Activity from MediaPortfolio

- Examples:
  - $MgSO_4$ added to water has $\Delta H_{soln} = -91.2$ kJ/mol.
  - $NH_4NO_3$ added to water has $\Delta H_{soln} = +26.4$ kJ/mol.
    - $MgSO_4$ is often used in instant heat packs and $NH_4NO_3$ is often used in instant cold packs.
- How can we predict if a solution will form?
  - In general, solutions form if the $\Delta H_{soln}$ is negative.
  - If $\Delta H_{soln}$ is too endothermic a solution will not form.
  - "Rule of thumb": Polar solvents dissolve polar solutes.
    - Nonpolar solvents dissolve nonpolar solutes.
  - Consider the process of mixing NaCl in gasoline.
    - Only weak interactions are possible because gasoline is nonpolar.
    - These interactions do not compensate for the separation of ions from one another.
      - Result: NaCl doesn't dissolve to any great extent in gasoline.
  - Consider the process of mixing water in octane ($C_8H_{18}$).
    - Water has strong H-bonds.
    - The energy required to break these H-bonds is not compensated for by interactions between water and octane.
      - Result: Water and octane do not mix.

### Solution Formation, Spontaneity, and Disorder[8]

- A spontaneous process occurs without outside intervention.
- When the energy of the system decreases (e.g., dropping a book and allowing it to fall to a lower potential energy), the process is spontaneous.
- Spontaneous processes tend to be exothermic.
  - However some spontaneous processes do not involve the movement of the system to a lower energy state (e.g., an endothermic reaction).
- The amount of randomness or disorder of the system is given by its **entropy**.
  - In most cases, solution formation is favored by the increase in entropy that accompanies mixing.
  - Example: A mixture of $CCl_4$ and $C_6H_{14}$ is less ordered than the two separate liquids.
  - Therefore, they spontaneously mix even though $\Delta H_{soln}$ is very close to zero.
  - A solution will form unless the solute-solute or solvent-solvent interactions are too strong relative to solute-solvent interactions.

### Solution Formation and Chemical Reactions[9]

- Some solutions form by physical processes and some by chemical processes.
  - Consider:

$$Ni(s) + 2HCl(aq) \rightarrow NiCl_2(aq) + H_2(g)$$

    - Note that the chemical form of the substance being dissolved has changed during this process ($Ni \rightarrow NiCl_2$)
    - When all the water is removed from the solution, no Ni is found, only $NiCl_2.6H_2O$ remains.
    - Therefore, the dissolution of Ni in HCl is a chemical process.
  - By contrast:

$$NaCl(s) + H_2O\,(l) \rightarrow Na^+(aq) + Cl^-(aq).$$

    - When the water is removed from the solution, NaCl is found.
    - Therefore, NaCl dissolution is a physical process.

## 13.2 Saturated Solutions and Solubility[10,11,12,13]

---

[8] Figure 13.6 from MediaPortfolio

[9] "Copper Sulfate: Blue to White" from Live Demonstrations

- As a solid dissolves, a solution forms:
  - Solute + solvent → solution
- The opposite process is **crystallization.**
  - Solution → solute + solvent
- If crystallization and dissolution are in equilibrium with undissolved solute, the solution is **saturated**.
  - There will be no further increase in the amount of dissolved solute.
- **Solubility** is the amount of solute required to form a saturated solution.
  - A solution with a concentration of dissolved solute that is less than the solubility is said to be **unsaturated**.
  - A solution is said to be **supersaturated** if more solute is dissolved than in a saturated solution.

## 13.3 Factors Affecting Solubility

- The tendency of a substance to dissolve in another depends on:
  - The nature of the solute.
  - The nature of the solvent.
  - The temperature.
  - The pressure (for gases).

### Solute-Solvent Interactions[14,15,16,17,18,19,20,21]

- Intermolecular forces are an important factor in determining solubility of a solute in a solvent.
  - The stronger the attraction between solute and solvent molecules, the greater the solubility.
    - For example, polar liquids tend to dissolve in polar solvents.
    - Favorable dipole-dipole interactions exist (solute-solute, solvent-solvent, and solute-solvent).
- Pairs of liquids that mix in any proportions are said to be **miscible**.
  - Example: Ethanol and water are miscible liquids.
- In contrast, **immiscible** liquids do not mix significantly.
  - Example: Gasoline and water are immiscible.
- Consider the solubility of alcohols in water.
  - Water and ethanol are miscible because the broken hydrogen bonds in both pure liquids are re-established in the mixture.
- However, not all alcohols are miscible with water.
  - Why?
  - The number of carbon atoms in a chain affects solubility.
    - The greater the number of carbons in the chain, the more the molecule behaves like a hydrocarbon.
    - Thus, the more C atoms in the alcohol, the lower its solubility in water.

---

[10] Figure 13.9 from MediaPortfolio
[11] "Crystallization from a Supersaturated Solution of Sodium Acetate" from Further Readings
[12] "Supersaturation" from Live Demonstrations
[13] "Crystallization from Supersaturated Solutions of Sodium Acetate" from Live Demonstrations
[14] "Nonadditivity of Volumes" from Live Demonstrations
[15] "Polarity, Miscibility, and Surface Tension" from Further Readings
[16] "An Analogy to Illustrate Miscibility of Liquids" from Further Readings
[17] "Solubility of Alcohols" from Live Demonstrations
[18] Table 13.3 from MediaPortfolio
[19] "Using Computer-Based Visualization Strategies to Improve Students' Understanding of Molecular Polarity and Miscibility" from Further Readings
[20] Figure 13.13 from MediaPortfolio and Transparency Pack
[21] "Why Don't Water and Oil Mix" from Live Demonstrations

- Increasing the number of –OH groups within a molecule increases its solubility in water.
  - The greater the number of –OH groups along the chain, the more solute-water H-bonding is possible.
- Generalization: "Like dissolves like".
  - Substances with similar intermolecular attractive forces tend to be soluble in one another.
    - The more polar bonds in the molecule, the better it dissolves in a polar solvent.
    - The less polar the molecule the less likely it is to dissolve in a polar solvent and the more likely it is to dissolve in a nonpolar solvent.
- Network solids do not dissolve because the strong intermolecular forces in the solid are not reestablished in any solution.

### Pressure Effects[22,23,24,25,26]

- The solubility of a gas in a liquid is a function of the pressure of the gas over the solution.
  - Solubilities of solids and liquids are not greatly affected by pressure.
- With higher gas pressure, more molecules of gas are close to the surface of the solution and the probability of a gas molecule striking the surface and entering the solution is increased.
  - Therefore, the higher the pressure, the greater the solubility.
- The lower the pressure, the smaller the number molecules of gas close to the surface of the solution resulting in a lower solubility.
  - The solubility of a gas is directly proportional to the partial pressure of the gas above the solution.
  - This statement is called **Henry's law**.
  - Henry's law may be expressed mathematically as:

$$S_g = kP_g$$

    - Where $S_g$ is the solubility of gas, $P_g$ the partial pressure, $k$ = Henry's law constant.
    - Note: The Henry's law constant differs for each solute-solvent pair and differs with temperature.
- An application of Henry's law: preparation of carbonated soda.
  - Carbonated beverages are bottled under $P_{CO_2} > 1$ atm.
  - As the bottle is opened, $P_{CO_2}$ *decreases* and the solubility of $CO_2$ decreases.
  - Therefore, bubbles of $CO_2$ escape from solution.

### Temperature Effects[27,28]

- Experience tells us that sugar dissolves better in warm water than in cold water.
  - As temperature increases, solubility of solids generally increases.
  - Sometimes solubility decreases as temperature increases (e.g., $Ce_2(SO_4)_3$).
- Experience tells us that carbonated beverages go flat as they get warm.
  - Gases are less soluble at higher temperatures.
- An environmental application of this is thermal pollution.
  - Thermal pollution: If lakes get too warm, $CO_2$ and $O_2$ become less soluble and are not available for plants or animals.
  - Fish suffocate.

---

[22] Figure 13.14 from MediaPortfolio
[23] "Effect of Temperature and Pressure on the Solubility of Gases in Liquids" from Live Demonstrations
[24] "Henry's Law and Noisy Knuckles" from Further Readings
[25] "Henry's Law" Animation from MediaPortfolio
[26] "Soft Drink Bubbles" from Further Readings
[27] Figure 13.17 from MediaPortfolio and Transparency Pack
[28] Figure 13.18 from MediaPortfolio and Transparency Pack

## 13.4 Ways of Expressing Concentration

- All methods involve quantifying the amount of solute per amount of solvent (or solution).
- Concentration may be expressed qualitatively or quantitatively.
  - The terms *dilute* and *concentrated* are qualitative ways to describe concentration.
    - A dilute solution has a relatively small concentration of solute.
    - A concentrated solution has a relatively high concentration of solute.
- Quantitative expressions of concentration require specific information regarding such quantities as masses, moles, or liters of the solute, solvent, or solution.
  - The most commonly used expressions for concentration are:
    - Mass percentage.
    - Mole fraction.
    - Molarity.
    - Molality.

### Mass percentage, ppm, and ppb[29]

- **Mass percentage** is one of the simplest ways to express concentration.
  - By definition:

$$\text{Mass \% of component} = \frac{\text{mass of component in soln}}{\text{total mass of solution}} \times 100$$

- Similarly, **parts per million (ppm)** can be expressed as the number of mg of solute per kilogram of solution.
  - By definition:

$$\text{Parts per million (ppm) of component} = \frac{\text{mass of component in soln}}{\text{total mass of solution}} \times 10^6$$

  - If the density of the solution is 1g/ml, then 1 ppm = 1 mg solute per liter of solution.
- We can extend this again!
  - **Parts per billion (ppb)** can be expressed as the number of μg of solute per kilogram of solution.
  - By definition:

$$\text{Parts per billion (ppb) of component} = \frac{\text{mass of component in soln}}{\text{total mass of solution}} \times 10^9$$

  - If the density of the solution is 1g/ml, then 1 ppb = 1 μg solute per liter of solution.

### Mole Fraction, Molarity, and Molality[30,31,32,33]

- Common expressions of concentration are based on the number of moles of one or more components.
- Recall that mass can be converted to moles using the molar mass.
- Recall:

$$\text{Mole fraction of component, } X = \frac{\text{moles of component}}{\text{total moles of all components}}$$

  - Note: Mole fraction has no units.
  - Note: Mole fractions range from 0 to 1.
- Recall:

$$\text{Molarity, } M = \frac{\text{moles of solute}}{\text{liters of solution}}$$

---

[29] "Candy Sprinkles to Illustrate One Part Per Million" from Further Readings
[30] "An Alternative Introduction to the Mole Fraction" from Further Readings
[31] "Mole Fraction Analogies" from Further Readings
[32] Figure 13.19 from MediaPortfolio and Transparency Pack

- Note: Molarity will change with a change in temperature (as the solution volume increases or decreases).
- We can define **molality** ($m$), yet another concentration unit:

$$\text{Molality}, m = \frac{\text{moles of solute}}{\text{kilograms of solvent}}$$

  - Molality does not vary with temperature.
  - Note: converting between molarity ($M$) and molality ($m$) requires density.

## 13.5 Colligative Properties

- Colligative properties depend on number of solute particles.
- There are four colligative properties to consider:
  - Vapor pressure lowering (Raoult's Law).
  - Boiling point elevation.
  - Freezing point depression.
  - Osmotic pressure.

### Lowering the Vapor Pressure[34,35]

- Nonvolatile solutes (with no measurable vapor pressure) reduce the ability of the surface solvent molecules to escape the liquid.
  - Therefore, vapor pressure is lowered.
  - The amount of vapor pressure lowering depends on the amount of solute.
- **Raoult's law** quantifies the extent to which a nonvolatile solute lowers the vapor pressure of the solvent.
  - If $P_A$ is the vapor pressure with solute, $P^\circ_A$ is the vapor pressure of the pure solvent, and $X_A$ is the mole fraction of A, then

$$P_A = X_A P_A^o$$

- **Ideal solution**: one that obeys Raoult's law.
  - Real solutions show approximately ideal behavior when:
    - The solute concentration is low.
    - The solute and solvent have similarly sized molecules.
    - The solute and solvent have similar types of intermolecular attractions.
  - Raoult's law breaks down when the solvent-solvent and solute-solute intermolecular forces are much greater or weaker than solute-solvent intermolecular forces.

### Boiling-Point Elevation[36,37]

- A nonvolatile solute lowers the vapor pressure of a solution.
- At the normal boiling point of the pure liquid, the solution has a has a vapor pressure less than 1 atm.
  - Therefore, a higher temperature is required to reach a vapor pressure of 1 atm for the solution ($\Delta T_b$).
- The **molal boiling-point-elevation constant**, $K_b$, expresses how much $\Delta T_b$ changes with molality, $m$:

$$\Delta T_b = K_b m$$

- The boiling-point elevation is proportional to the concentration of solute particles.
  - A 1 $m$ solution of NaCl is 2 $m$ in total solute particles.

---

33 "Molarity Calculation" Activity from MediaPortfolio
34 Figure 13.20 from MediaPortfolio and Transparency Pack
35 "Boiling Point Elevation and Freezing Point Depression" Activity from MediaPortfolio
36 Figure 13.22 from MediaPortfolio and Transparency Pack
37 Table 13.4 from MediaPortfolio

## Freezing-Point Depression[38,39]

- When a solution freezes, crystals of almost pure solvent are formed first.
  - Solute molecules are usually not soluble in the solid phase of the solvent.
  - Therefore, the triple point occurs at a lower temperature because of the lower vapor pressure for the solution.
- The melting-point (freezing-point) curve is a vertical line from the triple point.
  - Therefore, the solution freezes at a lower temperature ($\Delta T_f$) than the pure solvent.
  - The decrease in freezing point ($\Delta T_f$) is directly proportional to molality.
- $K_f$ is the **molal freezing-point-depression constant**.

$$\Delta T_f = K_f m$$

## Osmosis[40,41,42,43,44,45,46,47]

- Semipermeable membranes permit passage of some components of a solution.
  - Often they permit passage of water but not larger molecules or ions.
  - Examples of semipermeable membranes are cell membranes and cellophane.
- **Osmosis** is the net movement of a solvent from an area of low solute concentration to an area of high solute concentration.
- Consider a U-shaped tube with a two liquids separated by a semipermeable membrane.
  - One arm of the tube contains pure solvent.
  - The other arm contains a solution.
  - There is movement of solvent in both directions across a semipermeable membrane.
    - The rate of movement of solvent from the pure solvent to the solution is faster than the rate of movement in the opposite direction.
  - As solvent moves across the membrane, the fluid levels in the arms become uneven.
    - The vapor pressure of solvent is higher in the arm with pure solvent.
  - Eventually the pressure difference due to the difference in height of liquid in the arms stops osmosis.
- **Osmotic pressure**, $\pi$, is the pressure required to prevent osmosis.
  - Osmotic pressure obeys a law similar in form to the ideal-gas law.
    - For $n$ moles, $V$= volume, $M$= molarity, $R$= the ideal gas constant, and an absolute temperature, $T$, the osmotic pressure is:

$$\pi V = nRT$$

$$\pi = \left(\frac{n}{V}\right)RT = MRT$$

  - Two solutions are said to be *isotonic* if they have the same osmotic pressure.
    - *Hypotonic* solutions have a lower $\pi$, relative to a more concentrated solution.
    - *Hypertonic* solutions have a higher $\pi$, relative to a more dilute solution.
- We can illustrate this with a biological system: red blood cells.

---

[38] "Antifreeze Solutions: The Colligative Properties of Antifreeze" from Further Readings
[39] "Freeze-Proof Bugs" from Further Readings
[40] "A Simple Demonstration Model of Osmosis" from Live Demonstrations
[41] "Osmotic Pressure of a Sugar Solution" from Live Demonstrations
[42] "Osmosis Through the Membrane of an Egg" from Live Demonstrations
[43] Figure 13.23 from MediaPortfolio
[44] Figure 13.24 from MediaPortfolio and Transparency Pack
[45] "Seawater Gets Fresh" from Further Readings
[46] Figure 13.25 from MediaPortfolio
[47] "Osmosis and the Egg Membrane" from Live Demonstrations

- Red blood cells are surrounded by semipermeable membranes.
  - If red blood cells are placed in a hypertonic solution (relative to intracellular solution), there is a lower solute concentration in the cell than the surrounding tissue.
    - Osmosis occurs and water passes through the membrane out of the cell.
    - The cell shrivels up.
    - This process is called *crenation.*
  - If red blood cells are placed in a hypotonic solution, there is a higher solute concentration in the cell than outside the cell.
    - Osmosis occurs and water moves into the cell.
    - The cell bursts (*hemolysis*).
- To prevent crenation or hemolysis, IV (intravenous) solutions must be isotonic relative to the intracellular fluids of cells.

- Everyday examples of osmosis include:
  - If a cucumber is placed in NaCl solution, it will lose water to shrivel up and become a pickle.
  - A limp carrot placed in water becomes firm because water enters via osmosis.
  - Eating large quantities of salty food causes retention of water and swelling of tissues (*edema*).
  - Water moves into plants, to a great extent, through osmosis.
  - Salt may be added to meat (or sugar added to fruit) as a preservative.
    - Salt prevents bacterial infection: A bacterium placed on the salt will lose water through osmosis and die.
  - *Active transport* is the movement of nutrients and waste material through a biological membrane against a concentration gradient.
    - Movement is from an area of low concentration to an area of high concentration.
    - Active transport is not spontaneous.
      - Energy must be expended by the cell to accomplish this.

### Determination of Molar Mass[48,49,50,51]

- Any of the four colligative properties may be used to determine molar mass.

## 13.6 Colloids[52,53,54]

- **Colloids** or **colloidal dispersions** are suspensions in which the suspended particles are larger than molecules but too small to separate out of the suspension due to gravity.
  - Particle size: 10 to 2000 Å.
- There are several types of colloids:
  - Aerosol: gas + liquid or solid (e.g., fog and smoke),
  - Foam: liquid + gas (e.g., whipped cream),
  - Emulsion: liquid + liquid (e.g., milk),
  - Sol: liquid + solid (e.g., paint),
  - Solid foam: solid + gas (e.g., marshmallow),
  - Solid emulsion: solid + liquid (e.g., butter),
  - Solid sol: solid + solid (e.g., ruby glass).
- **Tyndall effect**: ability of colloidal particles to scatter light.

---

[48] "Determination of Molar Mass" Activity from MediaPortfolio
[49] Figure 13.26 from MediaPortfolio and Transparency Pack
[50] "Salts Are Mostly NOT Ionized " from Further Readings
[51] "J. H van't Hoff" from Further Readings
[52] "Colloidal Systems" from Further Readings
[53] "Color of the Sunset: The Tyndall Effect" from Live Demonstrations
[54] Table 13.6 from MediaPortfolio

- The path of a beam of light projected through a colloidal suspension can be seen through the suspension.

## Hydrophilic and Hydrophobic Colloids[55,56,57,58,59,60]

- Focus on colloids in water.
  - Water-loving colloids: **hydrophilic**.
  - Water-hating colloids: **hydrophobic**.
- In the human body, large biological molecules such as proteins are kept in suspension by association with surrounding water molecules.
  - These macromolecules fold up so that hydrophobic groups are away from the water (inside the folded molecule).
  - Hydrophilic groups are on the surface of these molecules and interact with solvent (water) molecules.
    - Typical hydrophilic groups are polar (containing C–O, O–H, N–H bonds) or charged.
- Hydrophobic colloids need to be stabilized in water.
  - One way to stabilize hydrophobic colloids is to adsorb ions on their surface.
    - *Adsorption*: When something sticks to a surface we say that it is adsorbed.
  - If ions are adsorbed onto the surface of a colloid, the colloid appears hydrophilic and is stabilized in water.
  - Consider a small drop of oil in water.
    - Add a small amount of sodium stearate.
    - Sodium stearate has a long hydrophobic hydrocarbon tail and a small hydrophilic head.
    - The hydrophobic tail can be absorbed into the oil drop, leaving the hydrophilic head on the surface.
    - The hydrophilic heads then interact with the water and the oil drop is stabilized in water.
  - A soap acts in a similar fashion.
    - Soaps are molecules with long hydrophobic tails and hydrophilic heads that remove dirt by stabilizing the colloid in water.
    - Most dirt stains on people and clothing are oil-based.
- Biological application of this principle:
  - The gallbladder excretes a fluid called bile.
  - Bile contains substances (bile salts) that form an emulsion with fats in our small intestine.
  - Emulsifying agents help form an emulsion.
    - Emulsification of dietary fats and fat-soluble vitamins is important in their absorption and digestion by the body.

## Removal of Colloid Particles[61,62,63]

- We often need to separate colloidal particles from the dispersing medium.
- This may be problematic:
  - Colloid particles are too small to be separated by physical means (e.g., filtration).

---

[55] Figure 13.29 from MediaPortfolio
[56] Figure 13.30 from MediaPortfolio
[57] "Illustrating the Properties of Magic Sand" from Live Demonstrations
[58] Figure 13.31 from MediaPortfolio
[59] "Put the Brakes on Wastewater Emulsions" from Further Readings
[60] "Sodium Stearate" 3-D Model from MediaPortfolio
[61] "Chemistry and Physics in the Kitchen" from Further Readings
[62] "Clearly Cleaner" from Further Readings
[63] "Blood-Chemistry Tutorials: Teaching Biological Applications of General Chemistry Material" from Further Readings

- However, colloid particles often may be coagulated (enlarged) until they can be removed by filtration.
- Methods of coagulation include:
  - Colloid particles move more rapidly when the collodial dispersion is heated, increasing the number of collisions. The particles stick to each other when they collide.
  - Adding an electrolyte neutralizes the surface charges on the colloid particles.
- A biological application of another approach to separating colloidal particles from the suspending medium is dialysis.
  - In dialysis a semipermeable membrane is used to separate ions from colloidal particles.
  - In kidney dialysis, the blood is allowed to pass through a semipermeable membrane immersed in a washing solution.
  - The washing solution is isotonic in ions that must be retained.
  - The washing solution does not have the waste products that are found in the blood.
    - Wastes therefore dialyze out of the blood (move from the blood into the washing solution).
    - The "good" ions remain in the blood.

## Further Readings:

1. Jamil Ahmad, "Crystallization from a Supersaturated Solution of Sodium Acetate," *J. Chem. Educ.*, Vol. 77, **2000**, 1446.

2. Todd P. Silverstein, "Polarity, Miscibility, and Surface Tension," *J. Chem. Educ.*, Vol. 70., **1993**, 253.

3. Barry K. Thornton, "An Analogy to Illustrate Miscibility of Liquids," *J. Chem. Educ.*, Vol. 71, **1994**, 156.

4. Michael J. Sanger and Steven M. Badger III, "Using Computer-Based Visualization Strategies to Improve Students' Understanding of Molecular Polarity and Miscibility," *J. Chem. Educ.*, Vol. 78, **2001**, 1412–1416.

5. Doris R. Kimbrough, "Henry's Law and Noisy Knuckles," *J. Chem. Educ.*, Vol. 76, **1999**, 1509–1510.

6. James H. Cragin, "Soft Drink Bubbles," *J. Chem. Educ.*, Vol. 60, **1983**, 71. A short Henry's Law reference.

7. Clifton E Meloan, Mindy L. Meloan, and John M. Meloan, "Candy Sprinkles to Illustrate One Part Per Million," *J. Chem. Educ.*, Vol. 71, **1994**, 658.

8. Alvin D. White, "An Alternative Introduction to the Mole Fraction," *J. Chem. Educ.*, Vol. 59, **1982**, 153.

9. Ronald DeLorenzo, "Mole Fraction Analogies," *J. Chem. Educ.*, Vol. 57, **1980**, 733.

10. Sarah F. McDuffie and Catherine E. Matthews, "Antifreeze Solutions: The Colligative Properties of Antifreeze," *The Science Teacher*, Vol. 63, **1996**, 41–43.

11. Ronald DeLorenzo, "Freeze-Proof Bugs," *J. Chem. Educ.*, Vol. 58, **1981**, 788.

12. Stephen J. Hawkes, "Salts are Mostly NOT Ionized," *J. Chem. Educ.*, Vol. 73, **1996**, 421–423.

13. W. A. E. McBryde, "J. H. van't Hoff," *J. Chem. Educ.*, Vol. 64, **1987**, 573–575.

14. Gerald Parkinson, Charlene Crabb, and Takeshi Kamiya, "Seawater Gets Fresh," *Chemical Engineering*, Vol. 106(3), **March, 1999**, 32–35. An article that looks at the role of desalination and reverse osmosis in providing drinking water.

15. Jerry Sarquis, "Colloidal Systems," *J. Chem. Educ.*, Vol. 57, **1980**, 602–605.

16. Jia-Qian Jiang and Nigel Graham, "Clearly Cleaner," *Chemistry in Britain*, Vol. 34(3), **March 1998**, 38–41. An article that explores the use of coagulants to help treat water.

17. Nicholas Kurti and Herve´ This-Benckhard, "Chemistry and Physics in the Kitchen," *Scientific American*, **April 1994**, 66–71.

18. Rachel E. Casiday, Dewey Holten, Richard Krathen, and Regina F. Frey, "Blood–Chemistry Tutorials: Teaching Biological Applications of General Chemistry Material," *J. Chem. Educ.*, Vol. 78, **2001**, 1210–1214. The relationship between oxygen transport, iron transport, blood buffering, kidney dialysis and general chemistry topics is discussed.

19. George Alther, "Put the Brakes On Wastewater Emulsions," *Chemical Engineering*, Vol. 105(3), **1998**, 82–88.

## Live Demonstrations:

1. Lee R. Summerlin, Christie L. Borgford, and Julie B. Ealy, "Supersaturation," *Chemical Demonstrations, A Sourcebook for Teachers, Volume 2* (Washington: American Chemical Society, **1988**), pp. 121–122. Disruption of a supersaturated solution of sodium acetate results in a sudden formation of solid in this demonstration.

2. Bassam Z. Shakhashiri, "Crystallization from Supersaturated Solutions of Sodium Acetate," *Chemical Demonstrations: A Handbook for Teachers of Chemistry, Volume 1* (Madison: The University of Wisconsin Press, **1983**), pp. 27–30.

3. Lee. R. Summerlin,, Christie L. Borgford, and Julie B. Ealy, "Copper Sulfate: Blue to White," *Chemical Demonstrations, A Sourcebook for Teachers*, *Volume 2* (Washington: American Chemical Society, **1988**), pp. 69–70. An exploration of color change associated with the dehydration of copper sulfate.

4. Walter H. Corkern and Linda L Munchausen, "Solubility of Alcohols," *J. Chem. Educ.*, Vol. 69, **1992**, 928. An overhead projector demonstration of solubility.

5. Lee. R. Summerlin, Christie L. Borgford, and Julie B. Ealy, "Nonadditivity of Volumes," *Chemical Demonstrations, A Sourcebook for Teachers*, *Volume 2* (Washington: American Chemical Society, **1988**), p.14. Two miscible liquids are mixed and the final volume measured in this short demonstration.

6. Katia Pravia and David F. Maynard, "Why Don't Water and Oil Mix?" *J. Chem. Educ.*, Vol. 73, **1996**, 497. A simple overhead projector demonstration.

7. Bassam Z. Shakhashiri, "Effect of Temperature and Pressure on the Solubility of Gases in Liquids," *Chemical Demonstrations: A Handbook for Teachers of Chemistry, Volume 3* (Madison: The University of Wisconsin Press, **1989**), pp. 280–282.

8. Bassam Z. Shakhashiri, "Osmosis Through the Membrane of an Egg," *Chemical Demonstrations: A Handbook for Teachers of Chemistry, Volume 3* (Madison: The University of Wisconsin Press, **1989**), pp. 283–285.

9. Lee. R. Summerlin, Christie L. Borgford, and Julie B. Ealy, "Osmosis and the Egg Membrane," *Chemical Demonstrations, A Sourcebook for Teachers*, *Volume 2* (Washington: American Chemical Society, **1988**), pp. 136–137. Movement of water through the membrane of an egg is explored in this demonstration of osmosis.

10. Bassam Z. Shakhashiri, "Osmotic Pressure of a Sugar Solution," *Chemical Demonstrations: A Handbook for Teachers of Chemistry, Volume 3* (Madison: The University of Wisconsin Press, **1989**), pp. 286–289. A sugar solution placed in dialysis tubing is used to demonstrate osmotic pressure.

11. Joseph G. Morse, "A Simple Demonstration Model of Osmosis," *J. Chem. Educ.*, Vol. 76, **1999**, 64–65.

12. Bassam Z. Shakhashiri, "Color of the Sunset: The Tyndall Effect," *Chemical Demonstrations: A Handbook for Teachers of Chemistry, Volume 3* (Madison: The University of Wisconsin Press, **1989**), pp. 353–357. Several procedures for demonstrating the Tyndall Effect are presented in this demonstration.

13. Robert H. Goldsmith, "Illustrating the Properties of Magic Sand," *J. Chem. Educ.*, Vol. 76, **1999**, 41. An overhead projector demonstration illustrating the differences between hydrophobic and hydrophilic materials.

# Chapter 14. Chemical Kinetics

## Media Resources

### Figures and Tables

| **In Transparency Pack and on MediaPortfolio:** | **Section:** |
|---|---|
| Table 14.1 Rate Data for Reaction of $C_4H_9Cl$ with Water | 14.2 Reaction Rates |
| Figure 14.4 Concentration of Butyl Chloride as a Function of Time | 14.2 Reaction Rates |
| Figure 14.5 Basic Components of a Spectrometer | 14.2 Reaction Rates |
| Table 14.2 Rate Data for the Reaction of Ammonium and Nitrate Ions in Water at 25°C | 14.3 Concentration and Rate |
| Figure 14.7 Partial Pressure of $CH_3NC$ With Time | 14.4 The Change of Concentration with Time |
| Figure 14.8 Plots of Kinetic Data for the Decomposition of $NO_2$ | 14.4 The Change of Concentration with Time |
| Figure 14.12 Variation in Rate Constant As a Function of Temperature | 14.5 Temperature and Rate |
| Figure 14.13 Collision of Cl and NOCl | 14.5 Temperature and Rate |
| Figure 14.15 Energy Profile for Rearrangement Of Methyl Isonitrile | 14.5 Temperature and Rate |
| Figure 14.16 Kinetic Energies of Gas Molecules | 14.5 Temperature and Rate |
| Figure 14.20 Energy Profiles for an Uncatalyzed And a Catalyzed Reaction | 14.7 Catalysis |
| Figure 14.21 Mechanism of Catalysis | 14.7 Catalysis |
| Figure 14.24 Lock-And-Key Model for Enzymes | 14.7 Catalysis |
| Figure 14.26 Nitrogen Cycle | 14.7 Catalysis |

| **On MediaPortfolio:** | **Section:** |
|---|---|
| Figure 14.3 Progress of a Hypothetical Reaction | 14.2 Reaction Rates |
| Figure 14.9 Pressure of Methyl Isonitrile as a Function of Time | 14.4 The Change of Concentration with Time |
| Figure 14.17 Ln of Rate Constant as a Function of $1/T$ | 14.6 Reaction Mechanisms |
| Table 14.3 Elementary Steps and Their Rate Laws | 14.6 Reaction Mechanisms |

| **Animations:** | **Section:** |
|---|---|
| Bimolecular Reaction | 14.6 Reaction Mechanisms |
| Surface Reactions–Hydrogenation | 14.7 Catalysis |

| **Movie:** | **Section:** |
|---|---|
| Catalysis | 14.7 Catalysis |

| **Activities:** | **Section:** |
|---|---|
| Decomposition of $N_2O_5$ | 14.2 Reaction Rates |
| Rates of Reactions | 14.3 Concentration and Rate |
| Integrated Rate Law | 14.4 The Changes of Concentration with Time |
| Rates of Reaction | 14.5 Temperature and Rate |
| Arrhenius Activity | 14.5 Temperature and Rate |

| | |
|---|---|
| Bimolecular Reaction | 14.6 Reaction Mechanisms |

## Other Resources

| Further Readings: | Section: |
|---|---|
| The Fizz Keeper, a Case Study in Chemical Education, Equilibrium, and Kinetics | 14.1 Factors that Affect Reaction Rates |
| Inflation Rates, Car Devaluation, and Chemical Kinetics | 14.3 Concentration and Rate |
| An Analogy to Help Students Understand Reaction Orders | 14.3 Concentration and Rate |
| Mice in the Box for Zero-Order Kinetics | 14.3 Concentration and Rate |
| Don't Be Tricked by Your Integrated Rate Plot | 14.4 The Change of Concentration with Time |
| Light Sticks | 14.5 Temperature and Rate |
| The Collision Theory and an American Tradition | 14.5 Temperature and Rate |
| Audience-Appropriate Analogies: Collision Theory | 14.5 Temperature and Rate |
| The Arrhenius Law and Storage of Food | 14.5 Temperature and Rate |
| Just What Is a Transition State? | 14.5 Temperature and Rate |
| Pictorial Analogies XIII: Kinetics and Mechanisms | 14.6 Reaction Mechanisms |
| Doing the Dishes: An Analogy for Use in Teaching Reaction Kinetics | 14.6 Reaction Mechanisms |
| Another Auto Analogy: Rate-Determining Steps | 14.6 Reaction Mechanisms |
| Auto Analogies | 14.6 Reaction Mechanisms |
| Catalysis | 14.7 Catalysis |
| Catalysis on Surfaces | 14.7 Catalysis |
| Solid Acid Catalysts | 14.7 Catalysis |
| Catalysis: New Reaction Pathways, Not Just a Lowering of the Activation Energy | 14.7 Catalysis |
| Practical Enzyme Kinetics | 14.7 Catalysis |
| Environmental Catalysts | |
| Breaking Bonds versus Chopping Heads: The Enzyme as Butcher | 14.7 Catalysis |
| Enzyme Activity: A Simple Analogy | 14.7 Catalysis |
| The Catalytic Function of Enzymes | 14.7 Catalysis |
| Enzyme Catalysis: Cleaner, Safer, Energy Efficient | 14.7 Catalysis |
| Biocatalysis Makes Headway in Chemicals | 14.7 Catalysis |
| Getting Auto Exhausts to Pristine | 14.7 Catalysis |

| Live Demonstrations: | Section: |
|---|---|
| Appearing Red | 14.1 Factors that Affect Reaction Rates |
| A New Twist on the Iodine Clock Reaction: Determining the Order of a Reaction | 14.1 Factors that Affect Reaction Rates |
| Hydrogen Peroxide Iodine Clock: Oxidation of Potassium Iodide by Hydrogen Peroxide | 14.1 Factors that Affect Reaction Rates |
| The Starch-Iodine Clock Reaction | 14.1 Factors that Affect Reaction Rates |
| Lightsticks | 14.5 Temperature and Rate |
| Cool-Light Chemiluminescence | 14.5 Temperature and Rate |

| | |
|---|---|
| Catalytic Decomposition of Hydrogen Peroxide: Foam Production | 14.7 Catalysis |
| Enzyme Kinetics: Effects of Temperature and an Inhibitoron Catalase Extracted from Potato | 14.7 Catalysis |

# Chapter 14. Chemical Kinetics

## Common Student Misconceptions

- It is possible for mathematics to get in the way of some students' understanding of the chemistry of this chapter.
- Students often assume that reaction orders may be determined from stoichiometric coefficients.
- Students often confuse intermediates and transition states.
- Students often confuse adsorption and absorption.

## Lecture Outline

### 14.1 Factors that Affect Reaction Rates[1,2,3,4,5]

- **Chemical kinetics** is the study of how fast chemical reactions occur.
- There are several important factors which affect rates of reactions:
  - Physical state of the reactants.
  - Concentration of the reactants.
  - Temperature of the reaction.
  - Presence or absence of a catalyst.
- Goal: to understand chemical reactions at the molecular level.

### 14.2 Reaction Rates[6]

- The speed of a reaction is defined as the change that occurs per unit time.
  - It is often determined by measuring the change in concentration of a reactant or product with time.
  - The speed of the chemical reaction is its **reaction rate**.
- For a reaction A → B

$$\text{Average rate with respect to B} = \frac{\text{Change in the concentration of B}}{\text{Change in time}}$$

  - Here the change in the concentration of B is defined as:

  Δ (concentration of B) = (concentration of B at final time) – (concentration of B at initial time)
- Illustrate this with an example:
  - Suppose A reacts to form B. Let us begin with 1.00 $M$ A.
  - At $t = 0$ (time zero) there is 1.00 $M$ A and no B present.
  - At $t = 20$ sec, there is 0.54 $M$ A and 0.46 $M$ B.
  - At $t = 40$ sec, there is 0.30 $M$ A and 0.70 $M$ B.
  - We can uses this information to find the average rate with respect to B:

---

1 "Appearing Red" from Live Demonstrations

2 "A New Twist on the Iodine Clock Reaction: Determining the Order of a Reaction" from Live Demonstrations

3 "Hydrogen Peroxide Iodine Clock: Oxidation of Potassium Iodide by Hydrogen Peroxide" from Live Demonstrations

4 "The Starch-Iodine Clock Reaction" from Live Demonstrations

5 "The Fizz Keeper, a Case Study in Chemical Education, Equilibrium, and Kinetics" from Further Readings

6 Figure 14.3 from MediaPortfolio

$$\text{Avg Rate} = \frac{\Delta\,(\text{Conc B})}{\Delta t} = \frac{(\text{Conc of B at } t = 20s) - (\text{Conc of B at } t = 0\text{ s})}{20s - 0\text{ min}}$$

- For the reaction A → B there are two ways of measuring rate:
  - The rate of appearance of product B (i.e., change in moles of B per unit time) as in the preceding example.

$$\text{Avg Rate} = \frac{0.46\text{M} - 0.00\text{ M}}{20\text{ s} - 0\text{ s}} = 0.023\frac{\text{M}}{\text{s}}$$

  - The rate of disappearance of reactant A (i.e., the change in moles of A per unit time).

$$\text{Average Rate} = \frac{-\Delta[A]}{\Delta t}$$

  - Note the negative sign! This reminds us that rate is being expressed in terms of the d*isappearance* of a reactant.
  - A plot of number of moles versus time shows that as the reactants (A) disappear, the products (B) appear.

## Change of Rate with Time[7,8]

- In most chemical reactions we will determine the reaction rate by monitoring a change in concentration (of a reactant or product).
  - The most useful unit to use for rate is molarity.
    - Since volume is constant, molarity and moles are directly proportional.
  - Consider the following reaction:

$$C_4H_9Cl(aq) + H_2O(l) \rightarrow C_4H_9OH(aq) + HCl(aq)$$

  - We can calculate the average rate in terms of the disappearance of $C_4H_9Cl$.
  - The units for average rate are mol/L·s or *M/s*.
  - The average rate decreases with time.
  - We can plot $[C_4H_9Cl]$ versus time.
    - The rate at any instant in time is called the **instantaneous rate.**
    - It is the slope of the straight line tangent to the curve at that instant.
    - Instantaneous rate is different from average rate.
      - It is the rate at that particular instant in time.
      - For our discussion we will call the "instantaneous rate" the rate, unless otherwise indicated.

## Reaction Rates and Stoichiometry[9,10]

- For the reaction:

$$C_4H_9Cl(aq) + H_2O(l) \rightarrow C_4H_9OH(aq) + HCl(aq)$$

  - The rate of appearance of $C_4H_9OH$ must equal the rate of disappearance of $C_4H_9Cl$.

$$\text{Rate} = -\frac{\Delta[C_4H_9Cl]}{\Delta t} = \frac{\Delta[C_4H_9OH]}{\Delta t}$$

- What if the stoichiometric relationships are not one-to-one?
  - For the reaction:

$$2HI(g) \rightarrow H_2(g) + I_2(g)$$

---

[7] Table 14.1 from MediaPortfolio and Transparency Pack
[8] Figure 14.4 from MediaPortfolio and Transparency Pack
[9] "Decomposition of $N_2O_5$" Activity from MediaPortfolio
[10] Figure 14.5 from MediaPortfolio and Transparency Pack

- The rate may be expressed as:

$$\text{Rate} = -\frac{1}{2}\frac{\Delta[\text{HI}]}{\Delta t} = \frac{\Delta[\text{H}_2]}{\Delta t} = \frac{\Delta[\text{I}_2]}{\Delta t}$$

- We can generalize this equation a bit.
  - For the reaction:

$$aA + bB \rightarrow cC + dD$$

  - The rate may be expressed as:

$$\text{Rate} = -\frac{1}{a}\frac{\Delta[A]}{\Delta t} = -\frac{1}{b}\frac{\Delta[B]}{\Delta t} = \frac{1}{c}\frac{\Delta[C]}{\Delta t} = \frac{1}{d}\frac{\Delta[D]}{\Delta t}$$

## 14.3 Concentration and Rate[11,12,13]

- In general, rates:
  - Increase when reactant concentration is increased.
  - Decrease as the concentration of reactants is reduced.
- We often examine the effect of concentration on reaction rate by measuring the way in which reaction rate at the beginning of a reaction depends on starting conditions.
- Consider the reaction:

$$NH_4^+(aq) + NO_2^-(aq) \rightarrow N_2(g) + 2H_2O(l)$$

  - We measure initial reaction rates.
    - The initial rate is the instantaneous rate at time $t = 0$.
  - We find this at various initial concentrations of each reactant.
  - As $[NH_4^+]$ doubles with $[NO_2^-]$ constant the rate doubles.
    - We conclude the rate is proportional to $[NH_4^+]$.
  - As $[NO_2^-]$ doubles with $[NH_4^+]$ constant the rate doubles.
    - We conclude that the rate is proportional to $[NO_2^-]$.
- The overall concentration dependence of reaction rate is given in a **rate law** or rate expression.
  - For our example, the rate law is:

$$\text{Rate} = k[NH_4^+][NO_2^-]$$

  - The proportionality constant $k$ is called the **rate constant.**
  - Once we have determined the rate law and the rate constant, we can use them to calculate initial reaction rates under any set of initial concentrations.

### Exponents in the Rate Law[14,15]

- For a general reaction with rate law:

$$\text{Rate} = k[\text{reactant 1}]^m[\text{reactant 2}]^n$$

- The exponents $m$ and $n$ are called **reaction orders.**
  - The **overall reaction order** is the sum of the reaction orders.
    - The overall order of reaction is $m + n + \ldots$.
  - For the reaction:

$$NH_4^+(aq) + NO_2^-(aq) \rightarrow N_2(g) + 2H_2O(l)$$

  - The reaction is said to be first order in $[NH_4^+]$, first order in $[NO_2^-]$, and second order overall.
- Note that reaction orders must be determined experimentally.

---

[11] "Inflation Rates, Car Devaluation, and Chemical Kinetics" from Further Readings
[12] Table 14.2 from MediaPortfolio and Transparency Pack
[13] "Rates of Reactions" Activity from MediaPortfolio
[14] "An Analogy to Help Students Understand Reaction Orders" from Further Readings
[15] "Mice in the Box for Zero-Order Kinetics" from Further Readings

- They do not necessarily correspond to the stoichiometric coefficients in the balanced chemical equation!
- We commonly encounter reaction orders of 0, 1 or 2.
- Even fractional or negative values are possible.

### Units of Rate Constants

- Units of the rate constant depend on the overall reaction order.
- For example, for a reaction that is second order overall:
- Units of rate are:

$$\text{Units of rate} = (\text{Units of rate constant})(\text{Units of concentration})^2$$

$$\text{Units of rate constant} = \frac{(\text{Units of rate})}{(\text{Units of concration})^2} = \frac{M/s}{M^2} = M^{-1}s^{-1}$$

- Thus the units of the rate constant are:

### Using Initial Rates to Determine Rate Laws

- To determine the rate law, we observe the effect of changing initial concentrations.
  - If a reaction is zero order in a reactant, changing the initial concentration of that reactant will have no effect on rate (as long as *some* reactant is present).
  - If a reaction is first order, doubling the concentration will cause the rate to double.
  - If a reaction is second order, doubling the concentration will result in a $2^2$ increase in rate.
    - Similarly, tripling the concentration results in a $3^2$ increase in rate.
  - A reaction is *n*th order if doubling the concentration causes a $2^n$ increase in rate.
- Note that the rate, not the rate constant, depends on concentration.
- The rate constant IS affected by temperature and by the presence of a catalyst.

## 14.4 The Change of Concentration with Time

- Goal: Convert the rate law into a convenient equation that gives concentration as a function of time.

### First-Order Reactions[16,17]

- For a **first-order reaction**, the rate doubles as the concentration of a reactant doubles.
  - Therefore:

$$\text{Rate} = -\frac{\Delta[A]}{\Delta t} = k[A]$$

  - Integrating:

$$\int_{[A]_0}^{[A]_t} \frac{d[A]}{[A]} = -k\int_0^t dt$$

  - We get:

$$\ln[A]_t - \ln[A]_0 = -kt$$

  - Rearranging:

$$\ln[A]_t = -kt + \ln[A]_0$$

  - An alternate form:

$$\ln\frac{[A]_t}{[A]_0} = -kt$$

---

16 "Integrated Rate Law" Activity from MediaPortfolio

17 "Don't be Tricked by Your Integrated Rate Plot!" from Further Readings

- A plot of $\ln[A]_t$ versus t is a straight line with slope $-k$ and intercept $\ln[A]_0$.
- Note that in this equation we use the natural logarithm, ln (log to the base *e*).

## Second-Order Reactions[18,19]

- A **second-order reaction** is one whose rate depends on the reactant concentration to the second power or on the concentration of two reactants, each raised to the first power.
- For a second-order reaction with just one reactant:

$$\text{Rate} = -\frac{\Delta[A]}{\Delta t} = k[A]^2$$

- Integrating,

$$\int_{[A]_0}^{[A]_t} \frac{d[A]}{[A]^2} = -k\int_0^t dt$$

- We get:

$$\frac{1}{[A]_t} = kt + \frac{1}{[A]_0}$$

- A plot of $1/[A]_t$ versus $t$ is a straight line with slope $k$ and intercept $1/[A]_0$.
  - For a second order reaction, a plot of $\ln[A]_t$ vs. $t$ is not linear.
- Note that a second-order process can have a rate constant expression of the form:

$$\text{Rate} = k[A][B]$$

- That is, the reaction is second order overall, but has first order dependence on A and B.

## Half-life[20]

- **Half-life**, $t_{1/2}$, is the time required for the concentration of a reactant to decrease to half its original value.
  - That is, half life, $t_{1/2}$, is the time taken for $[A]_0$ to reach ½ $[A]_0$.
  - Mathematically, the half life of a first-order reaction is:

$$\ln\frac{[A]_t}{[A]_0} = -kt$$

$$\text{So, for } t = t_{1/2} \text{ and } [A]_t = 1/2[A]_0$$

$$\ln\frac{1/2[A]_0}{[A]_0} = -kt_{1/2}$$

$$\ln 1/2 = -kt_{1/2}$$

$$\therefore t_{1/2} = -\frac{\ln 1/2}{k} = \frac{0.693}{k}$$

[18] Figure 14.7 from MediaPortfolio and Transparency Pack
[19] Figure 14.8 from MediaPortfolio and Transparency Pack
[20] Figure 14.9 from MediaPortfolio

- Note that the half-life of a first-order reaction is independent of the initial concentration of the reactant.
- We can show that the half-life of a second order reaction is:
- Note that the half-life of a second-order reaction is dependent on the initial concentration of reactant.

## 14.5 Temperature and Rate[21,22,23]

- Most reactions speed up as temperature increases.
- We can illustrate this with chemiluminescent Cyalume® light sticks.
  - A chemiluminescent reaction produces light.
  - Two light sticks are placed in water, one at room temperature and one in ice.
    - The one at room temperature is brighter than the one in ice.
    - Its luminescence also fades more quickly.
  - The chemical reaction responsible for chemiluminescence is dependent on temperature, the higher the temperature, the faster the reaction and the brighter the light.

$$t_{1/2} = \frac{1}{k[A]_0}$$

- As temperature increases, the rate increases.
- How is the relationship between temperature and rate reflected in the rate expression?
  - The rate law has no temperature term in it, so the rate constant must depend on temperature.
  - Consider the first-order reaction $CH_3NC \rightarrow CH_3CN$.
    - As temperature increases from 190°C to 250°C the rate constant increases.
      - The temperature effect is quite dramatic.
      - We see an approximate doubling of the rate with each 10°C increase in temperature.

### The Collision Model[24,25,26,27]

- Rates of reactions are affected by concentration and temperature.
- We need to develop a model that explains this observation.
- An explanation is provided by the **collision model**, based on kinetic-molecular theory.
  - In order for molecules to react they must collide.
  - The greater the number of collisions the faster the rate.
  - The more molecules present, the greater the probability of collision and the faster the rate.
    - Thus reaction rate should increase with an increase in the concentration of reactant molecules.
  - The higher the temperature, the more energy available to the molecules and the more frequently the molecules collide.
    - Thus reaction rate should increase with an increase in temperature.
  - However, not all collisions lead to products.
    - In fact, only a small fraction of collisions lead to products.
    - In order for a reaction to occur the reactant molecules must collide in the correct orientation and with enough energy to form products.

### The Orientation Factor[28]

---

[21] "Lightsticks" from Live Demonstrations
[22] "Cool-Light Chemiluminescence" from Live Demonstrations
[23] "Light Sticks" from Further Readings
[24] "Rates of Reaction" Activity from MediaPortfolio
[25] "The Collision Theory and an American Tradition" from Further Readings
[26] Figure 14.12 from MediaPortfolio and Transparency Pack
[27] "Audience-Appropriate Analogies: Collision Theory" from Further Readings

- The orientation of a molecule during collision can have a profound effect on whether or not a reaction occurs.
- Consider the reaction between Cl and NOCl:
  - If the Cl collides with the Cl of NOCl, the products are $Cl_2$ and NO.
  - If the Cl collides with the O of NOCl, no products are formed.

## Activation Energy[29,30,31,32,33]

- Arrhenius: Molecules must posses a minimum amount of energy to react. Why?
  - In order to form products, bonds must be broken in the reactants.
  - Bond breakage requires energy.
  - Molecules moving too slowly, with too little kinetic energy, don't react when they collide.
- **Activation energy, $E_a$,** is the minimum energy required to initiate a chemical reaction.
  - $E_a$ will vary with the reaction.
- Consider the rearrangement of methyl isonitrile to form acetonitrile:
  - Energy is required to stretch the bond between the $CH_3$ group and the N≡C group to allow the N≡C to rotate.
  - The C–C bond begins to form.
  - The energy associated with the molecule drops.
  - The energy barrier between the starting molecule and the highest energy state found along the reaction pathway is the activation energy.
    - The species at the top of the barrier is called the **activated complex** or **transition state.**
  - The change in energy for the reaction is the difference in energy between $CH_3NC$ and $CH_3CN$.
    - $\Delta E_{rxn}$ has no effect on reaction rate.
  - The activation energy is the difference in energy between reactants, ($CH_3NC$) and the transition state.
    - The rate depends on the magnitude of the $E_a$.
      - In general, the lower the $E_a$, the faster the rate.
- Notice that if a forward reaction is exothermic ($CH_3NC \rightarrow CH_3CN$), then the reverse reaction is endothermic ($CH_3CN \rightarrow CH_3NC$).
- How does this relate to temperature?
  - At any particular temperature, the molecules present have an average kinetic energy associated with the population.
  - In the same distribution, some molecules have less energy than the average while others have more than the average value.
    - The fraction of molecules with an energy equal to or greater than $E_a$ is given by:

$$f = e^{\frac{-Ea}{RT}}$$

  - Molecules that have an energy equal to or greater than $\Delta E_a$ have sufficient energy to react.
  - As we increase the temperature, the fraction of the population that has an energy equal to or greater than $E_a$ increases.
    - Thus more molecules can react.

## The Arrhenius Equation

---

[28] Figure 14.13 from MediaPortfolio and Transparency Pack
[29] "Arrhenius Activity" Activity from MediaPortfolio
[30] "Just What Is a Transition State?" from Further Readings
[31] Figure 14.15 from MediaPortfolio and Transparency Pack
[32] "Figure 14.16 from MediaPortfolio and Transparency Pack
[33] "The Arrhenius Law and Storage of Food" from Further Readings

- Arrhenius discovered that most reaction-rate data obeyed an equation based on three factors:
  - The number of collisions per unit time.
  - The fraction of collisions that occur with the correct orientation.
  - The fraction of the colliding molecules that have an energy equal to or greater than $\Delta E_a$.
- From these observations Arrhenius developed the **Arrhenius equation**.

$$k = Ae^{\frac{-Ea}{RT}}$$

  - Where $k$ is the rate constant, $E_a$ is the activation energy, $R$ is the ideal-gas constant (8.314 J/K·mol) and $T$ is the temperature in K.
  - $A$ is called the **frequency factor**.
    - It is related to the frequency of collisions and the probability that a collision will have a favorable orientation.
  - Both $A$ and $E_a$ are *specific to a given reaction.*

### Determining the Activation Energy[34]

- $E_a$ may be determined experimentally.
  - We need to take the natural log of both sides of the Arrhenius equation:

$$\ln k = -\frac{E_a}{RT} + \ln A$$

  - A graph of ln $k$ vs $1/T$ will have a slope of $-E_a/R$ and a y-intercept of ln $A$.
- Alternatively we can use:

$$\ln\frac{k_1}{k_2} = \frac{Ea}{R}\left(\frac{1}{T_2} - \frac{1}{T_1}\right)$$

## 14.6 Reaction Mechanisms[35,36]

- The balanced chemical equation provides information about substances present at the beginning and end of the reaction.
- The **reaction mechanism** is the process by which the reaction occurs.
- Mechanisms provide a picture of which bonds are broken and formed during the course of a reaction.

### Elementary Steps[37]

- **Elementary steps** are any processes that occur in a single step.
- The number of molecules present in an elementary step is the **molecularity** of that elementary step.
  - **Unimolecular**: one molecule in the elementary step.
  - **Bimolecular**: two molecules in the elementary step.
  - **Termolecular**: three molecules in the elementary step.
    - It is not common to see termolecular processes (statistically improbable).

### Multistep Mechanisms

- A multistep mechanism consists of a sequence of elementary steps.
  - The elementary steps must add to give the balanced chemical equation.
  - Some multistep mechanisms will include **intermediates.**
  - These are species that appear in an elementary step but are neither a reactant nor product.
  - Intermediates are formed in one elementary step and consumed in another.

---

[34] Figure 14.17 from MediaPortfolio
[35] "Pictorial Analogies XIII: Kinetics and Mechanisms" from Further Readings
[36] "Doing the Dishes: An Analogy for Use in Teaching Reaction Kinetics" from Further Readings
[37] "Bimolecular Reaction" Animation from MediaPortfolio

- They are not found in the balanced equation for the overall reaction.

## Rate Laws for Elementary Steps[38]

- The rate laws of the elementary steps determine the overall rate law of the reaction.
- The rate law of an elementary step is determined by its molecularly.
  - Unimolecular processes are first order.
  - Bimolecular processes are second order.
  - Termolecular processes are third order.

## Rate Laws for Multistep Mechanisms[39,40]

- Most reactions occur by mechanisms with more than one elementary step.
  - Often one step is much slower than the others.
  - The slow step limits the overall reaction rate.
    - This is called the **rate-determining step** (rate-limiting step) of the reaction.
    - This step governs the overall rate law for the overall reaction.
- Consider the reaction:

$$NO_2(g) + CO(g) \rightarrow NO(g) + CO_2(g)$$

  - The experimentally derived rate law is: Rate = $k[NO_2]^2$
  - We propose a mechanism for the reaction:
    - Step 1: $NO_2(g) + NO_2(g) \xrightarrow{k_1} NO_3(g) + NO(g)$ slow step
    - Step 2: $NO_3(g) + CO(g) \xrightarrow{k_2} NO_2(g) + CO_2(g)$ fast step
    - Note that $NO_3$ is an intermediate.
  - If $k_2 >> k_1$, then the overall reaction rate will depend on the first step (the rate-determining step).
    - Rate = $k_1[NO_2]^2$
    - This theoretical rate law is in agreement with the experimental rate law.
    - This supports (but does not prove) our mechanism.

## Mechanisms with an Initial Fast Step

- Consider the reaction:

$$2NO(g) + Br_2(g) \rightarrow 2NOBr(g)$$

  - The experimentally determined rate law is:

$$\text{Rate} = k[NO]^2[Br_2]$$

  - Consider the following proposed mechanism:
    - Step 1: $NO(g) + Br_2(g) \underset{k_{-1}}{\overset{k_1}{\rightleftharpoons}} NOBr_2(g)$ fast step
    - Step 2: $NOBr_2(g) + NO(g) \xrightarrow{k_2} 2NOBr(g)$ slow step
    - The theoretical rate law for this mechanism is based on the rate-determining step, step 2:

$$\text{Rate} = k_2[NOBr_2][NO]$$

  - Problem: This rate law depends on the concentration of an intermediate species.
    - Intermediates are usually unstable and have low/unknown concentrations.
    - We need to find a way to remove this term from our rate law.

---

[38] Table 14.3 from MediaPortfolio
[39] "Auto Analogies" from Further Readings
[40] "Another Auto Analogy: Rate-Determining Steps" from Further Readings

- We can express the concentration of [$NOBr_2$] in terms of NOBr and $Br_2$ by assuming that there is an equilibrium in step 1.
- In a dynamic equilibrium, the forward rate equals the reverse rate.
  - Therefore, by definition of equilibrium we get:

$$k_1[NO][Br_2] = k_{-1}[NOBr_2]$$

  - Rearranging we get:

$$[NOBr_2] = \frac{k_1}{k_{-1}}[NO][Br_2]$$

  - Therefore, the overall rate law becomes

$$\text{Rate} = k_2 \frac{k_1}{k_{-1}}[NO][Br_2][NO] = k[NO]^2[Br_2]$$

- Note the final rate law is consistent with the experimentally observed rate law.

## 14.7 Catalysis[41,42]

- A **catalyst** is a substance that changes the rate of a chemical reaction without itself undergoing a permanent chemical change in the process.
- There are two types of catalyst.
  - Homogeneous.
  - Heterogeneous.
- Catalysts are common in the body, in the environment, and in the chemistry lab!

### Homogeneous Catalysis[43,44,45]

- A **homogeneous catalyst** is one that is present in the same phase as the reacting molecules.
- For example, hydrogen peroxide decomposes very slowly in the absence of a catalyst:

$$2H_2O_2(aq) \rightarrow 2H_2O(l) + O_2(g)$$

- In the presence of bromide ion, the decomposition occurs rapidly in acidic solution:

$$2Br^-(aq) + H_2O_2(aq) + 2H^+(aq) \rightarrow Br_2(aq) + 2H_2O(l)$$
$$Br_2(aq) + H_2O_2(aq) \rightarrow 2Br^-(aq) + 2H^+(aq) + O_2(g)$$

  - $Br^-$ is a catalyst because it is regenerated at the end of the reaction.
  - The net reaction is still:

$$2H_2O_2(aq) \rightarrow 2H_2O(l) + O_2(g)$$

- How do catalysts increase reaction rates?
  - In general, catalysts operate by lowering the overall activation energy for a reaction.
  - However, catalysts can operate by increasing the number of effective collisions.
    - That is, from the Arrhenius equation catalysts increase $k$ by increasing $A$ or decreasing $E_a$.
  - A catalyst usually provides a completely different mechanism for the reaction.
    - In the preceding peroxide decomposition example, in the absence of a catalyst, $H_2O_2$ decomposes directly to water and oxygen.
    - In the presence of $Br^-$, $Br_2(aq)$ is generated as an intermediate.
  - When a catalyst adds an intermediate, the activation energies for *both* steps must be lower than the activation energy for the uncatalyzed reaction.

---

41 "Catalysis" from Further Readings
42 "Catalytic Decomposition of Hydrogen Peroxide: Foam Production" from Live Demonstrations
43 "Catalysis" Movie from MediaPortfolio
44 "Catalysis: New Reaction Pathways, Not Just a Lowering of the Activation Energy" from Further Readings
45 Figure 14.20 from MediaPortfolio and Transparency Pack

## Heterogeneous Catalysis[46,47,48,49,50,51]

- A **heterogeneous catalyst** exists in a different phase than the reactants.
- Often we encounter a situation involving a solid catalyst in contact with gaseous reactants and gaseous products (example: catalytic converters in cars) or with reactants in a liquid.
  - Many industrial catalysts are heterogeneous.
- How do they do their job?
  - The first step is **adsorption** (the binding of reactant molecules to the catalyst surface).
  - Adsorption occurs due to the high reactivity of atoms or ions on the surface of the solid.
  - Molecules are adsorbed onto **active sites** on the catalyst surface.
    - The number of active sites on a given amount of catalyst depends on several factors such as:
      - The nature of the catalyst.
      - How the catalyst was prepared.
      - How the catalyst was treated prior to use.
  - For example, consider the hydrogenation of ethylene to form ethane:

$$C_2H_4(g) + H_2(g) \rightarrow C_2H_6(g) \qquad \Delta H^\circ = -137 \text{ kJ/mol}$$

    - The reaction is slow in the absence of a catalyst.
    - In the presence of a finely divided metal catalyst (Ni, Pt or Pd) the reaction occurs quickly at room temperature.
    - First, the ethylene and hydrogen molecules are adsorbed onto active sites on the metal surface.
    - The H–H bond breaks and the H atoms migrate about the metal surface.
    - When an H atom collides with an ethylene molecule on the surface, the C–C $\pi$ bond breaks and a C–H $\sigma$ bond forms.
    - An *ethyl group*, $C_2H_5$, is weakly bonded to the metal surface with a metal-carbon $\sigma$ bond.
    - When $C_2H_6$ forms it desorbs from the surface.
    - When ethylene and hydrogen are adsorbed onto a surface, less energy is required to break the bonds.
    - The activation energy for the reaction is lowered.
      - Thus the reaction rate is increased.

## Enzymes[52,53,54,55,56,57,58,59]

- **Enzymes** are biological catalysts.
- Most enzymes are large protein molecules.
  - Molar masses are in the range of $10^4$ to $10^6$ amu.

---

46 "Catalysis on Surfaces" from Further Readings
47 "Surface Reactions–Hydrogenation" Animation from MediaPortfolio
48 "Solid Acid Catalysts" from Further Readings
49 "Getting Auto Exhausts to Pristine" from Further Readings
50 "Environmental Catalysts" from Further Readings
51 Figure 14.21 from MediaPortfolio and Transparency Pack
52 "Practical Enzyme Kinetics" from Further Readings
53 "Breaking Bonds Versus Chopping Heads: The Enzyme as Butcher" from Further Readings
54 "Biocatalysis Makes Headway in Chemicals" from Further Readings
55 "The Catalytic Function of Enzymes" from Further Readings
56 Figure 14.24 from MediaPortfolio and Transparency Pack
57 "Enzyme Activity" A Simple Analogy" from Further Readings
58 "Enzyme Kinetics: Effects of Temperature and an Inhibitor on Catalase Extracted from Potato" from Live Demonstrations
59 "Enzyme Catalysis: Cleaner, Safer, Energy Efficient" from Further Readings

- Enzymes are capable of catalyzing very specific reactions.
- For example, *catalase* is an enzyme found in blood and liver cells.
  - It catalyzes the decomposition of hydrogen peroxide:

$$2H_2O_2(aq) \rightarrow 2H_2O(l) + O_2(g)$$

  - This reaction is important in removing peroxide, a potentially harmful oxidizing agent.
- The enzyme catalyzes the reaction at its active site.
- The substances that undergo reaction at the active site on enzymes are called **substrates**.
- A simple view of enzyme specificity is the **lock-and-key model**.
  - Here, a substrate is pictured as fitting into the active site of an enzyme in a manner similar to a specific key fitting into a lock. This forms an *enzyme-substrate (ES) complex*.
  - Only substrates that fit into the enzyme lock can be involved in the reaction.
  - The enzyme's active site and the substrate thus have complementary shapes.
  - However, there may be a significant amount of flexibility at the active site.
    - It may change shape as it binds substrate.
  - A reaction occurs very quickly once substrate is bound.
  - Products depart the active site at the end of the reaction.
  - This allows new substrate molecules to bind to the enzyme.
- If a molecule binds so tightly to an enzyme that substrate molecules cannot displace it, then the active site is blocked and the catalyst is inhibited.
  - Such molecules are called *enzyme inhibitors*.
  - Many poisons act by binding to the active site blocking the binding of substrates.
  - Some poisons bind to *other* locations on the enzyme.
    - Binding ultimately causes a change in the enzyme that interferes with enzyme activity.
- Enzymes are extremely efficient catalysts.
  - The number of individual catalytic events occurring at an active site per unit time is called the *turnover number*.
  - Large turnover numbers correspond to very low $E_a$ values.
  - For enzymes, turnover numbers are very large (typically $10^3 - 10^7$ per second).

### *Nitrogen Fixation and Nitrogenase*[60]

- Nitrogen gas cannot be used in the soil for plants or animals.
- Nitrogen compounds, $NH_3$, $NO_2^-$, and $NO_3^-$ are used in the soil.
- The conversion between $N_2$ and $NH_3$ is a process with a high activation energy (the N≡N triple bond needs to be broken).
- Nitrogenase, an enzyme in bacteria that lives in root nodules of legumes such as clover and alfalfa, catalyses the reduction of nitrogen to ammonia.
- The fixed nitrogen ($NH_3$, $NO_2^-$, and $NO_3^-$) is consumed by plants and then eaten by animals.
- Animal waste and dead plants are attacked by bacteria that break down the fixed nitrogen and produce $N_2$ gas for the atmosphere.

---

[60] Figure 14.26 from MediaPortfolio and Transparency Pack

## Further Readings:

1. Reed A. Howald, "The Fizz Keeper, a Case Study in Chemical Education, Equilibrium, and Kinetics," *J. Chem. Educ.*, Vol. 76, **1999**, 208–209.

2. Francisco J. Arnaiz, "Mice in the Box for Zero-Order Kinetics," *J. Chem. Educ.*, Vol. 76, **1999**, 1458.

3. Edward Todd Urbansky, "Don't Be Tricked by Your Integrated Rate Plot!," *J. Chem. Educ.*, Vol. 78, **2001**, 921–923.

4. Elizabeth Wilson, "Light Sticks," *Chemical and Engineering News*, **January 18, 1999**, 65. A brief article on chemiluminescent light sticks.

5. Lee A. Krug, "The Collision Theory and an American Tradition," *J. Chem. Educ.*, Vol. 64, **1987**, 1000.

6. Kent W. Piepgrass, "Audience-Appropriate Analogies: Collision Theory," *J. Chem. Educ.*, Vol. 75, **1998**, 72.

7. Keith J. Laidler, "Just What Is A Transition State?," *J. Chem. Educ.*, Vol. 64, **1988**, 540–542.

8. Ilya A. Leenson, "The Arrhenius Law and Storage of Food," *J. Chem. Educ.*, Vol. 76, **1999**, 504–505.

9. John J. Fortman, "Pictorial Analogies XIII: Kinetics and Mechanisms," *J. Chem. Educ.*, Vol. 71, **1994**, 848–849.

10. Arthur M. Last, "Doing the Dishes: An Analogy for Use in Teaching Reaction Kinetics," *J. Chem. Educ.*, Vol. 62, **1985**, 1015–1016.

11. David W. Ball, "Another Auto Analogy: Rate Determining Steps," *J. Chem. Educ.*, Vol. 64, **1987**, 486–487.

12. Richard A. Potts, "Auto Analogies," *J. Chem. Educ.*, Vol. 62, **1985**, 579. This brief article includes analogies for reaction mechanisms and rate-determining steps of a reaction.

13. Charles J. Marzzacco, "An Analogy to Help Students Understand Reaction Orders," *J. Chem. Educ.*, Vol. 75, **1998**, 482.

14. Lionello Pobliani and Mario N. Berberan-Santos, "Inflation Rates, Car Devaluation, and Chemical Kinetics," *J. Chem. Educ.*, Vol. 73, **1996**, 950–952.

15. Doris Kolb, "Catalysis," *J. Chem. Educ.*, Vol. 56, **1979**, 743–747.

16. Cynthia M. Friend, "Catalysis on Surfaces," *Scientific American*, **April 1993**, 74–79.

17. Sir John Meurig Thomas, "Solid Acid Catalysts," *Scientific American*, **April 1992**, 112–118.

18. Albert Haim, "Catalysis: New Reaction Pathways, Not Just a Lowering of the Activation Energy," *J. Chem. Educ.*, Vol. 66, **1989**, 935–937.

19. H. Alan Rowe and Morris Brown, "Practical Enzyme Kinetics," *J. Chem. Educ*., Vol. 65, **1988**, 548–549.

20. Robert J. Farrauto, Ronald M. Heck, and Barry K. Speronello, "Environmental Catalysts," *Chemical and Engineering News*, **September 7, 1992**, 34–44.

21. Todd P. Silverstein, "Breaking Bonds versus Chopping Heads: The Enzyme as Butcher," *J. Chem. Educ*., Vol. 72, **1995**, 645–646.

22. Kenton B. Abel and Donald R. Halenz, "Enzyme Activity: A Simple Analogy," *J. Chem. Educ*., Vol. 69, **1992**, 9.

23. Allan G. Splittgerber, "The Catalytic Function of Enzymes," *J. Chem. Educ*., Vol. 62, **1985**, 1008–1010.

24. Jim Lalonde, "Enzyme Catalysis: Cleaner, Safer, Energy Efficient," *Chemical Engineering*, Vol. 104(9), **1997**, 108–112.

25. Rita L. D'Aquino, "Biocatalysis Makes Headway in Chemicals," *Chemical Engineering*, Vol. 106(3), **1999**, 37–43.

26. Mitch Jacoby, "Getting Auto Exhausts to Pristine," *Chemical and Engineering News*, **January 25, 1999**, 36–44.

## Live Demonstrations:

1. Lee. R. Summerlin, Christie L. Borgford, and Julie B. Ealy, "Appearing Red," *Chemical Demonstrations, A Sourcebook for Teachers, Volume 2* (Washington: American Chemical Society, **1988**), pp. 145–146. An introductory kinetics experiment.

2. Xavier Creary and Karen M. Morris, "A New Twist on the Iodine Clock Reaction: Determining the Order of a Reaction," *J. Chem. Educ.*, Vol. 76, **1999**, 530–531.

3. Bassam Z. Shakhashiri, "Hydrogen Peroxide Iodine Clock: Oxidation of Potassium Iodide by Hydrogen Peroxide", *Chemical Demonstrations: A Handbook for Teachers of Chemistry, Volume 4* (Madison: The University of Wisconsin Press, **1992**), pp. 37–43.

4. Lee. R. Summerlin, and James. L. Ealy, Jr., "The Starch-Iodine Clock Reaction," *Chemical Demonstrations, A Sourcebook for Teachers, Volume 1* (Washington: American Chemical Society, 1988), pp.107–108. The classic iodine clock experiment.

5. Bassam Z. Shakhashiri, "Lightsticks," *Chemical Demonstrations: A Handbook for Teachers of Chemistry, Volume 1* (Madison: The University of Wisconsin Press, **1983**), pp. 146–152.

6. Bassam Z Shakhashiri, Lloyd G. Williams, Glen E. Dirreen, and Ann Francis, "Cool-Light Chemiluminescence," *J. Chem. Educ*., Vol. 58, **1981**, 70–72. The dependence of reaction rates on temperature is demonstrated with chemiluminescent light sticks.

7. Lee. R. Summerlin, Christie L. Borgford, and Julie B. Ealy, "Enzyme Kinetics: Effects of Temperature and an Inhibitor on Catalase Extracted from Potato," *Chemical Demonstrations, A Sourcebook for Teachers*, *Volume 2* (Washington: American Chemical Society, **1988**), pp. 152–153. An exploration of enzyme-catalyzed decomposition of hydrogen peroxide.

# Chapter 15. Chemical Equilibrium

## Media Resources

### Figures and Tables

| **In Transparency Pack and on MediaPortfolio:** | **Section:** |
|---|---|
| Figure 15.2 Establishing Equilibrium between $N_2O_4$ and $NO_2$ | 15.1 The Concept of Equilibrium |
| Figure 15.3 Achieving Chemical Equilibrium for a Hypothetical Reaction | 15.1 The Concept of Equilibrium |
| Figure 15.4 Haber Process | 15.1 The Concept of Equilibrium |
| Figure 15.6 Achieving Equilibrium for the Reaction of $N_2$ and $H_2$ to form $NH_3$ | 15.2 The Equilibrium Constant |
| Table 15.1 Initial and Equilibrium Partial Pressures ($P$) of $N_2O_4$ and $NO_2$ at 100°C | 15.2 The Equilibrium Constant |
| Figure 15.12 Illustration of Le Châtelier's Principle | 15.6 Le Châtelier's Principle |

| **On MediaPortfolio:** | **Section:** |
|---|---|
| Figure 15.1 Structures of $N_2O_4$ and $NO_2$ | 15.1 The Concept of Equilibrium |
| Figure 15.7 Equilibrium Mixture Starting With Either $NO_2$ or $N_2O_4$ | 15.2 The Equilibrium Constant |
| Figure 15.8 Diagram Illustrating $K >> 1$ and $K << 1$ | 15.2 The Equilibrium Constant |
| Figure 15.9 Heterogeneous Equilibrium | 15.3 Heterogeneous Equilibria |
| Figure 15.10 Relative Magnitudes of $K$ and $Q$ | 15.5 Applications of Equilibrium Constants |
| Figure 15.11 Effect of $T$ and $P$ on $\%NH_3$ | 15.6 Le Châtelier's Principle |
| Figure 15.13 Industrial Production of $NH_3$ | 15.6 Le Châtelier's Principle |
| Figure 15.15 Effect of Temperature on Equilibrium | 15.6 Le Châtelier's Principle |
| Figure 15.16 Reaction Pathway for Equilibrium | 15.6 Le Châtelier's Principle |
| Figure 15.17 Variation in Equilibrium Constant as a Function of Temperature | 15.6 Le Châtelier's Principle |

| **Animations:** | **Section:** |
|---|---|
| $NO_2/NO_4$ Equilibrium | 15.2 The Equilibrium Constant |
| $NO_2/N_2O_4$ Equilibrium | 15.6 Le Châtelier's Principle |
| Temperature Dependence of Equilibrium | 15.6 Le Châtelier's Principle |

| **Activities:** | **Section:** |
|---|---|
| Chemical Equilibrium | 15.1 The Concept of Equilibrium |
| Equilibrium Constant | 15.2 Equilibrium Constant |
| Using an Equilibrium Table I | 15.5 Applications of Equilibrium Constants |
| Using an Equilibrium Table II | 15.5 Applications of Equilibrium Constants |

## Other Resources

| **Further Readings:** | **Section:** |
|---|---|
| Fritz Haber | 15.1 The Concept of Equilibrium |
| The Complexity of Teaching and Learning Chemical Equilibrium | 15.2 The Equilibrium Constant |

| | |
|---|---|
| Equilibrium: A Teaching/Learning Activity | 15.2 The Equilibrium Constant |
| Introducing Dynamic Equilibrium as an Explanatory Model | 15.2 The Equilibrium Constant |
| Chemical Equilibrium in the General Chemistry Course | 15.2 The Equilibrium Constant |
| An Elementary Discussion of Chemical Equilibrium | 15.2 The Equilibrium Constant |
| Simulations for Teaching Chemical Equilibrium | 15.2 The Equilibrium Constant |
| Amounts Tables as a Diagnostic Tool for Flawed Stoichiometric Reasoning | 15.5 Applications of Equilibrium Constants |
| Chemical Equilibrium and Polynomial Equations: Beware of Roots | 15.5 Applications of Equilibrium Constants |
| Calculating Equilibrium Concentrations by Iteration: Recycle Your Approximations | 15.5 Applications of Equilibrium Constants |
| Le Châtelier's Principle | 15.6 Le Châtelier's Principle |
| Global Population and the Nitrogen Cycle | 15.6 Le Châtelier's Principle |
| The Fizz Keeper, a Case Study in Chemical Education, Equilibrium, and Kinetics | 15.6 Le Châtelier's Principle |

| **Live Demonstrations:** | **Section:** |
|---|---|
| Equilibrium and Le Châtelier's Principle | 15.2 The Equilibrium Constant |
| Effect of Concentration on Equilibrium: Cobalt Complex | 15.6 Le Châtelier's Principle |
| Equilibrium in the Gas Phase | 15.6 Le Châtelier's Principle |
| Effect of Temperature Change on Equilibrium: Cobalt Complex | 15.6 Le Châtelier's Principle |
| From Chicken Breath to the Killer Lakes of Cameroon: Uniting Seven Interesting Phenomena with a Single Chemical Underpinning | 15.6 Le Châtelier's Principle |

# Chapter 15. Chemical Equilibrium

## Common Student Misconceptions

- Many students need to see how the numerical problems in this chapter are solved.
- Students confuse the arrows used for resonance and equilibrium.
- Students often have problems distinguishing between *K* and *Q*.
- Students who have difficulty with some of the mathematical manipulations in this chapter should be directed to Appendix A of the text.
- Sometimes students worry about approximations used in solving equilibrium problems. They feel that ignoring a small number when it is subtracted from a significantly larger number is wrong.

## Lecture Outline

### 15.1 The Concept of Equilibrium[1,2,3,4,5]

- Consider colorless frozen $N_2O_4$.
    - At room temperature, it decomposes to brown $NO_2$.

      $$N_2O_4(g) \rightarrow 2NO_2(g)$$
    - At some time, the color stops changing and we have a mixture of $N_2O_4$ and $NO_2$.
    - **Chemical equilibrium** is the point at which the concentrations of all species are constant.
- Consider a simple reaction.
    - $A(g) \rightarrow B(g)$
    - Assume that both the forward and reverse reactions are elementary processes.
    - We can write rate expressions for each reaction.
        - Forward reaction: $A \rightarrow B$
            - Rate = $k_f[A]$ $k_f$ = rate constant (forward reaction)
        - Reverse reaction: $B \rightarrow A$
            - Rate = $k_r[B]$ $k_r$ = rate constant (reverse reaction)
    - For gaseous substances we can use the ideal gas equation to convert between concentration and pressure:
        - $PV = nRT$ so $M = (n/V) = (P/RT)$
        - For substances A and B:
            - $[A] = (P_A/RT)$ and $[B] = (P_B/RT)$
            - $\text{Rate}_{fwd} = k_f P_A/RT$ and $\text{Rate}_{rev} = k_r P_B/RT$
    - Place some pure compound A into a closed container.
        - As A reacts to form B, the partial pressure of A will decrease and the partial pressure of B will increase.
        - Thus we expect the forward reaction rate to slow and the reverse reaction rate to increase.
        - Eventually we get to equilibrium where the forward and reverse rates are equal.
        - At equilibrium:

          $$k_f P_A/RT = k_r P_B/RT$$
        - Rearranging, we get:

---

[1] Figure 15.1 from MediaPortfolio
[2] Figure 15.2 from MediaPortfolio and Transparency Pack
[3] Figure 15.3 from MediaPortfolio and Transparency Pack
[4] "Chemical Equilibrium" Activity from MediaPortfolio
[5] "Frantz Haber" from Further Readings

$$\frac{(P_B / RT)}{(P_A / RT)} = \frac{P_B}{P_A} = \frac{k_f}{k_r} = \text{a constant}$$

- At equilibrium the partial pressures of A and B do not change.
  - This mixture is called an *equilibrium mixture*.
  - This is an example of a *dynamic* equilibrium.
    - A dynamic equilibrium exists when the rates of the forward and reverse reactions are equal.
    - No further net change in reactant or product concentration occurs.
    - The double arrow ⇋ implies that the process is dynamic.
- **Haber process**: industrial preparation of ammonia from nitrogen and hydrogen:

$$N_2(g) + 3H_2(g) \rightleftharpoons 2NH_3(g)$$

  - The process is carried out at high temperature (500°C) and pressure (200 atm).
  - Ammonia is a good source of fixed nitrogen for plants.
    - Much of the $NH_3$ produced industrially is used as a fertilizer.

## 15.2 The Equilibrium Constant[6,7,8,9,10,11,12,13,14,15,16,17]

- Consider the reaction:

$$N_2(g) + 3H_2(g) \rightleftharpoons 2NH_3(g)$$

- If we start with a mixture of nitrogen and hydrogen (in any proportions), the reaction will reach equilibrium with constant concentrations of nitrogen, hydrogen and ammonia.
- However, if we start with just ammonia and no nitrogen or hydrogen, the reaction will proceed and $N_2$ and $H_2$ will be produced until equilibrium is achieved.
- No matter the starting composition of reactants and products is, the equilibrium mixture contains the same relative concentrations of reactants and products.
  - Equilibrium can be reached from either direction.
- We can write an expression for the relationship between the concentration of the reactants and products at equilibrium.
  - This expression is based on the **law of mass action**.
  - For a general reaction

$$aA + bB \rightleftharpoons cC + dD$$

  - The **equilibrium expression** is given by:

$$K_{eq} = \frac{P_C^c P_D^d}{P_A^a P_B^b}$$

---

6 Figure 15.4 from MediaPortfolio and Transparency Pack
7 Figure 15.6 from MediaPortfolio and Transparency Pack
8 "An Elementary Discussion of Chemical Equilibrium" from Further Readings
9 "Equilibrium and Le Châtelier's Principle" from Live Demonstrations
10 "Chemical Equilibrium in the General Chemistry Course" from Further Readings
11 "The Complexity of Teaching and Learning Chemical Equilibrium" from Further Readings
12 "Equilibrium: A Teaching/Learning Activity" from Further Readings
13 "Introducing Dynamic Equilibrium as an Explanatory Model" from Further Readings
14 Table 15.1 from MediaPortfolio and Transparency Pack
15 "Equilibrium Constant" Activity from MediaPortfolio
16 "Simulations for Teaching Chemical Equilibrium" from Further Readings
17 Figure 15.7 from MediaPortfolio

- Where $K_{eq}$ is the **equilibrium constant.**
- Note that the equilibrium constant expression has products in the numerator and reactants in the denominator.

- When the reactants and products are all in solution, the equilibrium constant is expressed in terms of molarities:

$$K_{eq} = \frac{[C]^c[D]^d}{[A]^a[B]^b}$$

- The value of $K_{eq}$ does not depend on initial concentrations of products or reactants.
  - Consider the reaction:

$$N_2O_4(g) \rightleftharpoons 2NO_2(g)$$

  - The equilibrium constant is given by:

$$K_{eq} = \frac{P^2{}_{NO_2}}{P_{N_2O_4}}$$

  - The value of this constant (at 100°C) is 6.49 (regardless of the initial $N_2O_4$(g) or $NO_2$(g) partial pressures.
- The equilibrium expression depends on stoichiometry.
  - It does not depend on the reaction mechanism.
  - The value of $K_{eq}$ varies with temperature.
- We generally omit the units of the equilibrium constant.

## The Magnitude of Equilibrium Constants[18]

- The equilibrium constant, $K_{eq}$, is the ratio of products to reactants.
  - Therefore, the larger $K_{eq}$ the more products are present at equilibrium.
  - Conversely, the smaller $K_{eq}$ the more reactants are present at equilibrium.
    - If $K_{eq} >> 1$, then products dominate at equilibrium and equilibrium lies to the right.
    - If $K_{eq} << 1$, then reactants dominate at equilibrium and the equilibrium lies to the left.

## The Direction of the Chemical Equation and $K$[19]

- An equilibrium can be approached from any direction.
- Consider the reaction:

$$N_2O_4(g) \rightleftharpoons 2NO_2(g)$$

  - The equilibrium constant for this reaction (at 100°C) is:

$$K_{eq} = \frac{P^2{}_{NO_2}}{P_{N_2O_4}} = 6.49$$

  - However, when we write the equilibrium expression for the reverse reaction,

$$2NO_2(g) \rightleftharpoons N_2O_4(g)$$

  - The equilibrium constant for this reaction (at 100°C) is:

$$K_{eq} = \frac{P_{N_2O_4}}{P^2{}_{N_2O}} = 0.154$$

- The equilibrium constant for a reaction in one direction is the reciprocal of the equilibrium constant of the reaction in the opposite direction.

## Other Ways to Manipulate Chemical Equations and $K_{eq}$ Values

---

[18] Figure 15.8 from MediaPortfolio

[19] "$NO_2/N_2O_4$" Animation from MediaPortfolio

- The equilibrium constant of a reaction in the reverse direction is the inverse of the equilibrium constant of the reaction in the forward direction.
- The equilibrium constant of a reaction that has been multiplied by a number is the equilibrium constant raised to a power equal to that number.
- The equilibrium constant for a net reaction made up of two or more steps is the product of the equilibrium constants for the individual steps.

## 15.3 Heterogeneous Equilibria[20]

- Equilibria in which all reactants and products are present in the same phase are called **homogeneous equilibria**.
- Equilibria in which one or more reactants or products are present in a different phase are called **heterogeneous equilibria**.
- Consider the decomposition of calcium carbonate:

$$CaCO_3(s) \leftrightharpoons CaO(s) + CO_2(g)$$

  - Experimentally, the amount of $CO_2$ does not depend on the amounts of CaO and $CaCO_3$.
    - Why?
  - The concentration of a pure solid or pure liquid equals its density divided by its molar mass.
  - Neither density nor molar mass is a variable.
    - Thus the concentrations of solids and pure liquids are constant.
  - For the decomposition of $CaCO_3$:

$$K_{eq} = \frac{[\text{CaO}]P_{CO_2}}{[\text{CaCO}_3]}$$

  - CaO and $CaCO_3$ are pure solids and have constant concentrations.

$$K_{eq} = \frac{(\text{constant }1)P_{CO_2}}{(\text{constant }2)}$$

  - Rearranging:

$$\therefore K_{eq}' = K_{eq}\frac{(\text{constant }2)}{(\text{constant }1)} = P_{CO_2}$$

- If a pure solid or pure liquid is involved in a heterogeneous equilibrium, its concentration is not included in the equilibrium constant expression.
- Therefore, we anticipate that the amount of $CO_2$ formed will not depend on the amounts of CaO and $CaCO_3$ present.
- Note: Although the *concentrations* of these species are not included in the equilibrium expression, they *do* participate in the reaction and *must* be present for an equilibrium to be established!

## 15.4 Calculating Equilibrium Constants

- Proceed as follows:
  - Tabulate initial and equilibrium concentrations (or partial pressures) for all species in the equilibrium.
  - If an initial *and* an equilibrium concentration is given for a species, calculate the change in concentration.
  - Use the coefficients in the balanced chemical equation to calculate the changes in concentration of all species.
  - Deduce the equilibrium concentrations of all species.
  - Use these equilibrium concentrations to calculate the value of the equilibrium constant.

---

[20] Figure 15.9 from MediaPortfolio

## 15.5 Applications of Equilibrium Constants[21,22]

### Predicting the Direction of Reaction[23]

- For a general reaction:

$$aA + bB \rightleftharpoons cC + dD$$

- We define $Q$, the **reaction quotient**, as:

$$Q = \frac{[C]^c[D]^d}{[A]^a[B]^b}$$

  - Where [A], [B], [C], and [D] are molarities (for substances in solution) or partial pressures (for gases) at any given time.
  - Note: $Q = K_{eq}$ only at equilibrium.
    - If $Q < K_{eq}$ then the forward reaction must occur to reach equilibrium.
    - If $Q > K_{eq}$ then the reverse reaction must occur to reach equilibrium.
      - Products are consumed, reactants are formed.
      - $Q$ decreases until it equals $K_{eq}$.

### Calculating Equilibrium Concentrations[24,25]

- The same steps used to calculate equilibrium constants are used to calculate equilibrium concentrations.
- Generally, we do not have a number for the change in concentration.
  - Therefore, we need to assume that $x$ mol/L of a species is produced (or used).
- The equilibrium concentrations are given as algebraic expressions.

## 15.6 Le Châtelier's Principle

- Consider the Haber process:

$$N_2(g) + 3H_2(g) \rightleftharpoons 2NH_3(g)$$

  - As the pressure increases, the amount of ammonia present at equilibrium increases.
  - As the temperature increases, the amount of ammonia at equilibrium decreases.
  - Can this be predicted?
- **Le Châtelier's principle**: If a system at equilibrium is disturbed by a change in temperature, a change in pressure, or a change in the concentration of one or more components, the system will shift its equilibrium position in such a way as to counteract the effects of the disturbance.

### Change in Reactant or Product Concentration[26,27,28,29,30,31,32]

---

[21] "Using an Equilibrium Table I" Activity from MediaPortfolio
[22] "Using an Equilibrium Table II" Activity from MediaPortfolio
[23] "Figure 15.10 from MediaPortfolio
[24] "Amounts Tables as a Diagnostic Tool for Flawed Stoichiometric Reasoning" from Further Readings
[25] "Chemical Equilibrium and Polynomial Equations: Beware of Roots" from Further Readings
[26] "Calculating Equilibrium Concentrations by Iteration: Recycle your Approximations" from Further Readings
[27] "Le Châtelier's Principle" from Further Readings
[28] Figure 15.11 from MediaPortfolio
[29] "Effect of Concentration on Equilibrium: Cobalt Complex" from Live Demonstrations
[30] Figure 15.12 from MediaPortfolio and Transparency Pack
[31] Figure 15.13 from MediaPortfolio
[32] "Global Population and the Nitrogen Cycle" from Further Readings

- If a chemical system is at equilibrium and we add or remove a product or reactant, the reaction will shift so as to reestablish equilibrium.
  - For example, consider the Haber process again:

$$N_2(g) + 3H_2(g) \leftrightharpoons 2NH_3(g)$$

  - If $H_2$ is added while the system is at equilibrium, $Q < K_{eq}$.
    - The system must respond to counteract the added $H_2$ (by Le Châtelier's principle).
  - That is, the system must consume the $H_2$ and produce products until a new equilibrium is established.
    - Therefore, $[H_2]$ and $[N_2]$ will decrease and $[NH_3]$ increase until $Q = K_{eq}$.
- We can exploit this industrially.
  - Suppose that we wanted to optimize the amount of ammonia we formed from the Haber process.
  - We might flood the reaction vessel with reactants and continuously remove product.
  - The amount of ammonia produced is optimized because the product ($NH_3$) is continuously removed and the reactants ($N_2$ and $H_3$) are continuously being added.

## Effects of Volume and Pressure Changes[33]

- Consider a system at equilibrium.
- If the equilibrium involves gaseous products or reactants, the concentration of these species will be changed if we change the volume of the container.
  - For example, if we decrease the volume of the container, the partial pressures of each gaseous species will increase.
  - Le Châtelier's principle predicts that if pressure is increased, the system will shift to counteract the increase.
    - That is, the system shifts to remove gases and decrease pressure.
    - An increase in pressure favors the direction that has fewer moles of gas.
- Consider the following system:

$$N_2O_4(g) \leftrightharpoons 2NO_2(g)$$

  - An increase in pressure (by decreasing the volume) favors the formation of colorless $N_2O_4$.
  - The instant the pressure increases, the concentration of both gases increases and the system is not at equilibrium.
  - The system moves to reduce the number moles of gas.
  - A new equilibrium is established.
    - The mixture is lighter in color.
    - Some of the brown $NO_2$ has been converted into colorless $N_2O_4(g)$
- In a reaction with the same number of moles of gas in the products and reactants, changing the pressure has no effect on the equilibrium.
- In addition, no change will occur if we increase the total gas pressure by the addition of a gas that is not involved in the reaction.

## Effect of Temperature Changes[34,35,36,37,38,39]

- The equilibrium constant is temperature dependent.

---

[33] "$NO_2/N_2O_4$ Equilibrium" from MediaPortfolio
[34] "Effect of Temperature Change on Equilibrium: Cobalt Complex" from Live Demonstrations
[35] "Equilibrium in the Gas Phase" from Live Demonstrations
[36] Figure 15.15 from MediaPortfolio
[37] "From Chicken Breath to the Killer Lakes of Cameroon: Uniting Seven Interesting Phenomena with a Single Chemical Underpinning" from Live Demonstrations
[38] "The Fizz Keeper, a Case Study in Chemical Education, Equilibrium, and Kinetics" from Further Readings
[39] "Temperature Dependence of Equilibrium" Animation from MediaPortfolio

- How will a change in temperature alter a system at equilibrium?
  - It depends on the particular reaction.
  - For example, consider the endothermic reaction:

$$Co(H_2O)_6^{2+}(aq) + 4Cl^-(aq) \rightleftharpoons CoCl_4^{2-}(aq) + 6H_2O(l) \quad \Delta H > 0$$

  - $Co(H_2O)_6^{2+}$ is pale pink and $CoCl_4^{2-}$ is a deep blue.
  - At room temperature, an equilibrium mixture (light purple) is placed in a beaker of warm water.
    - The mixture turns deep blue.
    - This indicates a shift toward products (blue $CoCl_4^{2-}$).
    - This reaction is endothermic.
    - For an endothermic reaction ($\Delta H > 0$), heat can be considered as a reactant.
      - Thus adding heat causes a shift in the forward direction.
  - The room-temperature equilibrium mixture is placed in a beaker of ice water.
    - The mixture turns bright pink.
    - This indicates a shift toward reactants (pink $Co(H_2O)_6^{2+}$).
    - In this case, by cooling the system we are removing a reactant (heat).
    - Thus the reaction is shifted in the reverse reaction.

## The Effect of Catalysts[40,41]

- A catalyst lowers the activation energy barrier for the reaction.
  - Therefore, a catalyst will decrease the time taken to reach equilibrium.
  - A catalyst *does not* effect the composition of the equilibrium mixture.

[40] Figure 15.16 from MediaPortfolio
[41] Figure 15.17 from MediaPortfolio

## Further Readings:

1. Louise Tyson, David F. Treagust, and Robert B. Bucat, "The Complexity of Teaching and Learning Chemical Equilibrium," *J. Chem. Educ.*, Vol. 76, **1999**, 554–558.

2. Audrey H. Wilson, "Equilibrium: A Teaching/Learning Activity," *J. Chem. Educ.*, Vol. 75, **1998**, 1176–1177.

3. Jan H. Van Driel, Wobbe de Vos, and Nico Verloop, "Introducing Dynamic Equilibrium as an Explanatory Model," *J. Chem. Educ.*, Vol. 76, **1999**, 559–561.

4. Penelope A. Huddle, Margie W. White, and Fiona Rogers, "Simulations for Teaching Chemical Equilibrium," *J. Chem. Educ.*, Vol. 77, **2000**, 920–926.

5. John Olmsted III, "Amounts Tables as a Diagnostic Tool for Flawed Stoichiometric Reasoning," *J. Chem. Educ.*, Vol. 76, **1999**, 52–54.

6. Carl W. David, "An Elementary Discussion of Chemical Equilibrium," *J. Chem. Educ.*, Vol. 65, **1988**, 407–409.

7. Martin R. Feldman and Monica L. Tarver, "Fritz Haber," *J. Chem. Educ.*, Vol. 60, **1983**, 463–464.

8. Vaclav Smith, "Global Population and the Nitrogen Cycle," *Scientific American*, **July 1997**, 76–81.

9. William R. Smith and Ronald W. Missen, "Chemical Equilibrium and Polynomial Equations: Beware of Roots," *J. Chem. Educ.*, Vol. 66, **1989**, 489–490.

10. E. Weltin, "Calculating Equilibrium Concentrations by Iteration: Recycle Your Approximations," *J. Chem. Educ.*, Vol. 72, **1995**, 36–38.

11. Richard S. Treptow, "Le Châtelier's Principle," *J. Chem. Educ.*, Vol. 57, **1980**, 417–420.

12. Vladimir E. Fainzilberg and Stewart Karp, "Chemical Equilibrium in the General Chemistry Course," *J. Chem. Educ.*, Vol. 71, **1994**, 769–770.

13. Reed A. Howald, "The Fizz Keeper, a Case Study in Chemical Education, Equilibrium, and Kinetics," *J. Chem. Educ.*, Vol. 76, **1999**, 208–209.

## Live Demonstrations:

1. Lee R. Summerlin and James L. Ealy, Jr., "Equilibrium in the Gas Phase," *Chemical Demonstrations, A Sourcebook for Teachers* (Washington: American Chemical Society, **1985**), pp. 60–61. Color changes in a mixture of $NO_2$ and $N_2O_4$ as a sealed tube of gas is heated or cooled are used to demonstrate Le Châtelier's principle.

2. Lee. R. Summerlin, and James. L. Ealy, Jr., "Effect of Temperature Change on Equilibrium: Cobalt Complex," *Chemical Demonstrations, A Sourcebook for Teachers, Volume 1* (Washington: American Chemical Society, **1988**), pp. 79–80. An equilibrium system containing the dehydrated-hydrated cobalt complex is shifted in response to changes in temperature.

3. Lee. R. Summerlin, and James. L. Ealy, Jr., “Equilibrium and Le Châtelier's Principle,” *Chemical Demonstrations, A Sourcebook for Teachers*, *Volume 1* (Washington: American Chemical Society, **1988**), pp. 77–78. An overhead projector demonstration of the effect of reactant concentration on equilibrium.

4. Lee. R. Summerlin, and James. L. Ealy, Jr., “Effect of Concentration on Equilibrium: Cobalt Complex,” *Chemical Demonstrations, A Sourcebook for Teachers*, *Volume 1* (Washington: American Chemical Society, **1988**), pp. 81–82.

5. Ron DeLorenzo, “From Chicken Breath to the Killer Lakes of Cameroon: Uniting Seven Interesting Phenomena with a Single Chemical Underpinning,” *J. Chem. Educ.*, Vol. 78, **2001**, 191–194. A collection of demonstrations dealing with equilibria associated with a sodium bicarbonate solution.

# Chapter 16. Acid-Base Equilibria

## Media Resources

### Figures and Tables

| In Transparency Pack and on MediaPortfolio: | Section: |
|---|---|
| Figure 16.4 Relative Strengths of Common Conjugate Acid-Base Pairs | 16.2 Brønsted-Lowry Acids and Bases |
| Figure 16.5 $H^+$ Concentrations and pH Values of Common Substances | 16.4 The pH Scale |
| Figure 16.7 pH Ranges for Indicators | 16.4 The pH Scale |
| Table 16.3 Acid-Dissociation Constants of Some Common Polyprotic Acids | 16.6 Weak Acids |
| Table 16.5 Some Conjugate Acid-Base Pairs | 16.8 Relationship Between $K_a$ and $K_b$ |

| On MediaPortfolio: | Section: |
|---|---|
| Figure 16.2 Proton Transfer from HCl to $H_2O$ | 16.2 Brønsted-Lowry Acids and Bases |
| Table 16.2 Some Weak Acids in Water at 25°C | 16.6 Weak Acids |
| Figure 16.9 Percent Ionization of A Weak Acid as a Function of Concentration | 16.6 Weak Acids |
| Table 16.4 Some Weak Bases and Their Aqueous Solution Equilibria | 16.7 Weak Bases |
| Figure 16.12 Acid-Base Properties Of Binary Compounds of H | 16.10 Acid-Base Behavior and Chemical Structure |
| Figure 16.13 Dependence of Acid Strength on the Polarity of the O-H Bond | 16.11 Lewis Acids and Bases |
| Figure 16.15 Interaction of $H_2O$ with Cation of 1+ or 3+ Charge | 16.11 Lewis Acids and Bases |

| Animations: | Section: |
|---|---|
| Introduction to Aqueous Acids | 16.1 Acids and Bases: A Brief Review |
| Introduction to Aqueous Bases | 16.1 Acids and Bases: A Brief Review |
| Introduction to Aqueous Bases | 16.5 Strong Acids and Bases |
| Lewis Acid-Base Theory | 16.11 Lewis Acids and Bases |

| Movies: | Section: |
|---|---|
| Natural Indicators | 16.5 Strong Acids and Bases |

| Activities: | Section: |
|---|---|
| $K_w$ Activity | 16.3 The Autoionization of Water |
| pH Estimation | 16.4 The pH Scale |
| Acids and Bases | 16.5 Strong Acids and Bases |

## Other Resources

| Further Readings: | Section: |
|---|---|
| Acids and Bases | 16.1 Acids and Bases: A Brief Review |
| The Brønsted-Lowry Acid-Base Concept | 16.2 Brønsted-Lowry Acids and Bases |

| | |
|---|---|
| Teaching Brønsted-Lowry Acid-Base Theory in a Direct Comprehensive Way | 16.2 Brønsted-Lowry Acids and Bases |
| An Analogy for the Leveling Effect in Acid-Base Chemistry | 16.2 Brønsted-Lowry Acids and Bases |
| Acid and Base Dissociation Constants of Water and Its Associated Ions | 16.2 Brønsted-Lowry Acids and Bases |
| Do pH in your Head | 16.4 The pH Scale |
| Teaching the Truth about pH | 16.4 The pH Scale |
| The pH Concept | 16.4 The pH Scale |
| Fruit Anthocyanins: Colorful Sensors of Molecular Milieu | 16.4 The pH Scale |
| Pictorial Analogies XI: Concentrations and Acidity of Solutions | 16.6 Weak Acids |
| Weak vs Strong Acids and Bases: The Football Analogy | 16.6 Weak Acids |
| Kinetic Classroom: Acid-Base and Redox Demonstrations with Student Movement | 16.6 Weak Acids |
| The Relative Strength of Oxyacids and Its Application | 16.10 Acid-Base Behavior and Chemical Structure |
| The Research Style of Gilbert N. Lewis: Acids and Bases | 16.11 Lewis Acids and Bases |

| **Live Demonstrations:** | **Section:** |
|---|---|
| Food is Usually Acidic, Cleaners Are Usually Basic | 16.4 The pH Scale |
| Colorful Acid-Base Indicators | 16.4 The pH Scale |
| Rainbow Colors with Mixed Acid-Base Indicators | 16.4 The pH Scale |
| Colorful Effects of Hydrochloric Acid Dilution | 16.4 The pH Scale |
| Acid-Base Indicators Extracted from Plants | 16.4 The pH Scale |
| Disappearing Ink | 16.5 Strong Acids and Bases |
| Differences Between Acid Strength and Concentration | 16.6 Weak Acids |
| Hydrolysis: Acidic and Basic Properties of Salts | 16.9 Acid-Base Properties of Salt Solutions |
| Effect of Molecular Structure on the Strength of Organic Acids and Bases in Aqueous Solutions | 16.10 Acid-Base Behavior and Chemical Structure |

# Chapter 16. Acid-Base Equilibria

## Common Student Misconceptions

- Students often confuse a weak acid with a dilute acid.
- Students have problems with the numerical parts of this chapter. They should be strongly encouraged to do many problems on their own.

## Lecture Outline

### 16.1 Acids and Bases: A Brief Review[1,2,3]

- Acids: taste sour and cause certain dyes to change color.
- Bases: taste bitter and feel soapy.
- Arrhenius concept of acids and bases:
  - An acid is a substance that, when dissolved in water, increases the concentration of $H^+$ ions.
    - Example: HCl is an acid.
  - An Arrhenius base is a substance that, when dissolved in water, increases the concentration of $OH^-$.
    - Example: NaOH is a base.
  - This definition is quite narrow in scope as it limits us to aqueous solutions.

### 16.2 Brønsted-Lowry Acids and Bases[4,5]

- We can use a broader, more general definition for acids and bases that is based on the fact that acid-base reactions involve proton transfers.

#### The $H^+$ Ion in Water

- The $H^+(aq)$ ion is simply a proton with no surrounding valence electrons.
- In water, clusters of hydrated $H^+(aq)$ ions form.
- The simplest cluster is $H_3O^+(aq)$.
  - We call this a **hydronium ion**.
  - Larger clusters are also possible (such as $H_5O_2^+$ and $H_9O_4^+$).
- Generally we use $H^+(aq)$ and $H_3O^+(aq)$ interchangeably.

#### Proton-Transfer Reactions[6]

- **We will focus our attention on $H^+(aq)$:**
- According to the Arrhenius definitions, an acid increases $[H^+]$ and a base increases $[OH^-]$.
- Another definition of acids and bases was proposed by Brønsted and Lowry.
- In the Brønsted-Lowry system, a **Brønsted-Lowry acid** is a species that donates $H^+$ and a **Brønsted-Lowry base** is a species that accepts $H^+$.
  - Therefore a Brønsted-Lowry base does not need to contain $OH^-$.
    - $NH_3$ is a Brønsted-Lowry base but not an Arrhenius base.

---

[1] "Introduction to Aqueous Acids" Animation from MediaPortfolio
[2] "Introduction to Aqueous Bases" Animation from MediaPortfolio
[3] "Acids and Bases" from Further Readings
[4] "The Brønsted-Lowry Acid-Base Concept" from Further Readings
[5] "Teaching Brønsted-Lowry Acid-Base Theory in a Direct Comprehensive Way" from Further Readings
[6] Figure 16.2 from MediaPortfolio

- Consider $NH_3(aq) + H_2O(l) \leftrightharpoons NH_4^+(aq) + OH^-(aq)$:
- $H_2O$ donates a proton to ammonia.
  - Therefore, water is acting as an acid.
- $NH_3$ accepts a proton from water.
  - Therefore, ammonia is acting as a base.
  - **Amphoteric substances** can behave as acids and bases.
  - Thus water is an example of an amphoteric species.

### Conjugate Acid-Base Pairs

- Whatever is left of the acid after the proton is donated is called its conjugate base.
- Similarly, a conjugate acid is formed by adding a proton to the base.
- Consider $HA(aq) + H_2O(l) \leftrightharpoons H_3O^+(aq) + A^-(aq)$:
  - HA and $A^-$ differ only in the presence or absence of a proton.
    - These are said to be a **conjugate acid-base pair**.
    - $A^-$ is called the **conjugate base**.
  - After HA (acid) loses its proton it is converted into $A^-$ (base).
    - Therefore HA and $A^-$ are a conjugate acid-base pair.
  - After $H_2O$ (base) gains a proton it is converted into $H_3O^+$ (acid).
    - $H_3O^+$ is the **conjugate acid**.
    - Therefore, $H_2O$ and $H_3O^+$ are a conjugate acid-base pair.

### Relative Strengths of Acids and Bases[7,8]

- The stronger an acid is, the weaker its conjugate base will be.
- We can categorize acids and bases according to their behavior in water.
  - 1. *Strong acids* completely transfer their protons to water.
    - No undissociated molecules remain in solution.
    - Their conjugate bases have negligible tendencies to become protonated.
      - Example: HCl.
  - 2. *Weak acids* only partially dissociate in aqueous solution.
    - They exist in solution as a mixture of molecules and component ions.
    - Their conjugate bases show a slight tendency to abstract protons from water.
    - These conjugate bases are weak bases.
      - Example: Acetic acid is a weak acid; acetate ion (conjugate base) is a weak base.
  - 3. *Substances with negligible acidity* do not transfer a proton to water.
    - Example: $CH_4$.
- In every acid-base reaction, the position of the equilibrium favors the transfer of a proton from the stronger acid to the stronger base.
  - $H^+$ is the strongest acid that can exist in equilibrium in aqueous solution.
  - $OH^-$ is the strongest base that can exist in equilibrium in aqueous solution.

## 16.3 The Autoionization of Water

- In pure water the following equilibrium is established:

$$2H_2O(l) \leftrightharpoons H_3O^+(aq) + OH^-(aq)$$

- This process is called the **autoionization** of water.

### The Ion Product of Water[9,10]

---

[7] Figure 16.4 from MediaPortfolio and Transparency Pack
[8] "An Analogy for the Leveling Effect in Acid-Base Chemistry" from Further Readings
[9] "Acid and Base Dissociation Constants of Water and its Associated Ions" from Further Readings
[10] "$K_w$ Activity" from MediaPortfolio

- We can write an equilibrium constant expression for the autoionization of water.

$$K_{eq} = \frac{[H_3O^+][OH^-]}{[H_2O]^2}$$

- Because $H_2O(l)$ is a pure liquid, we can simplify this expression:

$$[H_2O]^2 K_{eq} = [H_3O^+][OH^-] = K_w$$

- $K_w$ is called the ion-product constant.
  - At 25°C the ion-product of water is:

$$1.0 \times 10^{-14} = K_w = [H_3O^+][OH^-]$$

- This applies to pure water as well as to aqueous solutions.
  - A solution is *neutral* if $[OH^-] = [H_3O^+]$.
  - If the $[H_3O^+] > [OH^-]$, the solution is *acidic*.
  - If the $[H_3O^+] < [OH^-]$, the solution is *basic*.

## 16.4 The pH Scale[11,12,13,14,15,16]

- In most solutions $[H^+]$ is quite small.
- We express the $[H^+]$ in terms of **pH**.

$$pH = -\log[H^+] = -\log[H_3O^+]$$

  - Note that this is a logarithmic scale.
  - Thus a change in $[H^+]$ by a factor of 10 causes the pH to change by 1 unit.
- Most pH values fall between 0 and 14.
  - In neutral solutions at 25°C, pH = 7.00.
  - In acidic solutions, $[H^+] > 1.0 \times 10^{-7}$, so pH < 7.00.
    - As the pH decreases, the acidity of the solution increases.
  - In basic solutions, $[H^+] < 1.0 \times 10^{-7}$, so pH > 7.00.
    - As the pH increases, the basicity of the solution increases (acidity decreases).

### Other "p" Scales

- We can use a similar system to describe the $[OH^-]$.

$$pOH = -\log[OH^-]$$

- Recall that the value of $K_w$ at 25°C is $1.0 \times 10^{-14}$.
  - Thus we can describe a relationship between pH and pOH:

$$-\log[H^+] + (-\log[OH^-]) = pH + pOH = -\log K_w = 14.00$$

### Measuring pH[17,18,19,20,21,22,23]

---

[11] "Do pH in Your Head" from Further Readings
[12] "Teaching the Truth about pH" from Further Readings
[13] The pH Concept" from Further Readings
[14] "Food is Usually Acidic, Cleaners are Usually Basic" from Live Demonstrations
[15] Figure 16.5 from MediaPortfolio and Activity Pack
[16] "pH Estimation" Activity from MediaPortfolio
[17] "Fruit Anthocyanins: Colorful Sensors of Molecular Milieu" from Further Readings
[18] "Colorful Acid-Base Indicators" from Live Demonstrations
[19] Figure 16.7 from MediaPortfolio and Transparency Pack

- The most accurate method to measure pH is to use a pH meter.
  - However, certain dyes change color as pH changes.
    - They are called acid-base indicators.
  - Indicators are less precise than pH meters.
  - Many indicators do not have a sharp color change as a function of pH.
  - Most acid-base indicators can exist as either an acid or a base.
    - These two forms have different colors.
    - The relative concentration of the two different forms is sensitive to the pH of the solution.
    - Thus, if we know the pH at which the indicator turns color, we can use this color change to determine whether a solution has a higher or lower pH than this value.
  - Some natural products can be used as indicators (tea is colorless in acid and brown in base; red cabbage extract is another natural indicator).

## 16.5 Strong Acids and Bases[24,25]

### Strong Acids

- The most common strong acids are HCl, HBr, HI, $HNO_3$, $HClO_3$, $HClO_4$, and $H_2SO_4$.
- Strong acids are strong electrolytes.
  - All strong acids ionize completely in solution:
  - Example: Nitric acid ionizes completely in solution.

$$HNO_3(aq) + H_2O(l) \rightarrow H_3O^+(aq) + NO_3^-(aq)$$

    - Since $H^+$ and $H_3O^+$ are used interchangeably, we write

$$HNO_3(aq) \rightarrow H^+(aq) + NO_3^-(aq)$$

- In solution the strong acid is usually the only source of $H^+$.
  - Therefore, the pH of a solution of a monoprotic acid may usually be calculated directly from the initial molarity of the acid.
  - Caution: If the molarity of the acid is less than $10^{-6}$ *M* then the autoionization of water needs to be taken into account.

### Strong Bases[26]

- The most common strong bases are ionic hydroxides of the alkali metals or the heavier alkaline earth metals (e.g., NaOH, KOH, and $Ca(OH)_2$ are all strong bases).
- Strong bases are strong electrolytes and dissociate completely in solution.
  - For example:

$$NaOH(aq) \rightarrow Na^+(aq) + OH^-(aq)$$

- The pOH (and thus the pH) of a strong base may be calculated using the initial molarity of the base.
- Not all bases contain the $OH^-$ ion.
  - Ionic metal oxides, hydrides, and nitrides are basic.
  - The oxide, hydride and nitride ions are stronger bases than hydroxide.
  - They are thus able to abstract a proton from water and generate $OH^-$.

$$O^{2-}(aq) + H_2O(l) \rightarrow 2OH^-(aq)$$

$$H^-(aq) + H_2O(l) \rightarrow H_2(g) + OH^-(aq)$$

---

[20] "Natural Indicators" Movie from MediaPortfolio
[21] "Rainbow Colors with Mixed Acid-Base Indicators" from Live Demonstrations
[22] "Colorful Effects of Hydrochloric Acid Dilution" from Live Demonstrations
[23] "Acid-Base Indicators Extracted from Plants" from Live Demonstrations
[24] "Introduction to Aqueous Bases" Animation from MediaPortfolio
[25] "Acids and Bases" Activity from MediaPortfolio
[26] "Disappearing Ink" from Live Demonstrations

$$N^{3-}(aq) + 3H_2O(l) \rightarrow NH_3(aq) + 3OH^-(aq)$$

## 16.6 Weak Acids[27,28,29,30,31]

- Weak acids are only partially ionized in aqueous solution.
  - There is a mixture of ions and un-ionized acid in solution.
  - Therefore, weak acids are in equilibrium:

$$HA(aq) + H_2O(l) \rightleftharpoons H_3O^+(aq) + A^-(aq)$$

  - Or:

$$HA(aq) \rightleftharpoons H^+(aq) + A^-(aq)$$

  - We can write an equilibrium constant expression for this dissociation:

$$K_a = \frac{[H_3O^+][A^-]}{[HA]} \text{ or } K_a = \frac{[H^+][A^-]}{[HA]}$$

  - $K_a$ is called the **acid-dissociation constant**.
  - Note that the subscript "a" indicates that this is the equilibrium constant for the dissociation of an acid.
  - Note that $[H_2O]$ is omitted from the $K_a$ expression. ($H_2O$ is a pure liquid.)
- The larger the $K_a$, the stronger the acid.
  - $K_a$ is larger since there are more ions present at equilibrium relative to un-ionized molecules.
  - If $K_a >> 1$, then the acid is completely ionized and the acid is a strong acid.

### Calculating $K_a$ from pH

- In order to find the value of $K_a$, we need to know all of the equilibrium concentrations.
  - The pH gives the equilibrium concentration of $H^+$.
  - Thus, to find $K_a$, we use the pH to find the equilibrium concentration of $H^+$ and then the stoichiometric coefficients of the balanced equation to help us determine the equilibrium concentration of the other species.
  - We then substitute these equilibrium concentrations into the equilibrium constant expression and solve for $K_a$.

### Using $K_a$ to Calculate pH[32]

- Using $K_a$, we can calculate the concentration of $H^+$ (and hence the pH).
- Write the balanced chemical equation clearly showing the equilibrium.
- Write the equilibrium expression. Look up the value for $K_a$ (in a table).
- Write down the initial and equilibrium concentrations for everything except pure water.
  - We usually assume that the equilibrium concentration of $H^+$ is $x$.
- Substitute into the equilibrium constant expression and solve.
  - Remember to convert $x$ to pH if necessary.
- What do we do if we are faced with having to solve a quadratic equation in order to determine the value of $x$?
  - Often this cannot be avoided.
  - However, if the $K_a$ value is quite small, we find that we can make a simplifying assumption.
    - Assume that $x$ is negligible compared to the initial concentration of the acid.

---

27 "Pictorial Analogies XI: Concentrations and Acidity of Solutions" from Further Readings
28 "Weak vs Strong Acids and Bases: The Football Analogy" from Further Readings
29 "Differences Between Acid Strength and Concentration" from Live Demonstrations
30 Table 16.2 from MediaPortfolio
31 "Kinetic Classroom: Acid-Base and Redox" from Further Readings
32 Figure 16.9 from MediaPortfolio

    - This will simplify the calculation.
    - It is always necessary to check the validity of any assumption.
    - Once we have the value of $x$, check to see how large it is compared to the initial concentration.
    - If $x$ is <5% of the initial concentration, the assumption is probably a good one.
    - If $x$>5% of the initial concentration, then it may be best to solve the quadratic equation or use successive approximations.
  - Weak acids are only partially ionized.
  - Percent ionization is another method to assess acid strength.
  - For the reaction

$$HA(aq) \rightleftharpoons H^+(aq) + A^-(aq)$$

$$\%\,\text{ionization} = \frac{[H^+]_{\text{equilibrium}}}{[HA]_{initial}} \times 100$$

  - Percent ionization relates the *equilibrium* $H^+$ concentration, $[H^+]_{\text{equilibrium}}$, to the *initial* HA concentration, $[HA]_{\text{initial}}$.
  - The higher the percent ionization, the stronger the acid.
  - However, we need to keep in mind that percent ionization of a weak acid decreases as the molarity of the solution increases.

### Polyprotic Acids[33]

- **Polyprotic acids** have more than one ionizable proton.
- The protons are removed in successive steps.
  - Consider the weak acid, $H_2SO_3$ (sulfurous acid):

$$H_2SO_3(aq) \rightleftharpoons H^+(aq) + HSO_3^-(aq) \qquad K_{a1} = 1.7 \times 10^{-2}$$
$$HSO_3^-(aq) \rightleftharpoons H^+(aq) + SO_3^{2-}(aq) \qquad K_{a2} = 6.4 \times 10^{-8}$$

  - Where $K_{a1}$ is the dissociation constant for the first proton released, $K_{a2}$ is for the second, etc.
- It is always easier to remove the first proton in a polyprotic acid than the second.
  - Therefore, $K_{a1} > K_{a2} > K_{a3}$, etc.
- The majority of the $H^+(aq)$ at equilibrium usually comes from the first ionization (i.e., the $K_{a1}$ equilibrium).
  - If the successive $K_a$ values differ by a factor of $\geq 10^3$, we can usually get a good approximation of the pH of a solution of a polyprotic acid by considering the first ionization only.

## 16.7 Weak Bases[34]

- Weak bases remove protons from substances.
- There is an equilibrium between the base and the resulting ions:

$$\text{Weak base} + H_2O(l) \rightleftharpoons \text{conjugate acid} + OH^-(aq)$$

  - Example:

$$NH_3(aq) + H_2O(l) \rightleftharpoons NH_4^+(aq) + OH^-(aq).$$

  - The **base-dissociation constant**, $K_b$, is defined as

$$K_b = \frac{[NH_4^+][OH^-]}{[NH_3]}$$

    - The larger $K_b$, the stronger the base.

### Types of Weak Bases

---

[33] Table 16.3 from MediaPortfolio and Transparency Pack
[34] Table 16.4 from MediaPortfolio

- Weak bases generally fall into one of two categories.
  - Neutral substances with a lone pair of electrons that can accept protons.
    - Most neutral weak bases contain nitrogen.
    - **Amines** are related to ammonia and have one or more N–H bonds replaced with N–C bonds (e.g., $CH_3NH_2$ is methylamine).
  - Anions of weak acids are also weak bases.
  - Example: $ClO^-$ is the conjugate base of HClO (weak acid):

$$ClO^-(aq) + H_2O(l) \rightleftharpoons HClO(aq) + OH^-(aq) \qquad K_b = 3.3 \times 10^{-7}$$

## 16.8 Relationship Between $K_a$ and $K_b$[35]

- We can quantify the relationship between strength of an acid and the strength of its conjugate base.
- Consider the following equilibria:

$$NH_4^+(aq) \rightleftharpoons NH_3(aq) + H^+(aq)$$
$$NH_3(aq) + H_2O(l) \rightleftharpoons NH_4^+(aq) + OH^-(aq)$$

  - We can write equilibrium expressions for these reactions:

$$K_a = \frac{[NH_3][H^+]}{[NH_4^+]} \qquad K_b = \frac{[NH_4^+][OH^-]}{[NH_3]}$$

  - If we add these equations together:

$$NH_4^+(aq) \rightleftharpoons NH_3(aq) + H^+(aq)$$
$$NH_3(aq) + H_2O(l) \rightleftharpoons NH_4^+(aq) + OH^-(aq)$$

  - The net reaction is the autoionization of water.

$$H_2O(l) \rightleftharpoons H^+(aq) + OH^-(aq)$$

- Recall that:

$$K_w = [H^+][OH^-]$$

  - We can use this information to write an expression that relates the values of $K_a$, $K_b$ and $K_w$ for a conjugate acid-base pair:

$$K_a \times K_b = K_w$$

    - Alternatively, we can express this as:

$$pK_a + pK_b = pK_w = 14.00 \text{ (at 25°C)}$$

- Thus, the larger $K_a$ (and the smaller $pK_a$), the smaller $K_b$ (and the larger $pK_b$).
  - The stronger the acid, the weaker its conjugate base and vice versa.

## 16.9 Acid-Base Properties of Salt Solutions[36]

- Nearly all salts are strong electrolytes.
  - Therefore, salts in solution exist entirely of ions.
  - Acid-base properties of salts are a consequence of the reactions of their *ions* in solution.
- Many salt ions can react with water to form $OH^-$ or $H^+$.
  - This process is called **hydrolysis**.
  - Anions from weak acids are basic.
  - Anions from strong acids are neutral.
  - Anions with ionizable protons (e.g., $HSO_4^-$) are amphoteric.
    - They are capable of acting as an acid *or* a base.
  - All cations, except those of the alkali metals or heavier alkaline earth metals, are weak acids.
- The pH of a solution may be qualitatively predicted using the following guidelines:
  - Salts derived from a strong acid and strong base are neutral.
    - Examples: NaCl, $Ca(NO_3)_2$.

---

[35] Table 16.5 from MediaPortfolio and Transparency Pack

[36] "Hydrolysis: Acidic and Basic Properties of Salts" from Live Demonstrations

- Salts derived from a strong base and weak acid are basic.
  - Examples: NaClO, $Ba(C_2H_3O_2)_2$.
- Salts derived from a weak base and strong acid are acidic.
  - Example: $NH_4Cl$.
- Salts derived from a weak acid and weak base can be either acidic or basic.
  - Equilibrium rules apply!
  - We need to compare $K_a$ and $K_b$ for hydrolysis of the anion and the cation.
  - For example, consider $NH_4CN$.
    - Both ions undergo significant hydrolysis.
    - Is the salt solution acidic or basic?
    - • The $K_a$ of $NH_4^+$ is smaller than the $K_b$ of $CN^-$, so the solution should be basic.

## 16.10 Acid-Base Behavior and Chemical Structure

### Factors That Affect Acid Strength[37]

- Consider H–X.
- For this substance to be an acid:
  - The H–X bond must be polar with $H^{\delta+}$ and $X^{\delta-}$.
- In ionic hydrides, the bond polarity is reversed.
  - The H–X bond is polar with $H^{\delta-}$ and $X^{\delta+}$.
  - In this case, the substance is a base.
- Other factors important in determining acid strength include:
  - The strength of the bond.
    - The H–X bond must be weak enough to be broken.
  - The stability of the conjugate base, $X^-$.
    - The greater the stability of the conjugate base, the more acidic the molecule.

### Binary Acids[38]

- The H–X bond strength is important in determining relative acid strength in any *group* in the periodic table.
  - The H–X bond strength tends to decrease as the element X increases in size.
  - Acid strength increases down a group; base strength decreases down a group.
- H–X bond polarity is important in determining relative acid strength in any *period* of the periodic table.
  - Acid strength increases and base strength decreases from left to right across a period as the electronegativity of X increases.
- For example, consider the molecules HF and $CH_4$.
  - HF is a weak acid because the bond energy is high.
  - The electronegativity difference between C and H is so small that the C–H bond is nonpolar, and $CH_4$ is neither an acid nor a base.

### Oxyacids[39,40]

- Many acids contain one or more O–H bonds.
  - Acids that contain OH groups (and often additional oxygen atoms) bound to the central atom are called **oxyacids.**

---

[37] "Effect of Molecular Structure on the Strength of Organic Acids and Bases in Aqueous Solutions" from Live Demonstrations

[38] Figure 16.12 from MediaPortfolio

[39] "The Relative Strength of Oxyacids and Its Application" from Further Readings

[40] Figure 16.13 from MediaPortfolio and Transparency Pack

    - All oxyacids have the general structure Y–O–H.
- The strength of the acid depends on Y and the atoms attached to Y.
    - As the electronegativity of Y increases, so does the acidity of the substance.
    - The bond polarity increases and the stability of the conjugate base (usually an anion) increases.
- A general trend is thus:
    - If Y is a metal (low electronegativity), then the substances are bases.
    - If Y has an intermediate electronegativity (e.g., I, EN = 2.5), the electrons are between Y and O and the substance is a weak oxyacid.
    - If Y has a large electronegativity (e.g., Cl, EN = 3.0), the electrons are located closer to Y than O and the O–H bond is more polar, making it easier to lose $H^+$.
    - As the number of O atoms attached to Y increases the O–H bond polarity, and consequently the strength of the acid increases.
        - Example, HClO is a weaker acid than $HClO_2$ which is weaker than $HClO_3$ which is weaker than $HClO_4$.

### Carboxylic Acids

- There is a large class of acids that contain a –COOH group (a *carboxyl* group).
    - Acids that contain this group are called **carboxylic acids.**
        - Examples: acetic acid, benzoic acid, formic acid.
- Why are these molecules acidic?
    - 1. The additional oxygen atom on the carboxyl group increases the polarity of the O–H bond and stabilizes the conjugate base.
    - 2. The conjugate base exhibits resonance.
        - This gives it the ability to delocalize the negative charge over the carboxylate group, further increasing the stability of the conjugate base.
- The acid strength also increases as the number of electronegative groups in the acid increases.
    - For example, acetic acid is much weaker than trichloroacetic acid.

## 16.11 Lewis Acids and Bases[41,42]

- A Brønsted-Lowry acid is a proton donor.
- Focusing on electrons: A Brønsted-Lowry acid can be considered as an electron pair acceptor.
- Lewis proposed a new definition of acids and bases that emphasizes the shared electron pair.
    - A **Lewis acid** is an electron pair acceptor.
    - A **Lewis base** is an electron pair donor.
        - Note: Lewis acids and bases do not need to contain protons.
        - Therefore, the Lewis definition is the most general definition of acids and bases.
- What types of compounds can act as Lewis acids?
    - Lewis acids generally have an incomplete octet (e.g., $BF_3$).
    - Transition-metal ions are generally Lewis acids.
    - Lewis acids must have a vacant orbital (into which the electron pairs can be donated).
    - Compounds with multiple bonds can act as Lewis acids.
        - For example, consider the reaction:

$$H_2O(l) + CO_2(g) \rightarrow H_2CO_3(aq)$$

        - Water acts as the electron pair donor and carbon dioxide as the electron pair acceptor in this reaction.
        - Overall, the water (Lewis base) has donated a pair of electrons to the $CO_2$ (Lewis acid).

### Hydrolysis of Metal Ions[43]

---

[41] "Lewis Acid-Base Theory" Animation from MediaPortfolio

[42] "The Research Style of Gilbert N. Lewis: Acids and Bases" from Further Readings

- The Lewis concept may be used to explain the acid properties of many metal ions.
- Metal ions are positively charged and attract water molecules (via the lone pairs on the oxygen atom of water).
- Hydrated metal ions act as acids.
    - For example:

$$Fe(H_2O)_6^{3+}(aq) \leftrightharpoons Fe(H_2O)_5(OH)^{2+}(aq) + H^+(aq) \qquad K_a = 2 \times 10^{-3}.$$

- In general:
    - The higher the charge, the stronger the M–$OH_2$ interaction.
        - $K_a$ values generally increase with increasing charge
    - The smaller the metal ion, the more acidic the ion.
        - $K_a$ values generally decrease with decreasing ionic radius
            - Thus the pH of an aqueous solution increases as the size of the ion increases (e.g., $Ca^{2+}$ vs. $Zn^{2+}$) and as the charge increases (e.g., $Na^+$ vs. $Ca^{2+}$ and $Zn^{2+}$ vs. $Al^{3+}$).

## The Amphoteric Behavior of Amino Acids

- Amino acids: building blocks of proteins.
- Each contains a carboxyl group AND an amine group.
- Thus amino acids have both acidic and basic groups.
    - They undergo a proton transfer in which the proton of the carboxyl is transferred to the basic nitrogen atom of the amine group.
        - A *zwitterion* or dipolar ion results.

---

[43] Figure 16.15 from MediaPortfolio

## Further Readings:

1. Doris Kolb, "Acids and Bases," *J. Chem. Educ.*, Vol. 55, **1978**, 459–464.

2. Joseph F. Lomax, "Kinetic Classroom: Acid-Base and Redox Demonstrations with Student Movement," *J. Chem. Educ.*, Vol. 71, **1994**, 428–430.

3. A. M. de Lange and J. H. Potgieter, "Acid and Base Dissociation Constants of Water and Its Associated Ions," *J. Chem. Educ.*, Vol. 68, **1991**, 304–305.

4. Stephen J. Hawkes, "Teaching the Truth about pH," *J. Chem. Educ.*, Vol. 71, **1994**, 747–749.

5. Doris Kolb, "The pH Concept," *J. Chem. Educ.*, Vol. 56, **1979**, 49–53.

6. Robert D. Curtright, James A. Rynearson, and John Markwell, "Fruit Anthocyanins: Colorful Sensors of Molecular Milieu," *J. Chem. Educ.*, Vol. 71, **1994**, 682–684.

7. Geoerge B. Kauffman, "The Brønsted-Lowry Acid-Base Concept," *J. Chem. Educ.*, Vol. 65, **1988**, 28–31.

8. Jamie L. Adcock, "Teaching Brønsted-Lowry Acid–Base Theory in a Direct Comprehensive Way," *J. Chem. Educ.*, Vol. 78, **2001**, 1495–1496.

9. F. Axtell Kramer, "An Analogy for the Leveling Effect in Acid-Base Chemistry," *J. Chem. Educ.*, Vol. 63, **1986**, 275.

10. John J. Fortman, "Pictorial Analogies XI: Concentrations and Acidity of Solutions," *J. Chem. Educ.*, Vol. 71, **1994**, 430–432.

11. Todd P. Silverstein, "Weak vs Strong Acids and Bases: The Football Analogy," *J. Chem. Educ.*, Vol. 77, **2000**, 849–850.

12. Addison Ault, "Do pH in Your Head," *J. Chem. Educ.*, Vol. 76, **1999**, 936–938.

13. Manus Monroe and Karl Abrams, "The Relative Strength of Oxyacids and Its Application," *J. Chem. Educ.*, Vol. 62, **1985**, 41–43.

14. Glen T. Seaborg, "The Research Style of Gilbert N. Lewis: Acids and Bases," *J. Chem. Educ.*, Vol. 61, **1984**, 93–100.

## Live Demonstrations:

1. Bassam Z. Shakhashiri, "Acid-Base Indicators Extracted from Plants," *Chemical Demonstrations: A Handbook for Teachers of Chemistry, Volume 3* (Madison: The University of Wisconsin Press, **1989**), pp. 50–57. A wide range of plant materials are used as sources of acid-base indicator. Included in this group is an old favorite: red cabbage.

2. Bassam Z. Shakhashiri, "Differences Between Acid Strength and Concentration," *Chemical Demonstrations: A Handbook for Teachers of Chemistry, Volume 3* (Madison: The University of Wisconsin Press, **1989**), pp. 136–139. The strength of three acids (acetic, hydrochloric, and sulfuric) are compared by reaction with sodium hydroxide. A companion procedure, involving base strength, is also included.

3. Lee. R. Summerlin, Christie L. Borgford, and Julie B. Ealy, "Disappearing Ink," *Chemical Demonstrations, A Sourcebook for Teachers, Volume 2* (Washington: American Chemical Society, **1988**), p. 176. "Disappearing ink" is made from thymolphthalein indicator and dilute sodium hydroxide.

4. Bassam Z. Shakhashiri, "Colorful Acid-Base Indicators," *Chemical Demonstrations: A Handbook for Teachers of Chemistry, Volume 3* (Madison: The University of Wisconsin Press, **1989**), pp. 33–40.

5. Bassam Z. Shakhashiri, "Hydrolysis: Acidic and Basic Properties of Salts," *Chemical Demonstrations: A Handbook for Teachers of Chemistry, Volume 3* (Madison: The University of Wisconsin Press, **1989**), pp. 103–108.

6. Bassam Z. Shakhashiri, "Effect of Molecular Structure on the Strength of Organic Acids and Bases in Aqueous Solutions," *Chemical Demonstrations: A Handbook for Teachers of Chemistry, Volume 3* (Madison: The University of Wisconsin Press, **1989**), pp. 158–161.

# Chapter 17. Additional Aspects of Aqueous Equilibria

## Media Resources

### Figures and Tables

| **In Transparency Pack and on MediaPortfolio:** | **Section:** |
|---|---|
| Figure 17.2 Buffer Action | 17.2 Buffered Solutions |
| Figure 17.3 Calculation of the pH of a Buffer | 17.2 Buffered Solutions |
| Figure 17.6 Strong Acid-Strong Base Titration Curve | 17.3 Acid-Base Titrations |
| Figure 17.9 Weak Acid-Strong Base Titration Curve | 17.3 Acid-Base Titrations |
| Figure 17.10 Titration Calculation | 17.3 Acid-Base Titrations |
| Figure 17.11 Effect of $K_a$ on the Titration Curve | 17.3 Acid-Base Titrations |
| Figure 17.12 Titration of $NH_3$ with HCl | 17.3 Acid-Base Titrations |
| Figure 17.13 Titration of a Polyprotic Acid | 17.3 Acid-Base Titrations |
| Figure 17.14 Interconverting Solubility and $K_{sp}$ | 17.4 Solubility Equilibria |
| Figure 17.22 Qualitative Analysis Scheme | 17.7 Qualitative Analysis for Metallic Elements |

| **On MediaPortfolio:** | **Section:** |
|---|---|
| Figure 17.8 Strong Base-Strong Acid Titration Curve | 17.3 Acid-Base Titrations |
| Table 17.1 Formation Constants for Some Metal Complex Ions in Water at 25°C | 17.5 Factors That Affect Solubility |

| **Animations:** | **Section:** |
|---|---|
| Common-Ion Effect | 17.1 The Common-Ion Effect |
| Acid-Base Titration | 17.3 Acid-Base Titrations |
| Dissolution of $Mg(OH)_2$ by Acid | 17.5 Factors That Affect Solubility |

| **Movies:** | **Section:** |
|---|---|
| Precipitation Reactions | 17.5 Factors That Affect Solubility |

| **Activities:** | **Section:** |
|---|---|
| Calculating pH Using Henderson-Hasselbalch Equation | 17.2 Buffered Solutions |
| Buffer pH | 17.2 Buffered Solutions |
| Acid-Base Titration | 17.3 Acid-Base Titrations |
| Weak Acid/Strong Base Titration Curve Activity | 17.3 Acid-Base Titrations |
| Weak Base/Strong Acid Titration Curve Activity | 17.3 Acid-Base Titrations |
| Polyprotic Acid/Strong Base Titration Curve Activity | 17.3 Acid-Base Titrations |
| $K_{sp}$ Activity | 17.4 Solubility Equilibria |

## Other Resources

| **Further Readings:** | **Section:** |
|---|---|
| A Good Idea Leads to a Better Buffer | 17.2 Buffered Solutions |
| Phosphate Buffers and Telephone Poles—A Useful Analogy with Limitations | 17.2 Buffered Solutions |
| The Henderson-Hasselbalch Equation: Its History and Limitations | 17.2 Buffered Solutions |

| | |
|---|---|
| Acid-Base Indicators: a New Look at an Old Topic | 17.3 Acid-Base Titrations |
| Edible Acid-Base Indicators | 17.3 Acid-Base Titrations |
| Predicting Acid-Base Titration Curves without Calculations | 17.3 Acid-Base Titrations |
| Blood-Chemistry Tutorials: Teaching Biological Applications of General Chemistry Material | 17.3 Acid-Base Titrations |
| The Useless Tea Kettle | 17.4 Solubility Equilibria |
| The Murky Pool | 17.4 Solubility Equilibria |
| The $K_{sp}$-Solubility Conundrum | 17.4 Solubility Equilibria |
| Assessing Students' Conceptual Understanding of Solubility Equilibrium | 17.4 Solubility Equilibria |
| What Should We Teach Beginners about Solubility and Solubility Products? | 17.4 Solubility Equilbiria |
| Chemical Aspects of Dentistry | 17.5 Factors That Affect Solubility |
| Acid-Base Chemistry of the Aluminum Ion in Aqueous Solution | 17.5 Factors That Affect Solubility |
| Complexometric Titrations: Competition of Complexing Agents in the Determination of Water Hardness with EDTA | 17.5 Factors That Affect Solubility |
| Swimming Pools, Hot Rods, and Qualitative Analysis | 17.6 Precipitation and Separation of Ions |

| **Live Demonstrations:** | **Section:** |
|---|---|
| The Common Ion Effect: Second Demonstration | 17.1 The Common-Ion Effect |
| Effect of Acetate Ion on the Acidity of Acetic Acid: The Common-Ion Effect | 17.1 The Common-Ion Effect |
| The Common-Ion Effect: Ammonium Hydroxide and Ammonium Acetate | 17.1 The Common-Ion Effect |
| Equilibrium: The Dissociation of Acetic Acid | 17.1 The Common-Ion Effect |
| Buffering Action and Capacity | 17.2 Buffered Solutions |
| Buffering Action of Alka-Seltzer | 17.2 Buffered Solutions |
| Teas as Natural Indicators | 17.3 Acid-Base Titrations |
| Solubility of Some Silver Compounds | 17.4 Solubility Equilibria |
| Silver Ion Solubilities: Red and White Precipitates | 17.4 Solubility Equilibria |
| Determination of Neutralizing Capacity of Antacids | 17.5 Factors That Affect Solubility |
| Milk of Magnesia versus Acid | 17.5 Factors That Affect Solubility |
| Fizzing and Foaming: Reactions of Acids with Carbonates | 17.5 Factors That Affect Solubility |
| Colorful Complex Ions in Ammonia | 17.5 Factors That Affect Solubility |
| Green and Blue Copper Complexes | 17.5 Factors That Affect Solubility |
| Acidic and Basic Properties of Oxides | 17.5 Factors That Affect Solubility |

# Chapter 17. Additional Aspects of Aqueous Equilibria

## Common Student Misconceptions

- Students often believe that the pH at the equivalence point for any titration is 7.00.
- In terms of problem-solving skills, this is probably the most difficult chapter for most students.
- Students tend to find buffers particularly difficult to understand.
- Students often forget to consider volume changes that occur when two solutions are mixed (this will have an effect on the concentration of the species present).
- Students tend to confuse $K_{sp}$ and solubility.

## Lecture Outline

### 17.1 The Common Ion Effect[1,2,3,4,5]

- The dissociation of a weak electrolyte is decreased by the addition of a strong electrolyte that has an ion in common with the weak electrolyte.
- For example, consider the ionization of a weak acid, acetic acid.

$$HC_2H_3O_2(aq) \leftrightharpoons H^+(aq) + C_2H_3O_2^-(aq)$$

  - If we add additional $C_2H_3O_2^-$ ions by the addition of a strong electrolyte, (e.g., $NaC_2H_3O_2$) the equilibrium is shifted to the left.
  - This causes a reduction in the $[H^+]$ and a decrease in the percent ionization of the acetic acid.
  - By adding sodium acetate, we have disturbed the acetic acid equilibrium.
  - In effect, we have added a product of this equilibrium (i.e., the acetate ion).
    - This phenomenon is called the **common-ion effect**.
- Common ion equilibrium problems are solved following the same pattern as other equilibrium problems.
  - However, the initial concentration of the common ion (from the salt) must be considered.

### 17. 2 Buffered Solutions

- A buffered solution or buffer is a solution that resists a change in pH upon addition of small amounts of strong acid or strong base.

#### Composition and Action of Buffered Solutions[6,7,8,9,10]

- A buffer consists of a mixture of a weak acid (HX) and its conjugate base ($X^-$).

$$HX(aq) \leftrightharpoons H^+(aq) + X^-(aq)$$

- Thus a buffer contains both:

---

[1] "The Common Ion Effect: Second Demonstration" from Live Demonstrations
[2] "Effect of Acetate Ion on the Acidity of Acetic Acid: The Common Ion Effect" from Live Demonstrations
[3] "Common Ion Effect" Animation from MediaPortfolio
[4] "The Common Ion Effect: Ammonium Hydroxide and Ammonium Acetate" from Live Demonstrations
[5] "Equilibrium: The Dissociation of Acetic Acid" from Live Demonstrations
[6] "A Good Idea Leads to a Better Buffer" from Further Readings
[7] "Phosphate Buffers and Telephone Poles—A Useful Analogy with Limitation" from Further Readings
[8] "Buffering Action and Capacity" from Live Demonstrations
[9] "Buffering Action of Alka-Seltzer" from Live Demonstrations
[10] Figure 17.2 from MediaPortfolio and Transparency Pack

- An acidic species (to neutralize $OH^-$) and
- A basic species (to neutralize $H^+$).
- When a small amount of $OH^-$ is added to the buffer, the $OH^-$ reacts with HX to produce $X^-$ and water.
  - But the [HX]/[ $X^-$] ratio remains more or less constant, so the pH is not significantly changed.
- When a small amount of $H^+$ is added to the buffer, $X^-$ is consumed to produce HX.
  - Once again, the [HX]/[ $X^-$] ratio is more or less constant, so the pH does not change significantly.

## Buffer Capacity and pH[11,12,13]

- **Buffer capacity** is the amount of acid or base that can be neutralized by the buffer before there is a significant change in pH.
- Buffer capacity depends on the concentrations of the components of the buffer.
  - The greater the concentrations of the conjugate acid-base pair, the greater the buffer capacity.
- The pH of the buffer is related to $K_a$ and to the relative concentrations of the acid and base.
- We can derive an equation that shows the relationship between conjugate acid-base concentrations, pH and $K_a$.
- By definition:

$$K_a = \frac{[H^+][X^-]}{[HX]}$$

- Rearranging, we get:

$$[H^+] = K_a \frac{[HX]}{[X^-]}$$

- If we take the negative log of each side of the equation we get:

$$-\log[H^+] = -\log K_a - \log\frac{[HX]}{[X^-]}$$

- By definition:

$$pH = pK_a - \log\frac{[HX]}{[X^-]}$$

- An alternate form of this equation is:

$$pH = pK_a + \log\frac{[X^-]}{[HX]} = pK_a + \log\frac{[\text{base}]}{[\text{acid}]}$$

- The above equation is the **Henderson-Hasselbalch equation.**
  - Note that this equation uses the equilibrium concentrations of the acid and conjugate base.
  - However, if $K_a$ is sufficiently small (i.e., if the equilibrium concentration of undissociated acid is close to the initial concentration), then we can use the initial values of the acid and base concentrations in order to get a good estimate of the pH.

## Addition of Strong Acids or Bases to Buffers[14,15]

---

[11] "The Henderson-Hasselbalch Equation: Its History and Limitations" from Further Readings
[12] "Calculating pH Using Henderson-Hasselbalch Equation" Activity from MediaPortfolio
[13] "Buffer pH" Activity from MediaPortfolio
[14] Figure 17.3 from MediaPortfolio and Transparency Pack

- We break the calculation into two parts.
  - A stoichiometric calculation.
  - An equilibrium calculation.
- The addition of strong acid or base results in a neutralization reaction:

$$X^- + H_3O^+ \rightarrow HX + H_2O$$
$$HX + OH^- \rightarrow X^- + H_2O$$

  - By knowing how much $H_3O^+$ or $OH^-$ was added we know how much HX or $X^-$ is formed.
    - This is the stoichiometric calculation.
  - With the concentrations of HX and $X^-$ (note the change in volume of solution) we can calculate the pH from the Henderson-Hasselbalch equation:

$$pH = pK_a + \log\frac{[X^-]}{[HX]}$$

    - This is the equilibrium calculation.

## 17.3 Acid-Base Titrations[16,17,18]

- In an acid-base titration:
  - A solution of base (or acid) of known concentration is added to an acid.
  - Acid-base indicators or a pH meter are used to signal the equivalence point.
  - The plot of pH versus volume during a titration is called a **pH titration curve**.

### Strong Acid-Strong Base Titrations[19,20,21,22]

- Consider adding a strong base (e.g., NaOH) to a solution of a strong acid (e.g., HCl).
- We can divide the titration curve into four regions.
  - 1. Initial pH (before any base is added).
    - The pH is given by the strong acid solution.
    - Therefore, pH < 7.
  - 2. Between the initial pH and the equivalence point.
    - When base is added before the equivalence point the pH is given by the amount of strong acid in excess.
    - Therefore, pH < 7.
  - 3. At the equivalence point.
    - The amount of base added is stoichiometrically equivalent to the amount of acid originally present.
    - Therefore, the pH is determined by the hydrolysis of the salt in solution.
    - Therefore, pH = 7.
  - 4. After the equivalence point.
    - The pH is determined by the excess base in the solution.
    - Therefore, pH > 7.
- How can we analyze the titration (i.e., how will we know when we are at the equivalence point?).

---

[15] "Blood-Chemistry Tutorials: Teaching Biological Applications of General Chemistry Material" from Further Readings

[16] "Acid-Base Indicators: A New Look at an Old Topic" from Further Readings

[17] "Teas as Natural Indicators" from Live Demonstrations

[18] "Edible Acid-Base Indicators" from Further Readings

[19] "Acid-Base Titration" Animation from MediaPortfolio

[20] "Acid-Base Titration" Activity from MediaPortfolio

[21] "Predicting Acid-Base Titration Curves Without Calculations" from Further Readings

[22] Figure 17.6 from MediaPortfolio and Transparency Pack

- Consider adding a strong base (e.g., NaOH) to a solution of a strong acid (e.g., HCl).
- We know the pH at the equivalence point is 7.00.
- To detect the equivalence point, we use an indicator that changes color somewhere near pH 7.00.
- Usually, we use phenolphthalein which changes color between pH 8.3 to 10.0.
    - In acid, phenolphthalein is colorless.
    - As NaOH is added, there is a slight pink color at the addition point.
    - When the flask is swirled and the reagents mixed, the pink color disappears.
    - At the end point, the solution is light pink.
    - If more base is added, the solution turns darker pink.
    - The equivalence point in a titration is the point at which the acid and base are present in stoichiometrically equivalent quantities.
    - The end point in a titration is the point where the indicator changes color.
        - The difference between the equivalence point and the end point is called the titration error.
- The shape of a strong base-strong acid titration curve is very similar to a strong acid-strong base titration curve.
    - Initially, the strong base is in excess, so the pH > 7.
    - As acid is added, the pH decreases but is still greater than 7.
    - At the equivalence point, the pH is given by the salt solution (i.e., pH = 7).
    - After the equivalence point, the pH is given by the strong acid in excess, so pH is less than 7.

### Weak Acid-Strong Base Titration[23,24,25,26,27,28,29]

- Consider the titration of acetic acid, $HC_2H_3O_2$ with NaOH.
- Again, we divide the titration into four general regions:
    - 1. Before any base is added:
        - The solution contains only weak acid.
        - Therefore, pH is given by the equilibrium calculation.
    - 2. Between the initial pH and the equivalence point.
        - As strong base is added it consumes a stoichiometric quantity of weak acid:

$$HC_2H_3O_2(aq) + OH^-(aq) \rightarrow C_2H_3O_2^-(aq) + H_2O(l)$$

        - However, there is an excess of acetic acid.
        - Therefore, we have a mixture of weak acid and its conjugate base.
            - Thus the composition of the mixture is that of a buffer.
            - The pH is given by the buffer calculation.
                - First the amount of $C_2H_3O_2^-$ generated is calculated, as well as the amount of $HC_2H_3O_2$ consumed. (Stoichiometry.)
                - Then the pH is calculated using equilibrium conditions. (Henderson-Hasselbalch equation.)
    - 3. At the equivalence point, all the acetic acid has been consumed and all the NaOH has been consumed.
        - However, $C_2H_3O_2^-$ has been generated.
        - Therefore, the pH depends on the $C_2H_3O_2^-$ concentration.

---

[23] Figure 17.8 from MediaPortfolio
[24] Figure 17.9 from MediaPortfolio and Transparency Pack
[25] "Weak Acid/Strong Base Titration Curve Activity" from MediaPortfolio
[26] Figure 17.10 from MediaPortfolio and Transparency Pack
[27] Figure 17.11 from MediaPortfolio and Transparency Pack
[28] Figure 17.12 from MediaPortfolio and Transparency Pack
[29] "Weak Base/Strong Acid Titration Curve Activity" from MediaPortfolio

- The pH > 7 at the equivalence point.
- More importantly, the pH of the equivalence point ≠ 7 for a weak acid-strong base titration.
- 4. After the equivalence point:
  - The pH is given by the concentration of the excess strong base.
- The pH curve for a weak acid-strong base titration differs significantly from that of a strong acid-strong base titration.
  - For a strong acid-strong base titration:
    - The pH begins at less than 7 and gradually increases as base is added.
    - Near the equivalence point, the pH increases dramatically.
  - For a weak acid-strong base titration:
    - The initial pH rise is more steep than the strong acid-strong base case.
    - However, then there is a leveling off due to buffer effects.
    - The inflection point is not as steep for a weak acid-strong base titration.
  - The shape of the two curves after the equivalence point is the same because pH is determined by the strong base in excess.
  - The pH at the equivalence point differs also:
    - The pH is 7.00 for the strong acid-strong base equivalence point.
    - The pH is >7.00 for the weak acid-strong base equivalence point.

### Titrations of Polyprotic Acids[30,31]

- In polyprotic acids, the ionizable protons dissociate in a series of steps.
  - Therefore, in a titration there are *n* equivalence points corresponding to each ionizable proton.
- In the titration of $H_2CO_3$ with NaOH there are two equivalence points:
  - One for the formation of $HCO_3^-$.
  - One for the formation of $CO_3^{2-}$.

## 17.4 Solubility Equilibria[32,33]

### The Solubility-Product Constant, $K_{sp}$[34,35,36,37,38,39]

- Consider a saturated solution of $BaSO_4$ in contact with solid $BaSO_4$.
  - We can write an equilibrium expression for the dissolving of the slightly soluble solid.

$$BaSO_4(s) \rightleftharpoons Ba^{2+}(aq) + SO_4^{2-}(aq)$$

  - Because $BaSO_4(s)$ is a pure solid, the equilibrium expression depends only on the concentration of the ions.
  - $K_{sp}$ is the equilibrium constant for the equilibrium between an ionic solid solute and its saturated aqueous solution.
    - $K_{sp}$ is called the **solubility-product constant** or the **solubility product**.
    - $K_{sp}$ for $BaSO_4$ is:

$$K_{sp} = [Ba^{2+}][SO_4^{2-}]$$

---

30 Figure 17.13 from MediaPortfolio and Transparency Pack
31 "Polyprotic Acid/Strong Base Titration Curve Activity" from MediaPortfolio
32 "Solubility of some Silver Compounds" from Live Demonstrations
33 "Silver Ion Solubilities: Red and White Precipitates" from Live Demonstrations
34 "$K_{sp}$ Activity" from Media Portfolio
35 "The Murky Pool" from Further Readings
36 "The $K_{sp}$-Solubility Conundrum" from Further Readings
37 "The Useless Tea Kettle" from Further Readings
38 "Assessing Students' Conceptual Understanding of Solubility Equilibrium" from Further Readings
39 "What Should We Teach Beginners about Solubility and Solubility Products" from Further Readings

- In general: the solubility product is equal to the product of the molar concentration of ions raised to powers corresponding to their stoichiometric coefficients.

### Solubility and $K_{sp}$[40]

- *Solubility* is the amount of substance that dissolves to form a saturated solution.
  - This is often expressed as grams of solid that will dissolve per liter of solution.
- *Molar solubility* is the number of moles of solute that dissolve to form a liter of saturated solution.
- We can use the solubility to find $K_{sp}$ and vice versa.
  - To convert solubility to $K_{sp}$:
    - Convert solubility into molar solubility (via molar mass).
    - Convert molar solubility into the molar concentration of ions at equilibrium (equilibrium calculation).
    - Use the equilibrium concentration of ions in the $K_{sp}$ expression.
  - To convert $K_{sp}$ to solubility:
    - Write the $K_{sp}$ expression.
    - Let $x$ = the molar solubility of the salt.
    - Use the stoichiometry of the reaction to express the concentration of each species in terms of $x$.
    - Substitute these concentrations into the equilibrium expression and solve for $x$.
    - This calculation works best for salts whose ions have low charges.

## 17.5 Factors That Affect Solubility

- Three factors that have a significant impact on solubility are:
  - The presence of a common ion.
  - The pH of the solution.
  - The presence or absence of complexing agents.

### Common-Ion Effect

- Solubility is decreased when a common ion is added.
  - This is an application of Le Châtelier's principle:
- Consider the solubility of $CaF_2$:

$$CaF_2(s) \leftrightharpoons Ca^{2+}(aq) + 2F^-(aq)$$

  - If more $F^-$ is added (i.e., by the addition of NaF), the equilibrium shifts to offset the increase.
  - Therefore, $CaF_2(s)$ is formed and precipitation occurs.
    - As NaF is added to the system, the solubility of $CaF_2$ decreases.

### Solubility and pH[41,42,43,44,45]

- Again we apply Le Châtelier's principle:

$$Mg(OH)_2(s) \leftrightharpoons Mg^{2+}(aq) + 2OH^-(aq)$$

  - If $OH^-$ is removed, then the equilibrium shifts toward the right and $Mg(OH)_2$ dissolves.
  - $OH^-$ can be removed by adding a strong acid:

$$OH^-(aq) + H^+(aq) \leftrightharpoons H_2O(aq)$$

  - As pH decreases, $[H^+]$ increases and the solubility of $Mg(OH)_2$ increases.
- Another example:

---

[40] Figure 17.14 from MediaPortfolio and Transparency Pack
[41] "Dissolution of $Mg(OH)_2$ by Acid" Animation from MediaPortfolio
[42] "Precipitation Reactions" Movie from MediaPortfolio
[43] "Fizzing and Foaming: Reactions of Acids with Carbonates" from Live Demonstrations
[44] "Milk of Magnesia Versus Acid" from Live Demonstrations
[45] "Determination of the Neutralizing Capacity of Antacids" from Live Demonstrations

$$CaF_2(s) \rightleftharpoons Ca^{2+}(aq) + 2F^-(aq)$$

- If the $F^-$ is removed, then the equilibrium shifts towards the right and $CaF_2$ dissolves.
- $F^-$ can be removed by adding a strong acid:

$$F^-(aq) + H^+(aq) \rightleftharpoons HF(aq)$$

- As pH decreases, $[H^+]$ increases and solubility of $CaF_2$ increases.

- The effect of pH on solubility can be dramatic.
- The effect is most significant if one or both ions involved are at least somewhat acidic or basic.
  - In general:
    - The solubility of slightly soluble salts containing basic ions increases as pH decreases.
    - The more basic the anion, the greater the effect.

## Formation of Complex Ions[46,47,48,49,50]

- Recall that metal ions may act as Lewis acids in aqueous solution (water may act as the Lewis base).
  - Such an interaction may have a significant impact on metal salt solubility.
  - For example, AgCl has a very low solubility.
    - $K_{sp}$ for AgCl = $1.8 \times 10^{-10}$
    - However, the solubility is greatly increased if ammonia is added.
      - Why?
- Consider the formation of $Ag(NH_3)_2^+$:

$$Ag^+(aq) + 2NH_3(aq) \rightleftharpoons Ag(NH_3)_2^+(aq)$$

  - The $Ag(NH_3)_2^+$ is called a **complex ion.**
  - $NH_3$ (the attached Lewis base) is called a *ligand.*
  - The equilibrium constant for the reaction is called the **formation constant,** $K_f$:

$$K_f = \frac{[Ag(NH_3)_2^+]}{[Ag^+][NH_3]^2} = 1.7 \times 10^7$$

  - Consider the addition of ammonia to AgCl (white salt):

$$AgCl(s) \rightleftharpoons Ag^+(aq) + Cl^-(aq)$$
$$Ag^+(aq) + 2NH_3(aq) \rightleftharpoons Ag(NH_3)_2^+(aq)$$

    - The overall reaction is:

$$AgCl(s) + 2NH_3(aq) \rightleftharpoons Ag(NH_3)_2^+(aq) + Cl^-(aq)$$

    - Effectively, the $Ag^+(aq)$ has been removed from solution.
    - By Le Châtelier's principle, the forward reaction (the dissolving of AgCl) is favored.

## Amphoterism[51,52]

- Amphoteric metal hydroxides and oxides will dissolve in either a strong acid or a strong base.
  - Examples: hydroxides and oxides of $Al^{3+}$, $Cr^{3+}$, $Zn^{2+}$, and $Sn^{2+}$.
  - The hydroxides generally form complex ions with several hydroxide ligands attached to the metal:

$$Al(OH)_3(s) + OH^-(aq) \rightleftharpoons Al(OH)_4^-(aq)$$

- Hydrated metal ions act as weak acids.

---

[46] Table 17.1 from MediaPortfolio
[47] "Colorful Complex Ions in Ammonia" from Live Demonstrations
[48] "Green and Blue Copper Complexes" from Live Demonstrations
[49] "Chemical Aspects of Dentistry" from Further Readings
[50] "Complexometric Titrations: Competition of Complexing Agents in the Determination of Water Hardness With EDTA" from Further Readings
[51] "Acid-Base Chemistry of the Aluminum Ion in Aqueous Solution" from Further Readings
[52] "Acidic and Basic Properties of Oxides" from Live Demonstrations

- As strong base is added, protons are removed:

$$Al(H_2O)_6^{3+}(aq) + OH^-(aq) \leftrightharpoons Al(H_2O)_5(OH)^{2+}(aq) + H_2O(l)$$
$$Al(H_2O)_5(OH)^{2+}(aq) + OH^-(aq) \leftrightharpoons Al(H_2O)_4(OH)_2^{+}(aq) + H_2O(l)$$
$$Al(H_2O)_4(OH)_2^{+}(aq) + OH^-(aq) \leftrightharpoons Al(H_2O)_3(OH)_3(s) + H_2O(l)$$
$$Al(H_2O)_3(OH)_3(s) + OH^-(aq) \leftrightharpoons Al(H_2O)_2(OH)_4^{-}(aq) + H_2O(l)$$

- Addition of an acid reverses these reactions

## 17.6 Precipitation and Separation of Ions

- Consider the following:

$$BaSO_4(s) \leftrightharpoons Ba^{2+}(aq) + SO_4^{2-}(aq)$$

- At any instant in time, $Q = [Ba^{2+}][SO_4^{2-}]$
  - If $Q > K_{sp}$, precipitation occurs until $Q = K_{sp}$.
  - If $Q = K_{sp}$ equilibrium exists (saturated solution).
  - If $Q < K_{sp}$, solid dissolves until $Q = K_{sp}$.

### Selective Precipitation of Ions

- Ions can be separated from each other based on the solubilities of their salts.
  - Example: If HCl is added to a solution containing $Ag^+$ and $Cu^{2+}$, the silver precipitates ($K_{sp}$ for AgCl is $1.8 \times 10^{-10}$) while the $Cu^{2+}$ remains in solution.
    - Removal of one metal ion from a solution is called *selective precipitation*.
- Sulfide ion is often used to separate metal ions.
  - Example: Consider a mixture of $Zn^{2+}(aq)$ and $Cu^{2+}(aq)$.
    - CuS ($K_{sp} = 6 \times 10^{-37}$) is less soluble than ZnS ($K_{sp} = 2 \times 10^{-25}$).
    - Thus, CuS will be removed from solution before ZnS.
    - As $H_2S$ is bubbled through the acidified green solution, black CuS forms.
    - When the precipitate is removed, a colorless solution containing $Zn^{2+}(aq)$ remains.
    - When more $H_2S$ is added to the solution, a second precipitate of white ZnS forms.

## 17.7 Qualitative Analysis for Metallic Elements[53,54]

- **Quantitative analysis** is designed to determine how much metal ion is present.
- **Qualitative analysis** is designed to detect the presence of metal ions.
  - Typical qualitative analysis of a metal ion mixture involves:
    - 1. Separation of ions into five major groups on the basis of their differential solubilities.
      - Insoluble chlorides.
      - Acid-insoluble sulfides.
      - Base-insoluble sulfides and hydroxides.
      - Insoluble phosphates.
      - Alkali metals and ammonium ion.
    - 2. Individual ions within each group are separated by selectively dissolving members of the group.
    - 3. Specific tests are used to determine whether a particular ion is present or absent.

---

[53] "Swimming Pools, Hot Rods, and Qualitative Analysis" from Further Readings

[54] Figure 17.22 from MediaPortfolio and Transparency Pack

## Further Readings:

1. Charles L. Bering, "A Good Idea Leads to a Better Buffer," *J. Chem. Educ.*, Vol. 64, **1987**, 803–805.

2. Edwin S. Gould, "Phosphate Buffers and Telephone Poles —A Useful Analogy with Limitations," *J. Chem. Educ.*, Vol. 76, **1999**, 1511.

3. Henry N. Po and N. M. Senozan, "The Henderson-Hasselbalch Equation: Its History and Limitations," *J. Chem. Educ.*, Vol. 78, **2001**, 1499–1503.

4. Robert C. Mebane and Thomas R. Rybolt, "Edible Acid-Base Indicators," *J. Chem. Educ.*, Vol. 62, **1985**, 285.

5. Dennis Barnum, "Predicting Acid-Base Titration Curves without Calculations," *J. Chem. Educ.*, Vol. 76, **1999**, 938–942.

6. Robert Perkins, "The Useless Tea Kettle," *J. Chem. Educ.*, Vol. 61, **1984**, 383.

7. Rachel E. Casiday, Dewey Holten, Richard Krathen, and Regina F. Frey, "Blood-Chemistry Tutorials: Teaching Biological Applications of General Chemistry Material," *J. Chem. Educ.*, Vol. 78, **2001**, 1210–1214. The relationship between oxygen transport, iron transport, blood buffering, kidney dialysis and general chemistry topics is discussed.

8. Robert Perkins, "The Murky Pool," *J. Chem. Educ.*, Vol. 61, **1984**, 383–384.

9. Murry Helfman, "Chemical Aspects of Dentistry," *J. Chem. Educ.*, Vol. 59, **1982**, 666–668.

10. Edward Koubek, Cole McWherter, and George L. Gilbert, "Acid-Base Chemistry of the Aluminum Ion in Aqueous Solution," *J. Chem. Educ.*, Vol. 75, **1998**, 60.

11. Roy W. Clark and Judith M. Bonicamp, "The $K_{sp}$-Solubility Conundrum," *J. Chem. Educ.*, Vol. 75, **1998**, 1182–1185.

12. Andres Raviolo, "Assessing Students' Conceptual Understanding of Solubility Equilibrium," *J. Chem. Educ.*, Vol. 78, **2001**, 629–631.

13. Stephen J. Hawkes, "What Should We Teach Beginners about Solubility and Solubility Products?" *J. Chem. Educ.*, Vol. 75, **1998**, 1179–1181.

14. M. Cecilia Yappert and Donald B. DuPre, "Complexometric Titrations: Competition of Complexing Agents in the Determination of Water hardness with EDTA," *J. Chem. Educ.*, Vol. 74, **1997**, 1422–1423.

15. Edward Koubek, Cole McWherter, and George L. Gilbert, "Acid-Base Chemistry of the Aluminum Ion in Aqueous Solution," *J. Chem. Educ.*, Vol. 75, **1998**, 60.

15. Dale D. Clyde, "Swimming Pools, Hot Rods, and Qualitative Analysis," *J. Chem. Educ.*, Vol. 65, **1988**, 911–913.

## Live Demonstrations:

1. Dianne N. Epp, "Teas as Natural Indicators," *J. Chem. Educ.*, Vol. 70, **1993**, 326. The use of teas as natural acid-base indicators is demonstrated.

2. Lee R. Summerlin, Christie L Borgford, and Julie B. Ealy, "Silver Ion Solubilities: Red and White Precipitates," *Chemical Demonstrations, a Sourcebook for Teachers, Volume 2* (Washington: American Chemical Society, **1988**), pp. 124–125. An effective introduction to equilibrium; the relative solubilities of silver chromate and silver chloride are investigated.

3. Lee. R. Summerlin, Christie L. Borgford, and Julie B. Ealy, "Solubility of Some Silver Compounds," *Chemical Demonstrations, A Sourcebook for Teachers*, *Volume 2* (Washington: American Chemical Society, **1988**), pp. 83–85. The solubility of a series of silver salts and complexes is explored in this colorful demonstration.

4. Lee. R. Summerlin, and James. L. Ealy, Jr., "The Common Ion Effect: Second Demonstration," *Chemical Demonstrations, A Sourcebook for Teachers*, *Volume 1* (Washington: American Chemical Society, **1988**), pp. 93–94. The reaction of calcium carbonate and acetic acid is used to demonstrate the common ion effect.

5. Bassam Z. Shakhashiri, "Effect of Acetate Ion on the Acidity of Acetic Acid: The Common Ion Effect," *Chemical Demonstrations: A Handbook for Teachers of Chemistry, Volume 3* (Madison: The University of Wisconsin Press, **1989**), pp. 155–157.

6. Lee. R. Summerlin, and James. L. Ealy, Jr., "The Common Ion-Effect: Ammonium Hydroxide and Ammonium Acetate," *Chemical Demonstrations, A Sourcebook for Teachers*, *Volume 1* (Washington: American Chemical Society, 1988), p. 95.

7. Lee. R. Summerlin, Christie L. Borgford, and Julie B. Ealy, "Equilibrium: The Dissociation of Acetic Acid," *Chemical Demonstrations, A Sourcebook for Teachers*, *Volume 2* (Washington: American Chemical Society, **1988**), pp.160–161. Changes in indicator color upon addition of base or acetate to acetic acid are explored.

8. Bassam Z. Shakhashiri, "Buffering Action and Capacity," *Chemical Demonstrations: A Handbook for Teachers of Chemistry, Volume 3* (Madison: The University of Wisconsin Press, **1989**), pp. 173–185.

9. Bassam Z. Shakhashiri, "Buffering Action of Alka-Seltzer," *Chemical Demonstrations: A Handbook for Teachers of Chemistry, Volume 3* (Madison: The University of Wisconsin Press, **1989**), pp. 186–187.

10. Bassam Z. Shakhashiri, "Determination of Neutralizing Capacity of Antacids," *Chemical Demonstrations: A Handbook for Teachers of Chemistry, Volume 3* (Madison: The University of Wisconsin Press, **1989**), pp. 162–166.

11. Lee. R. Summerlin, Christie L. Borgford, and Julie B. Ealy, "Milk of Magnesia versus Acid," *Chemical Demonstrations, A Sourcebook for Teachers*, *Volume 2* (Washington: American Chemical Society, **1988**), p. 173. An antacid, milk of magnesia, is mixed with acid in this demonstration.

12. Bassam Z. Shakhashiri, "Fizzing and Foaming: Reactions of Acids with Carbonates", *Chemical Demonstrations: A Handbook for Teachers of Chemistry, Volume 3* (Madison: The University of Wisconsin Press, **1989**), pp. 96–99.

13. Lee. R. Summerlin, Christie L. Borgford, and Julie B. Ealy, " Colorful Complex Ions in Ammonia," *Chemical Demonstrations, A Sourcebook for Teachers*, *Volume 2* (Washington: American Chemical Society, **1988**), pp. 75-76. Ammine complexes of copper and cobalt are prepared in this demonstration.

14. Lee. R. Summerlin, Christie L. Borgford, and Julie B. Ealy, " Green and Blue Copper Complexes," *Chemical Demonstrations, A Sourcebook for Teachers*, *Volume 2* (Washington: American Chemical Society, **1988**), pp.71-72. Three copper complexes are prepared in this demonstration.

15. Bassam Z. Shakhashiri, "Acidic and Basic Properties of Oxides", *Chemical Demonstrations: A Handbook for Teachers of Chemistry, Volume 3* (Madison: The University of Wisconsin Press, **1989**), pp. 109-113.

# Chapter 18. Chemistry of the Environment

## Media Resources

### Figures and Tables

| In Transparency Pack and on MediaPortfolio: | Section: |
|---|---|
| Figure 18.1 Variation of *T* and *P* with Altitude | 18.1 Earth's Atmosphere |
| Table 18.1 Composition of Dry Air Near Sea Level | 18.1 Earth's Atmosphere |
| Figure 18.3 Variation of Ozone Concentration with Altitude | 18.3 Ozone in the Upper Atmosphere |
| Figure 18.6 Removal of $SO_2$ from Combusted Fuel | 18.4 Chemistry of the Troposphere |
| Figure 18.10 Wavelengths of Infrared Radiation Absorbed by $CO_2$ and $H_2O$ | 18.4 Chemistry of the Troposphere |
| Figure 18.11 Change in Atmospheric $CO_2$ Over Time | 18.4 Chemistry of the Troposphere |
| Table 18.6 Ionic Constituents of Seawater Present in Concentrations Greater than 0.001 g/kg (1ppm) | 18.5 World Ocean |
| Figure 18.17 Steps in Public Water Treatment | 18.7 Green Chemistry |

| Animations: | Section: |
|---|---|
| Stratospheric Ozone | 18.3 Ozone in the Upper Atmosphere |
| CFCs and Stratospheric Ozone | 18.3 Ozone in the Upper Atmosphere |
| Catalytic Destruction of Stratospheric Ozone | 18.3 Ozone in the Upper Atmosphere |

| Movies: | Section: |
|---|---|
| Carbon Dioxide Behaves as an Acid in Water | 18.4 Chemistry of the Troposphere |

## Other Resources

| Further Readings: | Section: |
|---|---|
| Introducing Atmospheric Reactions: A Systematic Approach for Students | 18.1 Earth's Atmosphere |
| Thermal Physics (and Some Chemistry) of the Atmosphere | 18.1 Earth's Atmosphere |
| Ozone Depletion: 20 Years after the Alarm | 18.3 Ozone in the Upper Atmosphere |
| Ozone Depletion Research Wins Nobel | 18.3 Ozone in the Upper Atmosphere |
| Drop in Ozone Killers Means Global Gain | 18.3 Ozone in the Upper Atmosphere |
| Understanding Ozone | 18.3 Ozone in the Upper Atmosphere |
| Local and Regional Ozone: A Student Study Project | 18.3 Ozone in the Upper Atmosphere |
| Acid-Rain Effects on Stone Monuments | 18.4 Chemistry of the Troposphere |
| Atmospheric Dust and Acid Rain | 18.4 Chemistry of the Troposphere |
| Outdoor Carbon Monoxide: Risk to Millions | 18.4 Chemistry of the Troposphere |
| Carbon Monoxide Poisoning. Some Surprising Aspects of the Equilibrium between Hemoglobin, Carbon Monoxide, and Oxygen | 18.4 Chemistry of the Troposphere |
| Global Population and the Nitrogen Cycle | 18.4 Chemistry of the Troposphere |
| Getting Auto Exhausts to Pristine | 18.4 Chemistry of the Troposphere |

| | |
|---|---|
| Ocean Carbon Cycle | 18.5 The World Ocean |
| The Expiration of Respiration: Oxygen—The Missing Ingredient in Many Bodies of Water | 18.6 Freshwater |
| The Water Softener — A Relevant, Unifying Example of Many Common Chemical Principles and Calculations | 18.6 Freshwater |
| A Discovery-Based Experiment Illustrating How Iron Metal is Used to Remediate Contaminated Groundwater | 18.6 Freshwater |
| Topics in Green Chemistry | 18.7 Green Chemistry |

| **Live Demonstrations:** | **Section:** |
|---|---|
| Acid-Neutralizing Capacity of Lake Beds | 18.6 Freshwater |

# Chapter 18. Chemistry of the Environment

## Lecture Outline

### 18.1 Earth's Atmosphere[1,2,3]

- The temperature of the atmosphere varies with altitude.
- The atmosphere is divided into four regions based on the temperature profile:
  - The **troposphere** (below an altitude of 12 km).
  - The temperature decreases from 290 K to 215 K as altitude increases.
  - This region is where we spend most of our time.
  - The boundaries between regions are given the suffix *-pause*.
    - The area at the boundary of the troposphere is the *tropopause*.
  - 75% of the mass of the atmosphere is within the troposphere.
  - The **stratosphere** (12 km – 50 km).
    - The temperature increases from 215 K to 275 K.
  - The mesosphere (50 km – 85 km).
    - The temperature decreases (275 K to 190 K).
  - The **thermosphere** (>85 km).
    - The temperature increases.
  - There is only slow mixing of gases between regions in the atmosphere.
- The variation of pressure with altitude is simpler, pressure decreases as altitude increases.
  - The pressure at sea level is 760 torr; that at 200 km is $1 \times 10^{-6}$ torr.

#### Composition of the Atmosphere[4]

- The composition of the atmosphere is not uniform.
  - Temperature and pressure vary over a wide range with altitude.
  - Gases in the atmosphere are bombarded by radiation and energetic particles from the sun.
  - Gravity also plays a role.
    - Lighter molecules and atoms are found at higher altitudes.
- Two major components of the atmosphere are nitrogen, $N_2$, and oxygen, $O_2$.
  - $CO_2$ and noble gases make up most of the remainder.
  - The concentration of gases in the atmosphere is given in parts per million (ppm).
    - The definition of ppm in this instance is on a per volume basis.
    - 1 ppm = 1 part by volume per million volumes of the whole.
  - The concentration of $N_2$ is about 0.78 ppm; $O_2$ is about 0.21 ppm.
  - These two components differ significantly with respect to reactivity.
    - The O=O bond is much weaker than the N≡N bond.
    - Therefore, $O_2$ is significantly more reactive than $N_2$.

### 18.2 The Outer Regions of the Atmosphere

#### Photodissociation

- Recall:

$$E = h\nu = hc/\lambda$$

---

[1] Figure 18.1 from MediaPortfolio and Transparency Pack
[2] "Introducing Atmospheric Reactions: A Systematic Approach for Students" from Further Readings
[3] "Thermal Physics (and Some Chemistry) of the Atmosphere" from Further Readings
[4] Table 18.1 from MediaPortfolio and Transparency Pack

- Thus the higher the frequency, the shorter the wavelength and the higher the energy of radiation.
- For a chemical reaction induced by radiation to occur, the photons must have sufficient energy to break the required bonds and the molecules must absorb the photons.
- **Photodissociation** is the rupture of a chemical bond induced by absorption of a photon by a molecule.
  - Ions do not form.
  - Bond cleavage leaves half the bonding electrons with each of the two atoms forming two neutral particles.
- In the upper atmosphere, photodissociation causes the formation of oxygen atoms:

$$O_2(g) + h\nu \rightarrow 2O(g)$$

  - The minimum energy required to induce this depends on the dissociation energy of $O_2$ (495 kJ/mol).
  - The longest wavelength of light that causes the formation of oxygen atoms is 242 nm.

### Photoionization

- 1924: Electrons were discovered in the upper atmosphere.
  - Therefore, cations must be present in the upper atmosphere.
- **Photoionization** is the ionization of molecules (and atoms) caused by radiation.
  - A molecule absorbs energy causing the loss of an electron.
  - Thus the photon must have sufficient energy to remove an electron when it is absorbed by a molecule.
  - Wavelengths of light that cause photoionization and photodissociation are absorbed by the upper atmosphere.
    - This filters them out and prevents them from reaching the Earth.

## 18.3 Ozone in the Upper Atmosphere[5,6]

- Ozone absorbs photons with wavelengths between 240 and 310 nm.
- Most of the ozone is present in the stratosphere; 90% of it is found at 10–50 km.
- Between altitudes of 30 and 90 km photodissociation of oxygen is possible:

$$O_2(g) + h\nu \rightarrow 2O(g)$$

  - Here the concentration of $O_2$ is greater than that of O.
  - The oxygen atoms can collide with oxygen molecules to form ozone with excess energy, $O_3^*$:

$$O(g) + O_2(g) \rightarrow O_3^*(g)$$

  - The excited ozone ($O_3^*$) can lose energy by decomposing to oxygen atoms and oxygen molecules (the reverse reaction) or by transferring the energy to M (usually $N_2$ or $O_2$):

$$O(g) + O_2(g) \leftrightharpoons O_3^*(g)$$
$$O_3^*(g) + M(g) \rightarrow O_3(g) + M^*(g)$$

- Why does maximum ozone formation occur in the stratosphere?
  - The formation of ozone in the atmosphere depends on the presence of O(*g*).
    - At low altitudes, the radiation with sufficient energy to form O(*g*) has been absorbed.
  - The release of energy from $O_3^*$ depends on collisions which generally occur at lower altitudes.
    - The concentration of molecules is generally greater at lower altitudes, thus more frequent collisions occur.
  - Combining these factors results in maximum ozone formation in the stratosphere.
- The *ozone shield* in the stratosphere protects plant and animal life on Earth's surface from being bombarded with high-energy radiation.

### Depletion of the Ozone Layer[7,8,9,10,11,12,13]

---

[5] "Stratospheric Ozone" Animation from MediaPortfolio

[6] Figure 18.3 from MediaPortfolio and Transparency Pack

- 1970: Cratzen demonstrated that naturally occurring nitrogen oxides can catalytically degrade ozone.
- 1974: Rowland and Molina demonstrated that chlorine atoms from **chlorofluorocarbons** (CFCs) deplete the ozone layer.
    - CFCs such as $CFCl_3$ (Freon-11) and $CF_2Cl_2$ (Freon-12) were commonly used as propellants in spray cans, as refrigerants, and in the plastics industry.
    - CFCs are relatively insoluble in water.
    - Thus they are not removed from the atmosphere by rain.
    - Their lack of chemical reactivity allows them to survive in the atmosphere and diffuse into the stratosphere.
- In the stratosphere, CFCs undergo photochemical rupture of a C–Cl bond:

$$CF_2Cl_2(g) + h\nu \rightarrow CF_2Cl(g) + Cl(g) \qquad \text{(optimal at 30 km)}.$$

    - The free chlorine atoms subsequently react with ozone:

$$Cl(g) + O_3(g) \rightarrow ClO(g) + O_2(g)$$

        - Rate = $k[Cl][O_3]$, $k = 7.2 \times 10^9\ M^{-1}s^{-1}$ at 298 K.
    - In addition, the ClO generated may produce Cl as well:

$$2ClO(g) \rightarrow O_2(g) + 2Cl(g)$$

    - These chlorine atoms can react with more ozone.
    - The overall reaction is:

$$2O_3(g) \rightarrow 3O_2(g)$$

- The use and production of CFCs was completely banned as of 1996 (by 100 nations).
- Rowland and Molina were awarded the Nobel prize in 1995.

## 18.4 Chemistry in the Troposphere

- The troposphere consists mostly of $O_2$ and $N_2$.
- Even though other gases are present in low concentrations, their effects on the environment can be profound.
    - Typical minor components include $CO_2$, CO, $CH_4$, NO, $O_3$ and $SO_2$.

### Sulfur Compounds and Acid Rain[14,15,16,17]

- Sulfur dioxide, $SO_2$, is produced by natural events (volcanic gases, bacterial action, forest fires).
    - The major source is linked to human activities such as the combustion of sulfur-containing fuels.
    - The amount of $SO_2$ produced depends on the sulfur content of the coal or oil.
    - More than 30 million tons per year of $SO_2$ are released into the atmosphere in the United States.
    - The $SO_2$ can be oxidized to $SO_3$, which dissolves in water to produce sulfuric acid (a component of **acid rain**):

$$SO_3(g) + H_2O(l) \rightarrow H_2SO_4(aq)$$

- Nitrogen oxides also contribute to acid rain by forming nitric acid.
- Normal rainwater has a pH of about 5.6 (due to the $H_2CO_3$ produced from $CO_2$).

---

[7] "Catalytic Destruction of Stratospheric Ozone" Animation from MediaPortfolio
[8] "CFC's and Stratospheric Ozone" Animation from MediaPortfolio
[9] "Drop in Ozone Killers Means Global Gain" from Further Readings
[10] "Understanding Ozone" from Further Readings
[11] "Ozone Depletion Research Wins Nobel" from Further Readings
[12] "Ozone Depletion: 20 Years After the Alarm" from Further Readings
[13] "Local and Regional Ozone: A Student Study Project" from Further Readings
[14] "Acid Rain Effects on Stone Monuments" from Further Readings
[15] "Atmospheric Dust and Acid Rain" from Further Readings
[16] Figure 18.6 from MediaPortfolio and Transparency Pack
[17] "Carbon Dioxide Behaves as an Acid in Water" Animation from MediaPortfolio

- Acid rain has a pH around 4, whereas the pH of natural waters containing living organisms is 6.5 to 8.5.
- Natural waters with a pH below 4 cannot sustain life.
  - All vertebrates, most invertebrates and many microorganisms cannot survive at such a low pH.
- The acids in acid rain are problematic.
  - They react with metals and cause corrosion.
  - They react with carbonates (such as the calcium carbonate in marble and limestone).
- How can we reduce the amount of $SO_2$ produced from fuel combustion?
  - It is too expensive to remove sulfur from oil and coal prior to its use.
    - Therefore, the $SO_2$ is removed from fuel on combustion.
  - $SO_2$ is commonly removed from the gases formed by the combustion of fuels (oil and coal) as follows:
    - Powdered limestone decomposes into CaO in the furnace of a power plant.
    - CaO reacts with $SO_2$ to form $CaSO_3$ in the furnace.
    - $CaSO_3$ and unreacted $SO_2$ are passed into a scrubber (purification chamber) where the $SO_2$ is converted to $CaSO_3$ by jets of CaO.
    - $CaSO_3$ is precipitated into a watery slurry and is removed.

## Carbon Monoxide[18,19]

- CO is produced by incomplete combustion of carbon-containing materials such as fossil fuels.
- In terms of total mass, CO is the most abundant of all gaseous pollutants.
  - About $10^{14}$ g of CO is produced in the United States per year (mostly from automobiles).
- CO interferes with the binding of oxygen to **hemoglobin**, the iron-containing protein in red blood cells that is responsible for transport of oxygen in the blood.
- Hemoglobin consists of four protein chains or subunits.
  - Each subunit contains a heme molecule.
  - The heme molecule contains an iron in its center.
  - The oxygen molecule is able to bind reversibly to this iron.
    - Hemoglobin with oxygen bound is called *oxyhemoglobin*.
- Hemoglobin is responsible for oxygen transport.
  - In the lungs, where the partial pressure of oxygen is relatively high, $O_2$ binds to the heme iron in hemoglobin.
  - In the tissues, where the partial pressure of oxygen is lower, $O_2$ is released from the hemoglobin.
  - Thus $O_2$ is delivered to the tissues.
- CO binds very tightly to the iron in hemoglobin.
  - CO binds to human hemoglobin about 210 times more strongly than does oxygen.
  - When CO binds to iron in hemoglobin, forming *carboxyhemoglobin* (COHb), it cannot be easily displaced by $O_2$.
  - Therefore, in sufficient concentrations, CO can stop oxygen transport in living systems.
    - CO poisoning occurs with little warning, since the gas is odorless and colorless.

## Nitrogen Oxides and Photochemical Smog[20,21]

- **Photochemical smog** is the result of photochemical reactions on pollutants.
  - Oxides of nitrogen are the primary components of smog.

---

[18] "Outdoor Carbon Monoxide: Risk to Millions" from Further Readings
[19] "Carbon Monoxide Poisoning. Some Surprising Aspects of the Equilibrium between Hemoglobin, Carbon Monoxide, and Oxygen" from Further Readings
[20] "Global Population and the Nitrogen Cycle" from Further Readings
[21] "Getting Auto Exhausts to Pristine" from Further Readings

- In car engines, NO forms as follows:
  $$N_2(g) + O_2(g) \leftrightharpoons 2NO(g) \qquad \Delta H = 181 \text{ kJ}$$
  - In air NO is rapidly oxidized:
    $$2NO(g) + O_2(g) \leftrightharpoons 2NO_2(g) \qquad \Delta H = -113.1 \text{ kJ}$$
  - Light with a wavelength of 393 nm causes photodissociation of $NO_2$:
    $$NO_2(g) + h\nu \rightarrow NO(g) + O(g)$$
  - The O can react with $O_2$ to form $O_3$ which is the key component of smog:
    $$O(g) + O_2(g) + M(g) \rightarrow O_3(g) + M^*(g)$$
  - In the troposphere ozone is undesirable because it is toxic and reactive.
- A further pollutant is emitted by automobiles: unburned hydrocarbons.
- Catalytic converters reduce the level of $NO_x$ and hydrocarbon emissions.

### Water Vapor, Carbon Dioxide, and Climate[22,23]

- There is a thermal balance between the Earth and its surroundings.
- Therefore, radiation is emitted from the Earth at the same rate as it is absorbed by the Earth.
- The troposphere is transparent to visible light.
- However, the troposphere is not transparent to IR radiation (heat).
- Therefore, the troposphere insulates the Earth making it appear colder from the outside than it is on the surface.
- $CO_2$ and $H_2O$ absorb IR radiation escaping from the Earth's surface.
  - The effect of $CO_2$, $H_2O$ and other gases on Earth's temperature is called the *greenhouse effect*.
- At night, the Earth emits radiation.
  - Water vapor plays a major role in maintaining atmospheric temperature at night.
  - $CO_2$ also plays a role in maintaining surface temperature.
- The carbon dioxide level on Earth has been increasing over the years.
  - Much of the increase is due to the combustion of fuels.
  - We speculate that the increased $CO_2$ concentration is resulting in a gradual warming of the Earth's surface.
  - Between 2050 and 2100 the $CO_2$ concentration is expected to be twice the present level.
  - This will result in a global temperature increase of 1 to 3°C. (Assuming we continue to use fossil fuels in the present manner.)

## 18.5 The World Ocean

- 72% of the Earth's surface is covered with water.
- Water plays an important role in our environment.
- The properties of water are important.
  - Water exhibits extensive H-bonding (thus water has a high melting point, a high boiling point, and a high heat capacity).
  - Water is highly polar and can dissolve many ionic and polar-covalent substances.
  - Water may participate in many reactions (e.g., acid-base, redox).

### Seawater[24,25]

- The volume of oceans in the world is $1.35 \times 10^9$ km$^3$.
- The oceans contain 97.2% of Earth's water.
- The remainder is primarily in ice caps/glaciers (2.1%) and freshwater sources (0.6%).
- The **salinity** of seawater is defined as the mass (in grams) of dry salts present in 1 kg seawater.

---

[22] Figure 18.10 from MediaPortfolio and Transparency Pack
[23] Figure 18.11 from MediaPortfolio and Transparency Pack
[24] Table 18.6 from MediaPortfolio and Transparency Pack
[25] "Ocean Carbon Cycle" from Further Readings

- Seawater has an average salinity of about 35.
- Most elements in seawater are only present in low concentration.
  - Only NaCl, bromine and magnesium are currently obtained from seawater in commercially important amounts.

### Desalination

- Seawater has a salt concentration too high for drinking.
  - Water used for drinking should contain less than 500 ppm dissolved salts (United States municipal water).
- **Desalination**: removal of salts from seawater or brackish water.
- Common methods for isolation of drinking water include *distillation* (small scale) and **reverse osmosis** (used commercially; small and large scale).
  - Recall that osmosis involves the transport of solvent molecules across a semipermeable membrane.
  - In reverse osmosis pressure is applied to cause solvent to move from the more concentrated solution to the more dilute solution.
    - Seawater is introduced under pressure and water passes through the hollow fibers of semipermeable membranes.
    - The water is thus separated from the ions.

## 18.6 Freshwater

- An adult needs about 2 L of water a day for drinking.
- In the United States, the average person uses about 300 L of freshwater per day.
- Industry uses even more freshwater than this (e.g., about $10^5$ L of water is used to make 1000 kg of steel).
- Freshwater is only a small fraction of the total water on Earth.
  - Its source is evaporation of ocean water.
  - The water accumulates as water vapor in the atmosphere.
  - It returns to Earth as rain or snow.
  - After rain and snow falls, the water flows into rivers and dams.
  - As the water flows over the Earth it dissolves many substances.
  - Freshwater usually contains some ions ($Na^+$, $K^+$, $Mg^{2+}$, $Ca^{2+}$, $Fe^{2+}$, $Cl^-$, $SO_4^{2-}$, and $HCO_3^-$) and dissolved gases ($O_2$, $N_2$, and $CO_2$).

### Dissolved Oxygen and Water Quality[26,27,28,29]

- Water fully saturated with air at 1 atm and 20°C has 9 ppm of $O_2$ dissolved in it.
- Cold-water fish require about 5 ppm of dissolved oxygen for life.
- Aerobic bacteria consume oxygen to oxidize **biodegradable** organic material.
  - Biodegradable materials are *oxygen-demanding wastes.*
  - Examples: sewage, industrial waste from food-processing plants and paper mills, and effluent from meat packing plants.
  - Aerobic bacteria oxidize organic material into $CO_2$, $HCO_3^-$, $H_2O$, $NO_3^-$, $SO_4^{2-}$, and phosphates.
- These oxidation reactions may deplete the dissolved oxygen so that aerobic bacteria can no longer survive.

---

[26] "The Expiration of Respiration: Oxygen—The Missing Ingredient in Many Bodies of Water" from Further Readings

[27] "Acid-Neutralizing Capacity of Lake Beds" from Live Demonstrations

[28] Figure 18.17 from MediaPortfolio and Transparency Pack

[29] "A Discovery-Based Experiment Illustrating How Iron Metal is Used to Remediate Contaminated Groundwater" from Further Readings

- Anaerobic bacteria then complete the decomposition process forming $CH_4$, $NH_3$, $H_2S$, $PH_3$, and other foul smelling products.
- *Eutrophication* is the increase in dead and decaying plant matter resulting from excessive plant growth.

### Treatment of Municipal Water Supplies

- There are five steps:
  - Coarse filtration.
    - Occurs as water is taken from a lake, river or reservoir and passed through a screen.
  - Sedimentation.
    - Water is allowed to stand so that solid particles (e.g., sand) can settle out.
    - To remove small components (like bacteria), CaO and $Al_2(SO_4)_3$ are added.
      - They cause a gelatinous precipitate of $Al(OH)_3$ to form and settle slowly.
      - As the $Al(OH)_3$ settles it carries small particles with it.
  - Sand Filtration.
    - Water is filtered through a sand bed to remove $Al(OH)_3$ and anything it trapped in it.
  - Aeration.
    - Air hastens oxidation of any organic material that may be present.
  - Sterilization.
    - Chlorine or ozone may be used to kill bacteria, viruses, and other microorganisms.

#### *Water Softening*[30]

- Water containing a high concentration of $Ca^{2+}$ and $Mg^{2+}$ and other divalent cations is called **hard water**.
- The presence of these ions may cause the water to be unsuitable for some uses.
  - For example, soaps form an insoluble soap "scum" and water in water heaters forms a deposit (*scale*) via reactions involving the divalent cations.
  - These ions can be removed by a process called *water softening*.
    - Municipal water supplies utilize the **lime-soda process** for large-scale water softening.
      - Water is treated with CaO (lime) and soda ash ($Na_2CO_3$).
      - They cause the $Ca^{2+}$ and $Mg^{2+}$ to precipitate as $CaCO_3$ and $Mg(OH)_2$.
    - **Ion exchange** is often used for household water softening.
      - The divalent cations are removed and replaced with sodium ions.
      - The sodium ions do not form precipitates.

## 18.7 Green Chemistry[31]

- Basic principles of **green chemistry:**
  - Waste prevention is preferred to waste treatment or clean up.
  - Efforts should be made to devise synthetic methods that generate as little waste as possible.
    - The waste should not be toxic to people or the environment.
    - Processes should be energy efficient.
  - Catalysts that permit the use of safe reagents should be used if possible.
  - Renewable raw materials should be used if possible.
  - The use of auxiliary substances (e.g., solvents) should be eliminated or made as innocuous as possible.

### Solvents and Reagents

---

[30] "The Water Softener-A Relevant, Unifying Example of Many Common Chemical Principles and Calculations" from Further Readings

[31] "Topics in Green Chemistry" from Further Readings

- The release of toxic volatile solvents to the atmosphere must be avoided.
    - Alternative environmentally-friendly methods need to be developed.
    - Examples:
        - Use of nontoxic supercritical fluids (e.g., $CO_2$) to replace toxic conventional solvents (e.g., chlorofluorocarbons) in the production of Teflon$^{TM}$.
        - Use of supercritical water in the synthesis of plastics.
- Substitution of an environmentally friendly reagent in place of a particularly toxic reagent should be encouraged.
    - Examples:
        - Use of dimethylcarbonate in place of dimethylsulfate and methylsulfates in methyl group reactions.
        - Use of dimethylcarbonate in place of phosgene in the synthesis of polycarbonate plastics.

## Other Processes

- Earth friendly alternatives are being developed for many processes important to modern society.
    - Examples:
        - Dry-cleaning solvents.
        - Lead-free automotive coatings.

## Water Purification

- Access to clean water is essential.
    - Disinfection of public water supplies have dramatically decreased the risk of water-borne illnesses.
        - Chlorination is a commonly used method of disinfection.
            - Trihalomethanes (THMs) are byproducts of this process.
            - THMs are suspected carcinogens.
    - Alternate methods of disinfection need to be developed.
        - Examples: ozone or chlorine dioxide.

## Further Readings:

1. N. Colin Baird, "Introducing Atmospheric Reactions: A Systematic Approach for Students," *J. Chem. Educ.*, Vol. 72, **1995**, 153–157.

2. Stephen K. Lower, "Thermal Physics (and Some Chemistry) of the Atmosphere," *J. Chem. Educ.*, Vol. 75, **1998**, 837–840.

3. F. Sherwood Rowland and Mario J. Molina, "Ozone Depletion: 20 Years After the Alarm," *Chemical and Engineering News*, **August 15, 1994**, 8–15.

4. R. Lipkin, "Ozone Depletion Research Wins Nobel," *Science News*, **October 21, 1995**, 262.

5. R. Monastersky, "Drop in Ozone Killers Means Global Gain," *Science News*, **March 9, 1996**, 151.

6. Muhammad Hanif, "Understanding Ozone," *The Science Teacher*, **December 1995**, 20–23.

7. Otto Klemm, "Local and Regional Ozone: A Student Study Project," *J. Chem. Educ.*, Vol. 78, **2001**, 1641–1646.

8. Jorge L. Sarmiento, "Ocean Carbon Cycle," *Chemical and Engineering News*, **May 31, 1993**, 30–43.

9. A. Elena Charola, "Acid Rain Effects on Stone Monuments," *J. Chem. Educ.*, Vol. 64, **1987**, 436–437.

10. Lars O. Hedin and Gene E. Likens, "Atmospheric Dust and Acid Rain," *Scientific American*, **December 1996**, 88–92.

11. Janet Raloff, "Outdoor Carbon Monoxide: Risk to Millions," *Science News*, **October 14, 1995**, 247.

12. N. M. Senozan and J. A Devore, "Carbon Monoxide Poisoning. Some Surprising Aspects of the Equilibrium between Hemoglobin, Carbon Monoxide, and Oxygen," *J. Chem. Educ.*, Vol. 73, **1996**, 767–770.

13. Tina Adler, "The Expiration of Respiration: Oxygen-The Missing Ingredient in Many Bodies of Water," *Science News*, **February 10, 1996**, 88–89.

14. Barbara A. Balko and Paul G Tratnyek, "A Discovery-Based Experiment Illustrating How Iron Metal Is Used to Remediate Contaminated Groundwater," *J. Chem. Educ.,* Vol. 78, **2001**, 1661–1663.

15. Vaclav Smith, "Global Population and the Nitrogen Cycle," *Scientific American*, **July 1997**, 76–81.

16. Mitch Jacoby, "Getting Auto Exhausts to Pristine," *Chemical and Engineering News*, **January 25, 1999**, 36–44.

17. John E. Fulkrod, "The Water Softener—A Relevant, Unifying Example of Many Common Chemical Principles and Calculations," *J. Chem. Educ.*, Vol. 62, **1985**, 529.

18. Mary M. Kirchhoff, "Topics in Green Chemistry," *J. Chem. Educ.*, Vol. 78, **2001**, 1577.

## Live Demonstrations:

1. Bassam Z. Shakhashiri, "Acid-Neutralizing Capacity of Lake Beds," *Chemical Demonstrations: A Handbook for Teachers of Chemistry, Volume 3* (Madison: The University of Wisconsin Press, **1989**), pp. 125–127.

# Chapter 19. Chemical Thermodynamics

## Media Resources

### Figures and Tables

| In Transparency Pack and on MediaPortfolio: | Section: |
|---|---|
| Conversion of Potential Energy to Work | 19.1 Spontaneous Processes |
| Figure 19.4 Irreversible Process | 19.1 Spontaneous Processes |
| Figure 19.6 Possible Locations of Gas Molecules in the Expansion of a Gas | 19.2 Entropy and the Second Law of Thermodynamics |
| Figure 19.7 Structure of Ice | 19.2 Entropy and the Second Law of Thermodynamics |
| Figure 19.8 Changes in Disorder On Dissolving an Ionic Solid in Water | 19.2 Entropy and the Second Law of Thermodynamics |
| Figure 19.12 Vibrational and Rotational Motion | 19.3 The Molecular Interpretation of Energy |
| Figure 19.13 Perfect Crystal at Absolute Zero | 19.3 The Molecular Interpretation of Energy |
| Figure 19.14 Entropy Changes with Increasing Temperature | 19.3 The Molecular Interpretation of Energy |
| Table 19.2 Standard Molar Entropies of Selected Substances at 298 K | 19.4 Entropy Changes in Chemical Reactions |
| Figure 19.18 Free Energy Changes in the Synthesis of $NH_3$ | 19.5 Gibbs Free Energy |

| On MediaPortfolio: | Section: |
|---|---|
| Figure 19.5 Spontaneous Expansion of an Ideal Gas | 19.2 Entropy and the Second Law of Thermodynamics |
| Figure 19.11 Decrease in Entropy Due to a Decrease in the Number of Gas Molecules | 19.3 The Molecular Interpretation of Energy |
| Figure 19.17 Potential Energy Analogy | 19.5 Gibbs Free Energy |
| Table 19.3 Conventions Used in Establishing Standard Free Energies | 19.5 Gibbs Free Energy |
| Table 19.4 The Effect of Temperature on the Spontaneity of Reactions | 19.6 Free Energy and Temperature |
| Figure 19.19 Free Energy Changes in a Cell | 19.7 Free Energy and the Equilibrium Constant |

| Animations: | Section: |
|---|---|
| Air Bags | 19.6 Free Energy and Temperature |

| Movies: | Section: |
|---|---|
| Thermite | 19.1 Spontaneous Processes |
| Nitrogen Triiodide | 19.1 Spontaneous Processes |
| Formation of Water | 19.6 Free Energy and Temperature |

| Activities: | Section: |
|---|---|
| Expansion of Gas into a Vacuum | 19.2 Entropy and the Second Law of Thermodynamics |
| Possible Orientation of Three Gas Molecules | 19.2 Entropy and the Second Law of Thermodynamics |

| | |
|---|---|
| Molecular Entropy | 19.3 The Molecular Interpretation of Entropy |
| Entropy and Temperature | 19.3 The Molecular Interpretation of Entropy |
| Gibbs Free Energy | 19.6 Free Energy and Temperature |

# Other Resources

| **Further Readings:** | **Section:** |
|---|---|
| Thermodynamics and Spontaneity | 19.1 Spontaneous Processes |
| Demystifying Introductory Chemistry. Part 4: An Approach to Reaction Thermodynamics through Enthalpies, Entropies, and Free Energies of Atomization | 19.1 Spontaneous Processes |
| A Model of Thermal Equilibrium: A Tool for the Introduction of Thermodynamics | 19.1 Spontaneous Processes |
| Visualizing Entropy | 19.2 Entropy and the Second Law of Thermodynamics |
| Pictorial Analogies III: Heat Flow, Thermodynamics, and Entropy | 19.2 Entropy and the Second Law of Thermodynamics |
| Order, Chaos, and All That! | 19.2 Entropy and the Second Law of Thermodynamics |
| Another Face of Entropy | 19.2 Entropy and the Second Law of Thermodynamics |
| Entropy: Conceptual Disorder | 19.2 Entropy and the Second Law of Thermodynamics |
| Derivation of the Second Law of Thermodynamics from Boltzmann's Distribution Law | 19.3 The Molecular Interpretation of Energy |
| The Boltzmann Distribution | 19.3 The Molecular Interpretation of Energy |
| Periodic Trends for the Entropy of Elements | 19.4 Entropy Changes in Chemical Reactions |
| J. Willard Gibbs (1839–1903): A Modern Genius | 19.5 Gibbs Free Energy |
| Josiah Willard Gibbs and Wilhelm Ostwald: A Contrast in Scientific Style | 19.5 Gibbs Free Energy |
| The Free-Energy Prediction and the Principle of Le Châtelier | 19.7 Free Energy and the Equilibrium Constant |
| The Conversion of Chemical Energy. Part 2: Biochemical Examples | 19.7 Free Energy and the Equilibrium Constant |

| **Live Demonstrations:** | **Section:** |
|---|---|
| Entropy, Disorder, and Freezing | 19.2 Entropy and the Second Law of Thermodynamics |
| A Chemical Hand Warmer | 19.6 Gibbs Free Energy |

# Chapter 19. Chemical Thermodynamics

## Common Student Misconceptions

- Students often believe that a spontaneous process should occur very quickly. They do not appreciate the difference between kinetics and thermodynamics.
- Students have a problem distinguishing between absolute thermodynamic quantities and the change in thermodynamic quantities.

## Lecture Outline

### 19.1 Spontaneous Processes[1,2,3]

- *Chemical thermodynamics* is concerned with energy relationships in chemical reactions.
  - We consider enthalpy.
  - We also consider *randomness* or *disorder* in the reaction.
- Recall the first law of thermodynamics: energy is conserved.

$$\Delta E = q + w$$

  - Where $\Delta E$ is the change in internal energy, $q$ is the heat absorbed by the system from the surroundings and $w$ is the work done.
- Any process that occurs without outside intervention is a **spontaneous** process.
  - When two eggs are dropped they spontaneously break.
  - The reverse reaction (two eggs leaping into your hand with their shells back intact) is not spontaneous.
  - We can conclude that a spontaneous process has a direction.
- A process that is spontaneous in one direction is not spontaneous in the opposite direction.
- Temperature may also effect the spontaneity of a process.

#### Reversible and Irreversible Processes[4,5,6,7]

- A **reversible process** is one that can go back and forth between states along the same path.
  - The reverse process restores the system to its original state.
  - The path taken back to the original state is *exactly* the reverse of the forward process.
  - There is no net change in the system or the surroundings when this cycle is completed.
  - Completely reversible processes are too slow to be attained in practice.
- Consider the interconversion of ice and water at 1 atm, 0°C.
  - Ice and water are in equilibrium.
  - We now add heat to the system from the surroundings.
    - We melt 1 mole of ice to form 1 mole of liquid water.
      - $q = \Delta H_{fus}$

---

[1] "Demystifying Introductory Chemistry. Part 4: An Approach to Reaction Thermodynamics through Enthalpies, Entropies, and Free Energies of Atomization" from Further Readings
[2] "A Model of Thermal Equilibrium: A Tool for the Introduction of Thermodynamics" from Further Readings
[3] "Thermodynamics and Spontaneity" from Further Readings
[4] "Thermite" Movie from MediaPortfolio
[5] "Nitrogen Triiodide" Movie from MediaPortfolio
[6] Figure 19.4 from MediaPortfolio and Transparency Pack
[7] "Conversion of Potential Energy to Work" Figure from MediaPortfolio

- To return to the original state we reverse the procedure.
  - We remove the same amount of heat from the system to the surroundings.
- An **irreversible process** cannot be reversed to restore the system and surroundings back to their original state.
  - A different path (with different values of $q$ and $w$) must be taken.
- Consider a gas in a cylinder with a piston.
  - Remove the partition and the gas expands to fill the space.
  - No $P$-$V$ work is done on the surroundings.
    - $w = 0$.
  - Now use the piston to compress the gas back to the original state.
  - The surroundings must do work on the system.
    - $w > 0$.
  - A different path is required to get the system back to its original state.
    - Note that the surroundings are NOT returned to their original conditions.
- For a system at equilibrium, reactants and products can interconvert *reversibly*.
- For a spontaneous process, the path between reactants and products is *irreversible*.

## 19.2 Entropy and the Second Law of Thermodynamics

### The Spontaneous Expansion of a Gas[8,9]

- Consider the expansion of an ideal gas:
- Consider an initial state: two 1-liter flasks connected by a closed stopcock.
  - One flask is evacuated and the other contains 1 atm of gas.
  - We open the stopcock while maintaining the system at constant temperature.
  - Initial state: an ideal gas confined to a cylinder kept at constant temperature in a water bath.
  - The process is isothermal: at constant temperature.
  - $\Delta E = 0$ for an isothermal process.
  - Thus, $q = -w$.
- Allow the gas to expand from $V_1$ to $V_2$.
- Pressure decreases from $P_1$ to $P_2$.
  - The final state: two flasks connected by an open stopcock.
    - Each flask contains gas at 0.5 atm.
  - Therefore the gas does no work and heat is not transferred.
- Why does the gas expand?
  - Why is the process spontaneous?
  - Why is the reverse process nonspontaneous?
  - When the gas molecules spread out into the 2 liter system there is an increase in the *randomness* or *disorder*.
  - Processes in which the disorder or entropy of the system increases tend to be spontaneous.

### Entropy[10,11,12,13,14,15,16]

---

[8] Figure 19.5 from MediaPortfolio
[9] Figure 19.6 from MediaPortfolio and Transparency Pack
[10] Figure 19.7 from MediaPortfolio and Transparency Pack
[11] "Visualizing Entropy" from Further Readings
[12] "Another Face of Entropy" from Further Readings
[13] "Pictorial Analogies III: Heat Flow, Thermodynamics, and Entropy" from Further Readings
[14] "Order, Chaos, and All That!" from Further Readings
[15] "Entropy: Conceptual Disorder" from Further Readings
[16] Figure 19.8 from MediaPortfolio and Transparency Pack

- Consider the melting of ice.
  - In the ice, the molecules are held rigidly in a lattice.
  - When it melts, the molecules have more freedom to move (increases degrees of freedom).
  - The molecules are more randomly distributed.
- Consider a KCl crystal dissolving in water.
  - The solid KCl has ions in a highly ordered arrangement.
  - When the crystal dissolves the ions have more freedom.
  - They are more randomly distributed.
  - However, now the water molecules are more ordered.
  - Some must be used to hydrate the ions.
  - Thus this example involves both ordering and disordering.
  - The disordering usually predominates (for most salts).
- **Entropy**, $S$, is a thermodynamic term that reflects the disorder or randomness of the system.
  - The more disordered or random the system, the larger the value of $S$.

## Relating Entropy to Heat Transfer and Temperature[17]

- Entropy is a state function.
  - It is independent of path.
  - For a system, $\Delta S = S_{final} - S_{initial}$.
- If $\Delta S > 0$ the randomness increases, if $\Delta S < 0$ the order increases.
- Suppose a system changes reversibly between state 1 and state 2.
  - Then, the change in entropy is given by:

$$\Delta S = \frac{q_{rev}}{T}$$

  - Where $q_{rev}$ is the amount of heat added reversibly to the system.
    - The subscript "rev" reminds us that the path between states is reversible.
    - Example: A phase change occurs at constant $T$ with the reversible addition of heat.

## The Second Law of Thermodynamics[18,19]

- The **second law of thermodynamics** explains why spontaneous processes have a direction.
- In any spontaneous process, the entropy of the universe increases.
- The change in entropy of the universe is the sum of the change in entropy of the system and the change in entropy of the surroundings.

$$\Delta S_{univ} = \Delta S_{sys} + \Delta S_{surr}$$

  - For a reversible process:

$$\Delta S_{univ} = \Delta S_{sys} + \Delta S_{surr} = 0$$

  - For a spontaneous process (i.e., irreversible):

$$\Delta S_{univ} = \Delta S_{sys} + \Delta S_{surr} > 0$$

    - Entropy is not conserved: $\Delta S_{univ}$ is continually increasing.
- Note: The second law states that the entropy of the universe must increase in a spontaneous process.
  - It is possible for the entropy of a system to decrease as long as the entropy of the surroundings increases.
- Consider an **isolated system**.
  - The system does not exchange energy or matter with the surroundings.
  - $\Delta S_{sys} = 0$ for a reversible process and $\Delta S_{sys} > 0$ for a spontaneous process.

---

[17] "Entropy, Disorder, and Freezing" from Live Demonstrations
[18] "Expansion of Gas into a Vacuum" Activity from MediaPortfolio
[19] "Possible Orientation of Three Gas Molecules" Activity from MediaPortfolio

## 19.3 The Molecular Interpretation of Entropy[20,21,22,23,24,25,26,27]

- The entropy of a system indicates its disorder.
  - A gas is less ordered than a liquid which is less ordered than a solid.
  - Any process that increases the number of gas molecules leads to an increase in entropy.
  - When $NO(g)$ reacts with $O_2(g)$ to form $NO_2(g)$, the total number of gas molecules decreases.

$$2NO(g) + O_2(g) \rightarrow 2NO_2(g)$$

    - Therefore, the entropy decreases.
- How can we relate changes in entropy to changes at the molecular level?
  - Formation of the new N-O bonds "ties up" more of the atoms in the products than in the reactants.
  - The *degrees of freedom* associated with the atoms have changed.
  - The greater the freedom of movement and degrees of freedom, the greater the entropy of the system.
- Individual molecules have degrees of freedom associated with motions within the molecule.
  - There are three atomic modes of motion:
  - **Translational motion.**
    - The moving of a molecule from one point in space to another.
  - **Vibrational motion.**
    - The shortening and lengthening of bonds, including the change in bond angles.
  - **Rotational motion.**
    - The spinning of a molecule about some axis.
  - Energy is required to get a molecule to translate, vibrate or rotate.
    - These forms of motion are ways molecules can store energy.
    - The more energy stored in translation, vibration and rotation, the greater the entropy.
- In a perfect crystal at 0 K there is no translation, rotation or vibration of molecules.
  - Therefore, this is a state of perfect order.
  - **Third law of thermodynamics**: The entropy of a perfect pure crystal at 0 K is zero.
- Entropy will increase as we increase the temperature of the perfect crystal.
  - Molecules gain vibrational motion.
  - The degrees of freedom increase.
- As we heat a substance from absolute zero, the entropy must increase.
- The entropy changes dramatically at a phase change.
  - When a solid melts, the molecules and atoms have a large increase in freedom of movement.
  - Boiling corresponds to a much greater change in entropy than melting.
- In general, entropy will increase when:
  - Liquids or solutions are formed from solids.
  - Gases are formed from solids or liquids.
  - The number of gas molecules increase.

## 19.4 Entropy Changes in Chemical Reactions[28,29]

---

[20] Figure 19.11 from MediaPortfolio
[21] "Molecular Entropy" Activity from MediaPortfolio
[22] Figure 19.12 from MediaPortfolio and Transparency Pack
[23] Figure 19.13 from MediaPortfolio and Transparency Pack
[24] "Derivation of the Second Law of Thermodynamics from Boltzmann's Distribution Law" from Further Readings
[25] Figure 19.14 from MediaPortfolio and Transparency Pack
[26] "The Boltzmann Distribution" from Further Readings
[27] "Entropy and Temperature" Activity from MediaPortfolio

- Absolute entropy can be determined from complicated measurements.
  - Values are based on a reference point of zero for a perfect crystalline solid at 0K (the 3rd law).
- **Standard molar entropy, $S^\circ$**: molar entropy of a substance in its standard state.
  - Similar in concept to $\Delta H^\circ$.
  - Units: J/mol-K.
    - Note: the units of $\Delta H$ are kJ/mol.
- Some observations about $S^\circ$ values:
  - Standard molar entropies of elements are not zero.
  - $S^\circ_{gas} > S^\circ_{liquid}$ or $S^\circ_{solid}$.
  - $S^\circ$ tends to increase with increasing molar mass of the substance.
  - $S^\circ$ tends to increase with the number of atoms in the formula of the substance.
- For a chemical reaction which produces $n$ products from $m$ reactants:

$$\Delta S^\circ = \sum nS^\circ(\text{products}) - \sum mS^\circ(\text{reactants})$$

- Example: Consider the reaction:

$$N_2(g) + 3H_2(g) \rightarrow 2NH_3(g)$$
$$\Delta S^\circ = \{2S^\circ(NH_3) - [S^\circ(N_2) + 3S^\circ(H_2)]\}$$

### Entropy Changes in the Surroundings[30,31]

- For an isothermal process,
  - $\Delta S_{surr} = -q_{sys} / T$
- For a reaction at constant pressure,
  - $q_{sys} = \Delta H$
- Example: consider the reaction:

$$N_2(g) + 3H_2(g) \rightarrow 2NH_3(g)$$

- The entropy gained by the surroundings is greater than the entropy lost by the system.
- This is the sign of a spontaneous reaction: the overall entropy change of the universe is positive.
- $\Delta S_{univ} > 0$

## 19.5 Gibbs Free Energy[32,33]

- For a spontaneous reaction the entropy of the universe must increase.
- Reactions with large negative $\Delta H$ values tend to be spontaneous.
- How can we use $\Delta S$ and $\Delta H$ to predict whether a reaction is spontaneous?
- The **Gibbs free energy, (free energy)**, $G$, of a state is:

$$G = H - TS$$

  - Free energy is a state function.
  - For a process occurring at constant temperature, the free energy change is:

$$\Delta G = \Delta H - T\Delta S$$

- Recall:
  - $\Delta S_{univ} = \Delta S_{sys} + \Delta S_{surr} = \Delta S_{sys} + [-\Delta H_{sys} / T]$
    - Thus,
      - $-T\Delta S_{univ} = \Delta H_{sys} - T\Delta S_{sys}$
- The sign of $\Delta G$ is important in predicting the spontaneity of the reaction.

---

[28] Table 19.2 from MediaPortfolio and Transparency Pack
[29] "Periodic Trends for the Entropy of Elements" from Further Readings
[30] "Josiah Willard Gibbs and Wilhelm Ostwald: A Contrast in Scientific Style" from Further Readings
[31] "J. Willard Gibbs (1839 – 1903): A Modern Genius" from Further Readings
[32] Figure 19.17 from MediaPortfolio
[33] Figure 19.18 from MediaPortfolio and Transparency Pack

- If $\Delta G < 0$ then the forward reaction is spontaneous.
- If $\Delta G = 0$ then the reaction is at equilibrium and no net reaction will occur.
- If $\Delta G > 0$ then the forward reaction is not spontaneous.
  - However, the reverse reaction is spontaneous.
  - If $\Delta G > 0$, work must be supplied from the surroundings to drive the reaction.
- The equilibrium position in a spontaneous process is given by the minimum free energy available to the system.
  - The free energy decreases until it reaches this minimum value.

### Standard Free-Energy Changes[34]

- We can tabulate **standard free energies of formation,** $\Delta G^\circ_f$.
  - Standard states are: pure solid, pure liquid, 1 atm (gas), 1 $M$ concentration (solution), and $\Delta G^\circ = 0$ for elements.
    - We most often use 25°C (or 298 K) as the temperature.
  - The standard free-energy change for a process is given by:

$$\Delta G^\circ = \sum n\Delta G^\circ_f(\text{products}) - \sum m\Delta G^\circ_f(\text{reactants})$$

  - The quantity $\Delta G^\circ$ for a reaction tells us whether a mixture of substances will spontaneously react to produce more reactants ($\Delta G^\circ > 0$) or products ($\Delta G^\circ < 0$).

## 19.6 Free Energy and Temperature[35,36,37,38,39]

- The sign of $\Delta G$ tells us if the reaction is spontaneous.
- Focus on $\Delta G = \Delta H - T\Delta S$.
  - If $\Delta H < 0$ and $-T\Delta S < 0$:
    - $\Delta G$ will always be <0.
    - Thus the reaction will be spontaneous.
  - If $\Delta H > 0$ and $-T\Delta S > 0$:
    - $\Delta G$ will always be >0.
    - Thus the reaction will not be spontaneous.
  - If $\Delta H$ and $-T\Delta S$ have different signs:
    - The sign of $\Delta G$ will depend on the sign and magnitudes of the other terms.
    - Temperature will be an important factor.
  - For example, consider the following reaction:

$$H_2O(s) \rightarrow H_2O(l) \qquad \Delta H > 0,\ \Delta S > 0$$

    - At a temperature less than 0°C:
      - $\Delta H > T\Delta S$
      - $\Delta G > 0$
      - The melting of ice is not spontaneous when the temperature is less than 0°C.
    - At a temperature greater than 0°C:
      - $\Delta H < T\Delta S$
      - $\Delta G < 0$
      - The melting of ice is spontaneous when the temperature is greater than 0°C.
    - At 0°C:

---

[34] Table 19.3 from MediaPortfolio
[35] Table 19.4 from MediaPortfolio
[36] "Gibbs Free Energy" Activity from MediaPortfolio
[37] "Air Bags" Animation from MediaPortfolio
[38] "Formation of Water" Movie from MediaPortfolio
[39] "A Chemical Hand Warmer" from Live Demonstrations

  - $\Delta H = T\Delta S$
  - $\Delta G = 0$
  - Ice and water are in equilibrium at 0°C.
- Even though a reaction has a negative $\Delta G$ it may occur too slowly to be observed.
  - Thermodynamics gives us the direction of a spontaneous process; it does not give us the rate of the process.

## 19.7 Free Energy and the Equilibrium Constant[40]

- Recall that $\Delta G^{\circ}$ and $K_{eq}$ (equilibrium constant) apply to *standard conditions*.
- Recall that $\Delta G$ and $Q$ (equilibrium quotient) apply to *any conditions*.
- It is useful to determine whether substances will react under specific conditions:

$$\Delta G = \Delta G^{\circ} + RT\ln Q$$

- At equilibrium, $Q = K_{eq}$ and $\Delta G = 0$, so:

$$\Delta G = \Delta G^{\circ} + RT\ln Q$$
$$0 = \Delta G^{\circ} + \mathrm{RT}\ln K_{eq}$$
$$\therefore \Delta G^{\circ} = -RT\ln K_{eq}$$

- From the above we can conclude:
  - If $\Delta G^{\circ} < 0$, then $K_{eq} > 1$.
  - If $\Delta G^{\circ} = 0$, then $K_{eq} = 1$.
  - If $\Delta G^{\circ} > 0$, then $K_{eq} < 1$.

### *Driving Nonspontaneous Reactions*[41,42]

- If $\Delta G > 0$, work must be supplied from the surroundings to drive the reaction.
- Biological systems often use one *spontaneous* reaction to drive another *nonspontaneous* reaction.
  - These reactions are *coupled reactions*.
- The energy required to drive most nonspontaneous reactions comes from the metabolism of foods.
  - Example: Consider the oxidation of glucose:

$$C_6H_{12}O_6(s) + 6O_2(g) \rightarrow 6CO_2(g) + 6H_2O(l) \qquad \Delta G^{\circ} = -2880 \text{ kJ.}$$

  - The free energy released by glucose oxidation is used to convert low energy adenosine diphosphate (ADP) and inorganic phosphate into high energy adenosine triphosphate (ATP).
  - When ATP is converted back to ADP the energy released may be used to "drive" other reactions.

---

[40] "The Free Energy Prediction and the Principle of Le Châtelier" from Further Readings
[41] Figure 19.19 from MediaPortfolio
[42] "The Conversion of Chemical Energy. Part 2: Biochemical Examples" from Further Readings

## Further Readings:

1. James N. Spencer, Richard S. Moog, and Ronald J. Gillespie, "Demystifying Introductory Chemistry. Part 4: An Approach to Reaction Thermodynamics Through Enthalpies, Entropies, and Free Energies of Atomization," *J. Chem. Educ.*, Vol. 73, **1996**, 631-636.

2. Ruth Ben-Zvi, Judith Silberstein, and Rachel Mamiok, "A Model of Thermal Equilibrium: A Tool for the Introduction of Thermodynamics," *J. Chem. Educ.*, Vol. 70, **1993**, 31-34.

3. John J Fortman, "Pictorial Analogies III: Heat Flow, Thermodynamics, and Entropy," *J. Chem. Educ.*, Vol. 70, **1993**, 102-103.

4. L. Glasser, "Order, Chaos, and All That!" *J. Chem. Educ.*, Vol. 66, **1989**, 997-1001.

5. John P. Lowe, "Entropy: Conceptual Disorder," *J. Chem. Educ.*, Vol. 65, **1988**, 403-406.

6. Joseph H. Lechner, "Visualizing Entropy," *J. Chem. Educ.*, Vol. 76, **1999**, 1382-1387.

7. P. G. Nelson, "Derivation of the Second Law of Thermodynamics from Boltzmann's Distribution Law," *J. Chem. Educ.*, Vol. 65, **1989**, 390-393.

8. Douglas K. Russell, "The Boltzmann Distribution," *J. Chem. Educ.*, Vol. 73, **1996**, 299-300.

9. Travis Thoms, "Periodic Trends for the Entropy of Elements," *J. Chem. Educ.*, Vol. 72, **1995**, 16.

10. Sidney Rosen, "J. Willard Gibbs (1839-1903): A Modern Genius," *J. Chem. Educ.*, Vol. 60, **1983**, 593-594.

11. Robert J. Deltete and David L. Thorsell, "Josiah Willard Gibbs and Wilhelm Ostwald: A Contrast in Scientific Style," *J. Chem. Educ.*, Vol. 73, **1996**, 289-295.

12. Zheng Xianmin, "The Free Energy Prediction and the Principle of Le Châtelier," *J. Chem. Educ.*, Vol. 66, **1989**, 401-402.

13. Raymond S. Ochs, "Thermodynamics and Spontaneity," *J. Chem. Educ.*, Vol. 73, **1996**, 952-954.

14. Peter Weiss, "Another Face of Entropy," *Science News*, Vol. 154, **August 15, 1998**, 108-109.

15. Donald J. Wink, "The Conversion of Chemical Energy. Part 2: Biochemical Examples," *J. Chem. Educ.*, Vol. 69, **1992**, 264-267.

## Literature Demonstrations:

1. Lee R. Summerlin, Christie L. Borgford, and Julie B. Ealy, "A Chemical Hand Warmer," *Chemical Demonstrations: A Sourcebook for Teachers, Volume 2* (Washington: American Chemical Society, 1988), pp. 99-100.

2. Brian B. Laird, "Entropy, Disorder, and Freezing," *J. Chem. Educ.*, Vol. 76, **1999**, 1388-1390.

# Chapter 20. Electrochemistry

## Media Resources

### Figures and Tables

| In Transparency Pack and on MediaPortfolio: | Section: |
|---|---|
| Figure 20.5 Voltaic Cell | 20.3 Voltaic Cells |
| Figure 20.6 Terminology Used for Voltaic Cells | 20.3 Voltaic Cells |
| Figure 20.7 Reaction between Zn(*s*) and $Cu^{2+}(aq)$ at the Atomic Level | 20.3 Voltaic Cells |
| Figure 20.11 Voltaic Cell Using a Standard Hydrogen Electrode | 20.4 Cell EMF |
| Table 20.1 Standard Reduction Potentials in Water at 25°C | 20.4 Cell EMF |
| Figure 20.14 Relation Between $E^{\circ}_{red}$ and Ease of Oxidation or Reduction | 20.4 Cell EMF |
| Figure 20.16 Concentration Cell | 20.6 Effect of Concentration on Cell EMF |
| Figure 20.21 Schematic of Lead-Acid Battery | 20.7 Batteries |
| Figure 20.25 Corrosion of Iron | 20.8 Corrosion |
| Figure 20.26 Cathodic Protection of Iron With Zinc | 20.8 Corrosion |
| Figure 20.28 Electrolysis of Molten NaCl | 20.9 Electrolysis |
| Figure 20.31 Steps to Convert Quantity of Electrical Charge to Amounts of Substances | 20.9 Electrolysis |

| On MediaPortfolio: | Section: |
|---|---|
| Figure 20.8 Depiction of a Voltaic Cell at the Atomic Level | 20.3 Voltaic Cells |
| Figure 20.10 Standard Hydrogen Electrode | 20.4 Cell EMF |
| Figure 20.20 Batteries Connected in Series | 20.7 Batteries |
| Figure 20.22 Cutaway View of Alkaline Battery | 20.7 Batteries |
| Figure 20.27 Cathodic Protection of an Iron Pipe | 20.8 Corrosion |
| Figure 20.30 Electrolytic Cell With Active Metal Electrode | 20.9 Electrolysis |

| Animations: | Section: |
|---|---|
| Oxidation-Reduction Reactions—Part I | 20.1 Oxidation-Reduction Reactions |
| Oxidation-Reduction Reactions—Part II | 20.1 Oxidation-Reduction Reactions |
| Voltaic Cells I: The Copper-Zinc Cell | 20.3 Voltaic Cells |
| Voltaic Cells II: The Zinc-Hydrogen Cell | 20.4 Cell EMF |
| Standard Reduction Potentials | 20.4 Cell EMF |
| Electrolysis of Water | 20.9 Electrolysis |

| Movies: | Section: |
|---|---|
| Redox Chemistry of Iron and Copper | 20.5 Spontaneity of Redox Reactions |
| Electroplating | 20.9 Electrolysis |

| **Activities:** | **Section:** |
|---|---|
| Balancing Redox Equations in Acid | 20.2 Balancing Oxidation-Reduction Equations |
| Balancing Redox Equations in Base | 20.2 Balancing Oxidation-Reduction Equations |
| Nernst Equation Activity | 20.6 Effect of Concentration on Cell EMF |
| Electrolysis | 20.9 Electrolysis |

## Other Resources

| **Further Readings:** | **Section:** |
|---|---|
| Redox Balancing without Puzzling | 20.2 Balancing Oxidation-Reduction Equations |
| Electrochemical Errors | 20.3 Voltaic Cells |
| Dental Filling Discomforts Illustrate Electrochemical Potentials of Metals | 20.3 Voltaic Cells |
| Using a Teaching Model to Correct Known Misconceptions in Electrochemistry | 20.3 Voltaic Cells |
| Alleviating the Common Confusion Caused by Polarity in Electrochemistry | 20.4 Cell EMF |
| Using the Biological Cell in Teaching Electrochemistry. | 20.5 Spontaneity of Redox Reactions |
| Batteries: Full Speed Ahead | 20.7 Batteries |
| Structure and Content of Some Primary Batteries | 20.7 Batteries |
| Evaluation of Corrosion Susceptibility of a Metal: Student Corrosion Experiment II | 20.8 Corrosion |

| **Live Demonstrations:** | **Section:** |
|---|---|
| Visible Oxidation-Reduction in Electrochemical Cells | 20.3 Voltaic Cells |
| An Activity Series: Zinc, Copper, and Silver Half Cells | 20.5 Spontaneity of Redox Reactions |
| Activity Series for Some Metals | 20.5 Spontaneity of Redox Reactions |
| Making a Simple Battery: The Gerber Cell | 20.7 Batteries |
| Floating Pennies | 20.8 Corrosion |
| Electrolytic Cells in Series: A Red, White, and Blue Electrolysis | 20.9 Electrolysis |
| Electroplating Copper | 20.9 Electrolysis |

# Chapter 20. Electrochemistry

## Common Student Misconceptions

- Students often have trouble balancing redox equations.

## Lecture Outline

### 20.1 Oxidation-Reduction Reactions[1,2]

- Chemical reactions in which the oxidation state of one or more substance changes are called **oxidation-reduction reactions** (*redox reactions*).
    - Recall:
        - Oxidation involves loss of electrons (OIL).
        - Reduction involves gain of electrons (RIG).
- **Electrochemistry** is the branch of chemistry that deals with relationships between electricity and chemical reactions.
- Consider the spontaneous reaction that occurs when Zn is added to HCl.

$$Zn(s) + 2H^{+}(aq) \rightarrow Zn^{2+}(aq) + H_2(g)$$

    - The oxidation numbers of Zn and $H^+$ have changed.
        - The oxidation number of Zn has increased from 0 to +2.
        - The oxidation number of H has decreased from +1 to 0.
            - Therefore, Zn is oxidized to $Zn^{2+}$ while $H^+$ is reduced to $H_2$.
    - $H^+$ causes Zn to be oxidized.
        - Thus, $H^+$ is the **oxidizing agent** or **oxidant**.
    - Zn causes $H^+$ to be reduced.
        - Thus, Zn is the **reducing agent** or **reductant**.
    - Note that the reducing agent is oxidized and the oxidizing agent is reduced.

### 20.2 Balancing Oxidation-Reduction Equations

- Recall the *law of conservation of mass*: The amount of each element present at the beginning of the reaction must be present at the end.
- *Conservation of charge*: Electrons are not lost in a chemical reaction.
- Some redox equations may be easily balanced by inspection.
    - However, for many redox reactions we need to look carefully at the transfer of electrons.

#### Half-Reactions

- **Half-reactions** are a convenient way of separating oxidation and reduction reactions.
- Consider the reaction:

$$Sn^{2+}(aq) + 2Fe^{3+}(aq) \rightarrow Sn^{4+}(aq) + 2Fe^{2+}(aq)$$

- The oxidation half-reaction is:

$$Sn^{2+}(aq) \rightarrow Sn^{4+}(aq) + 2e^{-}$$

    - Note that electrons are a product here.
- The reduction half-reaction is:

$$2Fe^{3+}(aq) + 2e^{-} \rightarrow 2Fe^{2+}(aq)$$

    - Note that electrons are a reactant here.

#### Balancing Equations by the Method of Half-Reactions[3,4]

---

[1] "Oxidation-Reduction Reactions—Part I" Animation from MediaPortfolio
[2] "Oxidation-Reduction Reactions—Part II" Animation from MediaPortfolio

- Consider the titration of an acidic solution of $Na_2C_2O_4$ (sodium oxalate, colorless) with $KMnO_4$ (deep purple).
  - $MnO_4^-$ is reduced to $Mn^{2+}$ (pale pink) while the $C_2O_4^{2-}$ is oxidized to $CO_2$.
  - The equivalence point is indicated by the presence of a pale pink color.
  - If more $KMnO_4$ is added, the solution turns purple due to the excess $KMnO_4$.
- What is the balanced chemical equation for this reaction?
- We can determine this using the method of half-reactions:
  - Write down the two incomplete half reactions.

$$MnO_4^-\,(aq) \rightarrow Mn^{2+}(aq)$$
$$C_2O_4^{2-}\,(aq) \rightarrow CO_2(g)$$

  - Balance each half reaction:
    - First, balance elements other than H and O.

$$MnO_4^-\,(aq) \rightarrow Mn^{2+}(aq)$$
$$C_2O_4^{2-}\,(aq) \rightarrow 2CO_2(g)$$

    - Then balance O by adding water.

$$MnO_4^-\,(aq) \rightarrow Mn^{2+}(aq) + 4H_2O(l)$$
$$C_2O_4^{2-}\,(aq) \rightarrow 2CO_2(g)$$

    - Then balance H by adding $H^+$.

$$8H^+(aq) + MnO_4^-\,(aq) \rightarrow Mn^{2+}(aq) + 4H_2O(l)$$
$$C_2O_4^{2-}\,(aq) \rightarrow 2CO_2(g)$$

    - Finish by balancing charge by adding electrons.
      - This is an easy place to make an error!
        - For the permanganate half-reaction, note that there is a charge of 7+ on the left and 2+ on the right.
        - Therefore, 5 electrons need to be added to the left:

$$5e^- + 8H^+(aq) + MnO_4^-\,(aq) \rightarrow Mn^{2+}(aq) + 4H_2O(l)$$

        - In the oxalate half-reaction, there is a 2– charge on the left and a 0 charge on the right, so we need to add two electrons to the products:

$$C_2O_4^{2-}\,(aq) \rightarrow 2CO_2(g) + 2e^-$$

    - Multiply each half-reaction to make the number of electrons equal.
      - To balance the 5 electrons for permanganate and 2 electrons for oxalate, we need 10 electrons for both.
        - Multiplying gives:

$$10e^- + 16H^+(aq) + 2MnO_4^-\,(aq) \rightarrow 2Mn^{2+}(aq) + 8H_2O(l)$$
$$5C_2O_4^{2-}\,(aq) \rightarrow 10CO_2(g) + 10e^-$$

    - Now add the reactions and simplify.

$$16H^+(aq) + 2MnO_4^-\,(aq) + 5C_2O_4^{2-}\,(aq) \rightarrow 2Mn^{2+}(aq) + 8H_2O(l) + 10CO_2(g)$$

    - The equation is now balanced!
    - Note that all of the electrons have cancelled out!

### Balancing Equations for Reactions Occurring in Basic Solution[5]

- The same method as above is used, but $OH^-$ is added to "neutralize" the $H^+$ used.
- The equation must again be simplified by canceling like terms on both sides of the equation.

## 20.3 Voltaic Cells[6,7,8,9,10,11,12]

---

[3] "Redox Balancing Without Puzzling" from Further Readings
[4] "Balancing Redox Equations in Acid" Activity from MediaPortfolio
[5] "Balancing Redox Equations in Base" Activity from MediaPortfolio
[6] "Voltaic Cells I: The Copper-Zinc Cell" Animation from MediaPortfolio

- The energy released in a spontaneous redox reaction may be used to perform electrical work.
- **Voltaic** or **galvanic cells** are devices in which electron transfer occurs via an external circuit.
- Voltaic cells utilize spontaneous reactions.
- If a strip of Zn is placed in a solution of $CuSO_4$, Cu is deposited on the Zn and the Zn dissolves by forming $Zn^{2+}$.

$$Zn(s) + Cu^{2+}(aq) \rightarrow Zn^{2+}(aq) + Cu(s)$$

  - Zn is spontaneously oxidized to $Zn^{2+}$ by $Cu^{2+}$.
  - The $Cu^{2+}$ is spontaneously reduced to $Cu^0$ by Zn.
  - The entire process is spontaneous.
- This voltaic cells consists of:
  - An oxidation half-reaction:

$$Zn(s) \rightarrow Zn^{2+}(aq) + 2e^-$$

    - Oxidation takes place at the **anode**.
  - A reduction half-reaction:

$$Cu^{2+}(aq) + 2e^- \rightarrow Cu(s)$$

    - Reduction takes place at the **cathode**.
  - A salt bridge (used to complete the electrical circuit).
    - Cations move from anode to cathode.
    - Anions move from cathode to anode.
  - The two solid metals are the **electrodes** (cathode and anode).
  - As oxidation occurs, Zn is converted to $Zn^{2+}$ and $2e^-$.
    - The electrons flow towards the cathode where they are used in the reduction reaction.
  - We expect the Zn electrode to lose mass and the Cu electrode to gain mass.
- Electrons flow from the anode to the cathode.
  - Therefore, the anode is negative and the cathode is positive.
  - Electrons cannot flow through the solution; they have to be transported through an external wire.
  - Anions and cations move through a porous barrier or salt bridge.
  - Cations move into the cathodic compartment to neutralize the excess negatively charged ions (Cathode: $Cu^{2+} + 2e^- \rightarrow Cu$, so the counter ion of Cu is in excess).
  - Anions move into the anodic compartment to neutralize the excess $Zn^{2+}$ ions formed by oxidation.

### A Molecular View of the Electrode Process[13,14]

- "Rules" of voltaic cells:
  - At the anode electrons are products.
    - Oxidation occurs at the anode.
  - At the cathode electrons are reagents.
    - Reduction occurs at the cathode.
  - The flow of electrons from anode to cathode requires an external wire.
    - The transfer of ions through a salt bridge maintains overall charge balance for the two compartments.

---

[7] "Visible Oxidation-Reduction in Electrochemical Cells" from Live Demonstrations
[8] Figure 20.5 from MediaPortfolio and Transparency Pack
[9] Figure 20.6 from MediaPortfolio and Transparency Pack
[10] "Electrochemical Errors" from Further Readings
[11] "Dental Filling Discomforts Illustrate Electrochemical Potentials of Metals" from Further Readings
[12] "Using a Teaching Model to Correct Known Misconceptions in Electrochemistry" from Further Readings
[13] Figure 20.7 from MediaPortfolio and Transparency Pack
[14] Figure 20.8 from MediaPortfolio

## 20.4 Cell EMF[15]

- The flow of electrons from anode to cathode is spontaneous.
    - What is the "driving force"?
- Electrons flow from anode to cathode because the cathode has a lower electrical potential energy than the anode.
    - *Potential difference*: difference in electrical potential.
    - The potential difference is measured in volts.
    - One volt (V) is the potential difference required to impart one joule (J) of energy to a charge of one coulomb (C):

$$1\text{V} = 1\frac{\text{J}}{\text{C}}$$

    - **Electromotive force (emf)** is the force required to push electrons through the external circuit.
        - **Cell potential**: $E_{cell}$ is the emf of a cell.
            - This is known as the *cell voltage*.
            - $E_{cell}$ is > 0 for a spontaneous reaction.
- For 1*M* solutions or 1 atm pressure for gases at 25°C (standard conditions), the **standard emf (standard cell potential)** is called $E°_{cell}$.
    - For example, for the reaction:

$$\text{Zn}(s) + \text{Cu}^{2+}(aq) \rightarrow \text{Zn}^{2+}(aq) + \text{Cu}(s)$$

    - $E°_{cell} = +1.10$ V

### Standard Reduction (Half-Cell) Potentials[16,17,18,19,20]

- We can conveniently tabulate electrochemical data.
- **Standard reduction potentials,** $E°_{red}$ are measured relative to a standard.
- The emf of a cell can be calculated from standard reduction potentials:

$$E°_{cell} = E°_{red}(\text{cathode}) - E°_{red}(\text{anode})$$

- We use the following half-reaction as our standard:

$$2\text{H}^{+}(aq, 1M) + 2\text{e}^{-} \rightarrow \text{H}_2(g, 1\text{ atm}) \qquad E°_{cell} = 0V.$$

    - This electrode is called a **standard hydrogen electrode** (SHE).
    - The SHE is *assigned* a standard reduction potential of zero.
- Consider the half-reaction:

$$\text{Zn}(s) \rightarrow \text{Zn}^{2+}(aq) + 2\text{e}^{-}$$

    - We can *measure* $E°_{cell}$ relative to the SHE (cathode):
        - It consists of a Pt electrode in a tube placed in 1 $M\,\text{H}^{+}$ solution.
        - $H_2$ is bubbled through the tube.

$$E°_{cell} = E°_{red}(\text{cathode}) - E°_{red}(\text{anode})$$
$$0.76\text{ V} = 0\text{ V} - E°_{red}(\text{anode}).$$

        - Therefore, $E°_{red}(\text{anode}) = -0.76$ V.
- Standard reduction potentials must be written as reduction reactions:

$$\text{Zn}^{2+}(aq, 1M) + 2\text{e}^{-} \rightarrow \text{Zn}(s) \qquad E°_{red} = -0.76\text{ V}.$$

    - Since $E°_{red} = -0.76$ V we conclude that the *reduction* of $Zn^{2+}$ in the presence of the SHE is *not* spontaneous.
        - However, the *oxidation* of Zn with the SHE *is* spontaneous.

---

15 "Alleviating the Common Confusion Caused by Polarity in Electrochemistry" from Further Readings
16 "Standard Reduction Potentials" Animation from MediaPortfolio
17 "Voltaic Cells II: The Zinc-Hydrogen Cell" Animation from MediaPortfolio
18 Figure 20.10 from MediaPortfolio
19 Figure 20.11 from MediaPortfolio and Transparency Pack
20 Table 20.1 from MediaPortfolio and Transparency Pack

- The standard reduction potential is an intensive property.
  - Therefore, changing the stoichiometric coefficient does not affect $E°_{red}$.

$$2Zn^{2+}(aq) + 4e^{-} \rightarrow 2Zn(s) \qquad E°_{red} = -0.76\ V$$

- Reactions with $E°_{red} > 0$ are spontaneous reductions relative to the SHE.
  - Reactions with $E°_{red} < 0$ are spontaneous oxidations relative to the SHE.
  - The larger the difference between $E°_{red}$ values, the larger $E°_{cell}$.
- The more positive the value of $E°_{red}$, the greater the driving force for reduction.

### Oxidizing and Reducing Agents[21]

- Consider a table of standard reduction potentials.
- We can use this table to determine the relative strengths of reducing (and oxidizing) agents.
  - The more positive the $E°_{red}$, the stronger the oxidizing agent (written in the table as a reactant)
  - The more negative the $E°_{red}$, the stronger the reducing agent (written as a product in the table).
  - We can use this to predict if one reactant can spontaneously oxidize another.
    - For example:
      - $F_2$ can oxidize $H_2$ or Li.
      - $Ni^{2+}$ can oxidize Al($s$).
  - We can use this table to predict if one reactant can spontaneously reduce another.
    - For example:
      - Li can reduce $F_2$.

## 20.5 Spontaneity of Redox Reactions[22,23,24]

- For any electrochemical process

$$E° = E°_{red}(\text{reduction process}) - E°_{red}(\text{oxidation process}).$$

  - A positive $E°$ indicates a spontaneous process (galvanic cell).
  - A negative $E°$ indicates a nonspontaneous process.
- The above equation is used to understand the activity series of metals.
  - Consider the reaction of nickel with silver ion:

$$Ni(s) + 2Ag^{+}(aq) \rightarrow Ni^{2+}(aq) + 2Ag(s)$$

    - The standard cell potential is:

$$\begin{aligned} E°_{cell} &= E°_{red}(Ag^{+}/Ag) - E°_{red}(Ni^{2+}/Ni) \\ &= (0.80\ V) - (-0.28\ V) \\ &= 1.08\ V \end{aligned}$$

    - This value indicates that the reaction is spontaneous.

### EMF and Free-Energy Change[25]

- We can show that:

$$\Delta G = -nFE$$

  - Where $\Delta G$ is the change in free energy, $n$ is the number of moles of electrons transferred, $F$ is *Faraday's constant* and $E$ is the emf of the cell.
- We define a **faraday** ($F$) as:

$$1F = 96{,}500 \frac{C}{\text{mol } e^{-}} = 96{,}500 \frac{J}{(V)(\text{mol } e^{-})}$$

---

[21] Figure 20.14 from MediaPortfolio and Transparency Pack
[22] "Redox Chemistry of Iron and Copper" Movie from MediaPortfolio
[23] "An Activity Series: Zinc, Copper, and Silver Half Cells" from Live Demonstrations
[24] "Activity Series for Some Metals" from Live Demonstrations
[25] "Using the Biological Cell in Teaching Electrochemistry" from Further Readings

- Since $n$ and $F$ are positive, if $\Delta G < 0$ then $E > 0$, and the reaction will be spontaneous.

## 20.6 Effect of Concentration on Cell EMF

- A voltaic cell is functional until $E = 0$ at which point equilibrium has been reached.
  - The cell is then "dead."
- The point at which $E = 0$ is determined by the concentrations of the species involved in the redox reaction.

### The Nernst Equation[26]

- We can calculate the cell potential under nonstandard conditions.
- Recall that:

$$\Delta G = \Delta G^{\circ} + RT\ln Q$$

- We can substitute in our expression for the free energy change:

$$-nFE = -nFE^{\circ} + RT\ln Q$$

- Rearranging, we get the **Nernst equation**:

$$E = E^{\circ} - \frac{RT}{nF}\ln Q$$

or

$$E = E^{\circ} - \frac{2.303RT}{nF}\log Q$$

  - Note the change from natural logarithm to log base 10.
- The Nernst equation can be simplified by collecting all the constants together and using a temperature of 298 K:

$$E = E^{\circ} - \frac{0.0592}{n}\log Q$$

- Example: If we have the reaction:

$$Zn(s) + Cu^{2+}(aq) \rightarrow Zn^{2+}(aq) + Cu(s)$$

  - If $[Cu^{2+}] = 5.0\ M$ and $[Zn^{2+}] = 0.050M$:

$$E_{cell} = 1.10V - \frac{0.0592}{2}\log\frac{0.050}{5.0} = 1.16V$$

### Concentration Cells[27]

- A **concentration cell** is one whose emf is generated solely because of a concentration difference.
- Example: Consider a cell with two compartments, each with a Ni($s$) electrode but with difference concentrations of $Ni^{2+}(aq)$.
  - One cell has $[Ni^{2+}] = 1.0$ M and the other has $[Ni^{2+}] = 0.001$ M.
  - The standard cell potential is zero.
  - But this cell is operating under nonstandard conditions!
  - The driving force is the difference in $Ni^{2+}$ concentrations.
    - Anode (dilute $Ni^{2+}$): $Ni(s) \rightarrow Ni^{2+}(aq) + 2e^-$
    - Cathode (concentrated $Ni^{2+}$): $Ni^{2+}(aq) + 2e^- \rightarrow Ni(s)$
- Using the Nernst equation we can calculate a cell potential of +0.0888 V for this concentration cell.

### Cell EMF and Chemical Equilibrium

---

26 "Nearnst Equation Activity" from MediaPortfolio

27 Figure 20.16 from MediaPortfolio and Transparency Pack

- A system is at equilibrium when $\Delta G = 0$.
- From the Nernst equation, at equilibrium

$$\log K = \frac{nE^\circ}{0.0592}$$

  - Thus, if we know the cell emf, we can calculate the equilibrium constant.

## 20.7 Batteries[28,29,30,31]

- A battery is a portable, self-contained electrochemical power source consisting of one or more voltaic cells.

### Lead-Acid Battery[32]

- A 12-V car battery consists of 6 cathode/anode pairs each producing 2 V.
- Cathode: $PbO_2$ on a metal grid in sulfuric acid:

$$PbO_2(s) + HSO_4^-(aq) + 3H^+(aq) + 2e^- \rightarrow PbSO_4(s) + 2H_2O(l)$$

- Anode: Pb:

$$Pb(s) + HSO_4^-(aq) \rightarrow PbSO_4(s) + H^+(aq) + 2e^-$$

- The overall electrochemical reaction is

$$PbO_2(s) + Pb(s) + 2HSO_4^-(aq) + 2H^+(aq) \rightarrow 2PbSO_4(s) + 2H_2O(l)$$

- The cell potential for this reaction is:

$$\begin{aligned} E^\circ_{cell} &= E^\circ_{red}(\text{cathode}) - E^\circ_{red}(\text{anode}) \\ &= (+1.685\text{ V}) - (-0.356\text{ V}) \\ &= +2.041\text{ V}. \end{aligned}$$

- Wood or glass-fiber spacers are used to prevent the electrodes form touching.
- An advantage of these cells is that they can be recharged.
  - An external source of energy is used to reverse the process.

### Alkaline Battery[33]

- The most common nonrechargeable battery is the alkaline battery.
- Powdered zinc metal is immobilized in a gel in contact with a concentrated solution of KOH.
- Thus these batteries are *alkaline*.
- The reaction at the anode is:

$$Zn(s) \rightarrow Zn^{2+}(aq) + 2e^-$$

- The reaction at the cathode is the reduction of $MnO_2$:

$$2MnO_2(s) + 2H_2O(l) + 2e^- \rightarrow 2MnO(OH)(s) + 2OH^-(aq)$$

- The cell potential of these batteries is 1.55 V at room temperature.

### Nickel–Cadmium, Nickel–Metal–Hydride, and Lithium–Ion Batteries

- A common rechargeable battery is the nickel–cadmium (NiCad) battery.
  - The reaction at the cathode is:

$$2NiO(OH)(s) + 2H_2O(l) + 2e^- \rightarrow 2Ni(OH)_2(s) + 2OH^-(aq)$$

  - The reaction at the anode is:

$$Cd(s) + 2OH^-(aq) \rightarrow Cd(OH)_2(s) + 2e^-$$

  - The cell potential of this battery is about 1.30 V at room temperature.

---

[28] "Batteries: Full Speed Ahead" from Further Readings
[29] Figure 20.20 from MediaPortfolio
[30] "Structure and Content of Some Primary Batteries" from Further Readings
[31] "Making a Simple Battery: The Gerber Cell" from Live Demonstrations
[32] Figure 20.21 from MediaPortfolio and Transparency Pack
[33] Figure 20.22 from MediaPortfolio

- Cadmium is a toxic heavy metal.
  - There are environmental concerns to be addressed with respect to disposal of such batteries.
- Other rechargeable batteries have been developed.
  - NiMH batteries (nickel–metal–hydride).
  - Li–ion batteries (lithium–ion batteries).

### Fuel Cells

- Direct production of electricity from fuels occurs in a **fuel** cell.
- Cathode: reduction of oxygen:

$$2H_2O(l) + O_2(g) + 4e^- \rightarrow 4OH^-(aq)$$

- Anode:

$$2H_2(g) + 4OH^-(aq) \rightarrow 4H_2O(l) + 4e^-$$

## 20.8 Corrosion

- An example of an undesirable redox reaction is the corrosion of metals.
- Metal is attacked by a substance in the environment and converted to an unwanted compound.

### Corrosion of Iron[34,35]

- Consider the rusting of iron:
  - Since $E°_{red}(Fe^{2+}) < E°_{red}(O_2)$, iron can be oxidized by oxygen.
  - Cathode: $O_2(g) + 4H^+(aq) + 4e^- \rightarrow 2H_2O(l)$ $E°_{red} = 1.23$ V.
  - Anode: $Fe(s) \rightarrow Fe^{2+}(aq) + 2e^-$ $E°_{red} = -0.44$ V.
- Dissolved oxygen in water usually causes the oxidation of iron.
- The $Fe^{2+}$ initially formed can be further oxidized to $Fe^{3+}$, which forms rust, $Fe_2O_3 \cdot xH_2O(s)$.
- Oxidation occurs at the site with the greatest concentration of $O_2$.
- Other factors to consider are the pH, presence of salts, stress on the iron, and contact with other metals.

### Preventing the Corrosion of Iron[36,37,38]

- Corrosion can be prevented by coating the iron with paint or another metal.
  - This prevents oxygen and water from reacting at the surface of the iron.
  - Galvanized iron is coated with a thin layer of zinc.
  - Zinc protects the iron since Zn is the anode and Fe the cathode:

$$Zn^{2+}(aq) + 2e^- \rightarrow Zn(s) \qquad E°_{red} = -0.76 \text{ V}$$
$$Fe^{2+}(aq) + 2e^- \rightarrow Fe(s) \qquad E°_{red} = -0.44 \text{ V}$$

  - The standard reduction potentials indicate that Zn is easier to oxidize than Fe.
  - This process is **cathodic protection** (the *sacrificial anode* is destroyed).
- We can use something similar to protect underground pipelines.
  - Often, Mg is used as a sacrificial anode:

$$Mg^{2+}(aq) + 2e^- \rightarrow Mg(s) \qquad E°_{red} = -2.37 \text{ V}$$
$$Fe^{2+}(aq) + 2e^- \rightarrow Fe(s) \qquad E°_{red} = -0.44 \text{ V}$$

## 20.9 Electrolysis[39,40]

---

[34] Figure 20.25 from MediaPortfolio and Transparency Pack
[35] "Evaluation of Corrosion Susceptibility of a Metal: Student Corrosion Experiment II" from Further Readings
[36] Figure 20.26 from MediaPortfolio and Transparency Pack
[37] Figure 20.27 from MediaPortfolio
[38] "Floating Pennies" from Live Demonstrations
[39] "Electrolytic Cells in Series: A Red, White, and Blue Electrolysis" from Further Readings

- **Electrolysis reactions** are nonspontaneous reactions that require an external current in order to force the reaction to proceed.
- In voltaic and electrolytic cells, reduction occurs at the cathode, and oxidation occurs at the anode.
  - However, in electrolytic cells, electrons are forced to flow from the anode to the cathode.
  - In **electrolytic cells** the anode is positive and the cathode is negative.
    - In voltaic cells the anode is negative and the cathode is positive.

### Electrolysis of Aqueous Solutions[41]

- Example, decomposition of molten NaCl.
  - Cathode: $2Na^+(l) + 2e^- \rightarrow 2Na(l)$
  - Anode: $2Cl^-(l) \rightarrow Cl_2(g) + 2e^-$.
  - Industrially, electrolysis is used to produce metals like Al.
- Electrolysis of high-melting ionic substances requires very high temperatures.
  - Do we get the same products if we electrolyze an aqueous solution of the salt?
  - Water complicates the issue!
  - Example: Consider the electrolysis of NaF(aq):

$$Na^+(aq) + e^- \rightarrow Na(s) \qquad E^\circ_{red} = -2.71 \text{ V}$$
$$2H_2O(l) + 2e^- \rightarrow H_2(g) + 2OH^-(aq) \qquad E^\circ_{red} = -0.83 \text{ V}$$

  - Thus water is more easily reduced the sodium ion.

$$2F^-(aq) \rightarrow F_2(g) + 2e^- \qquad E^\circ_{red} = +2.87 \text{ V}$$
$$2H_2O(l) \rightarrow O_2(g) + 4H^+(aq) + 4e^- \qquad E^\circ_{red} = +1.23 \text{ V}$$

  - Thus it is easier to oxidize water than the fluoride ion.

### Electrolysis with Active Electrodes[42,43,44]

- Active electrodes: electrodes that take part in electrolysis.
  - Example: electroplating.
- Consider an active Ni electrode and another metallic electrode (steel) placed in an aqueous solution of $NiSO_4$:
  - Anode: $Ni(s) \rightarrow Ni^{2+}(aq) + 2e^-$
  - Cathode: $Ni^{2+}(aq) + 2e^- \rightarrow Ni(s)$.
- Ni plates on the inert electrode.
- Electroplating is important in protecting objects from corrosion.

### Quantitative Aspects of Electrolysis[45,46]

- We want to know how much material we obtain with electrolysis.
- Consider the reduction of $Cu^{2+}$ to Cu.

$$Cu^{2+}(aq) + 2e^- \rightarrow Cu(s).$$

- Two mol of electrons will plate 1 mol of Cu.
- The charge of one mol of electrons is 96,500 C (1 *F*).
  - A coulomb is the amount of charge passing a point in one second when the current is one ampere.
- The amount of Cu can be calculated from the current ($I$) and time ($t$) required to plate.

$$Q = It$$

### Electrical Work

---

[40] Figure 20.28 from MediaPortfolio and Transparency Pack
[41] "Electrolysis of Water" Animation from MediaPortfolio
[42] "Electroplating" Movie from MediaPortfolio
[43] "Electroplating Copper" from Live Demonstrations
[44] Figure 20.30 from MediaPortfolio
[45] Figure 20.31 from MediaPortfolio and Transparency Pack
[46] "Electrolysis" Activity from MediaPortfolio

- Free energy is a measure of the maximum amount of useful work that can be obtained from a system.
  - We know:
$$\Delta G = w_{max}$$
  - And:
$$\Delta G = -nFE$$
  - Thus:
$$w_{max} = -nFE$$
  - If $E_{cell}$ is positive, $w_{max}$ will be negative.
    - Work is done *by* the system *on* the surroundings.
- The emf can be thought of as being a measure of the driving force for a redox process.
  - In an electrolytic cell an external source of energy is required to force the reaction to proceed.
$$w = nFE_{external}$$
  - In order to drive the nonspontaneous reaction the external emf must be greater than $E_{cell}$.
  - From physics: Work is measured in units of watts:
$$1\text{ W} = 1\text{ J/s}$$
  - Electric utilities use units of kilowatt-hours:
$$1\text{ kWh} = (1000\text{ W})(1\text{ hour}) = \left(\frac{3600\text{s}}{1\text{ hour}}\right)\left(\frac{1\text{ J/s}}{1\text{ W}}\right) = 3.6\times10^{6}\text{ J}$$

## Further Readings:

1. Marten J. ten Hoor, "Redox Balancing without Puzzling," *J. Chem. Educ.*, Vol. 74, **1997**, 1376–1368.

2. P. J. Moran and E. Gileadi, "Alleviating the Common Confusion Caused by Polarity in Electrochemistry," *J. Chem. Educ.*, Vol. 66, **1989**, 912.

3. Ron DeLorenzo, "Electrochemical Errors," *J. Chem. Educ.*, Vol. 62, **1985**, 424–425.

4. Richard S. Treptow, "Dental Filling Discomforts Illustrate Electrochemical Potentials of Metals," *J. Chem. Educ.*, Vol. 55, **1978**, 189.

5. Penelope Ann Huddle, Margaret Dawn White and Fiona Rogers, "Using a Teaching Model to Correct Known Misconceptions in Electrochemistry," *J. Chem. Educ.*, Vol. 77, **2000**, 104–110.

6. Gerald Ondrey, Charlene Crabb and Takeshi Kamiya, "Batteries: Full Speed Ahead," *Chemical Engineering,* Vol. 106(2), **1999**, 47–51. An article comparing many of the new up-and-coming batteries to older conventional batteries.

7. Michael J. Smith and Colin A. Vincent, "Structure and Content of Some Primary Batteries," *J. Chem. Educ.*, Vol. 78, **2001**, 519–521.

8. A. I. Onuchukwu, "Evaluation of Corrosion Susceptibility of a Metal: Student Corrosion Experiment II," *J. Chem. Educ.*, Vol. 65, **1988**, 934.

9. Eva Gankiewicz Merkel, "Using the Biological Cell in Teaching Electrochemistry," *J. Chem. Educ.*, Vol. 71, **1994**, 240.

## Live Demonstrations:

1. Bassam Z. Shakhashiri, "Electrolytic Cells in Series: A Red, White, and Blue Electrolysis," *Chemical Demonstrations, A Handbook for Teachers of Chemistry, Volume 4* (Wisconsin: The University of Wisconsin Press, **1992**), pp. 170–173. Electrolysis in a series of beakers results in color changes in pH indicators.

2. Lee R. Summerlin, Christie L. Borgford, and Julie B. Ealy, "Visible Oxidation-Reduction in Electrochemical Cells," *Chemical Demonstrations, A Sourcebook for Teachers, Volume 2* (Washington: American Chemical Society, **1988**), pp. 202–203. A nice visual demonstrations of basic operation of electrochemical cells.

3. Lee R. Summerlin, Christie L. Borgford, and Julie B. Ealy, "Making a Simple Battery: The Gerber Cell," *Chemical Demonstrations, A Sourcebook for Teachers, Volume 2* (Washington: American Chemical Society, **1988**), pp. 115–116. Mg/$CuSO_4$ and a baby food jar are used to construct a simple electrochemical cell.

4. Bassam Z. Shakhashiri, "An Activity Series: Zinc, Copper, and Silver Half Cells," *Chemical Demonstrations: A Handbook for Teachers of Chemistry, Volume 4* (Madison: The University of Wisconsin Press, **1992**), pp. 101–106.

5. Lee. R. Summerlin, and James. L. Ealy, Jr., "Activity Series for Some Metals," *Chemical Demonstrations, A Sourcebook for Teachers, Volume 1* (Washington: American Chemical Society, **1988**), p. 150. An overhead projector demonstration employing hydrogen gas formation.

6. Lee. R. Summerlin,, Christie L. Borgford, and Julie B. Ealy, "Floating Pennies," *Chemical Demonstrations, A Sourcebook for Teachers, Volume 2* (Washington: American Chemical Society, **1988**), p. 63. The zinc core of copper-coated pennies reacts with acid to form pennies that float in this demonstration.

7. Lee. R. Summerlin,, Christie L. Borgford, and Julie B. Ealy, "Electroplating Copper," *Chemical Demonstrations, A Sourcebook for Teachers, Volume 2* (Washington: American Chemical Society, **1988**), pp. 199-200. A stainless steel spoon is electroplated with copper in this demonstration.

# Chapter 21. Nuclear Chemistry

## Media Resources

### Figures and Tables

| In Transparency Pack and on MediaPortfolio: | Section: |
|---|---|
| Figure 21.2 Belt of Stability | 21.2 Patterns of Nuclear Stability |
| Figure 21.3 Effects of Various Types of Radiation on the Number of Protons and Neutrons | 21.2 Patterns of Nuclear Stability |
| Figure 21.4 Nuclear Disintegration Series for U-238 | 21.2 Patterns of Nuclear Stability |
| Figure 21.13 Nuclear Binding Energy | 21.6 Energy Changes in Nuclear Reactions |
| Figure 20.20 Nuclear Power Plant | 21.7 Nuclear Fission |
| Figure 21.23 Sources of Radiation in the U.S. | 21.9 Biological Effects of Radiation |

| On MediaPortfolio: | Section: |
|---|---|
| Table 21.1 Properties of Alpha, Beta, and Gamma Radiation | 21.1 Radioactivity |
| Table 21.2 Common Particles in Radioactive Decay and Nuclear Transformations | 21.1 Radioactivity |
| Figure 21.5 Schematic Drawing of a Cyclotron | 21.3 Nuclear Transmutations |
| Table 21.4 The Half-Lives and Type of Decay for Several Radioisotopes | 21.4 Rates of Radioactive Decay |
| Figure 21.10 Geiger Counter | 21.5 Detection of Radioactivity |
| Figure 21.16 Chain Reaction in Subcritical Mass and Supercritical Mass | 21.7 Nuclear Fission |
| Figure 21.19 Reactor Core | 21.7 Nuclear Fission |

| Animations: | Section: |
|---|---|
| Separation of Alpha, Beta, and Gamma Rays | 21.1 Radioactivity |
| First-Order Process | 21.4 Rates of Radioactive Decay |

| Activity: | Section: |
|---|---|
| Uranium-238 Decay Series | 21.2 Patterns of Nuclear Stability |
| Radioactive Decay | 21.4 Rates of Radioactive Decay |
| Half-Life Activity | 21.4 Rates of Radioactive Decay |

## Other Resources

| Further Readings: | Section: |
|---|---|
| Radioactivity in the Classroom | 21.1 Radioactivity |
| Nuclear Chemistry: State of the Art for Teachers | 21.1 Radioactivity |
| Teaching Aids for Nuclear Chemistry | 21.1 Radioactivity |
| Scientists Honor Centennial of the Discovery of Radioactivity | 21.1 Radioactivity |
| Radioactivity: A Natural Phenomenon | 21.1 Radioactivity |
| Teaching Nuclear Science: A Cosmological Approach | 21.1 Radioactivity |
| Radioactivity in Everyday Life | 21.1 Radioactivity |

| | |
|---|---|
| Beta Decay Diagram | 21.1 Radioactivity |
| Chemistry of the Heaviest Elements—One Atom at a Time | 21.2 Patterns of Nuclear Stability |
| Modeling Nuclear Decay: A Point of Integration between Chemistry and Mathematics | 21.3 Nuclear Transmutations |
| Nucleogenesis! A Game with Natural Rules for Teaching Nuclear Synthesis and Decay | 21.4 Rates of Radioactive Decay |
| Archaeological Dating | 21.4 Rates of Radioactive Decay |
| Radioactive Dating: A Method for Geochronology | 21.4 Rates of Radioactive Decay |
| California Earthquakes: Predicting the Next Big One Using Radiocarbon Dating | 21.4 Rates of Radioactive Decay |
| Development and Proliferation of Radioimmunoassay Technology | 21.5 Detection of Radioactivity |
| Radioactivity in the Service of Many | 21.5. Detection of Radioactivity |
| Special Agents | 21.6 Energy Changes in Nuclear Reactions |
| Positron Emission Tomography Merges Chemistry with Biological Imaging | 21.6 Energy Changes in Nuclear Reactions |
| Nuclear Medicine and Positron Emission Tomography: An Overview | 21.6 Energy Changes in Nuclear Reactions |
| Visualizing the Mind | 21.6 Energy Changes in Nuclear Reactions |
| The Role of Chemistry in Positron Emission Tomography | 21.6 Energy Changes in Nuclear Reactions |
| Lise Meitner and the Discovery of Nuclear Fission | 21.7 Nuclear Fission |
| Ten Years after Chernobyl: Consequences Are Still Emerging | 21.7 Nuclear Fission |
| Aspects of Nuclear Waste Disposal of Use in Teaching Basic Chemistry | 21.7 Nuclear Fission |
| Fusion—A Potential Power Source | 21.8 Nuclear Fusion |
| How Much Radon Is Too Much? | 21.9 Biological Effects of Radiation |
| Supercritical Solutions | 21.9 Biological Effects of Radiation |

# Chapter 21. Nuclear Chemistry

## Common Student Misconceptions

- This is new territory for students who have not taken advanced courses in physics.

## Lecture Outline

### 21.1 Radioactivity

- When nuclei change spontaneously, emitting energy, they are said to be **radioactive**.
- **Nuclear chemistry** is the study of nuclear reactions and their uses.
- **Nucleons** are particles in the nucleus:
    - $p^+$: proton
    - $n^0$: neutron.
    - Mass number: the number of $p^+ + n^0$.
        - The mass number is the total number of nucleons in the nucleus.
    - Atomic number: the number of $p^+$.
- *Isotopes* have the same number of $p^+$ but different numbers of $n^0$
    - Different isotopes of the same element are distinguished by their mass numbers.
    - Different isotopes have different natural abundances.
- **A radionuclide** is a radioactive nucleus.
    - Atoms containing these nuclei are called **radioisotopes**.

#### Nuclear Equations[1,2,3]

- Most nuclei are stable.
    - Radionuclides are unstable and spontaneously emit particles and/or electromagnetic radiation.
    - Example: Uranium-238 is radioactive.
        - It emits **alpha particles**.
        - These are helium-4 particles.
- When a nucleus spontaneously decomposes in this manner, we say it has decayed (*radioactive decay*).
- In nuclear equations, the total number of nucleons is conserved:
    - We can represent the uranium-238 decay by the following nuclear equation:

$$^{238}_{92}\text{U} \rightarrow {}^{234}_{90}\text{Th} + {}^{4}_{2}\text{He}$$

- The total number of protons and neutrons before a nuclear reaction must be the same as the total number of nucleons after reaction.

#### Types of Radioactive Decay[4,5,6,7,8,9,10,11]

---

1 "Radioactivity in the Classroom" from Further Readings
2 "Nuclear Chemistry: State of the Art for Teachers" from Further Readings
3 "Radioactivity: A Natural Phenomenon" from Further Readings
4 Table 21.1 from MediaPortfolio
5 "Separation of Alpha, Beta, and Gamma Rays" Animation from MediaPortfolio
6 "Scientists Honor Centennial of the Discovery of Radioactivity" from Further Readings
7 "Radioactivity in Everyday Life" from Further Readings
8 "Teaching Nuclear Science: A Cosmological Approach" from Further Readings
9 "Teaching Aids for Nuclear Chemistry" from Further Readings

- There are three types of radiation which we will consider:
  - α-Radiation is the loss of ${}^{4}_{2}He$ (**alpha particles**) from the nucleus.
  - β-Radiation is the loss of an electron from the nucleus.
    - These high-speed electrons are called **beta particles.**
  - **γ-Radiation** is the loss of high-energy photons from the nucleus.
- Nucleons can undergo two other types of decay:
  - **Positron emission.**
    - A positron is a particle with the same mass as an electron but an opposite sign.
  - **Electron capture.**
    - The nucleus captures an electron from the electron cloud surrounding the nucleus.
- Representations:
  - In nuclear chemistry to ensure conservation of nucleons we write all particles with their atomic and mass numbers: ${}^{4}_{2}He$ and ${}^{4}_{2}\alpha$ represent α-radiation.
- Nucleons can undergo decay:
  - (β-emission) ${}^{1}_{0}n \rightarrow {}^{1}_{1}p + {}^{0}_{-1}e$
  - (positron annihilation) ${}^{0}_{1}e + {}^{0}_{-1}e \rightarrow 2{}^{0}_{0}\gamma$
  - (positron or β⁺-emission) ${}^{1}_{1}p \rightarrow {}^{1}_{0}n + {}^{0}_{1}e$
  - (electron capture) ${}^{1}_{1}p + {}^{0}_{-1}e \rightarrow {}^{1}_{0}n$

## 21.2 Patterns of Nuclear Stability

### Neutron-to-Proton Ratio[12,13]

- The proton has high mass and high charge.
- Therefore the proton-proton repulsion is large.
- In the nucleus the protons are very close to each other.
- The cohesive forces in the nucleus are called *strong nuclear forces*.
  - Neutrons are involved with the strong nuclear force.
- As more protons are added (the nucleus gets heavier) the proton-proton repulsion gets larger.
  - Therefore, the heavier the nucleus, the more neutrons required for stability.
- The *belt of stability* is the portion of a graph of (number of protons) vs. (number of neutrons) that contains all stable nuclei.
  - All nuclei with 84 or more protons are radioactive.
  - Nuclei above the belt of stability undergo β-emission.
    - An ${}^{0}_{-1}e$ is lost and the number of neutrons decreases, the number of protons increases.
  - Nuclei below the belt of stability undergo $\beta^+$-emission or electron capture.
    - This results in the number of neutrons increasing and the number of protons decreasing.

---

10 Table 21.2 from MediaPortfolio
11 "Beta Decay Diagram" from Further Readings
12 Figure 21.2 from MediaPortfolio and Transparency Pack
13 Figure 21.3 from MediaPortfolio and Transparency Pack

- Nuclei with atomic numbers greater than 83 usually undergo α-emission.
  - The number of protons and neutrons decreases (in steps of 2).

### Radioactive Series[14,15,16]

- A nucleus usually undergoes more than one transition on its path to stability.
- The series of nuclear reactions that accompany this path is the **radioactive series** or a **nuclear disintegration series.**

### Further Observations

- **Magic numbers** are 2, 8, 20, 28, 50, or 82 protons or 2, 8, 20, 28, 50, 82, or 126 neutrons.
  - Nuclei with a "magic number" of nucleons are more stable than nuclei that do not have the magic number of nucleons.
  - The magic numbers correspond to filled, closed-shell nucleon configurations.
- Nuclei with even numbers of protons and neutrons are more stable than nuclei with any odd numbers of nucleons.
  - The *shell model* of the nucleus rationalizes these observations.
    - The shell model of the nucleus is similar to the shell model for the atom.
  - Pairs of protons and neutrons in the nucleus are analogous to pairs of electrons in the atom.

## 21.3 Nuclear Transmutations[17]

- **Nuclear transmutations** are nuclear reactions resulting from the collisions between nuclei or a nucleus and a neutron.

### Using Charged Particles[18]

- For example, nuclear transmutations can occur using high-velocity α-particles:

$$^{14}N + {}^{4}\alpha \rightarrow {}^{17}O + {}^{1}p$$

- In short-hand notation the preceding reaction is written as $^{14}N(\alpha,p)^{17}O$.
- To overcome electrostatic forces, charged particles need to be accelerated before they react.
  - **Particle accelerators** (atom smashers, cyclotrons, synchnotrons) are used to accelerate particles using strong magnetic and electrostatic fields.
  - A cyclotron consists of D-shaped electrodes (dees) with a large circular magnet above and below the chamber.
  - Particles enter the vacuum chamber and are accelerated as the dees are alternately made positive and negative.
  - The magnets above and below the dees keep the particles moving in a spiral path.
  - When the particles are moving at a sufficient velocity they are allowed to escape the cyclotron and strike the target.
  - The circumference of the ring at the Fermi National Accelerator Laboratory in Chicago is 6.3 km.

### Using Neutrons

- Most synthetic isotopes used in medicine and research are made using neutrons as projectiles.
- Example: The preparation of cobalt-60 for use in cancer radiation therapy.

### Transuranium Elements

---

[14] Figure 21.4 from MediaPortfolio and Transparency Pack
[15] "Uranium-238 Decay Series" Activity from MediaPortfolio
[16] "Chemistry of the Heaviest Elements—One Atom at a Time" from Further Readings
[17] "Modeling Nuclear Decay: A Point of Integration Between Chemistry and Mathematics" from Further Readings
[18] Figure 21.5 from MediaPortfolio

- **Transuranium elements** follow uranium in the periodic table.

## 21.4 Rates of Radioactive Decay[19,20,21,22,23]

- Radioactive decay is a first-order process.
- Each isotope has a characteristic **half-life.**
  - Half-lives are not affected by temperature, pressure or chemical composition.
  - Natural radioisotopes tend to have longer half-lives than synthetic radioisotopes.
  - Half-lives range from fractions of a second to millions of years.
  - Naturally occurring radioisotopes can be used to determine the age of a sample.
    - This process is radioactive dating.

### Dating[24,25,26]

- Carbon-14 ($^{14}C$) is used to determine the ages of organic compounds because half-lives are constant.
- For $^{14}C$ to be detected, the object must be less than 50,000 years old.
  - We assume the ratio of $^{12}C$ to $^{14}C$ has been constant over time.
  - The half-life of $^{14}C$ is 5,730 years.
  - $^{14}C$ undergoes decay to $^{14}N$ via β-decay:

$$^{14}_{6}C \rightarrow ^{14}_{7}N + ^{0}_{-1}e$$

- One of the more famous radiocarbon dating experiments was performed on the Shroud of Turin (thought to be the burial shroud of Jesus Christ).
  - Radiocarbon dating concluded that the linen was made between AD 1260 and 1390.
- Other dating methods are also used.
  - Uranium-lead dating has been used to estimate the age of the Earth at approximately 4.5 billion years.

### Calculations Based on Half-life

- Radioactive decay is a first-order process:

$$\text{Rate} = kN$$

  - If the activity of a sample at time = $t$ is $N_t$, and the activity at time = 0 is $N_0$, then:

$$\ln \frac{N_t}{N_o} = -kt$$

  - The half-life of the sample is given by:

$$t_{½} = \frac{0.693}{k}$$

  - In radioactive decay the constant, $k$, is called the *decay constant.*
  - The rate of decay is called **activity** (disintegrations per unit time).
- There are several units used to express activity or radioactivity:
  - The **becquerel** (Bq) is the SI unit of radioactivity.

---

[19] "First Order Process" Animation from MediaPortfolio
[20] "Radioactive Decay" Activity from MediaPortfolio
[21] "Half-Life Activity" from MediaPortfolio
[22] "Nucleogenesis! A Game with Natural Rules for Teaching Nuclear Synthesis and Decay" from Further Readings
[23] Table 21.4 from MediaPortfolio
[24] "Archeological Dating" from Further Readings
[25] "Radioactive Dating: A Method for Geochronology" from Further Readings
[26] "California Earthquakes: Predict the Next Big One Using Radiocarbon Dating" from Further Readings

- 1 Bq = 1 disintegration per second (dps).
- The **Curie** (Ci) is an older but still very widely used unit of activity.
- 1 Ci = $3.7 \times 10^{10}$ disintegrations per second.

## 21.5 Detection of Radioactivity[27,28,29]

- Matter is ionized by radiation.
- A **Geiger counter** determines the amount of ionization by detecting an electric current.
  - A thin window is penetrated by the radiation and causes the ionization of Ar gas.
  - The ionized gas carries a charge, so current is produced.
    - The current pulse generated when the radiation enters is amplified and counted.
  - Other methods are also used to detect radioactivity.
  - One common method employs an instrument called a **scintillation counter**.
    - A substance called a *phosphor* is allowed to interact with radiation.
    - Light is produced when radiation strikes a suitable phosphor.
    - This light is detected and used to quantify the amount of radiation.

### Radiotracers

- Photosynthesis has been studied using $^{14}C$:

$$6\,^{14}CO_2 + 6H_2O \xrightarrow[\text{chlorophyll}]{\text{sunlight}} {}^{14}C_6H_{12}O_6 + 6O_2$$

- The carbon dioxide is said to be $^{14}C$ labeled.
- The presence of $^{14}C$ in the intermediates or products of photosynthesis can be determined.
  - $^{14}C$ is detected as it moves from carbon dioxide to ultimately become incorporated into glucose.
    - Thus the path of the carbon atoms may be *traced.*
    - **Radiotracers** are used to follow an element through a chemical reaction.

## 21.6 Energy Changes in Nuclear Reactions[30,31,32,33,34,35]

- Einstein showed that mass and energy are proportional:

$$E = mc^2$$

  - If a system loses mass, it loses energy (exothermic).
  - If a system gains mass, it gains energy (endothermic).
- Since $c^2$ is a large number, small changes in mass cause large changes in energy.
- Mass and energy changes in nuclear reactions are much greater than in chemical reactions.
- Consider:

- For 1 mol of $^{238}_{92}U$, the $^{238}_{92}U \rightarrow {}^{234}_{90}Th + {}^{4}_{2}He$ masses are:

---

27 "Development and Proliferation of Radioimmunoassay Technology" from Further Readings
28 "Radioactivity in the Service of Many" from Further Readings
29 Figure 21.10 from MediaPortfolio
30 "Positron Emission Tomography Merges Chemistry with Biological Imaging" from Further Readings
31 "Special Agents" from Further Readings
32 "Visualizing the Mind" from Further Readings
33 "Nuclear Medicine and Positron Emission Tomography: An Overview" from Further Readings
34 "The Role of Chemistry in Positron Emission Tomography" from Further Readings
35 Figure 21.13 from MediaPortfolio and Transparency Pack

$$238.0003 \text{ g} \rightarrow 233.9942 \text{ g} + 4.0015 \text{ g}.$$

- The change in mass during the reaction is:

$$233.9942 \text{ g} + 4.0015 \text{ g} - 238.0003 \text{ g} = -0.0046 \text{ g}.$$

- The process is exothermic because the system has lost mass.

- To calculate the energy change per mole of $^{238}_{92}\text{U}$ :

$$\Delta E = \Delta\left(mc^2\right) = c^2(\Delta m)$$

$$\Delta E = \left(3.00\times10^8 \text{ m/s}\right)^2(-0.0046 \text{ g})\left(\frac{1 \text{ kg}}{1000 \text{ g}}\right)$$

$$\Delta E = -4.1\times10^{11}\,\frac{\text{kg m}^2}{\text{s}^2} = -4.1\times10^{11} \text{ J}$$

**Nuclear Binding Energies**

- The mass of a nucleus is less than the mass of its nucleons.
  - **Mass defect** is the difference in mass between the nucleus and the masses of nucleons.
  - **Nuclear binding energy** is the energy required to separate a nucleus into its nucleons.
  - Since $E = mc^2$, the binding energy is related to the mass defect.
- The larger the binding energy, the more likely a nucleus is to decompose.
- Heavy nuclei gain stability by splitting into smaller nuclei.
  - They give off energy if fragmented into two mid-sized nuclei.
  - This reaction is called **fission.**
- Very light nuclei are combined or fused together to form more massive nuclei.
  - Energy is released from this nuclear **fusion.**

## 21.7 Nuclear Fission[36]

- Splitting of heavy nuclei is exothermic for large mass numbers.
- Consider a neutron bombarding a $^{235}\text{U}$ nucleus:
  - The heavy $^{235}\text{U}$ nucleus can split in several different ways such as:

$$^{1}_{0}\text{n} + ^{235}_{92}\text{U} \rightarrow ^{142}_{56}\text{Ba} + ^{91}_{36}\text{Kr} + 3^{1}_{0}\text{n}$$

  - For every $^{235}\text{U}$ fission an average of 2.4 neutrons are produced.
  - Each neutron produced can cause the fission of another $^{235}\text{U}$ nucleus.
  - The number of fissions and the resulting energy increase rapidly.
  - Reactions that multiply this way are called **chain reactions.**
- Without controls, an explosion results.
  - Consider the fission of a nucleus which results in the production of neutrons.
  - Each neutron can cause another fission.
  - Eventually, a chain reaction forms.
  - A minimum mass of fissionable material is required for a chain reaction (or neutrons will escape before they can cause another fission).
    - This is called a **critical mass.**
  - When enough material is present for a chain reaction, we have a critical mass.
  - If the mass is lower than the critical mass (subcritical mass) the neutrons escape and a chain reaction does not occur.
  - At the critical mass one neutron from each fission is effective in causing another fission.
  - Any mass over critical mass is called **supercritical mass.**

---

[36] Figure 21.16 from MediaPortfolio

- Critical mass for $^{235}U$ is about 1 kg.

**Nuclear Reactors**[37,38,39,40,41]

- Use fission as a power source.
- Use a subcritical mass of $^{235}U$ ($^{238}U$ is enriched with about 3% $^{235}U$).
- Enriched $^{235}UO_2$ pellets are encased in Zr or stainless steel rods.
- *Control rods* are composed of Cd or B, which absorb neutrons.
    - They help to regulate the flux of neutrons.
- *Moderators* are inserted to slow down the neutrons to make them more easily captured.
- Heat produced in the reactor core is removed by a *cooling fluid* and carried to a steam generator.
- The steam is used to drive an electric generator.
- Storage of radioactive wastes from such reactions is not a simple problem.
- The potential for environmental contamination by long-lived isotopes is a serious consideration.

## 21.8 Nuclear Fusion[42]

- Light nuclei can fuse to form heavier nuclei.
    - Most reactions in the Sun are fusion.
- Fusion products are not usually radioactive, so fusion is a good energy source.
- Also, the hydrogen required for the reaction can easily be supplied by seawater.
    - However, high energies are required to overcome repulsion between nuclei before the reaction can occur.
    - High energies are achieved by high temperatures, the reactions are known as **thermonuclear reactions.**
- Fusion of tritium and deuterium requires a temperature of about 40,000,000 K:

$$^{2}_{1}H + ^{3}_{1}H \rightarrow ^{4}_{2}He + ^{1}_{0}n$$

- These temperatures can be achieved in a nuclear bomb or a *tokamak*.
- A tokamak is a magnetic bottle: strong magnetic fields contain a high-temperature plasma, so the plasma does not come into contact with the walls. (No known material can survive the temperatures required for fusion.)
- To date, temperatures of about 3,000,000 K have been achieved in a tokamak.
- Research continues.

## 21.9 Biological Effects of Radiation[43]

- **Ionizing radiation** involves ionization that occurs when radiation removes an electron from an atom or molecule.
    - This is generally more harmful to biological systems than **nonionizing radiation**.
        - Radiation absorbed by tissue causes excitation (nonionizing radiation) or ionization (ionizing radiation).
- Most ionizing radiation interacts with water in tissues to form $H_2O^+$.
    - The $H_2O^+$ ions react with water to produce $H_3O^+$ and OH.
    - OH has one unpaired electron.

---

[37] Figure 21.19 from MediaPortfolio
[38] "Lise Meitner and the Discovery of Nuclear Fission" from Further Readings
[39] "Ten Years After Chernobyl: Consequences Are Still Emerging" from Further Readings
[40] "Aspects of Nuclear Waste Disposal of Use in Teaching Basic Chemistry" from Further Readings
[41] Figure 21.20 from MediaPortfolio and Transparency Pack
[42] "Fusion—A Potential Power Source" from Further Readings
[43] "Supercritical Solutions" from Further Readings

    - It is called the *hydroxy radical*.
    - This is an example of a **free radical**, a substance with unpaired electrons.
    - Free radicals generally undergo chain reactions.
    - They are capable of causing substantial damage in biological tissues.
- The penetrating power of radiation is a function of the mass of the radiation.
  - Therefore, γ-radiation (zero mass) penetrates much further than β-radiation, which penetrates much further than α-radiation.

## Radiation Doses[44]

- Absorbed radiation is measured in:
  - **Gray**: 1 Gy is the SI unit for absorption of 1 J of energy per kg of tissue.
  - **Rad**: the *r*adiation *a*bsorbed *d*ose.
    - One rad is the absorption of $10^{-2}$ J of radiation per kg of tissue.
  - One gray is equivalent to 100 rads.
- Because not all forms of radiation have the same effect, we correct for the differences using the RBE (*relative biological effectiveness*).
  - The RBE is about 1 for β- and γ-radiation and 10 for α radiation.
  - A **rem** (*r*oentgen *e*quivalent for *m*an) = (rads) x (RBE).
  - The SI unit for effective dosage is the Sievert (1Sv = 1Gy = 100 rem).

## Radon[45]

- The nucleus is ${}^{222}_{86}\text{Rn}$ a decay product of ${}^{238}_{92}\text{U}$
- Radon exposure accounts for more than half the 360 mrem annual exposure to ionizing radiation.
- Rn is a noble gas; it is extremely stable.
  - Therefore, it is inhaled and exhaled without any chemical reactions occurring.
  - The half-life of ${}^{222}_{86}\text{Rn}$ is 3.82 days.
  - It decays as follows:

$${}^{222}_{86}\text{Rn} \rightarrow {}^{218}_{84}\text{Po} + {}^{4}_{2}\text{He}$$

- The α-particles produced have a high RBE.
  - Therefore, inhaled Rn is thought to be a cause of lung cancer.
- The situation is complicated because ${}^{218}_{84}\text{Po}$ has a short half-life (3.11 min) also:

$${}^{218}_{84}\text{Po} \rightarrow {}^{214}_{82}\text{Pb} + {}^{4}_{2}\text{He}$$

  - The ${}^{218}_{84}\text{Po}$ gets trapped in the lungs where it continually produces α-particles.
- The EPA recommends ${}^{222}_{86}\text{Rn}$ levels in homes be kept below four pCi per liter of air.
  - Radon testing kits are readily available in many areas of the country.

---

[44] Figure 21.23 from MediaPortfolio and Transparency Pack

[45] "How Much Radon is Too Much" from Further Readings

## Further Readings:

1. Enrique A. Hughes and Anita Zalts, "Radioactivity in the Classroom," *J. Chem. Educ.*, Vol. 77, **2000**, 613–614.

2. "Nuclear Chemistry: State of the Art for Teachers," a series of articles in the **October 1994** issue of the *Journal of Chemical Education*. Articles include a *J. Chem. Educ*. bibliography list.

3. Charles H. Atwood, "Teaching Aids for Nuclear Chemistry," *J. Chem. Educ.*, Vol. 71, **1994**, 845–847.

4. Stu Borman, "Scientists Honor Centennial of The Discovery of Radioactivity," *Chemical and Engineering News*, **April 29, 1996**, 55–65.

5. C. Ronneau, "Radioactivity: A Natural Phenomenon," *J. Chem. Educ.*, Vol. 67, **1990**, 736–737.

6. V. E. Viola, "Teaching Nuclear Science: A Cosmological Approach," *J. Chem. Educ.*, Vol. 71, **1994**, 840–944.

7. S. G. Hutchinson and F. I. Hutchinson, "Radioactivity in Everyday Life," *J. Chem. Educ.*, Vol. 74, **1997**, 501–505.

8. Darleane C. Hoffman and Diana M. Lee, "Chemistry of the Heaviest Elements–One Atom at a Time," *J. Chem. Educ.*, Vol. 76, **1999**, 332–347.

9. Robert Suder, "Beta Decay Diagram," *J. Chem. Educ.*, Vol. 66, **1989**, 231.

10. Kent J. Crippen and Robert D. Curtright, "Modeling Nuclear Decay: A Point of Integration between Chemistry and Mathematics," *J. Chem. Educ.*, Vol. 75, **1998**, 1434–1436.

11. Donald J. Olbris and Judith Herzfeld, "Nucleogenesis! A Game with Natural Rules for Teaching Nuclear Synthesis and Decay," *J. Chem. Educ.*, Vol. 76, **1999**, 349–352.

12. M. W. Rowe, "Archaeological Dating," *J. Chem. Educ.*, Vol. 63, **1986**, 16–20.

13. M. W. Rowe, "Radioactive Dating: A Method for Geochronology," *J. Chem. Educ.*, Vol. 62, **1985**, 580–584.

14. Ron DeLorenzo, "California Earthquakes: Predicting the Next Big One Using Radiocarbon Dating," *J. Chem. Educ.*, Vol. 57, **1980**, 601.

15. Rosalyn S. Yalow, "Development and Proliferation of Radioimmunoassay Technology," *J. Chem. Educ.*, Vol. 76, **1999**, 767–768.

16. Rosalyn S. Yalow, "Radioactivity in the Service of Many," *J. Chem. Educ.*, Vol. 59, **1982**, 735–738.

17. Helen Carmichael, "Special Agents," *Chemistry in Britain*, Vol. 34(8), **August 1998**, 30–33. An introduction to contrast agents for medical imaging.

18. Mairin B. Brennan, "Positron Emission Tomography Merges Chemistry with Biological Imaging," *Chemical and Engineering News*, **February 19, 1996**, 26–33.

19. Timothy J. McCarthy, Sally W. Schwarz, and Michael J. Welch, "Nuclear Medicine and Positron Emission Tomography: An Overview," *J. Chem. Educ.*, Vol. 71, **1994**, 830–836.

20. Marcus E. Raichle, "Visualizing the Mind," *Scientific American*, **April 1994**, 64.

21. Anthony L. Feliu, "The Role of Chemistry in Positron Emission Tomography," *J. Chem. Educ.*, Vol. 65, **1988**, 655–660.

22. Ruth Lewin Sime, "Lise Meitner and the Discovery of Nuclear Fission," *Scientific American*, **January 1998**, 80–85.

23. Torkil H. Jensen, "Fusion-A Potential Power Source," *J. Chem. Educ.*, Vol. 71, **1994**, 820–823.

24. Michael Freemantle, "Ten Years After Chernobyl: Consequences Are Still Emerging," *Chemical and Engineering News*, **April 29, 1996**, 18–28.

25. Gregory R. Choppin, "Aspects of Nuclear Waste Disposal of Use in Teaching Basic Chemistry," *J. Chem. Educ.*, Vol. 71, **1994**, 826–829.

26. Neil Smart, Chien Wai and Cindy Phelps, "Supercritical Solutions," *Chemistry in Britain*, Vol. 34(8), **August 1998**, 34–36. Supercritical fluids are considered for use in the nuclear industry.

27. Charles H. Atwood, "How Much Radon Is Too Much?" *J. Chem. Educ.*, Vol. 69, **1992**, 351–355.

# Chapter 22. Chemistry of the Nonmetals

## Media Resources

### Figures and Tables

| In Transparency Pack and on MediaPortfolio: | Section: |
|---|---|
| Figure 22.1 Periodic Trends | 22.1 General Concepts: Periodic Trends and Chemical Reactions |
| Table 22.2 Some Properties of the Halogens | 22.4 Group 7A: The Halogens |
| Table 22.4 Some Properties of the Group 6A Elements | 22.6 The Other Group 6A Elements: S, Se, Te, and Po |
| Figure 22.23 Frasch Process | 22.6 The Other Group 6A Elements: S, Se, Te, and Po |
| Figure 22.31 Conversion of $N_2$ into Compounds | 22.7 Nitrogen |
| Table 22.6 Properties of the Group 5A Elements | 22.8 The Other Group 5A Elements: P, As, Sb, and Bi |
| Figure 22.40 Structures of $P_4O_6$ and $P_4O_{10}$ | 22.8 The Other Group 5A Elements: P, As, Sb, and Bi |
| Table 22.7 Some Properties of the Group 4A Elements | 22.10 The Other Group 4A Elements: Si, Ge, Sn, and Pb |
| Figure 22.52 The $Si_2O_7^{6-}$ Ion | 22.10 The Other Group 4A Elements: Si, Ge, Sn, and Pb |
| Figure 22.53 Silicate Structures | 22.10 The Other Group 4A Elements: Si, Ge, Sn, and Pb |

| On MediaPortfolio: | Section: |
|---|---|
| Figure 22.2 Comparison of Pi-Bond Formation for C and S | 22.1 General Concepts: Periodic Trends and Chemical Reactions |
| Figure 22.3 Comparison of the Structures of $CO_2$ and $SiO_2$ | 22.1 General Concepts: Periodic Trends and Chemical Reactions |
| Figure 22.5 Laboratory Preparation of Hydrogen | 22.2 Hydrogen |
| Table 22.3 The Oxyacids of the Halogens | 22.5 Oxygen |
| Figure 22.19 Apparatus for Producing Ozone | 22.5 Oxygen |
| Figure 22.32 Structures of Hydrazine and Methylhydrazine | 22.7 Nitrogen |
| Table 22.5 Oxidation States of Nitrogen | 22.7 Nitrogen |
| Figure 22.34 Ostwald Process | 22.7 Nitrogen |
| Figure 22.48 Structures of HCN and $CS_2$ | 22.9 Carbon |
| Figure 22.50 Zone-Refining Apparatus | 22.10 The Other Group 4A Elements: Si, Ge, Sn, and Pb |

| Animations: | Sections: |
|---|---|
| Periodic Trends: Acid-Base Behavior of Oxides | 22.5 Oxygen |

| Movies: | Section: |
|---|---|
| Formation of Water | 22.2 Hydrogen |
| Physical Properties of the Halogens | 22.4 Group 7A: The Halogens |
| Formation of Sodium Chloride | 22.4 Group 7A: The Halogens |

| | |
|---|---|
| Reactions with Oxygen | 22.5 Oxygen |
| Carbon Dioxide Behaves as an Acid in Water | 22.5 Oxygen |
| Dehydration of Sugar | 22.6 The Other Group 6A Elements: S, Se, Te, And Po |
| Nitrogen Dioxide and Dinitrogen Tetraoxide | 22.7 Nitrogen |

| **Activities:** | **Section:** |
|---|---|
| Carbon-Silicon Sigma Overlap | 22.1 General Concepts: Periodic Trends and Chemical Reactions |

| **3-D Models** | **Section:** |
|---|---|
| Ozone | 22.5 Oxygen |
| Hydrogen Peroxide | 22.5 Oxygen |
| $S_8$ | 22.6 The Other Group 6A Elements: S, Se, Te, and Po |

## Other Resources

| **Further Readings:** | **Section:** |
|---|---|
| What's the Use? Hydrogen | 22.2 Hydrogen |
| Electronegativities of the Noble Gases | 22.3 Group 8A: The Noble Gases |
| Demonstrating a Lack of Reactivity Using a Teflon-Coated Pan | 22.4 Group 7A: The Halogens |
| Discovery and Early Uses of Iodine | 22.4 Group 7A: The Halogens |
| The Three Forms of Molecular Oxygen | 22.5 Oxygen |
| Joseph Priestley, Preeminent Amateur Chemist | 22.5 Oxygen |
| New Developments in Instant Photography | 22.6 The Other Group 6A Elements: S, Se, Te, and Po |
| Herman Frasch, Sulfur King | 22.6 The Other Group 6A Elements: S, Se, Te, and Po |
| The Discovery of Nitroglycerine: Its Preparation and Therapeutic Utility | 22.8 The Other Group 5A Elements: P, As, Sb, and Bi |
| Keeping the Fire Cold | 22.8 The Other Group 5A Elements: P, As, Sb, and Bi |
| Glass-Sand + Imagination | 22.10 The Other Group 4A Elements: Si, Ge, Sn, and Pb |
| Glass Doesn't Flow and it Isn't a Liquid | 22.10 The Other Group 4A Elements: Si, Ge, Sn, and Pb |

| **Literature Demonstrations:** | **Section:** |
|---|---|
| Making Hydrogen Gas from an Acid and a Base | 22.2 Hydrogen |
| An Overhead Demonstration of Some Descriptive Chemistry of the Halogens and Le Châtelier's Principle | 22.4 Group 7A: The Halogens |
| Preparation of Chlorine Gas from Laundry Bleach | 22.4 Group 7A: The Halogens |
| Combining Volume of Oxygen with Sulfur | 22.5 Oxygen |
| Plastic Sulfur | 22.6 The Other Group 6A Elements: S, Se, Te, and Po |

# Chapter 22. Chemistry of the Nonmetals

## Common Misconceptions:

- Students often find detailed discussions of descriptive chemistry to be difficult to digest.
- Students need to be encouraged to look for periodic trends in everything.

## Lecture Outline

### 22.1 General Concepts: Periodic Trends and Chemical Reactions[1,2,3,4]

- We divide the periodic table into metals, nonmetals and metalloids.
- Nonmetals occupy the upper right portion of the periodic table.
  - H is a special case.
- Electronegativity is important when determining whether an element is a metal.
- Nonmetals tend to have higher electronegativities than metals.
  - Thus reactions of metals and nonmetals often yield ionic compounds.
  - Compounds formed between nonmetals tend to be molecular.
- As we move down a group the chemistry of the elements can differ significantly from that of the first member of the group.
  - Elements in the third period and below have accessible *d* orbitals that can participate in bonding.
    - Therefore, the octet rule can be broken for elements in the third period and below.
  - The first member of a group can form $\pi$ bonds more readily than subsequent members.
    - This is due in part to the difference in atomic size.
    - For example, Si is much larger than C and the 3*p* orbitals are much larger than the 2*p* orbitals, so the overlap between 3*p* orbitals to form a $\pi_{3p}$ bond is less effective than for a $\pi_{2p}$ bond.
    - Because the Si–Si $\pi$ bond is much weaker than the C–C $\pi$ bond, Si tends to form $\sigma$ bonds.
      - Example: $CO_2$ is a gas with O=C=O bonds.
      - $SiO_2$ is a network solid with Si–O bonds.

#### Chemical Reactions

- In this chapter we focus on reactions involving $O_2$ (oxidation or combustion) and $H_2O$ (especially proton transfer).
- Combustion reactions with $O_2$ usually form $H_2O$ (with H–containing compounds), CO or $CO_2$ (with C–containing compounds), and $N_2$ or NO (with N–containing compounds).
- Water, nitrogen and $CO_2$ are thermodynamically stable because of the large bond energies for the H–O, N≡N, and C=O bonds.
- Examples:

$$2CH_3OH(l) + 3O_2(g) \rightarrow 2CO_2(g) + 4H_2O(l)$$
$$4CH_3NH_2(g) + 9O_2(g) \rightarrow 4CO_2(g)\ H_2O(l) + 2N_2(g)$$

- In proton-transfer reactions weaker the Brønsted-Lowry acid, the stronger the conjugate base.

### 2.2 Hydrogen

#### Isotopes of Hydrogen

---

[1] "Carbon-Silicon Sigma Overlap" Activity from MediaPortfolio
[2] Figure 22.1 from MediaPortfolio and Transparency Pack
[3] Figure 22.2 from MediaPortfolio
[4] Figure 22.3 from MediaPortfolio

- There are three isotopes of hydrogen: **protium** $\left({}^{1}_{1}\mathrm{H}\right)$, **deuterium** $\left({}^{2}_{1}\mathrm{H}\right)$, and **tritium** $\left({}^{3}_{1}\mathrm{H}\right)$.
  - Protium is the most abundant of these isotopes.
  - Deuterium (D) is about 0.0156% of naturally occurring H.
    - Deuteration (replacement of H for D) results in changes in the kinetics of reactions.
      - This phenomenon is called the *kinetic isotope effect.*
  - Tritium (T) is radioactive with a half-life of 12.3 yr.
- Deuterium and tritium are substituted for H in compounds in order to provide a molecular marker. Such compounds are said to be "labeled" (e.g., $D_2O$).
  - Replacement of protium with deuterium is called *deuteration*.

### Properties of Hydrogen[5]

- Hydrogen is unique.
- Hydrogen has a $1s^1$ electron configuration so it is placed above Li in the periodic table.
  - However, H is significantly less reactive than the alkali metals.
- Hydrogen can gain an electron to form the *hydride ion* ($H^-$) which has a He electron configuration.
  - Therefore, H could be placed above the halogens.
  - However, the electron affinity of H is lower than that of any halogen.
- Elemental hydrogen is a colorless, odorless diatomic gas at room temperature.
- Since $H_2$ is nonpolar and has only two electrons, its intermolecular forces are weak (boiling point –253°C, melting point –259°C).
- The H–H bond enthalpy is high (436 kJ/mol).
  - Therefore, reactions with hydrogen are slow at room temperature.
    - Often the molecules must be activated with heat, irradiation, or a catalyst.
- Hydrogen forms strong covalent bonds with many elements.
- When hydrogen is ignited in air, an explosion result (e.g., the *Challenger* explosion):

$$2H_2(g) + O_2(g) \rightarrow 2H_2O(l) \qquad \Delta H = -571.7\ \mathrm{kJ}$$

### Preparation of Hydrogen[6,7]

- In the laboratory hydrogen is usually prepared by reduction of an acid.
  - For example, Zn is added to an acidic solution and hydrogen bubbles form.
  - The hydrogen bubbles out of solution and is collected in a flask.
  - The collection flask is usually filled with water, so the volume of hydrogen collected is the volume of water displaced.
- Hydrogen can be prepared in larger quantities by the reduction of methane in the presence of steam at 1100°C:

$$CH_4(g) + H_2O(g) \rightarrow CO(g) + 3H_2(g)$$
$$CO(g) + H_2O(g) \rightarrow CO_2(g) + H_2(g)$$

- Alternatively:
  - Hydrogen gas can be prepared by reacting carbon with steam at high temperatures to make *water gas* (a mixture of $H_2$ and CO).
  - $H_2$ is a by-product of the electrolysis of NaCl(*aq*):

$$2NaCl(aq) + 2H_2O(l) \rightarrow H_2(g) + Cl_2(g) + 2NaOH(aq)$$

### Uses of Hydrogen[8]

---

[5] "Formation of Water" Movie from MediaPortfolio
[6] "Making Hydrogen Gas from and Acid and a Base" from Live Demonstrations
[7] Figure 22.5 from MediaPortfolio
[8] "What's the Use? Hydrogen" from Further Readings

- About two-thirds of the $2 \times 10^8$ kg of hydrogen produced in the United States is used for ammonia production via the Haber process.
- Hydrogen is used to manufacture methanol:

$$CO(g) + 2H_2(g) \rightarrow CH_3OH(g)$$

### Binary Hydrogen Compounds

- Three types of binary hydrogen compounds are formed:
  - **Ionic hydrides** (e.g., LiH)
    - Contain H and alkali metals or heavier alkaline earth metals.
    - $H^-$ is very reactive and basic.
      - Example: $H^-(aq) + H_2O(aq) \rightarrow H_2(g) + OH^-(aq)$
    - They are generally stored in an environment free from water and air.
  - **Metallic hydrides** (e.g., $TiH_2$)
    - Contain transition metals and H.
    - *Interstitial* hydrides can be made with less than stoichiometric amounts of H.
  - Example: $TiH_{1.8}$.
  - **Molecular hydrides** (e.g., $CH_4$)
    - Contain nonmetals or semimetals and H).
    - The thermal stability of molecular hydrides (measured by $\Delta G°_f$) decreases as we go down a group and increases from left to right across a period.

## 22.3 Group 8A: The Noble Gases[9]

### Noble-Gas Compounds

- The noble gases are all gases at room temperature.
  - He is the most important noble gas.
    - Liquid helium is used as a coolant.
    - It has the lowest boiling point of any substance.
  - Ar is the most abundant noble gas.
- The noble gases are very unreactive.
  - All noble gases have high ionization energies.
  - The heavier noble gases react more readily than the lighter ones.
- The first compounds of noble gases were prepared by Neil Bartlett in 1962.
  - He prepared xenon fluorides.
  - Xenon fluorides have Xe in the +2 to +8 oxidation states.
- In the presence of water, xenon fluorides form oxyfluorides:

$$XeF_6(s) + H_2O(l) \rightarrow XeOF_4(l) + 2HF(g)$$
$$XeF_6(s) + 3H_2O(l) \rightarrow XeO_3(aq) + 6HF(aq)$$

- Xenon fluorides are more stable than the oxides and oxyfluorides.
- Another noble gas compound known is $KrF_2$.
  - It decomposes to its elements at –10°C.

## 22.4 Group 7A: The Halogens

- Outer electron configurations: $ns^2np^5$.
- All halogens have large electron affinities.
  - They achieve a noble-gas configuration by gaining one electron.
  - Their most common oxidation state is –1, but oxidation states of +1, +3, +5 and +7 are possible.
- In the positive oxidation states, halogens are good oxidizing agents.

[9] "Electronegativities of the Noble Gases" from Further Readings

- Chlorine, bromine and iodine are found as halides in seawater and salt deposits.
- Fluorine occurs in several minerals (e.g., fluorspar, $CaF_2$).
- All isotopes of At are radioactive.

## Properties and Preparation of the Halogens[10,11,12,13,14,15,16]

- The properties of the halogens vary regularly with their atomic number.
- Each halogen is the most electronegative element in its row.
- Halogens exist as diatomic molecules.
  - In solids and liquids, the molecules are held together by weak London dispersion forces.
  - Iodine has the highest melting point and the strongest intermolecular forces.
  - At room temperature, $I_2$ is a solid, $Br_2$ is a liquid, and $Cl_2$ and $F_2$ are gases.
- The bond enthalpy of $F_2$ is low.
  - Hence, fluorine is very reactive.
  - The reduction potential of fluorine is very high.
  - Water is oxidized more readily than fluorine, so $F_2$ cannot be prepared by electrolysis of a salt solution.

$$F_2(aq) + H_2O(aq) \rightarrow 2HF(aq) + \tfrac{1}{2}O_2(g) \quad E° = +1.64\text{V}$$

- $Cl_2$ is produced by electrolysis of NaCl(*l*) or NaCl(*aq*).

## Uses of the Halogens

- Fluorine is an important industrial chemical .
  - It is used to make fluorocarbons (used as lubricants and plastics (Teflon)).
- Chlorine is used in plastics (PVC), dichloroethane and other organic chemicals, and as a bleaching agent in the paper and textile industries.
  - NaClO is the active ingredient in bleach.
- NaBr is used in photography.
- Iodine is a necessary nutrient.
  - It is used by the body in the synthesis of thyroid hormone.
  - Lack of iodine in the diet results in a thyroid condition called *goiter*.

## The Hydrogen Halides

- All halogens form diatomic molecules with hydrogen.
- Most hydrogen halides are prepared by treating a salt with a strong nonvolatile acid.
  - For example, we can utilize sulfuric acid in such a reaction to form HF or HCl:

$$CaF_2(s) + H_2SO_4(l) \rightarrow 2HF(g) + CaSO_4(s)$$
$$NaCl(s) + H_2SO_4(l) \rightarrow HCl(g) + NaHSO_4(s)$$

  - These reactions cannot be used to prepare HBr or HI.
- Hydrogen halides form hydrohalic acid solutions when dissolved in water.
- HF(*aq*) also reacts with silica to form hexafluorosilicic acid:

$$SiO_2(s) + 6HF(aq) \rightarrow H_2SiF_6(aq) + 2H_2O(l)$$

- HF must be stored in wax or plastic containers because it will react with the silicates in glass.

## Interhalogen Compounds

---

[10] Table 22.2 from MediaPortfolio and Transparency Pack
[11] "Physical Properties of the Halogens" Movie from MediaPortfolio
[12] "Formation of Sodium Chloride" Movie from MediaPortfolio
[13] "An Overhead Demonstration of Some Descriptive Chemistry of the Halogens and Le Châtelier's Principle" from Live Demonstrations
[14] "Discovery and Early Uses of Iodine" from Further Readings
[15] "Demonstrating a Lack of Reactivity Using a Teflon-Coated Pan" from Further Readings
[16] "Preparation of Chlorine Gas from Laundry Bleach" from Live Demonstrations

- Diatomic molecules containing two different halogens are called **interhalogen compounds.**
- Most higher interhalogen compounds have Cl, Br, or I as the central atom surrounded by 3, 5, or 7 F atoms.
  - The larger the halogen, the more interhalogen compounds it can form.
  - The compound $ICl_3$ is unique.
    - The large size of the I atom allows it to accommodate the three Cl atoms.
    - No other halogen is large enough to accommodate three Cl atoms.
- Interhalogen compounds are very reactive; they are powerful oxidizing agents.

### Oxyacids and Oxyanions[17]

- Acid strength increases as the oxidation state of the halogen increases.
- All are strong oxidizing agents.
- They are generally unstable and decompose readily.
  - The oxyanions are more stable than oxyacids.
- Oxyacids and oxyanions of chlorine include:
  - Hypochlorite salts (used in bleaches and disinfectants).
  - Perchlorates (particularly unstable when heated in the presence of organic material).
    - Ammonium perchlorate is a potent oxidizer.
    - In the presence of powdered aluminum, $NH_4ClO_4$ is used to launch the space shuttle.
    - Each launch uses 700 tons of ammonium perchlorate.
- There are two oxyacids of iodine in the +7 oxidation state:
  - Periodic acid ($HIO_4$) and paraperiodic acid ($H_5IO_6$).
  - Periodic acid is a strong acid while paraperiodic acid is a weak diprotic acid with acid dissociation constants of $K_{a1} = 2.8 \times 10^{-2}$ and $K_{a2} = 4.9 \times 10^{-9}$.
  - The large iodine atom allows six oxygen atoms around it.
  - Smaller halogens cannot form this type of compound.

## 22.5 Oxygen[18]

### Properties of Oxygen

- Oxygen has two allotropes: $O_2$ (*dioxygen*) and $O_3$ (*ozone*).
- $O_2$ is a colorless, odorless gas at room temperature.
  - The electron configuration is $[He]2s^22p^4$, which means the dominant oxidation state is –2.
  - It can complete an octet by gaining two $e^-$ to form an oxide anion ($O^{2-}$) or by sharing $2e^-$.
  - In covalent compounds it forms either two single bonds or a double bond.
  - The O=O bond is strong (bond enthalpy 495 kJ/mol).

### Preparation of Oxygen[19]

- Laboratory preparation of oxygen often involves the catalytic decomposition of $KClO_3$ in the presence of $MnO_2$:

$$2KClO_3(s) \rightarrow 2KCl(s) + 3O_2(g)$$

- Atmospheric oxygen is replenished by photosynthesis.

### Uses of Oxygen

- Oxygen is one of the most widely used oxidizing agents.
  - More than half of the oxygen produced is used in the steel industry to remove impurities.
- Oxygen is also used in medicine.

---

[17] Table 22.3 from MediaPortfolio
[18] "Joseph Preistly: Preeminent Amateur Chemist" from Further Readings
[19] "Reactions with Oxygen" Movie from MediaPortfolio

- It is used with acetylene, $C_2H_2$ for oxyacetylene welding:

$$2C_2H_2(g) + 5O_2(g) \rightarrow 4CO_2(g) + 2H_2O(g) \qquad \Delta H^\circ = -2570 \text{ kJ}$$

## Ozone[20,21,22,23]

- Ozone is a pale blue poisonous gas.
- Ozone dissociates to form oxygen:

$$O_3(g) \rightarrow O_2(g) + O(g) \qquad \Delta H^\circ = 105 \text{ kJ.}$$

- Ozone is a stronger oxidizing agent than oxygen:

$$O_3(g) + 2H^+(aq) + 2e^- \rightarrow O_2(g) + H_2O(l) \qquad E^\circ = 2.07 \text{ V}$$
$$O_2(g) + 4H^+(aq) + 4e^- \rightarrow 2H_2O(l) \qquad E^\circ = 1.23 \text{ V}$$

- Ozone can be made by passing an electric current through dry $O_2$:

$$3O_2(g) \rightarrow 2O_3(g) \qquad \Delta H^\circ = 285 \text{ kJ}$$

- Ozone is used to kill bacteria and in the preparation of pharmaceuticals and lubricants.
- Ozone is an important component of the atmosphere.
  - In the upper atmosphere ozone forms a shield to screen out harmful radiation.
  - In the lower atmosphere ozone is considered an air pollutant.

## Oxides[24,25]

- Oxygen is the second most electronegative element.
- Oxides are compounds with oxygen in the –2 oxidation state.
- Nonmetal oxides are covalent.
  - Most metal oxides combine with water to give oxyacids.
  - Oxides that react with water to form acids are called **acidic anhydrides** or **acidic oxides.**
    - Anhydride: without water.
  - Example:

$$SO_2(g) + H_2O(l) \rightarrow H_2SO_3(aq)$$

- Metal oxides are ionic.
  - Oxides that react with water to form hydroxides are called **basic anhydrides** or **basic oxides.**
  - Example: BaO in water produces $Ba(OH)_2$.

$$BaO(s) + H_2O(l) \rightarrow Ba(OH)_2(aq)$$

- Oxides that exhibit both acidic and basic properties are said to be *amphoteric* (e.g., $Cr_2O_3$).

## Peroxides and Superoxides[26]

- *Peroxides* have an O–O bond and O in the –1 oxidation state.
  - Example: hydrogen peroxide ($H_2O_2$).
- *Superoxides* have an O–O bond and O in an oxidation state of –½ .
  - The superoxide ion is $O_2^-$.
  - Superoxides usually form with very active metals ($KO_2$, $RbO_2$ and $CsO_2$).
- Properties and uses of peroxides:
  - Hydrogen peroxide is unstable and decomposes into water and oxygen:

$$2H_2O_2(l) \rightarrow 2H_2O(l) + O_2(g) \qquad \Delta H = -196.1 \text{ kJ.}$$

  - In dilute aqueous solution it is used as a mild antiseptic.
  - Peroxide is a by-product of some cellular metabolic processes.

---

[20] "Ozone" 3-D Model from MediaPortfolio
[21] Figure 22.19 from MediaPortfolio
[22] "Combining Volume of Oxygen with Sulfur" from Live Demonstrations
[23] "The Three Forms of Molecular Oxygen" from Further Readings
[24] "Periodic Trends: Acid-Base Behavior of Oxides" Animation from MediaPortfolio
[25] "Carbon Dioxide Behaves as an Acid in Water" Movie from MediaPortfolio
[26] "Hydrogen Peroxide" 3-D Model from MediaPortfolio

- These peroxides are reactive and potentially damaging to tissues.
- Cells contain enzymes (peroxidases, catalase) that convert peroxides into less harmful species.
- Peroxides are formed when active metals such as Na or Ca react with $O_2$ (i.e., to form metallic peroxides such as $Na_2O_2$, $CaO_2$).

- $H_2O_2$ can be used as either an oxidizing agent or a reducing agent.
  - Two molecules of $H_2O_2$ can react with each other in a process known as **disproportionation.**
    $$2H_2O_2(aq) \rightarrow 2H_2O(l) + O_2(g) \qquad E° = 1.10 \text{ V.}$$
  - Disproportionation occurs when an element is simultaneously oxidized and reduced:
    $$2H^+(aq) + H_2O_2(aq) + 2e^- \rightarrow 2H_2O(l) \qquad E° = 1.78 \text{ V}$$
    $$O_2(g) + 2H^+(aq) + 2e^- \rightarrow H_2O_2(aq) \qquad E° = 0.68 \text{ V}$$
- Uses of superoxides:
  - Superoxides generate oxygen gas when dissolved in water.
  - This process is used in oxygen masks used in rescue work.

## 22.6 The Other Group 6A Elements: S, Se, Te, and Po

### General Characteristics of Group 6A Elements[27,28]

- Outermost electron configuration: $ns^2np^4$.
- Dominant oxidation state: –2 ($ns^2np^6$).
- Other observed oxidation states: up to +6 (e.g., $SF_6$, $SeF_6$, $TeF_6$).
- There is a regular change in properties with increasing atomic number.

### Occurrences and Preparation of S, Se, and Te[29,30,31]

- *Frasch process*: recovery of underground elemental S deposits.
  - Superheated water is forced into the deposit to melt the S.
  - Compressed air is then injected into the sulfur deposit, which forces the $S(l)$ to the surface.
- S occurs widely as sulfates and in sulfide minerals.
  - Its presence in coal and petroleum poses an environmental problem when these fuels are burned.
- Se and Te occur in rare minerals ($Cu_2Se$, PbSe, $Ag_2Se$, $Cu_2Te$, PbTe, $Ag_2Te$, and $Au_2Te$) and are minor constituents in sulfide ores (usually of Cu, Fe, Ni and Pb).

### Properties and Uses of Sulfur, Selenium, and Tellurium

- Sulfur is yellow, tasteless and almost odorless.
  - Sulfur is insoluble in water.
  - Sulfur exists in allotropes (rhombic $S_8$ rings, plastic sulfur).
  - Sulfur is used in the manufacture of sulfuric acid and in vulcanizing rubber.
- Se and Te both form helical chains of atoms in crystals.
  - There is some sharing of electron pairs between chains.
  - Se is used in photoelectric cells, photocopiers, and light meters.
    - Its electrical conductivity is poor in the dark and increases greatly when exposed to light.

### Sulfides

- S is in the –2 oxidation state in *sulfides*.
- Many metals are found in the form of sulfides in ores.

---

27 "Plastic Sulfur" from Live Demonstrations
28 Table 22.4 from MediaPortfolio and Transparency Pack
29 "$S_8$" 3-D Model from MediaPortfolio
30 "Herman Frasch, Sulfur King" from Further Readings
31 Figure 22.23 from MediaPortfolio and Transparency Pack

- For example, PbS (galena) and HgS (cinnabar).
- S in pyrites is in the –1 oxidation state, $S_2^{2-}$.
  - $FeS_2$ is iron pyrite, often called "fools gold."
- Hydrogen sulfide (used for qualitative analysis of certain metals) is prepared by treating iron(II) sulfide with dilute acid:

$$FeS(s) + 2H^+(aq) \rightarrow H_2S(aq) + Fe^{2+}(aq)$$

  - Hydrogen sulfide is responsible for the odor of rotten eggs and is quite toxic.

### Oxides, Oxyacids, and Oxyanions of Sulfur[32,33]

- $SO_2$ is produced when sulfur is combusted in air.
- $SO_2$ in water produces sulfurous acid, $H_2SO_3$, a weak diprotic acid.
- $SO_2$ is toxic to fungi and is used to sterilize dried fruit and wine.
  - $Na_2SO_3$ and $NaHSO_3$ are used as preservatives.
    - Many people are allergic to these agents and must avoid foods treated with them.
- When sulfur burns in air both $SO_2$ (major product) and $SO_3$ are formed.
- Oxidation of $SO_2$ to $SO_3$ requires a catalyst (usually $V_2O_5$ or Pt).
- $SO_3$ is used to produce $H_2SO_4$:

$$SO_3(g) + H_2SO_4(l) \rightarrow H_2S_2O_7(l) \text{ [pyrosulfuric acid]}$$
$$H_2S_2O_7(l) + H_2O(l) \rightarrow 2H_2SO_4(l)$$

  - Commercially, sulfuric acid is 98% $H_2SO_4$.
  - Sulfuric acid is a powerful dehydrating agent, strong acid and moderate oxidizing agent.
  - In aqueous solutions of $H_2SO_4$ only the first proton is completely ionized:

$$H_2SO_4(aq) \rightarrow HSO_4^-(aq) + H^+(aq)$$

- Bisulfate ($HSO_4^-$) salts are important components of "dry acids" used in toilet bowl cleaners and in adjusting the pH of swimming pools and hot tubs.
- The sulfate ion, $SO_2^{2-}$, and the thiosulfate ion, $S_2O_3^{2-}$, are other important sulfur-containing ions:

$$8SO_3^{2-}(aq) + S_8(s) \rightarrow 8S_2O_3^{2-}(aq)$$

- *Hypo* (used in photography) is $Na_2S_2O_3 \cdot 5H_2O$.
  - Photographic film is a mixture of AgBr crystals on gelatin.
  - Exposure to light causes the AgBr to decompose to silver.
  - When the film is mildly reduced (developed) only the $Ag^+$ ions near the silver grains form an image of black metallic silver.
  - The film is treated with hypo to remove unexposed AgBr.

## 22.7 Nitrogen

### Properties of Nitrogen[34]

- Colorless, odorless, tasteless gas composed of $N_2$ molecules.
- It is unreactive because of the strong triple bond.
- Exception: Burning Mg or Li in air (78% nitrogen) forms nitrides:

$$3Mg(s) + N_2(g) \rightarrow Mg_3N_2(s)$$
$$6Li(s) + N_2(g) \rightarrow 2Li_3N(s)$$

- $N^{3-}$ is a strong Brønsted-Lowry base (forms $NH_3$ in water):

$$Mg_3N_2(s) + 6H_2O(l) \rightarrow 2NH_3(aq) + 3Mg(OH)_2(s)$$

- Nitrogen exhibits all oxidation states from –3 to +5.
  - The most common oxidation states are +5, 0 and –3 (nitrogen has a $[He]2s^22p^3$ electron configuration).

---

[32] "Dehydration of Sugar" Movie from MediaPortfolio
[33] "New Developments in Instant Photography" from Further Readings
[34] Table 22.5 from MediaPortfolio

## Preparation and Uses of Nitrogen[35]

- $N_2$ is produced by fractional distillation of air.
- Nitrogen is used as an inert gas to exclude oxygen from packaged foods and in the manufacture of chemicals, fabrication of metals, and production of electronics.
- Liquid nitrogen is an important coolant.
- The largest use of $N_2$ is in the manufacture of nitrogen-containing fertilizers to provide a source of *fixed* nitrogen.
  - Nitrogen is fixed by forming $NH_3$ (Haber Process).
  - $NH_3$ is converted into other useful chemicals.

## Hydrogen Compounds of Nitrogen[36]

- *Ammonia* is one of the most important compounds of nitrogen.
  - Ammonia is a colorless toxic gas with an irritating aroma.
  - In the laboratory, ammonia is produced by the reaction between NaOH and an ammonium salt:

$$NH_4Cl(aq) + NaOH(aq) \rightarrow NH_3(g) + H_2O(l) + NaCl(aq)$$

  - Commercially, ammonia is prepared by the Haber process.

$$N_2(g) + 3H_2(g) \rightarrow 2NH_3(g)$$

- *Hydrazine* contains an N–N single bond ($N_2H_4$).
  - Hydrazine (poisonous) is prepared by the reaction of ammonia and hypochlorite:

$$2NH_3(aq) + OCl^-(aq) \rightarrow N_2H_4(aq) + Cl^-(aq) + H_2O(l)$$

  - Poisonous chloramine, $NH_2Cl$, is an intermediate in the reaction.
    - It bubbles out of solution when household ammonia and bleach are mixed.
  - Pure hydrazine is an oily liquid which explodes on heating; it is used as a component of rocket fuels:

$$N_2H_4(l) + O_2(g) \rightarrow N_2(g) + 2H_2O(g) \qquad \Delta H^\circ = -534 \text{ kJ}$$

## Oxides and Oxyacids of Nitrogen[37,38,39]

- There are three common oxides of nitrogen:
  - $N_2O$ (*nitrous oxide*).
    - Laughing gas, used as an anesthetic.
  - NO (*nitric oxide*).
    - Toxic, colorless gas; an important neurotransmitter.
  - $NO_2$ (*nitrogen dioxide*).
    - Poisonous yellowish-brown gas which major constituent of smog.
- Some of the reactions used in their preparation include:

$$NH_4NO_3(s) \rightarrow N_2O(g) + 2H_2O(g)$$

$$3Cu(s) + 2NO_3^-(aq) + 8H^+(aq) \rightarrow 3Cu^{2+}(aq) + 2NO(g) + 4H_2O(l)$$

$$4HNO_3(aq) \rightarrow 4NO_2(g) + O_2(g) + 2H_2O(l) \text{ (in the presence of light)}$$

The **Ostwald process** is the commercial route to $HNO_3$:

- It takes place in 3 steps:
  - Oxidation of $NH_3$ by oxygen to form NO (usually using a Pt catalyst).

$$4NH_3(g) + 5O_2(g) \rightarrow 4NO(g) + 6H_2O(g)$$

  - Oxidation of NO by oxygen to form $NO_2$ (unreacted NO is recycled).
  - $NO_2$ dissolution in water to form nitric acid.

ommon oxyacids of nitrogen are $HNO_3$ (nitric) and $HNO_2$ (nitrous).

---

31 from MediaPortfolio and Transparency Pack

2 from MediaPortfolio

ioxide and Dinitrogen Tetraoxide" Movie from MediaPortfolio

from MediaPortfolio

v of Nitroglycerin: Its Preparation and Therapeutic Utility" from Further Readings

- Nitric acid is a strong acid and a powerful oxidizing agent.
  - Concentrated nitric acid will oxidize most metals (exceptions are Au, Pt, Rh and Ir):

$$NO_3^-(aq) + 2H^+(aq) + e^- \rightarrow NO_2(g) + H_2O(l) \qquad E° = 0.79V$$
$$NO_3^-(aq) + 4H^+(aq) + 3e^- \rightarrow NO(g) + 2H_2O(l) \qquad E° = 0.96V$$

  - Nitric acid is used to manufacture fertilizers ($NH_4NO_3$), drugs, plastics, and explosives (such as nitroglycerin and TNT (trinitrotoulene)).
- Nitrous acid (weak, $K_a = 4.5 \times 10^{-4}$) is not stable and disproportionates into NO and $HNO_3$.

## 22.8 The Other Group 5A Elements: P, As, Sb, and Bi

### General Characteristics of the Group 5A Elements[40]

- Outermost shell electron configuration $ns^2np^3$.
- The most common oxidation state is –3. Other common oxidation states are –1, +1, +3, and +5.
- The variation in atomic properties is very striking.
  - This group contains all three types of elements: metallic, nonmetallic, and semimetallic.
  - Size and metallic character increase with increasing atomic number within the group.
- The X–X bond enthalpies are difficult to measure.

### Occurrence, Isolation, and Properties of Phosphorus[41]

- Occurs mainly in phosphorus minerals (e.g., phosphate rock, $Ca_3(PO_4)_2$).
- Elemental $P_4$ is produced by reduction:

$$2\ Ca_3(PO_4)_2(s) + 6SiO_2(s) + 10C(s) \rightarrow P_4(g) + 6CaSiO_3(l) + 10CO(g)$$

- There are two allotropes of phosphorus: red and white.
  - $P_4$ is white phosphorus.
    - All P–P–P bond angles are 60° (small), therefore, the molecule is strained and unstable.
    - White phosphorus is poisonous and highly reactive (spontaneously reacts with oxygen in air).
      - Therefore, white phosphorus is stored under water.
- If white phosphorus is heated to 400°C in the absence of air, it converts into red phosphorus.
  - Red phosphorus is the more stable allotrope and is not usually stored under water.

### Phosphorus Halides

- Phosphorus forms a variety of compounds with halogens with the tri- and pentahalides being the most important.
- Most important: $PCl_3$ which is used in soap, detergent, plastic, and insecticide production.
- Preparation of phosphorus halides involves direct oxidation of elemental phosphorous with elemental halogen.
  - For example:

$$2P(s) + 3Cl_2(g) \rightarrow 2PCl_3(l)$$

  - In the presence of excess chlorine:

$$PCl_3(l) + Cl_2(g) \rightleftharpoons PCl_5(s)$$

- Exception: Since $F_2$ is a strong oxidant, we get

$$2P(s) + 5F_2(g) \rightarrow 2PCl_5(g)$$

- In the presence of water hydrolysis occurs readily:

$$PF_3(g) + 3H_2O(l) \rightarrow H_3PO_3(aq) + 3HF(aq)$$
$$PCl_5(l) + 4H_2O(l) \rightarrow H_3PO_4(aq) + 5HCl(aq)$$

### Oxy Compounds of Phosphorus[42]

---

[40] Table 22.6 from MediaPortfolio and Transparency Pack
[41] "Keeping the Fire Cold" from Further Readings
[42] Figure 22.40 from MediaPortfolio and Transparency Pack

- Oxygen-containing phosphorus compounds are extremely important.
  - Phosphorus(III) oxide, $P_4O_6$ is made by reacting white phosphorus with a limited supply of oxygen.
  - Phosphorus(V) oxide, $P_4O_{10}$ is made by reacting phosphorus with excess oxygen.
  - Phosphorus(III) oxide, $P_4O_6$ produces phosphorous acid, $H_3PO_3$ in water.
- The oxides of phosphorus are acidic.
  - $H_3PO_3$ is a weak *di*protic acid (the H attached to P is not acidic).
  - Phosphorus(V) oxide, $P_4O_{10}$ produces phosphoric acid, $H_3PO_4$.
    - $H_3PO_4$ is a weak *tri*protic acid.
    - $P_4O_{10}$ is used as a drying agent because of its affinity for water.
- Phosphoric and phosphorous acids undergo condensation reactions:

$$nH_3PO_4 \rightarrow (HPO_3)_n + nH_2O$$

  - Three acids containing P in the +5 oxidation state are:
    - Orthophosphoric acid: $H_3PO_4$
    - Pyrophosphoric acid: $H_4P_2O_7$
    - Metaphosphoric acid: $(HPO_3)_n$
- Phosphoric acid and its salts are used in detergents (as $Na_5P_3O_{10}$) and fertilizers (from mined phosphate rock).
- Phosphorus compounds are important in biological systems (e.g., RNA, DNA, and adenosine triphosphate (ATP)).

## 22.9 Carbon

### Elemental Forms of Carbon

- Carbon constitutes about 0.027% of the Earth's crust.
- Carbon is the main constituent of living matter.
- The study of carbon compounds (*organic compounds*) is called *organic chemistry*.
- There are three crystalline forms of carbon:
  - *Graphite* (soft, slippery, and black).
  - *Diamond* (clear, hard, and forms a covalent network).
  - *Buckminsterfullerene* (molecular form of carbon, $C_{60}$; the molecules look something like soccer balls).
- Microcrystalline and amorphous forms of C include:
  - **Carbon black**, formed when hydrocarbons are heated in a very limited supply of oxygen:

$$CH_4(g) + O_2(g) \rightarrow C(s) + 2H_2O(g)$$

    - Carbon black is used as a pigment in black inks and automobile tires.
  - **Charcoal**, formed by heating wood in the absence of air.
    - Activated charcoal is used to remove odors and impurities from air and water.
  - **Coke**, formed by heating coal in the absence of air.
    - Used as a reducing agent, especially in metallurgical processes.

### Oxides of Carbon

- Carbon forms two principal oxides: CO and $CO_2$.
- CO (*carbon monoxide*) is formed when carbon or hydrocarbons are burned in a limited supply of oxygen.

$$2C(s) + O_2(g) \rightarrow 2CO(g)$$

  - CO is very toxic (binds irreversibly to hemoglobin, interfering with oxygen transport).
    - It is odorless, colorless, and tasteless.
  - CO also has a lone pair of electrons on C, which is unusual.
  - CO is a good Lewis base and forms metal carbonyls with transition metals.
    - For example, $Ni(CO)_4$ forms readily when Ni is warmed in CO.

- CO can be used as a fuel:

$$2CO(g) + O_2(g) \rightarrow 2CO_2(g) \qquad \Delta H° = -566 \text{ kJ}$$

- CO is a good reducing agent

$$Fe_3O_4(s) + 4CO(g) \rightarrow 3Fe(s) + 4CO_2(g)$$

- $CO_2$ (*carbon dioxide*) is produced when organic compounds are burned in excess oxygen:

$$C(s) + O_2(g) \rightarrow CO_2(g)$$

$$C_2H_5OH(l) + 3O_2(g) \rightarrow 2CO_2(g) + 3H_2O(g)$$

  - $CO_2$ is produced by either heating carbonates or treating them with acids:

$$CaCO_3(s) \rightarrow CO_2(g) + CaO(s)$$

$$CO_3^{2-}(aq) + 2H^+(aq) \rightarrow CO_2(g) + H_2O(l)$$

  - Fermentation of sugar to produce alcohol also produces $CO_2$:

$$C_6H_{12}O_6(aq) \rightarrow 2C_2H_5OH(aq) + 2CO_2(g)$$

- Some of the major uses of $CO_2$ are in refrigeration (using Dry Ice™), in the carbonation of beverages, and in the production of both *washing soda* ($Na_2CO_3 \cdot 10H_2O$) and *baking soda* ($NaHCO_3$).

## Carbonic Acid and Carbonates

- When $CO_2$ dissolves in water (moderately soluble) a diprotic acid, carbonic acid, forms:

$$CO_2(aq) + H_2O(l) \rightleftharpoons H_2CO_3(aq)$$

- Carbonic acid is responsible for giving carbonated beverages a sharp acidic taste.
- Two salts of carbonic acid may be obtained by neutralization.
  - Partial neutralization of $H_2CO_3$ gives hydrogen carbonates (bicarbonates): $HCO_3^-$
    - Aqueous solutions of bicarbonates are weakly basic.
  - Full neutralization gives carbonates: $CO_3^{2-}$.
    - Aqueous solutions of carbonates are more strongly basic.
- Many minerals contain $CO_3^{2-}$.
- Example: Calcite ($CaCO_3$) is the principal mineral in limestone, marble, etc.
- $CaCO_3$ reacts readily with acid:

$$CaCO_3(s) + 2H^+(aq) \rightleftharpoons Ca^{2+}(aq) + CO_2(g) + H_2O(l)$$

- At elevated temperatures $CaCO_3$ decomposes:

$$CaCO_3(s) \rightarrow CaO(s) + CO_2(g)$$

  - This reaction is the commercial source of *lime*, CaO.
  - CaO reacts with water and $CO_2$ to form $CaCO_3$, which binds the sand in mortar:

$$CaO(s) + H_2O(l) \rightleftharpoons Ca^{2+}(aq) + 2OH^-(aq)$$

$$Ca^{2+}(aq) + 2OH^-(aq) + CO_2(aq) \rightarrow CaCO_3(s) + H_2O(l)$$

## Carbides

- **Carbides** are binary compounds of C and metals, metalloids, and certain nonmetals.
- There are three types of carbides:
  - Ionic (formed by active metals).
    - Most contain the *acetylide* ion, $C_2^{2-}$.
      - Example: $CaC_2$.
      - $CaC_2$ is used in the formation of acetylene:

$$CaC_2(s) + 2H_2O(l) \rightarrow Ca(OH)_2(aq) + C_2H_2(g)$$

  - Interstitial carbides are formed by many transition metals.
    - Example: Tungsten carbide.
    - The carbon atoms occupy the spaces or interstices between metal atoms.
  - Covalent carbides are formed by B and Si.
    - SiC is also called *carborundum*. It is nearly as hard as diamond.

### Other Inorganic Compounds of Carbon[43]

- Two interesting inorganic compounds of carbon are HCN and $CS_2$.
  - HCN (hydrogen cyanide) is an extremely toxic gas.
    - HCN is produced by reacting a salt, (e.g., NaCN) with acid.
    - Cyanides are used in the manufacture of plastics like nylon and Orlon.
    - $CN^-$ forms very stable complexes with transition metals.
    - One cause of its toxicity is its ability to combine with the iron(III) of a key enzyme in respiration (cytochrome oxidase).
  - $CS_2$ is an important solvent for waxes and greases.
    - $CS_2$ vapor is very toxic, colorless, and highly flammable.

## 22.10 The Other Group 4A Elements: Si, Ge, Sn, and Pb

### General Characteristics of Group 4A Elements[44]

- Outermost electron configuration: $ns^2np^2$.
- The electronegativities are low.
- Carbon has a coordination number of 4, the other members have higher coordination numbers.
  - Carbides ($C^{4-}$) are rare.
  - C–C bonds are very strong, so C shows the unusual ability to bond to itself to form long chains.
- The dominant oxidation state for Ge, Sn and Pb is +2.
- Because the Si–O bond is stronger than the Si–Si bond, Si tends to form oxides (silicates).

### Occurrence and Preparation of Silicon[45,46,47]

- Si is the second most abundant element in the Earth's crust.
- Elemental Si is prepared by reducing $SiO_2$:

$$SiO_2(l) + 2C(s) \rightarrow Si(l) + 2CO(g)$$

- Silicon has many important uses in the electronics industry.
  - Wafers of Si are cut from cylindrical Si crystals.
  - Si must be extremely pure when used as a semiconductor.
  - Impure Si is converted to $SiCl_4$ (with $Cl_2$), distilled and then reduced to pure Si:

$$SiCl_4(g) + 2H_2(g) \rightarrow Si(s) + 4HCl(g)$$

  - The Si is then further purified by zone refining.
    - Zone refining is used to produce ultrapure Si.
    - The silicon crystal is placed inside a tube with an inert atmosphere.
    - A heating coil is slowly moved down the Si.
    - As the coil melts the Si, any impurities dissolve and move down with the heating coil.
    - At the bottom of the crystal, the portion of Si containing all the impurities is cut off and discarded.
    - The remaining crystal is ultrapure.

### Silicates

- More than 90% of the Earth's crust is composed of compounds of Si and O.
- The most common oxidation state of Si is +4.
- **Silicates** are compounds in which Si has four O atoms surrounding it in a tetrahedral arrangement.
  - Other minerals like zircon, $ZrSiO_4$ have a similar structure.

---

[43] Figure 22.48 from MediaPortfolio
[44] Table 22.7 from MediaPortfolio and Transparency Pack
[45] Figure 22.50 from MediaPortfolio
[46] Figure 22.52 from MediaPortfolio and Transparency Pack
[47] Figure 22.53 from MediaPortfolio and Transparency Pack

- The silicate tetrahedra are building blocks for more complicated structures.
- If two $SiO_4^{4-}$ (*orthosilicate* ions) link together, one O atom is shared.
  - This structure is the *disilicate* ion, $Si_2O_7^{6-}$.
  - The mineral *thortveitite* ($Sc_2Si_2O_7$) contains disilicate ions.
- Many silicate tetrahedra can link together to form sheets, chains or three-dimensional structures.
  - Consider a structure with two vertices linked to two other tetrahedra:
  - A single-strand silicate chain can form with a $Si_2O_6^{4-}$ repeating unit.
    - Example: *enstatite* ($MgSiO_3$).
  - Consider a structure with two vertices linked to three other tetrahedra:
    - A two-dimensional sheet results.
  - The mineral *talc* (talcum powder, $Mg_3(Si_2O_5)_2(OH)_2$) results.
  - *Asbestos* is a general term applied to a group of fibrous silicate minerals.
    - They form chains or sheets of silicates.
    - The sheets in asbestos are formed into rolls.
    - The rolls make the asbestos fibrous.
    - The fibers can be woven into cloth (fireproof clothing).
      - Asbestos represents a significant health risk and has been linked to diseases such as lung cancer.
  - Three-dimensional silicate forms quartz.

### Glass

- Glasses result when silicates are heated (Si–O bonds are broken) and then rapidly cooled.
  - The Si–O bonds are re-formed before the atoms are able to organize into an ordered arrangement.
  - The amorphous solid is called quartz glass or silica glass.
- Additives are used to lower the melting point of the $SiO_2$.
  - **Glass** in windows and bottles is called *soda-lime glass* (CaO and $Na_2O$ are used as additives).
    - The CaO and $Na_2O$ are formed from limestone ($CaCO_3$) and soda ash ($Na_2CO_3$) when these inexpensive materials are heated.
- Other properties of glass may be altered by additives:
  - CoO produces blue cobalt glass.
  - $K_2O$ produces a harder glass than glass made with $Na_2O$.
  - PbO produces lead crystal glass (high refractive index).
  - $B_2O_3$ is used to make Pyrex® and Kimax®.
    - Pyrex® or Kimax® glassware has a very high melting point and resists thermal shock.

### Silicones[48,49]

- Silicones consist of O–Si–O chains with Si–R (R is an organic group such as $CH_3$) bonds filling the Si valency.
- Silicones can be oils or rubber-like materials depending on chain length and degree of cross-linking.
- Silicones are used in lubricants, car polishes, sealants, gaskets, and for waterproofing fabrics.

## 22.11 Boron

- **Boranes** are compounds of boron and hydrogen.
- $BH_3$ is the simplest borane.
  - It reacts with itself to form *diborane*, $B_2H_6$.
    - Hydrogen appears to form two bonds.
  - Diborane is very reactive:

$$B_2H_6(g) + 3O_2(g) \rightarrow B_2O_3(s) + 3H_2O(g) \quad \Delta H° = -2030 \text{ kJ}.$$

---

[48] "Glass-Sand + Imagination" from Further Readings
[49] "Glass Doesn't Flow and Doesn't Crystallize and it Isn't a Liquid" from Further Readings

- Some boranes such as pentaborane ($B_5H_9$), are reactive while some are stable in air at room temperature (e.g., decaborane: $B_{10}H_{14}$).
- Boron and hydrogen form a series of anions called *borane anions* such as $BH_4^-$.
  - They are used as reducing agents.
  - Sodium borohydride, $NaBH_4$, is used very commonly in organic chemistry.
- Boric oxide, $B_2O_3$, is the only important boron oxide.
  - It is the anhydride form of boric acid, $H_3BO_3$, a weak acid ($K_a = 5.8 \times 10^{-10}$).
  - Boric acid is used as an eyewash.
    - Heating causes a dehydration of boric acid, yielding a diprotic acid called tetraboric acid:

$$4H_3BO_3(s) \rightarrow H_2B_4O_7(s) + 5H_2O(g)$$

  - The hydrated sodium salt is called borax.
    - Solutions of borax are alkaline.
    - It is widely used as a cleaning agent.

## Further Readings:

1. Alton Banks, "What's the Use? Hydrogen," *J. Chem. Educ.*, Vol. 66, **1989**, 801. Each of the "What's the Use?" articles, written by Alton Banks, focuses on the uses of a specific element. See volumes 66 (**1989**), 67 (**1990**), 68 (**1991**) and 69 (**1992**) for other elements!

2. Thomas G. Richmond and Paul F. Kraus, "Demonstrating a Lack of Reactivity Using a Teflon-Coated Pan," *J. Chem. Educ.*, Vol. 72, **1995**, 731. A short demonstration of the wonders of Teflon.

3. Myron S. Simon, "New Developments in Instant Photography," *J. Chem. Educ.*, Vol. 71, **1994**, 132–140.

4. Terence P. Lee, "Keeping the Fire Cold," *Chemistry in Britain*, **January 1996**, 41–45. An article on the importance of phosphorous.

5. Michael Laing, "The Three Forms of Molecular Oxygen," *J. Chem. Educ.*, Vol. **66**, **1989**, 453–454.

6. Foil A. Miller, "Joseph Priestley, Preeminent Amateur Chemist," *J. Chem. Educ.*, Vol. 64, **1987**, 745–747.

7. Terry L. Meek, "Electronegativities of the Noble Gases," *J. Chem. Educ.*, Vol. 72, **1995**, 17–18.

8. Louis Rosenfeld, "Discovery and Early Uses of Iodine," *J. Chem. Educ.*, Vol. 77, **2000**, 984–987.

9. Miriam C. Nagel, "Herman Frasch, Sulfur King," *J. Chem. Educ.*, Vol. 58, **1981**, 60–61.

10. Natalie I. Foster and Ned D. Heindel, "The Discovery of Nitroglycerine: Its Preparation and Therapeutic Utility," *J. Chem. Educ.*, Vol 58, **1981**, 364–365.

11. Kenneth E. Kolb and Doris K. Kolb, "Glass-Sand + Imagination," *J. Chem. Educ.*, Vol. 77, **2000**, 812–816.

12. Stephen J. Hawkes, "Glass Doesn't Flow and Doesn't Crystallize and It Isn't a Liquid," *J. Chem. Educ.*, Vol. 77, **2000**, 846–848.

## Live Demonstrations:

1. Lee R. Summerlin, Christie L. Borgford, and Julie B. Ealy, "Making Hydrogen Gas from an Acid and a Base," *Chemical Demonstrations, A Sourcebook for Teachers, Volume 2* (Washington: American Chemical Society, **1987**), pp. 33–34. Gas-generating reactions are carried out in two flasks fitted with balloons; the balloons inflate as they collect the hydrogen gas generated.

2. Robert C. Hansen, "An Overhead Demonstration of Some Descriptive Chemistry of the Halogens and Le Châtelier's Principle," *J. Chem. Educ.*, Vol. 65, **1988**, 264–265.

3. Lee R. Summerlin and James L. Ealy, Jr., "Preparation of Chlorine Gas from Laundry Bleach," *Chemical Demonstrations, A Sourcebook for Teachers,* (Washington: American Chemical Society, **1985**), p. 13. The bleaching effect of chlorine is shown in this reaction; chlorine gas is prepared by reaction of laundry bleach with hydrochloric acid.

4. Bassam Z. Shakhashiri, "Combining Volume of Oxygen with Sulfur," *Chemical Demonstrations: A Handbook for Teachers of Chemistry, Volume 2* (Madison: The University of Wisconsin Press, **1985**), pp. 190–192. A demonstration of the production of $SO_2$, rather than $SO_3$, upon combustion of sulfur in $O_2$.

5. Lee R. Summerlin, Christie L. Borgford, and Julie B. Ealy, "Plastic Sulfur," *Chemical Demonstrations, A Sourcebook for Teachers, Volume 2* (Washington: American Chemical Society, **1987**), p. 53. Plastic sulfur is formed by pouring heated yellow sulfur into a beaker of water.

# Chapter 23. Metals and Metallurgy

## Media Resources

### Figures and Tables

| In Transparency Pack and on MediaPortfolio: | Section: |
|---|---|
| Table 23.1 Principal Mineral Sources of Some Common Metals | 21.1 Occurrence and Distribution of Some Metals |
| Figure 23.4 Blast Furnace | 23.2 Pyrometallurgy |
| Figure 23.7 Downs Cell | 23.4 Electrometallurgy |
| Figure 23.8 Hall Process | 23.4 Electrometallurgy |
| Figure 23.9 Quantities of Reactants and Energy Required to Produce 1000 kg of Aluminum | 23.4 Electrometallurgy |
| Figure 23.11 Electrolysis Cell for Copper Refining | 23.4 Electrometallurgy |
| Figure 23.14 Band of Molecular Orbitals in a Metal | 23.5 Metallic Bonding |
| Figure 23.18 Substitional and Interstitial Alloys | 23.6 Alloys |
| Figure 23.22 Variation in Atomic Radius of Transition Metals | 23.7 Transition Metals |
| Figure 23.24 Nonzero Oxidation States of the First Transition Series | 23.7 Transition Metals |

| On MediaPortfolio: | Section: |
|---|---|
| Figure 23.6 Converter for Refining Iron | 23.2 Pyrometallurgy |
| Figure 23.13 Electron Sea Model for Metals | 23.5 Metallic Bonding |
| Table 23.2 Melting Points of Selected Transition Metals | 23.5 Metallic Bonding |
| Figure 23.15 Conductors and Insulators | 23.5 Metallic Bonding |
| Figure 23.16 Effect of Doping | 23.5 Metallic Bonding |
| Table 23.4 Some Common Alloys | 23.6 Alloys |
| Figure 23.21 Transition Metals | 23.7 Transition Metals |
| Table 23.5 Properties of the First Transition-Series Elements | 23.7 Transition Metals |

| Movies: | Section: |
|---|---|
| Thermite | 23.2 Pyrometallurgy |
| Redox Chemistry of Iron and Copper | 23.8 Chemistry of Selected Transition Metals |

| Activities: | Section: |
|---|---|
| Mineral Sources of Mineral Ores | 23.1 Occurrence and Distribution of Metals |
| Electrolysis | 23.4 Electrometallurgy |
| Metallic Bonding | 23.5 Metallic Bonding |

## Other Resources

| Further Readings: | Section: |
|---|---|
| Teaching the Concepts of Metallurgy through the Use of Postage Stamps | 23.1 Occurrence and Distribution of Metals |

| | |
|---|---|
| A New Perspective on Rutile | 23.1 Occurrence and Distribution of Metals |
| Charles Martin Hall-The Young Man, His Mentor, and His Metal | 23.4 Electrometallurgy |
| On the Occurrence of Metallic Character in the Periodic Table of the Elements | 23.5 Metallic Bonding |
| An Ionic Model for Metallic Bonding | 23.5 Metallic Bonding |
| Conducting Midshipmen—A Classroom Activity Modeling Extended Bonding in Solids | 23.5 Metallic Bonding |
| A Stability Ruler for Metal-Ion Complexes | 23.8 Chemistry of Selected Transition Metals |

| **Live Demonstrations:** | **Section:** |
|---|---|
| Precipitates and Complexes of Copper(II) | 23.8 Chemistry of Selected Transition Metals |
| Green and Blue Copper Complexes | 23.8 Chemistry of Selected Transition Metals |
| Copper Sulfate: Blue to White | 23.8 Chemistry of Selected Transition Metals |
| The Copper Mirror | 23.8 Chemistry of Selected Transition Metals |

# Chapter 23. Metals and Metallurgy

## Common Misconceptions:

- Students have difficulty applying concepts of molecular orbital theory to metals.

## Lecture Outline

### 23.1 Occurrence and Distribution of Metals

- Early history is divided into the Stone Age, Bronze Age, and the Iron Age.
- Seven metals are present in a jet engine.
  - Although we think of Fe when we think of the dominant metal of industry, it is not present in the engine!
  - A modern jet engine consists mostly of Ti and Ni with smaller amounts of Cr, Co, Al, Nb and Ta.
- The solid portion of the Earth is called the **lithosphere**.
- *Concentrated* metal deposits are found beneath the Earth's surface.
- An **ore** is a deposit that contains a metal that can be extracted economically.
  - The metal of interest usually has to be extracted from a large amount of unwanted materials and treated to make it suit our requirements.

#### Minerals[1,2,3,4]

- Most metals are found in nature in the form of solid inorganic compounds called **minerals**.
- Names of minerals are based on the location of their discovery, the person who discovered them, or some characteristic of the mineral.
  - For example, some minerals are named after their colors:
    - Malachite comes from the Greek *malache* (the name of a tree with very green leaves).
- Most important sources of metals are oxide, sulfide and carbonate minerals.

#### Metallurgy

- **Metallurgy** is the science and technology of extracting metals from natural sources and preparing them for practical use.
- There are five important steps:
  - Mining (getting the ore out of the ground).
  - Concentrating (preparing it for further treatment).
  - Differences in the chemical and physical properties of the mineral of interest and the undesired material, called *gangue*, are used to separate these components.
    - Example: Iron can be separated from gangue in finely ground magnetite by using a magnet to attract the iron.
  - Reduction (to obtain the free metal in the 0 oxidation state).
  - Refining (to obtain the pure metal).
  - Mixing with other metals (to form an *alloy*).
    - Alloys are metallic materials composed of two or more elements.

---

[1] "Teaching the Concepts of Metallurgy Through the Use of Postage Stamps" from Further Readings
[2] "Mineral Sources of Mineral Ores" Activity from MediaPortfolio
[3] Table 23.1 from MediaPortfolio and Transparency Pack
[4] "A New Perspective on Rutile" from Further Readings

## 23.2 Pyrometallurgy[5]

- **Pyrometallurgy**: using high temperatures to obtain the free metal.
  - Several steps are employed:
    - **Calcination** is the heating of ore to cause decomposition and elimination of a volatile product:
$$PbCO_3(s) \xrightarrow{\Delta} PbO(s) + CO_2(g)$$
  - **Roasting** is a heat treatment that causes chemical reactions between the ore and the atmosphere of the furnace.
    - It may cause oxidation or reduction and be accompanied by calcination.
    - Examples of roasting include:
$$2ZnS(s) + 3O_2(g) \rightarrow 2ZnO(s) + 2SO_2(g)$$
$$2MoS_2(s) + 7O_2(g) \rightarrow 2MoO_3(s) + 4SO_2(g)$$
$$HgS(s) + O_2(g) \rightarrow Hg(g) + SO_2(g)$$
$$PbO(s) + CO(g) \rightarrow Pb(l) + CO_2(g)$$
    - **Smelting** is a melting process that causes materials to separate into two or more layers.
      - Two important kinds of layers are slag and molten metal.
      - Molten metal may be a single metal or a solution of several metals.
      - **Slag** consists mostly of molten silicates in addition to aluminates, phosphates, fluorides, and other inorganic materials.
    - **Refining** is the process during which a crude, impure metal is converted into a pure metal or a mixture with a well-defined composition.

### The Pyrometallurgy of Iron[6]

- Most important sources of iron are hematite, $Fe_2O_3$, and magnetite, $Fe_3O_4$.
  - Other ores such as *taconite*, are becoming increasingly important as sources of iron.
- Reduction occurs in a *blast furnace*, a chemical reactor capable of operating continuously.
- Ore, limestone and coke are added to the top of the blast furnace.
  - It takes about 2 kg of ore, 1 kg of coke, 0.3 kg of limestone and 1.5 kg of air to make 1 kg of crude iron, called *pig iron*.
  - Coke is coal that has been heated to drive off the volatile components.
  - Coke reacts with oxygen to form CO (the reducing agent):
$$2C(s) + O_2(g) \rightarrow 2CO(g) \qquad \Delta H = -221 \text{ kJ}$$
  - CO is also produced by the reaction of water vapor in the air with C:
$$C(s) + H_2O(g) \rightarrow CO(g) + H_2(g) \qquad \Delta H = +131 \text{ kJ}$$
    - Since this reaction is endothermic, if the blast furnace gets too hot, water vapor is added to cool it down without interrupting the chemistry.
  - At around 250°C limestone is calcinated (heated until it decomposes to form CaO and $CO_2$).
  - Also around 250°C iron oxides are reduced by CO:
$$Fe_3O_4(s) + 4CO(g) \rightarrow 3Fe(s) + 4CO_2(g) \qquad \Delta H = -15 \text{ kJ}$$
$$Fe_3O_4(s) + 4H_2(g) \rightarrow 3Fe(s) + 4H_2O(g) \qquad \Delta H = +150 \text{ kJ}$$
  - Molten iron is produced in the lower part of the furnace and removed at the bottom.
  - Slag (molten silicate materials) is removed from above the molten iron.
- If iron is going to be made into steel, it is poured directly into a basic oxygen converter.
  - The molten iron is converted to steel, an alloy of iron.
  - To remove impurities, $O_2$ is blown through the molten mixture.
  - The oxygen oxidizes the impurities.

---

[5] "Thermite" Movie from MediaPortfolio

[6] Figure 23.4 from MediaPortfolio and Transparency Pack

### Formation of Steel[7]

- Steel is an alloy of iron.
- From the blast furnace, the crude iron is poured into a *converter*.
  - A converter consists of a steel shell encasing a refractory brick liner.
  - After treatment in the blast furnace, there are impurities in the iron (e.g., Si, Mn, P, S, C) that must be removed by oxidation.
  - Air cannot be present in the converter because the nitrogen will form iron nitride (causes the steel to be brittle).
    - Oxygen diluted with Ar is used as the oxidizing agent.

## 23.3 Hydrometallurgy

- **Hydrometallurgy** is the extraction of metals from ores using aqueous reactions.
- **Leaching** is the selective dissolution of the desired mineral.
  - Typical leaching agents are dilute acids, bases, salts, and sometimes water.
  - The process often involves formation of a complex ion.
  - For example, gold can be extracted from low-grade ore by *cyanidation.*
- NaCN is sprayed over the crushed ore and the gold is oxidized:

$$4Au(s) + 8CN^-(aq) + O_2(g) + 2H_2O(l) \rightarrow 4Au(CN)_2^-(aq) + 4OH^-(aq)$$

- The gold is then obtained by reduction of the cyanide complex with Zn powder:

$$2Au(CN)_2^-(aq) + Zn(s) \rightarrow Zn(CN)_4^{2-}(aq) + 2Au(s)$$

### The Hydrometallurgy of Aluminum

- Aluminum is the second most useful metal.
- *Bauxite* is a mineral that contains Al as $Al_2O_3 \cdot xH_2O$.
  - The **Bayer process** is used to purify Al from bauxite.
- The crushed ore is digested in 30% NaOH (by mass) at 150°C to 230°C and high pressure (30 atm to prevent boiling).
- $Al_2O_3$ dissolves, forming the complex aluminate ion:

$$Al_2O_3 \cdot H_2O(s) + 2H_2O(l) + 2OH^-(aq) \rightarrow 2Al(OH)_4^-(aq)$$

- Impurities do not dissolve in the strongly basic solution. (Recall that $Al^{3+}$ is amphoteric while $Fe^{3+}$ is not.).
  - This allows for the separation of Al from Fe-containing solids.
- The pH of the aluminate solution is lowered; aluminum hydroxide precipitates.
- The aluminum hydroxide is calcined and reduced to produce the metal.

## 23.4 Electrometallurgy

### Electrometallurgy of Sodium[8]

- **Electrometallurgy** is the process of obtaining metals through electrolysis.
- Two different starting materials: molten salt or aqueous solution.
- Active metals cannot be obtained from aqueous solution.
  - Water is more easily reduced than the metal ions.
  - Sodium is produced by electrolysis of molten NaCl in a **Downs cell.**
  - $CaCl_2$ is used to lower the melting point of NaCl from 804°C to 600°C.
  - An iron screen is used to separate $Na(l)$ and $Cl_2(g)$ so that NaCl is not reformed.
  - At the cathode: $2Na^+(aq) + 2e^- \rightarrow 2Na(l)$
  - At the anode: $2Cl^-(aq) \rightarrow Cl_2(g) + 2e^-$

---

[7] Figure 23.6 from MediaPortfolio

[8] Figure 23.7 from MediaPortfolio and Transparency Pack

### Electrometallurgy of Aluminum[9,10,11,12]

- In the **Hall process** an electrolytic process is used to produce free aluminum.
  - $Al_2O_3$ melts at 2000°C, so it is impractical to perform electrolysis on the molten salt.
  - Hall used purified $Al_2O_3$ in molten cryolite ($Na_3AlF_6$, melting point 1012°C).
    - Anode: $C(s) + 2O^{2-}(l) \rightarrow CO_2(g) + 4e^-$
    - Cathode: $3e^- + Al^{3+}(l) \rightarrow Al(l)$
      - The graphite rods (anode) are consumed in the reaction.

### Electrorefining of Copper[13]

- Because of its good conductivity, Cu is used to make electrical wiring.
- Impurities reduce conductivity, therefore pure copper is required in the electronics industry.
- Slabs of impure Cu isolated by pyrometallurgical methods are used as anodes and thin sheets of pure Cu are the cathodes.
  - Acidic copper sulfate is used as the electrolyte.
  - The voltage across the electrodes is designed to produce copper at the cathode.
  - The metallic impurities do not plate out on the cathode.
  - Metal ions are collected in the sludge at the bottom of the cell.
- Copper sludge provides about 25% of U.S. silver production and 13% of U.S. gold production.

## 23.5 Metallic Bonding[14,15]

### Physical Properties of Metals

- Important physical properties of pure metals:
  - *Malleable*: can be hammered into thin sheets.
  - *Ductile*: can be pulled into wires
  - Good electrical and thermal conductivity.
- Most metals are solids with the atoms in a close-packed arrangement.
  - In Cu each atom is surrounded by 12 neighbors.
  - There are not enough electrons for the metal atoms to be covalently bonded to each other.
    - We need a model for bonding that explains this.

### Electron-Sea Model for Metallic Bonding[16,17]

- We use a delocalized model for electrons in a metal.
- The metal nuclei are seen to exist in an *electron-sea*.
- No electrons are localized between any two metal atoms.
- Therefore, the electrons can flow freely through the metal.
- Without any definite bonds, the metals are easy to deform (and are malleable and ductile).
- Problems with the electron-sea model:
  - As the number of electrons increases, the strength of bonding should increase, and the melting point should increase.

---

[9] Figure 23.8 from MediaPortfolio and Transparency Pack
[10] Figure 23.9 from MediaPortfolio and Transparency Pack
[11] "Electrolysis" Activity from MediaPortfolio
[12] "Charles Martin Hall-The Young Man, His Mentor, and His Metal" from Further Readings
[13] Figure 23.11 from MediaPortfolio and Transparency Pack
[14] "On the Occurrence of Metallic Character in the Periodic Table of the Elements" from Further Readings
[15] "An Ionic Model for Metallic Bonding" from Further Readings
[16] Figure 23.13 from MediaPortfolio
[17] Table 23.2 from MediaPortfolio

- *However*, group 6B metals (at the center of the transition metals) have the highest melting points in their respective periods.
- We turn to molecular-orbital theory for a more general model.

### Molecular-Orbital Model for Metals[18,19,20,21,22]

- Delocalized bonding requires the atomic orbitals on one atom to interact with atomic orbitals on neighboring atoms.
  - Example: Graphite electrons are delocalized over a whole plane, benzene molecules have electrons delocalized over a ring.
- Recall that the number of molecular orbitals is equal to the number of atomic orbitals.
- In metals there are a very large number of orbitals.
  - As the number of orbitals increases, their energy spacing decreases and they band together.
  - The available electrons do not completely fill the band of orbitals.
  - Therefore, electrons can be promoted to unoccupied energy *bands*.
  - Because the energy differences between orbitals are small the promotion of electrons requires little energy.
- As we move across the transition metal series, the antibonding band starts becoming filled.
  - Therefore, the first half of the transition metal series has only bonding-bonding interactions and the second half has bonding-antibonding interactions.
  - We expect the metals in the middle of the transition metal series (group 6B) to have the highest melting points.
- The energy gap between bands is called the *band gap*.
- The electron-sea model is a qualitative interpretation of *band theory* (molecular-orbital model for metals).

## 23.6 Alloys[23,24]

- **Alloys** contain more than one element and have the characteristic properties of metals.
  - Pure metals and alloys have different physical properties.
  - An alloy of gold and copper is used in jewelry (the alloy is harder than the relatively soft pure 24 karat gold).
    - Fourteen-karat gold is an alloy containing 58% gold.
- **Solution alloys** are homogeneous mixtures.
  - There are two types of solution alloys:
    - *Substitutional alloys* (the solute atoms take the positions normally occupied by a solvent atom).
      - The atoms must have similar atomic radii.
      - The elements must have similar bonding characteristics.
    - *Interstitial alloys* (the solute occupies interstitial sites in the metallic lattice).
      - One element (usually a nonmetal) must have a significantly smaller radius than the other (in order to fit into the interstitial site).

---

[18] "Metallic Bonding" Activity from MediaPortfolio
[19] Figure 23.14 from MediaPortfolio and Transparency Pack
[20] Figure 23.15 from MediaPortfolio
[21] "Conducting Midshipmen—A Classroom Activity Modeling Extended Bonding in Solids" from Further Readings
[22] Figure 23.16 from MediaPortfolio
[23] Table 23.4 from MediaPortfolio
[24] Figure 23.18 from MediaPortfolio and Transparency Pack

- The alloy is much harder, stronger and less ductile than the pure metal (increased bonding between nonmetal and metal).
    - Example steel (contains up to 3% carbon).
        - *Mild steels* (<0.2% carbon).
            - Useful for chains, nails, etc.
        - *Medium steels* (0.2–0.6% carbon).
            - Useful for girders, rails, etc.
        - *High-carbon steels* (0.6–1.5% carbon).
            - Used in cutlery, tools, springs.
- Other elements may also be added to make *alloy steels*.
    - Addition of V and Cr increases the strength of the steel and improves its resistance to stress and corrosion.
- The most important iron alloy is stainless steel. It contains C, Cr (from *ferrochrome*, $FeCr_2$), and Ni.

- **Heterogeneous alloys**: The components are not dispersed uniformly (e.g., pearlite steel has two phases: almost pure Fe and cementite, $Fe_3C$).

### Intermetallic Compounds

- Intermetallic compounds are homogeneous alloys with definite properties and compositions.
- Examples: Cu and Al form $CuAl_2$ (duraluminum), $Cr_3Pt$ is used to coat razor blades (to increase hardness and ability to maintain a sharp edge), and $Co_5Sm$ is used in permanent magnets in lightweight headsets.
- An interesting intermetallic compound is NiT, a *shape memory* metal.
    - Atoms can exist in two different bonding arrangements representing two different solid state phases.

## 23.7 Transition Metals[25]

- Transition metals occupy the *d* block of the periodic table.
    - Almost all have two *s* electrons (exceptions group 6B and group 1B).
- Most of these elements are very important in modern technology.

### Physical Properties[26,27]

- The physical properties of transition metals can be classified into two groups: atomic properties (e.g., atomic radius, ionization energy) and bulk properties (e.g., density, melting point).
- Most of the trends in bulk properties are less smooth than the atomic properties.
- The atomic trends tend to be smooth for the transition metals.
- The trends in atomic properties of the transition metals can be exemplified with atomic radii.
    - Atomic radius decreases and reaches a minimum around group 8B (Fe, Co, Ni) and then increases for groups 1 and 2.
    - This trend is again understood in terms of effective nuclear charge.
    - The increase in size of the Cu and Zn triads is rationalized in terms of the completely filled *d* orbital.
    - In general, atomic size increases down a group.
- An important exception: Hf has almost the same radius as Zr (group 4B): we would expect Hf to be larger than Zr.
    - Between La and Hf the 4*f* shell fills (lanthanides).
    - As 4*f* orbitals fill, the effective nuclear charge increases and the lanthanides contract smoothly.

---

[25] Figure 23.21 from MediaPortfolio
[26] Table 23.5 from MediaPortfolio
[27] Figure 23.22 from MediaPortfolio and Transparency Pack

- The **lanthanide contraction** balances the increase in size we anticipate between Hf and Zr.
- The second and third series are usually about the same size, with the first series being smaller.
- Second and third series metals are very similar in their properties (e.g., Hf and Zr are always found together in ores and are very difficult to separate).

### Electron Configurations and Oxidation States[28]

- Even though the $(n-1)d$ orbital is filled after the $ns$ orbital, electrons are lost from the orbital with highest $n$ first.
- That is, transition metals lose $s$ electrons before the $d$ electrons.
  - Example: Fe: $[Ar]3d^6 4s^2$ $Fe^{2+}$: $[Ar]3d^6$.
- $d$ Electrons are responsible for some important properties:
  - Transition metals have more than one oxidation state.
  - Transition-metal compounds are colored.
  - Transition-metal compounds have magnetic properties.
- Note: All oxidation states for metals are positive.
  - The +2 oxidation state is common because it corresponds to the loss of both $s$ electrons.
    - Exception: Sc where the +3 oxidation state is isoelectronic with Ar.
  - The maximum oxidation state for the first transition series is +7 for Mn.
  - For the second and third series, the maximum oxidation state is +8 for Ru and Os ($RuO_4$ and $OsO_4$).

### Magnetism

- Magnetism provides important bonding information.
- Electron spin generates a magnetic field with a magnetic moment.
- There are three types of magnetic behavior (shown here in order):
  - *Diamagnetic* (no atoms or ions with magnetic moments).
    - When two spins are opposite, the magnetic fields cancel (diamagnetic).
    - Diamagnetic substances are weakly repelled by external magnetic fields.
  - *Paramagnetic* (magnetic moments not aligned outside a magnetic field).
    - When spins are unpaired, the magnetic fields do not cancel (paramagnetic).
    - Generally, the unpaired electrons in a solid are not influenced by adjacent unpaired electrons.
      - That is, the magnetic moments are randomly oriented.
    - When paramagnetic materials are placed in a magnetic field, the electrons become aligned.
  - **Ferromagnetic** (coupled magnetic centers aligned in a common direction).
    - Ferromagnetism is a special case of paramagnetism where the magnetic moments are permanently aligned (e.g., Fe, Co and Ni).
    - Ferromagnetic oxides are used in magnetic recording tape (e.g., $CrO_2$ and $Fe_3O_4$).

## 23.8 Chemistry of Selected Transition Metals[29]

### Chromium

- In the absence of air, Cr reacts with acid to form a solution of blue $Cr^{2+}$:

$$Cr(s) + 2H^+(aq) \rightarrow Cr^{2+}(aq) + H_2(g)$$

- In the presence of air, the $Cr^{2+}$ readily oxidizes to $Cr^{3+}$:

$$4Cr^{2+}(aq) + O_2(g) + 4H^+(aq) \rightarrow 4Cr^{3+}(aq) + 2H_2O(l)$$

- In the presence of $Cl^-$, $Cr^{3+}$ forms the green $Cr(H_2O)_4Cl_2^+$ ion.
- In aqueous solution, Cr is usually present in the +6 oxidation state.
  - In base, chromate ($CrO_4^{2-}$, bright yellow ), is the most stable ion.

---

[28] Figure 23.24 from MediaPortfolio and Transparency Pack

[29] "Redox Chemistry of Iron and Copper" Movie from MediaPortfolio

- In acid, dichromate ($Cr_2O_7^{2-}$, deep orange), is the most stable ion.

## Iron

- In aqueous solution iron is present in the +2 (ferrous) or +3 (ferric) oxidation states.
- Iron reacts with nonoxidizing acids to form $Fe^{2+}(aq)$.
  - In the presence of air, $Fe^{2+}$ is oxidized to $Fe^{3+}$.
- As with most metal ions, iron forms complex ions in water (e.g., $Fe(H_2O)_6^{3+}$).
  - In acidic solution $Fe(H_2O)_6^{3+}$ is stable, but in base $Fe(OH)_3$ precipitates.
  - If NaOH is added to a solution of $Fe^{3+}(aq)$, the brownish $Fe(OH)_3$ precipitate is formed.

## Copper[30,31,32,33,34]

- In aqueous solution copper has two dominant oxidation states: +1 (cuprous) and +2 (cupric).
- $Cu^+$ has a $3d^{10}$ electronic configuration.
- Cu(I) salts tend to be white and insoluble in water.
- Cu(I) disproportionates easily in aqueous solution:

$$2Cu^+(aq) \rightarrow Cu^{2+}(aq) + Cu(s)$$

- Cu(II) is the more common oxidation state.
  - Many salts of $Cu^{2+}$ are water soluble.
  - One example is copper sulfate pentahydrate, $CuSO_4 \cdot 5H_2O$, which is often called *blue vitriol.*
  - In aqueous solution, four water molecules are coordinated to the $Cu^{2+}$ ion and one is hydrogen bonded to the sulfate ion.
  - Water-soluble copper(II) salts include $Cu(NO_3)_2$, $CuSO_4$, and $CuCl_2$.
- $Cu(OH)_2$ is insoluble and can be precipitated by adding NaOH to a solution containing $Cu^{2+}$ ions.
- CuS is one of the least soluble $Cu^{2+}$ compounds.
  - It is a black solid that dissolves in nitric acid:

$$3CuS(s) + 8H^+(aq) + 2NO_3^-(aq) \rightarrow 3Cu^{2+}(aq) + 3S(s) + 2NO(g) + 4H_2O(l)$$

  - It is not soluble in NaOH, $NH_3$ or in nonoxidizing acids (e.g., HCl).
- $CuSO_4$ is used commonly to inhibit fungal growth in water, etc.
- We require 2–5 mg of copper per day in our diet.

---

30 "Precipitates and Complexes of Copper(II)" from Live Demonstrations
31 "Green and Blue Copper Complexes" from Live Demonstrations
32 "Copper Sulfate: Blue to White" from Live Demonstrations
33 "The Copper Mirror" from Live Demonstrations
34 "A Stability Ruler for Metal Ion Complexes" from Further Readings

## Further Readings:

1. James K. Beattie, "A New Perspective on Rutile," *J. Chem Educ*., Vol. 75, **1998**, 641.

2. Daniel Bartet and Eugenia Aguila, "Teaching the Concepts of Metallurgy through the Use of Postage Stamps," *J. Chem. Educ*., Vol. 64, **1987**, 526–528.

3. Norman C. Craig, "Charles Martin Hall-The Young Man, His Mentor, and His Metal," *J. Chem. Educ*., Vol. 63, **1986**, 557–559.

4. Peter P. Edwards and M. J. Sienko, "On the Occurrence of Metallic Character in the Periodic Table of the Elements," *J. Chem. Educ*., Vol. 60, **1983**, 691–696.

5. Frank Rioux, "An Ionic Model for Metallic Bonding," *J. Chem. Educ*., Vol. 62, **1985**, 383–384.

6. Joseph F. Lomax, "Conducting Midshipmen-A Classroom Activity Modeling Extended Bonding in Solids," *J. Chem. Educ*., Vol. 69, **1992**, 794–795.

7. R. Bruce. Martin, "A Stability Ruler for Metal Ion Complexes," *J. Chem. Educ*., Vol. 64, **1987**, 402.

## Live Demonstrations:

1. Bassam Z. Shakhashiri, "Precipitates and Complexes of Copper (II)," *Chemical Demonstrations: A Handbook for Teachers of Chemistry, Volume 1* (Madison: The University of Wisconsin Press, **1983**), pp. 318–323. The color and solubility of various copper compounds is demonstrated.

2. Lee. R. Summerlin, Christie L. Borgford, and Julie B. Ealy, "Green and Blue Copper Complexes," *Chemical Demonstrations, A Sourcebook for Teachers, Volume 2* (Washington: American Chemical Society, **1988**), pp.71–72. Three copper complexes are prepared in this demonstration.

3. Lee. R. Summerlin,, Christie L. Borgford, and Julie B. Ealy, "Copper Sulfate: Blue to White," *Chemical Demonstrations, A Sourcebook for Teachers, Volume 2* (Washington: American Chemical Society, **1988**), pp. 69–70. An exploration of color change associated with the dehydration of copper sulfate.

4. Lee R. Summerlin, Christie L. Borgford, and Julie B. Ealy, "The Copper Mirror," *Chemical Demonstrations, A Sourcebook for Teachers, Volume 2* (Washington: American Chemical Society, **1987**), p. 184.

# Chapter 24. Chemistry of Coordination Compounds

## Media Resources

### Figures and Tables

| **In Transparency Pack and on MediaPortfolio:** | **Section:** |
|---|---|
| Figure 24.1 Isomers of $[Co(NH_3)_4Cl_2]^+$ | 24.1 Metal Complexes |
| Figure 24.3 Tetrahedral and Square-Planar Geometries | 24.1 Metal Complexes |
| Figure 24.4 Octahedral Coordination Sphere | 24.1 Metal Complexes |
| Figure 24.5 The $[Co(en)_3]^{3+}$ Ion | 24.2 Ligands with More Than One Donor Atom |
| Figure 24.6 Structures of Bidentate Ligands | 24.2 Ligands with More Than One Donor Atom |
| Figure 24.7 The $[CoEDTA]^-$ Ion | 24.2 Ligands with More Than One Donor Atom |
| Figure 24.11 Structure of Myoglobin | 24.2 Ligands with More Than One Donor Atom |
| Figure 24.12 Heme Group in Oxymyoglobin or Oxyhemoglobin | 24.2 Ligands with More Than One Donor Atom |
| Figure 24.14 Absorption Spectrum of Chlorophyll | 24.2 Ligands with More Than One Donor Atom |
| Figure 24.18 Isomerism in Coordination Compounds | 24.4 Isomerism |
| Figure 24.20 *cis* and *trans* $[Pt(NH_3)_2Cl_2]$ | 24.4 Isomerism |
| Figure 24.21 Nonsuperimposable Mirror Images | 24.4 Isomerism |
| Figure 24.22 Polarizer | 24.4 Isomerism |
| Figure 24.26 Determination of the Absorption Spectrum of a Solution | 24.5 Color and Magnetism |
| Figure 24.27 Visible Spectrum of $[Ti(H_2O)_6]^{3+}$ | 24.5 Color and Magnetism |
| Figure 24.29 Effects of Octahedral Crystal-Field on *d* Orbitals | 24.6 Crystal-Field Theory |
| Figure 24.30 Orientation of *d* Orbitals Relative to Octahedral Array of Negative Charges | 24.6 Crystal-Field Theory |
| Figure 24.32 Crystal-Field Splitting | 24.6 Crystal-Field Theory |
| Figure 24.38 Ligand-to-Metal Charge Transition | 24.6 Crystal-Field Theory |

| **On MediaPortfolio:** | **Section:** |
|---|---|
| Figure 24.10 Porphine Molecule | 24.2 Ligands with More Than One Donor Atom |
| Figure 24.13 Structure of Chlorophyll *a* | 24.2 Ligands with More Than One Donor Atom |
| Table 24.2 Some Common Ligands | 24.3 Nomenclature of Coordination Chemistry |
| Figure 24.28 Metal-Ligand Bond in a Complex Represented as a Lewis Acid-Base Interaction | 24.6 Crystal-Field Theory |
| Figure 24.34 Population of *d* Orbitals in High- and Low-Spin Complexes | 24.6 Crystal-Field Theory |
| Figure 24.36 Energies of *d* Orbitals in Square-Planar Complexes | 24.6 Crystal-Field Theory |

| **Animations:** | **Section:** |
|---|---|
| Isomerism | 24.3 Isomerism |
| Optical Activity | 24.3 Isomerism |

| **Activities:** | **Section:** |
|---|---|
| Color Wheel Activity | 24.5 Color and Magnetism |

| | |
|---|---|
| *d*-Orbital Populations in Cobalt Complexes | 24.6 Crystal-Field Theory |
| Crystal Field Theory: Chromium Complexes | 24.6 Crystal-Field Theory |

| **3-D Models:** | **Section:** |
|---|---|
| Ethylenediamine | 24.2 Ligands with More Than One Donor Atom |
| Oxalate Ion | 24.2 Ligands with More Than One Donor Atom |
| $[EDTA]^{4-}$ | 24.2 Ligands with More Than One Donor Atom |

# Other Resources

| **Further Readings:** | **Section:** |
|---|---|
| A Stability Ruler for Metal-Ion Complexes | 24.1 Metal Complexes |
| A Coordination Geometry Table of the *d*-Block Elements and Their Ions | 24.1 Metal complexes |
| Some Linguistic Detail on Chelation | 24.2 Ligands with More Than One Donor Atom |
| EDTA-Type Chelating Agents in Everyday Consumer Products: Some Medicinal and Personal Care Products | 24.2 Ligands with More Than One Donor Atom |
| Selecting and Using Chelating Agents | 24.2 Ligands with More Than One Donor Atom |
| Toxicity of Heavy Metals and Biological Defense: Principles and Applications in Bioinorganic Chemistry, Part VII. | 24.2 Ligands with More Than One Donor Atom |
| The Biochemistry of Some Iron Porphyrin Complexes | 24.2 Ligands with More Than One Donor Atom |
| Hemoglobin: Its Occurrence, Structure, and Adaptation | 24.2 Ligands with More Than One Donor Atom |
| Blood-Chemistry Tutorials: Teaching Biological Applications of General Chemistry Material | 24.2 Ligands with More Than One Donor Atom |
| Iron as Nutrient and Poison | 24.2 Ligands with More Than One Donor Atom |
| Iron Deficiency | 24.2 Ligands with More Than One Donor Atom |
| The Chemical Pigments of Plants | 24.2 Ligands with More Than One Donor Atom |
| Mirror-Image Molecules: New Techniques Promise More Potent Drugs and Pesticides | 24.4 Isomerism |
| Introducing Stereochemistry to Non-science Majors | 24.4 Isomerism |
| Chiral Drugs 24.4 Isomerism | |
| Pictorial Analogies VIII: Types of Formulas and Structural Isomers | 24.4 Isomerism |
| Color Classification of Coordination Compounds | 24.4 Color and Magnetism |
| Hope Springs Eternal | 24.4 Color and Magnetism |

| **Live Demonstrations:** | **Section:** |
|---|---|
| Cobalt Complexes: Changing Coordination Numbers | 24.1 Metal Complexes |
| Changing Coordination Numbers: Nickel Complexes | 24.1 Metal Complexes |
| Precipitates and Complexes of Copper (II) | 24.1 Metal Complexes |
| Separating Metallic Iron from Cereal | 24.2 Ligands with More Than One Donor Atom |

# Chapter 24. Chemistry of Coordination Compounds

## Lecture Outline

### 24.1 Metal Complexes[1,2]

- **Metal complexes** (or *complexes)* have a metal ion (which can have a 0 oxidation state) bonded to a number of molecules or ions.
  - If the complex has a net electrical charge it is called a **complex ion**.
- Compounds that contain complexes are known as **coordination compounds.**
- Most coordination compounds are metal compounds formed by Lewis acid-base interactions involving transition metal ions.
  - The molecules or ions surrounding the metal ion in a complex are called **ligands**.
    - The ligands act as Lewis bases.
      - Ligands are usually either anions or polar molecules.
      - They have at least one unshared pair of valence electrons.
    - The metal ion functions as a Lewis acid (electron-pair acceptor).
      - The ligands are said to *coordinate* to the metal.

### The Development of Coordination Chemistry: Werner's Theory[3,4]

- Alfred Werner proposed:
  - Metal ions exhibit a primary and secondary valence.
    - Primary valence: The oxidation state of the metal.
    - Secondary valence: The number of atoms directly bonded to the metal ion.
      - This is the **coordination number**.
  - The central metal and ligands bound to it are the **coordination sphere** of the complex.
    - Example: $[Co(NH_3)_6]Cl_3$
      - $Co^{3+}$ is the metal ion.
      - $NH_3$ groups are ligands.
  - When $Cl^-$ is part of the coordination sphere, it is tightly bound and not released when the complex is dissolved in water.
      - Example: $[Co(NH_3)_5Cl]Cl_2$.
- Different arrangements of ligands are possible.
  - Example: there are two ways to arrange the ligands in $[Co(NH_3)_4Cl_2]^+$.
    - In *cis*-$[Co(NH_3)_4Cl_2]^+$:
      - The chloride ligands occupy adjacent vertices of the octahedral arrangement.
    - In *trans*-$[Co(NH_3)_4Cl_2]^+$:
      - The chlorides are opposite each other.

### The Metal-Ligand Bond

- The metal-ligand bond is an interaction between:
- A Lewis acid (the metal ion with its empty valence orbitals) and
- A Lewis base (the ligand with its unshared pairs of electrons).
- Ligands can alter the properties of the metal.

---

[1] "A Stability Ruler for Metal Ion Complexes" from Further Readings
[2] "Cobalt Complexes: Changing Coordination Numbers" from Live Demonstrations
[3] Figure 24.1 from MediaPortfolio and Transparency Pack
[4] "Changing Coordination Numbers: Nickel Complexes" from Further Readings

- Complexes display physical and chemical properties different from those of the metal ion or the ligands.
- For example, consider the properties of $Ag^+$ and a complex involving $Ag^+$ and $CN^-$:

$$Ag^+(aq) + e^- \rightarrow Ag(s) \qquad E° = +0.799\ V$$
$$[Ag(CN)_2]^-(aq) + e^- \rightarrow Ag(s) + 2CN^-(aq) \qquad E° = -0.310\ V$$

### Charges, Coordination Numbers, and Geometries[5,6,7,8,9]

- The charge on a complex ion equals the sum of the charge on the metal plus the charges on the ligands.
- In a complex the **donor atom** is the atom bonded directly to the metal.
- The coordination number is the number of ligands attached to the metal.
  - The most common coordination numbers are 4 and 6.
  - Some metal ions have a constant coordination number (e.g., $Cr^{3+}$ and $Co^{3+}$ have coordination numbers of 6).
  - The size of the metal ion and the size of the ligand affect the coordination number (e.g., iron(III) can coordinate to six fluorides but only to four chlorides; thus $[FeF_6]^{3-}$ and $[FeCl_4]^-$ are stable).
  - The amount of charge transferred from ligand to metal affects the coordination number.
    - The greater the transfer of negative charge to the metal, the lower the coordination number tends to be.
    - For example, $[Ni(NH_3)_6]^{2+}$ and $[Ni(CN)_4]^{2-}$ are both stable.
- Four-coordinate complexes have two common geometries: tetrahedral and square planar.
  - Square-planar complexes are commonly seen for $d^8$ metal ions such as $Pt^{2+}$, $Au^{3+}$, and $Cu^{2+}$.
- Six-coordinate complexes are usually octahedral.

## 24.2 Ligands with More Than One Donor Atom[10,11,12,13,14,15,16,17]

- **Monodentate ligands** bind through one donor atom only.
  - Therefore they can occupy only one coordination site.
- **Polydentate** ligands (or **chelating agents**) have two or more donor atoms that can simultaneously coordinate to the metal ion.
  - They can thus occupy more than one coordination site.
  - Example: *ethylenediamine* ($H_2NCH_2CH_2NH_2$)
    - The abbreviation for ethylenediamine is "en."
    - There are two nitrogen atoms that can act as ligands.
    - They are far enough apart on the molecule that it can wrap around a metal ion.
    - The molecule can simultaneously coordinate to two sites on the metal ion.

---

[5] "A Coordination Geometry Table of the *d*-Block Elements and Their Ions" from Further Readings
[6] Figure 24.3 from MediaPortfolio and Transparency Pack
[7] Figure 24.4 from MediaPortfolio and Transparency Pack
[8] "Precipitates and Complexes of Copper(II)" from Live Demonstrations
[9] "Some Linguistic Detail on Chelation" from Further Readings
[10] "Ethylenediamine" 3-D Model from MediaPortfolio
[11] Figure 24.5 from MediaPortfolio and Transparency Pack
[12] "Oxalate Ion" 3-D Model from MediaPortfolio
[13] "$[EDTA]^{4-}$" 3-D Model from MediaPortfolio
[14] Figure 24.6 from MediaPortfolio and Transparency Pack
[15] "EDTA-Type Chelating Agents in Everyday Consumer Products: Some Medicinal and Personal Care Products" from Further Readings
[16] "Selecting and Using Chelating Agents" from Further Readings
[17] Figure 24.7 from MediaPortfolio and Transparency Pack

- Ethylenediamine is thus an example of a **bidentate ligand**.
- The octahedral $[Co(en)_3]^{3+}$ is a typical "en" complex.
- Chelating agents form more stable complexes than do monodentate ligands.
  - Example:

$$[Ni(H_2O)_6]^{2+}(aq) + 6NH_3 \leftrightharpoons [Ni(NH_3)_6]^{2+}(aq) + 6H_2O(l) \quad K_f = 1.2 \times 10^9$$
$$[Ni(H_2O)_6]^{2+}(aq) + 3en \leftrightharpoons [Ni(en)_3]^{2+}(aq) + 6H_2O(l) \quad K_f = 6.8 \times 10^{17}$$

  - The **chelate effect** refers to the larger formation constants for polydentate ligands as compared with corresponding monodentate ligands.
- Chelating agents are sometimes referred to as *sequestering agents* .
  - In medicine, sequestering agents are used to selectively remove toxic metal ions (e.g., $Hg^{2+}$ and $Pb^{2+}$) while leaving biologically important metals.
- One very important chelating agent is ethylenediaminetetraacetate ($EDTA^{4-}$).
  - EDTA occupies six coordination sites, for example $[CoEDTA]^-$ is an octahedral $Co^{3+}$ complex.
  - Both N atoms and O atoms coordinate to the metal.
  - EDTA is used in consumer products to complex the metal ions that would otherwise catalyze unwanted decomposition reactions.

## Metals and Chelates in Living Systems[18,19,20,21,22,23,24,25,26,27,28,29,30]

- Nine of the 24 elements required for human life are transition metals (V, Cr, Mn, Fe, Co, Cu, Zn, Mo, and Ni).
- Many natural chelates coordinate to the *porphine* molecule.
  - Porphine forms a tetradentate ligand with the loss of the two protons bound to its nitrogen atoms.
  - A **porphyrin** is a metal complex derived from porphine.
    - Two important porphyrins are heme (which contains $Fe^{2+}$) and chlorophyll (which contains $Mg^{2+}$).
- Two important heme-containing molecules are myoglobin and hemoglobin.
  - These proteins are important oxygen-binding proteins. Myoglobin is found in muscle tissue, while hemoglobin is found in red blood cells.
    - In each case the heme iron is coordinated to six ligands.
      - Four of these are nitrogen atoms of the porphyrin ring.
      - One ligand is a nitrogen atom that is part of one of the amino acids of the protein.
    - The sixth coordination site around the iron is occupied by either $O_2$ or water.
      - Other ligands, such as CO, can also serve as the sixth ligand.
- A different metal complex is important in the process of **photosynthesis**.

---

[18] "Toxicity of Heavy Metals and Biological Defense: Principles and Applications in Bioinorganic Chemistry" from Further Readings
[19] "The Biochemistry of Some Iron Porphyrin Complexes" from Further Readings
[20] Figure 24.10 from MediaPortfolio
[21] Figure 24.11 from MediaPortfolio and Transparency Pack
[22] "Hemoglobin: Its Occurrence, Structure, and Adaptation" from Further Readings
[23] Figure 24.12 from MediaPortfolio and Transparency Pack
[24] Figure 24.13 from MediaPortfolio
[25] Figure 24.14 from MediaPortfolio and Transparency Pack
[26] "Blood-Chemistry Tutorials: Teaching Biological Applications of General Chemistry Material" from Further Readings
[27] "The Chemical Pigments of Plants" from Further Readings
[28] "Iron as a Nutrient and Poison" from Further Readings
[29] "Iron Deficiency" from Further Readings
[30] "Separating Metallic Iron from Cereal" from Live Demonstrations

- Photosynthesis is the conversion of $CO_2$ and water to glucose and oxygen in plants in the presence of light.
- The synthesis of one mole of sugar requires the absorption and utilization of 48 moles of photons.
- **Chlorophylls** are the plant pigments that absorb these photons of light.
  - **Chlorophyll *a*** is the most abundant chlorophyll.
  - The other chlorophylls differ in the structure of the side chains.
  - $Mg^{2+}$ is in the center of the porphyrin-like ring.
  - The alternating double bonds give chlorophyll its green color (it absorbs red light).
  - Chlorophyll absorbs red light (655 nm) and blue light (430 nm).
  - The absorbed energy is ultimately used to drive the endothermic reaction:

$$6CO_2 + 6H_2O \rightarrow C_6H_{12}O_6 + 6O_2$$

- Plant photosynthesis sustains life on Earth.

## 24.3 Nomenclature of Coordination Chemistry[31]

- We can name complexes in a systematic manner using some simple nomenclature rules.
  - For salts, the name of the cation is given before the name of the anion.
    - Example: In $[Co(NH_3)_5Cl]Cl_2$ we name $[Co(NH_3)_5Cl]^{2+}$ before $Cl^-$.
  - Within a complex ion or molecule, the ligands are named (in alphabetical order) before the metal.
    - Example: $[Co(NH_3)_5Cl]^{2+}$ is pentaamminechlorocobalt(III).
    - Note that the *penta* portion indicates the number of $NH_3$ groups and is therefore not considered in alphabetizing the ligands.
  - The names of anionic ligands end in *o*, and for neutral ligands the name of the molecule is used.
    - Example: $Cl^-$ is *chloro* and $CN^-$ is *cyano.*
    - Exceptions: $H_2O$ (aqua) and $NH_3$ (ammine).
  - Greek prefixes are used to indicate the number of ligands (di-, tri-, tetra-, penta-, and hexa-).
    - Exception: If the ligand name already has a Greek prefix.
      - Then enclose the name of the ligand in parentheses and use bis-, tris-, tetrakis-, pentakis-, and hexakis-.
  - Example $[Co(en)_3]Cl_3$ is tris(ethylenediamine)cobalt(III) chloride.
  - If the complex is an anion, the name ends in -ate.
    - For example, $[CoCl_4]^{2-}$ is the tetrachlorocobaltate(II) ion.
  - The oxidation state of the metal is given in Roman numerals in parenthesis after the name of the metal.

## 24.4 Isomerism[32,33]

- Two compounds with the same formulas but different arrangements of atoms are called **isomers.**
- Two kinds of isomers are:
  - **Structural isomers** have different bonds.
  - **Stereoisomers** have the same bonds but different spatial arrangements of the bonds.

### Structural Isomerism

- Two examples of structural isomerism in coordination chemistry:
  - **Linkage isomerism:**
  - *Linkage isomers*: A ligand is capable of coordinating to a metal in two different ways.
    - Example: Nitrite can coordinate via a nitrogen or an oxygen atom.
      - If the nitrogen atom is the donor atom, the ligand is called *nitro*.

---

[31] Table 24.2 from MediaPortfolio

[32] "Pictorial Analogies VIII: Types of Formulas and Structural Isomers" from Further Readings

[33] Figure 24.18 from MediaPortfolio and Transparency Pack

- If the oxygen atom is the donor atom, the ligand is called *nitrito*.
- The ligand thiocyanate ($SCN^-$) is also capable of being involved in linkage isomerism.
- **Coordination-sphere isomerism**:
- *Coordination-sphere isomers* differ in the ligands that are directly bound to the metal.
  - Example: $CrCl_3(H_2O)_6$ exists in three different forms:
    - $[Cr(H_2O)_6]Cl_3$
    - $[Cr(H_2O)_5Cl]Cl_2 \cdot H_2O$
    - $[Cr(H_2O)_4Cl_2]Cl \cdot 2H_2O$

**Stereoisomerism**[34,35,36,37,38,39,40,41]

- Stereoisomers have the same connectivity but different spatial arrangements of atoms.
- Two types of stereoisomerism:
  - **Geometrical isomerism**:
    - In *geometrical isomerism* the arrangement of the atoms is different although the same bonds are present.
    - Example: *cis* and *trans* isomers.
      - Consider square planar $[Pt(NH_3)_2Cl_2]$.
        - The two $NH_3$ ligands can either be 90° apart or 180° apart.
        - Therefore, the spatial arrangement of the atoms is different.
      - In the *cis* isomer, the two $NH_3$ groups are adjacent.
        - The *cis* isomer (cisplatin) is used in chemotherapy.
      - In the *trans* isomer, the two $NH_3$ groups are across from each other.
      - It is possible to find *cis* and *trans* isomers in octahedral complexes.
        - For example, *cis*-$[Co(NH_3)_4Cl_2]^+$ is violet.
        - The *trans*-$[Co(NH_3)_4Cl_2]^+$ isomer is green.
        - The two isomers also have different solubilities.
  - **Optical isomerism**.
  - *Optical isomers* are nonsuperimposable mirror images.
    - These are referred to as **enantiomers**.
    - Complexes that exist as enantiomers are **chiral**.
      - Chiral species are molecules or ions that can not be superimposed on their mirror image.
    - Most physical and chemical properties of enantiomers are identical.
      - Therefore, enantiomers are very difficult to separate.
    - Optical isomers are differentiated from each other by their interaction with plane-polarized light.
      - Enantiomers are capable of rotating the plane of polarized light.
      - Horizontally polarized light is passed through an optically active solution.
      - As the light emerges from the solution, the plane of polarity has changed.
      - The mirror image of an enantiomer will rotate the plane of polarized light by the same amount in the opposite direction.

---

[34] "Introducing Stereochemistry to Non-science Majors" from Further Readings
[35] Figure 24.20 from MediaPortfolio and Transparency Pack
[36] "Isomerism" Animation from MediaPortfolio
[37] "Chiral Drugs" from Further Readings
[38] "Optical Activity" Animation from MediaPortfolio
[39] "Mirror-Image Molecules: New Techniques Promise More Potent Drugs and Pesticides" from Further Readings
[40] Figure 24.21 from MediaPortfolio and Transparency Pack
[41] Figure 24.22 from MediaPortfolio and Transparency Pack

- **Dextrorotatory** solutions rotate the plane of polarized light to the right.
  - This isomer is called the *dextro* or *d* isomer.
- **Levorotatory** solutions rotate the plane of polarized light to the left.
  - This isomer is called the *levo* or *l* isomer.

- Chiral molecules are said to be **optically active** because of their effect on light.
  - **Racemic** mixtures contain equal amounts of *l* and *d* isomers.
    - They have no overall effect on the plane of polarized light.
- The 2001 Nobel Prize in Chemistry was awarded to W.S. Knowles and K. B. Sharples of the United States and R. Noyori of Japan for work on the catalysis of chiral reactions.

## 24.5 Color and Magnetism

### Color[42,43,44,45,46]

- The color of a complex depends on the metal, the ligands present, and the oxidation state of the metal.
  - For example, pale blue $[Cu(H_2O)_6]^{2+}$ can be converted into dark blue $[Cu(NH_3)_6]^{2+}$ by adding $NH_3(aq)$.
- A partially filled *d* orbital is usually required for a complex to be colored.
  - Thus ions with completely empty (e.g., $Al^{3+}$ or $Ti^{4+}$) or completely filled (e.g., $Zn^{2+}$) *d* subshells are usually colorless.
- Colored compounds absorb visible light.
  - The color perceived is the sum of the light reflected or transmitted by the complex.
    - An object will have a particular color if it reflects or transmits that color or if it absorbs light of the **complementary** color.
      - An object appears black if it absorbs all wavelengths of light.
      - An object appears white or colorless if it absorbs no visible light.
- A plot of the amount of absorbed light versus wavelength is called the **absorption spectrum**.

### Magnetism

- Many transition-metal complexes are paramagnetic (i.e., they have unpaired electrons).
- Consider a $d^6$ metal ion:
  - Compounds of $[Co(NH_3)_6]^{3+}$ have no unpaired electrons, but compounds of $[CoF_6]^{3-}$ have four unpaired electrons per metal ion.
- We need to develop a bonding theory to account for both color and magnetism in transition metal complexes.

## 24.6 Crystal-Field Theory[47,48,49,50,51,52]

- **Crystal-field** theory describes bonding in transition-metal complexes.
- The formation of a complex is a Lewis acid-base reaction.

---

[42] "Color Wheel Activity" from MediaPortfolio
[43] "Color Classification of Coordination Compounds" from Further Readings
[44] "Hope Springs Eternal" from Further Readings
[45] Figure 24.26 from MediaPortfolio and Transparency Pack
[46] Figure 24.27 from MediaPortfolio and Transparency Pack
[47] Figure 24.28 from MediaPortfolio
[48] Figure 24.29 from MediaPortfolio and Transparency Pack
[49] Figure 24.30 from MediaPortfolio and Transparency Pack
[50] Figure 24.32 from MediaPortfolio and Transparency Pack
[51] "*d*-Orbital Population in Cobalt Complexes" Activity from MediaPortfolio
[52] "Crystal Field Theory: Chromium Complexes" Activity from MediaPortfolio

- Both electrons in the bond come from the ligand and are donated into an empty hybridized orbital on the metal.
- Charge is donated from the ligand to the metal.

- Assumption in crystal-field theory: The interaction between ligand and metal is electrostatic.
  - Orbitals which point directly at the ligands have their energies raised more than those that point between the ligands.
  - The complex metal ion has a lower energy than the separated metal and ligands.
  - However, repulsion occurs between the ligands and the *d* electrons of the metal.
- In an octahedral field, the five *d* orbitals do not have the same energy: three degenerate orbitals have a lower energy than two degenerate orbitals.
  - We assume an octahedral array of negative charges placed around the metal ion (which is positive).
    - The $d_{z^2}$ and $d_{x^2-y^2}$ orbitals lie on the same axes as negative charges.
      - Therefore, there is a large, unfavorable interaction between the ligand and these orbitals.
      - These orbitals form the degenerate high-energy pair of energy levels.
    - The $d_{xy}$, $d_{yz}$, and $d_{xz}$ orbitals are oriented between the negative charges.
      - Therefore, there is a smaller repulsion between ligands and these orbitals.
      - These orbitals form the degenerate low-energy set of energy levels.
    - The energy gap between these two sets of *d* orbitals is labeled Δ.
      - Δ is referred to as the *crystal-field splitting energy*.
- For example, consider the $[Ti(H_2O)_6]^{3+}$ complex.
  - $Ti^{3+}$ is a $d^1$ metal ion.
  - Therefore, the one electron is in a low energy orbital.
  - For $Ti^{3+}$, the gap between energy levels, Δ, is of the order of the wavelength of visible light.
  - As the $[Ti(H_2O)_6]^{3+}$ complex absorbs visible light the electron is promoted to a higher energy level.
    - This transition is called a ***d-d*-transition** because it involves exciting an electron from one set of *d* orbitals to the other.
  - Because there is only one *d*, electron there is only one possible absorption line for this molecule.
  - The color of a complex depends on the magnitude of Δ, which, in turn, depends on the metal and the type of ligand.
    - $[Ti(H_2O)_6]^{3+}$ is purple, $[Fe(H_2O)_6]^{3+}$ is light violet, $[Cr(H_2O)_6]^{3+}$ is violet, and $Cr(NH_3)_6]^{3+}$ is yellow
- A **spectrochemical series** is a listing of ligands in order of their ability to increase Δ:

$$Cl^- < F^- < H_2O < NH_3 < en < NO_2^- \text{ (N-bonded)} < CN^-$$

  - ***Weak-field ligands*** lie on the low end of the spectrochemical series.
  - ***Strong-field ligands*** lie on the high end of the spectrochemical series.
  - Example: When the ligand coordinated to $Cr^{3+}$ is changed from the weak-filed ligand $F^-$ to the strong-field ligand $CN^-$, Δ increases and the color of the complex changes from green (in $[CrF_6]^{3+}$) to yellow (in $[Cr(CN)_6]^{3-}$).

## Electron Configurations in Octahedral Complexes[53,54,55]

- Recall: that when transition metals form cations, *s* electrons are lost first.
  - Thus, $Ti^{3+}$ is a $d^1$ ion, $V^{3+}$ is a $d^2$ ion and $Cr^{3+}$ is a $d^3$ ion.
- If one to three electrons add to the *d* orbitals in an octahedral complex ion, Hund's rule applies.

---

[53] Figure 24.34 from MediaPortfolio
[54] Figure 24.36 from MediaPortfolio
[55] Figure 24.38 from MediaPortfolio and Transparency Pack

    - The first three electrons go into different *d* orbitals with their spins parallel.
- We have a choice for the placement of the fourth electron:
    - If it goes into a higher-energy orbital, then there is an energy cost ($\Delta$).
    - If it goes into a lower-energy orbital, there is a different energy cost (called the **spin-pairing energy** due to pairing with the electron already present).
        - Weak-field ligands (which have a small $\Delta$) tend to favor adding electrons to the higher-energy orbitals (**high-spin complexes**) because $\Delta$ is less than the spin-pairing energy.
        - Strong-field ligands (which have a large $\Delta$) tend to favor adding electrons to lower-energy orbitals (**low-spin complexes**) because $\Delta$ is greater than the spin-pairing energy.

## Tetrahedral and Square Planar Complexes

- By using the same arguments as for the octahedral case, we can derive the relative orbital energies for *d* orbitals in a tetrahedral field.
    - The splitting of the *d* orbitals is the opposite of that observed for an octahedral field.
        - The $d_{xy}$, $d_{yz}$, and $d_{xz}$ orbitals are of lower energy than the $d_{z^2}$ and $d_{x^2-y^2}$ orbitals).
    - Because there are only four ligands, $\Delta$ for a tetrahedral field is smaller than $\Delta$ for an octahedral field.
    - This causes all tetrahedral complexes to be high-spin.
- Square-planar complexes can be thought of as follows: Start with an octahedral complex and remove two ligands along the *z*-axis.
    - As a consequence the four planar ligands are drawn in towards the metal.
    - Relative to the octahedral field, the $d_{z^2}$ orbital is greatly lowered in energy, the $d_{yz}$, and $d_{xz}$ orbitals lowered in energy, the $d_{xy}$, and $d_{x^2-y^2}$ orbitals are raised in energy.
    - Most $d^8$ metal ions form square-planar complexes.
    - The majority of complexes are low-spin (i.e., diamagnetic).
    - Examples: $Pd^{2+}$, $Pt^{2+}$, $Ir^+$, and $Au^{3+}$.

## Further Readings:

1. D. Venkataraman, Yuhua Du. Scott R. Wilson, A. Hirsch, Peng Zhang, and Jeffrey S. Moore, "A Coordination Geometry Table of the *d*-Block Elements and Their Ions," *J. Chem. Educ.*, Vol. 74, **1997**, 915–918.

2. J. Roger Hart, "EDTA-Type Chelating Agents in Everyday Consumer Products: Some Medicinal and Personal Care Products," *J. Chem. Educ.*, Vol. 61, **1984**, 1060–1061.

3. Ei-Ichiro Ochiai, "Toxicity of Heavy Metals and Biological Defense: Principles and Applications in Bioinorganic Chemistry, Part VII," *J. Chem. Educ.*, Vol. 72, **1995**, 479–484.

4. N. M. Senozan and R. L. Hunt, "Hemoglobin: Its Occurrence, Structure, and Adaptation," *J. Chem. Educ.*, Vol. 59, **1982**, 173–178.

5. N. M. Senozan and M. P. Christiano, "Iron As Nutrient and Poison," *J. Chem. Educ.*, Vol. 74, **1997**, 1060–1063.

6. Nevin S. Scrimshaw, "Iron Deficiency," *Scientific American*, **October 1991**, 46–52.

7. Rachel E. Casiday, Dewey Holten, Richard Krathen, and Regina F. Frey, "Blood-Chemistry Tutorials: Teaching Biological Applications of General Chemistry Material," *J. Chem. Educ.*, Vol. 78, **2001**, 1210–1214. The relationship between oxygen transport, iron transport, blood buffering, kidney dialysis and general chemistry topics is discussed.

8. Colin J. Rix, "The Biochemistry of Some Iron Porphyrin Complexes," *J. Chem. Educ.*, Vol. 59, **1982**, 389-392.

9. Joy Alkema and Spencer L. Seager, "The Chemical Pigments of Plants," *J. Chem. Educ.*, Vol. 59, **1982**, 183–186.

10. Daniel T. Haworth, "Some Linguistic Detail on Chelation," *J. Chem. Educ.*, Vol. 75, **1998**, 47.

11. Mark Conway, Smallwood Holoman, Ladell Jones, Ray Leenhouts, and Gerald Williamson, "Selecting and Using Chelating Agents," *Chemical Engineering*, Vol. 106(3), **March 1999**, 86–90.

12. Karen F. Schmidt, "Mirror–Image Molecules: New Techniques Promise More Potent Drugs and Pesticides," *Science News*, **May 29, 1993**, 348–350.

13. Stephen C. Stinson, "Chiral Drugs," *Chemical and Engineering News*, **September 19, 1994**, 38–57.

14. John J. Fortman, "Pictorial Analogies VIII: Types of Formulas and Structural Isomers," *J. Chem. Educ.*, Vol. 70, **1993**, 755.

15. Hannia Lujan-Upton, "Introducing Stereochemistry to Non-science Majors," *J. Chem. Educ.*, Vol. 78, **2001**, 475–477.

16. Laurence Poncini and Franz L. Wimmer, "Color Classification of Coordination Compounds," *J. Chem. Educ.*, Vol. 64, **1987**, 1001–1002.

17. R. Bruce. Martin, "A Stability Ruler for Metal Ion Complexes," *J. Chem. Educ*., Vol. 64, **1987**, 402.

18. Anthony Butler and Rossyln Nicholson, "Hope Springs Eternal," *Chemistry in Britain*, Vol. 34, **December 1998**, 34–36. A brief article investigating the color of the Hope diamond and other colored gems.

## Live Demonstrations:

1. Bassam Z. Shakhashiri, "Precipatates and Complexes of Copper (II)," *Chemical Demonstrations: A Handbook for Teachers of Chemistry, Volume 1* (Madison: The University of Wisconsin Press, **1983**), pp. 318–323. The sequential addition of various agents to beakers of $CuSO_4$ or $Cu(NO_3)_2$ yield a variety of colored copper complexes and precipitates.

2. Lee R. Summerlin and James L. Ealy, Jr., "Cobalt Complexes: Changing Coordination Numbers," *Chemical Demonstrations, A Sourcebook for Teachers,* (Washington: American Chemical Society, **1985**), pp. 32–33. The coordination number of cobalt in cobalt chloride solutions is changed as the solutions are mixed with varying amounts of ethanol.

3. Lee R. Summerlin, Christie L. Borgford, and Julie B. Ealy, "Changing Coordination Numbers: Nickel Complexes," *Chemical Demonstrations, A Sourcebook for Teachers, Volume 2* (Washington: American Chemical Society, **1987**), pp. 73–74.

4. Lee. R. Summerlin,, Christie L. Borgford, and Julie B. Ealy, "Separating Metallic Iron from Cereal," *Chemical Demonstrations, A Sourcebook for Teachers*, *Volume 2* (Washington: American Chemical Society, **1988**), p. 62. Iron is removed from fortified cereal in this simple demonstration.

# Chapter 25. The Chemistry of Life: Organic and Biological Chemistry

## Media Resources

### Figures and Tables

| **In Transparency Pack and on MediaPortfolio:** | **Section:** |
|---|---|
| Figure 25.1 Molecular Models Molecules | 25.1 Some General Characteristics of Organic |
| Figure 25.3 Names, Structures and Molecular Formulas | 25.2 Introduction to Hydrocarbons |
| Table 25.1 First Several Members of the Straight-Chain Alkane Series | 25.3 Alkanes |
| Figure 25.4 Representations of Methane | 25.3 Alkanes |
| Figure 25.5 Three-Dimensional Models for Propane | 25.3 Alkanes |
| Table 25.2 Condensed Structural Formulas and Common Names for Several Alkyl Groups | 25.3 Alkanes |
| Figure 25.11 Rotation About a Carbon-Carbon Double Bond | 25.4 Unsaturated Hydrocarbons |
| Figure 25.12 Energy Profile for Addition of HBr to 2-Butene | 25.4 Unsaturated Hydrocarbons |
| Table 25.4 Common Functional Groups in Organic Compounds | 25.5 Functional Groups: Alcohols and Ethers |
| Figure 25.14 Important Alcohols | 25.5 Functional Groups: Alcohols and Ethers |
| Figure 25.17 Common Carboxylic Acids | 25.6 Compounds with a Carbonyl Group |
| Figure 25.19 Enantiomers of 2-Bromopentane | 25.7 Chirality in Organic Chemistry |
| Figure 25.20 S-Ibuprofen | 25.7 Chirality in Organic Chemistry |
| Figure 25.21 Some Amino Acids | 25.9 Proteins |
| Figure 25.22 Enantiomers of Alanine | 25.9 Proteins |
| Figure 25.24 Alpha-Helix | 25.9 Proteins |
| Figure 25.27 Cyclic Forms of Glucose | 25.10 Carbohydrates |
| Figure 25.31 Structures of Starch and Cellulose | 25.10 Carbohydrates |
| Figure 25.32 Structure of Deoxyadenylic Acid | 25.11 Nucleic Acids |
| Figure 25.33 Structure of a Polynucleotide | 25.11 Nucleic Acids |
| Figure 25.34 DNA Double Helix | 25.11 Nucleic Acids |
| Figure 25.35 Complementary Base Pairs | 25.11 Nucleic Acids |

| **On MediaPortfolio:** | **Section:** |
|---|---|
| Figure 25.6 Isomers of Butane and Pentane | 25.3 Alkanes |
| Figure 25.7 Structures of Cycloalkanes | 25.3 Alkanes |
| Figure 25.10 Isomers of Butene | 25.4 Unsaturated Hydrocarbons |
| Figure 25.13 Aromatic Compounds | 25.4 Unsaturated Hydrocarbons |
| Figure 25.26 Glucose and Fructose | 25.10 Carbohydrates |
| Figure 25.28 Structures of Sucrose and Lactose | 25.10 Carbohydrates |
| Figure 25.29 Structure of Starch | 25.10 Carbohydrates |
| Figure 25.30 Structure of Cellulose | 25.10 Carbohydrates |
| Figure 25.36 DNA Replication | 25.11 Nucleic Acids |

| **Animations:** | **Section:** |
|---|---|
| Chirality | 25.7 Chirality in Organic Chemistry |
| Optical Activity | 25.7 Chirality in Organic Chemistry |
| Proteins and Amino Acids | 25.9 Proteins |

| **Activities:** | **Section:** |
|---|---|
| Boiling Point | 25.2 Introduction to Hydrocarbons |
| Addition Reactions of Alkenes | 25.4 Unsaturated Hydrocarbons |

| **3-D Models:** | **Section:** |
|---|---|
| Ethane | 25.2 Introduction to Hydrocarbons |
| Ethylene | 25.2 Introduction to Hydrocarbons |
| Acetylene | 25.2 Introduction to Hydrocarbons |
| Benzene | 25.2 Introduction to Hydrocarbons |
| *cis*-2-Butene | 25.4 Unsaturated Hydrocarbons |
| *trans*-2-Butene | 25.4 Unsaturated Hydrocarbons |
| Enantiomers of Alanine | 25.9 Proteins |
| DNA | 25.11 Nucleic Acids |

## Other Resources

| **Further Readings:** | **Section:** |
|---|---|
| Alkanes: Abundant, Pervasive, Important, and Essential | 25.3 Alkanes |
| A Simple Method of Drawing Stereoisomers from Complicated Symmetrical Structures | 25.3 Alkanes |
| Chemistry in the Dyeing of Eggs | 25.4 Unsaturated Hydrocarbons |
| Ester, What's in My Food? | 25.6 Compounds with a Carbonyl Group |
| Trans Fatty Acids | 25.6 Compounds with a Carbonyl Group |
| Icie Macy Hoobler: Pioneer Woman Biochemist | 25.8 Introduction to Biochemistry |
| Why Teach Biochemistry | 25.8 Introduction to Biochemistry |
| Reversible Oxygenation of Oxygen Transport Proteins | 25.9 Proteins |
| The Use of Stick Figures to Visualize Fischer Projections | 25.10 Carbohydrates |
| The Biochemistry of Brewing | 25.10 Carbohydrates |
| Carbohydrate Stereochemistry | 25.10 Carbohydrates |
| A New Method to Convert the Fischer Projection of Monosaccharide to the Haworth Projection | 25.10 Carbohydrates |
| 'Absolutely' Simple Stereochemistry | 25.10 Carbohydrates |
| An Easy Way to Convert a Fischer Projection into a Zigzag Representation | 25.10 Carbohydrates |
| βrand the Name with the Linkage of the Same | 25.10 Carbohydrates |
| Rosalind Franklin: From Coal to DNA to Plant Viruses | 25.11 Nucleic Acids |
| DNAmonic | 25.11 Nucleic Acids |
| A Simple Demonstration of How Intermolecular Forces Make DNA Helical | 25.11 Nucleic Acids |

| **Live Demonstrations:** | **Section:** |
|---|---|
| Oxidation of Alcohol by $Mn_2O_7$ | 25.5 Functional Groups: Alcohols and Ethers |
| The Disappearing Coffee Cup | 25.6 Compounds with a Carbonyl Group |
| Making Canned Heat | 25.6 Compounds with a Carbonyl Group |
| A Variation of the Starch-Iodine Clock Reaction | 25.10 Carbohydrates |

# Chapter 25. The Chemistry of Life: Organic and Biological Chemistry

## Common Student Misconceptions

- Students interpret straight chain to mean geometrically linear. They need to be reminded of the tetrahedral C atom from VSEPR theory.
- Students should be encouraged to follow the chapter links to review earlier material as they progress through this chapter.

## Lecture Outline

### 25.1 Some General Characteristics of Organic Molecules

- Organic chemistry is the branch of chemistry that studies carbon compounds.
- Biochemistry or *biological chemistry* is the study of the chemistry of living things.

#### The Structures of Organic Molecules[1]

- The shapes of organic and biochemical molecules are important in determining their physical and chemical properties.
- Consider the element carbon:
  - Using the VSEPR model we find that the bonds to carbon involve four electron pairs.
    - The electron pairs are in a tetrahedral arrangement when all four bonds are single bonds.
      - The carbon is $sp^3$ hybridized.
    - A carbon with one double bond shows a trigonal arrangement.
      - The carbon is $sp^2$ hybridized.
    - If the carbon has a triple bond, the arrangement is linear.
      - The carbon is *sp* hybridized.
- C–H bonds occur in almost every organic molecule.

#### The Stabilities of Organic Substances

- The stability of organic substances varies.
- Substances such as benzene have a special stability due to the delocalization of $\pi$ electrons.
- A group of atoms that determines how an organic molecule functions or reacts is a functional group.
  - Functional groups are the center of reactivity in organic molecules.

#### Solubility and Acid-Base Properties of Organic Substances

- The most common bonds in organic substances are carbon-carbon bonds.
  - This results in a low overall polarity of many organic molecules.
    - Such molecules are soluble in nonpolar solvents.
- Organic substances that are soluble in water and other polar solvents have polar groups.
  - Examples: glucose and ascorbic acid (vitamin C).
- Soaps and detergents are examples of molecules that have both a polar part (which is water soluble) and a nonpolar part (which is soluble in nonpolar substances such as fat).
- Many organic molecules contain acidic or basic groups.
  - Carboxylic acids contain the functional group –COOH.
  - Amines are important organic bases.
    - These contain the functional groups $-NH_2$, –NHR or $-NR_2$.

---

[1] Figure 25.1 from MediaPortfolio and Transparency Pack

- Some molecules contain both an acidic and a basic group.

## 25.2 Introduction to Hydrocarbons[2,3,4,5,6,7]

- The simplest class of organic molecules is the *hydrocarbons*.
  - Hydrocarbons consist only of carbon and hydrogen.
  - There are four major classes of hydrocarbons: alkanes, alkenes, alkynes, and aromatics.
- **Alkanes** contain only single bonds.
  - These compounds are also called *saturated hydrocarbons* because they have the largest possible number of hydrogen atoms per carbon.
  - Example: ethane ($C_2H_6$).
- **Alkenes** contain at least one carbon-carbon double bond.
  - They are also called *olefins*.
  - Example: ethylene ($C_2H_4$).
- **Alkynes** contain a carbon-carbon triple bond.
  - Example: acetylene ($C_2H_2$)
- **Aromatic hydrocarbons** have carbon atoms connected in a planar ring structure.
  - The carbons are linked by both $\sigma$ and $\pi$ bonds.
  - The best known example is benzene ($C_6H_6$).
- Alkenes, alkynes and aromatic hydrocarbons are all examples of *unsaturated hydrocarbons*.

## 25.3 Alkanes[8,9]

- The name of the alkane varies according to the number of C atoms present in the chain.
- We can make a table of members of a homologous series of straight-chain alkanes.
  - In this table each member differs by one $CH_2$ unit.
  - The names each end in -ane.
  - The prefix assigned indicates the number of carbon atoms.
    - Example: $CH_4$ is the alkane with a single carbon atom; it is called *meth*ane.
    - The next member of the series is $C_2H_6$, with two carbon atoms; it is called *eth*ane.
- The formulas for alkanes may be written in a notation called *condensed structural formulas*.
  - This notation shows which atoms are bonded to one another but does not require that we draw in all of the bonds.
  - Notice that each carbon in an alkane has four single bonds.

### Structures of Alkanes[10,11]

- VSEPR theory predicts each C atom is tetrahedral.
  - Therefore, each C atom has $sp^3$-hybridized orbitals.
  - Rotation about the C–C bond in alkanes is relatively easy.

### Structural Isomers[12,13]

---

[2] Figure 25.3 from MediaPortfolio and Transparency Pack
[3] "Ethane" 3-D Model from MediaPortfolio
[4] "Ethylene" 3-D Model from MediaPortfolio
[5] "Acetylene" 3-D Model from MediaPortfolio
[6] "Benzene" 3-D Model from MediaPortfolio
[7] "Boiling Point" Activity from MediaPortfolio
[8] Table 25.1 from MediaPortfolio and Transparency Pack
[9] "Alkanes: Abundant, Pervasive, Important, and Essential" from Further Readings
[10] Figure 25.4 from MediaPortfolio and Transparency Pack
[11] Figure 25.5 from MediaPortfolio and Transparency Pack

- In *straight-chain hydrocarbons* the C atoms are joined in a continuous chain.
  - In a straight-chain hydrocarbon no one C atom may be attached to more than two other C atoms.
  - Straight chain hydrocarbons are not linear.
    - Each C atom is tetrahedral, so the chains are bent.
- *Branched-chain hydrocarbons* are possible for alkanes with four or more C atoms.
  - Structures with different branches can be written for the same formula.
    - These compounds are **structural isomers.**
    - Structural isomers have somewhat different physical and chemical properties.

### Nomenclature of Alkanes[14]

- Organic compounds are named according to rules established by the International Union for Pure and Applied Chemistry (IUPAC).
- To name alkanes:
  - Find the longest chain and use it as the base name of the compound.
    - Groups attached to the main chain are called *substituents*.
  - Number the carbon atoms in the longest chain starting with the end closest to a substituent.
    - The preferred numbering will give substituents the lowest numbers.
  - Name and give the location of each substituent.
    - A substituent group formed by removing an H atom from an alkane is called an **alkyl group**.
    - Alkyl groups are named by replacing the *–ane* ending with *-yl*.
      - Example: $CH_4$ is meth*ane*, and a $-CH_3$ group is a meth*yl* group.
  - When two or more substituents are present, list them in alphabetical order.
    - When there are two or more of the same substituent, the number of that type of substituent is indicated by a prefix: (i.e., "dimethyl" indicates two methyl group substituents).

### Cycloalkanes[15]

- Alkanes that form rings are called **cycloalkanes.**
- Cyclopropane and cyclobutane are strained because the C–C–C bond angles in the ring are less than the 109.5° required for a tetrahedral geometry.
  - Because of the strain in the ring, cyclopropane is very reactive.

### Reactions with Alkanes

- The C–C and C–H bonds are very strong.
  - Therefore, alkanes are very unreactive.
- At room temperature alkanes do not react with acids, bases, or strong oxidizing agents.
- Alkanes do undergo *combustion* in air (making them good fuels):

$$2C_2H_6(g) + 7O_2(g) \rightarrow 4CO_2(g) + 6H_2O(l) \qquad \Delta H = -2855 \text{ kJ}$$

## 25.4 Unsaturated Hydrocarbons

### Alkenes[16,17,18,19]

---

[12] Figure 25.6 from MediaPortfolio

[13] "A Simple Method of Drawing Stereoisomers from Complicated Symmetrical Structures" from Further Readings

[14] Table 25.2 from MediaPortfolio and Transparency Pack

[15] Figure 25.7 from MediaPortfolio

[16] Figure 25.10 from MediaPortfolio

[17] Figure 25.11 from MediaPortfolio and Transparency Pack

[18] "*cis*-2-Butene" 3-D Model from MediaPortfolio

[19] "*trans*-2-Butene" 3-D Model from MediaPortfolio

- Alkenes are unsaturated hydrocarbons that contain C and H atoms and at least one C-C double bond.
- The simplest alkenes are $H_2C{=}CH_2$ (ethene) and $CH_3CH{=}CH_2$ (propene):
  - Their common names are ethylene and propylene.
- Alkenes are named in the same way as alkanes with the suffix *-ene* replacing the *-ane* in alkanes.
  - The location of the double bond is indicated by a number.
  - If a substance has two or more double bonds, the number of double bonds is indicated with a prefix .
- **Geometric isomers** are possible in alkenes since there is no rotation about a C=C $\pi$ bond.
  - Note that the overlap between orbitals is above and below the plane of the $\sigma$ bonds.
  - As the C–C bond begins to rotate (moving from *cis* to *trans*) the overlap decreases.
  - At 90° the $\pi$ bond breaks completely.
    - Therefore, there is no "free" rotation about a $\pi$ bond.
  - Therefore, *cis* and *trans* isomers do not readily interconvert.

## Alkynes

- Alkynes are hydrocarbons with one or more C≡C bond.
  - The triple bond has one $\sigma$ and two $\pi$ bonds between two C atoms.
- Ethyne (acetylene) is the simplest alkyne: HC≡CH.
- Alkynes are named in the same way as alkenes with the suffix *-yne* replacing the *-ene* for alkenes.

## Addition Reactions of Alkenes and Alkynes[20]

- The dominant reactions for alkenes and alkynes are **addition reactions.**
  - They involve the addition of something to the two atoms that form the double or triple bond.
    - Example: The addition of a halogen (bromine) to ethylene:

$$H_2C{=}CH_2 + Br_2 \rightarrow H_2BrC{-}CBrH_2$$

    - Note that the C–C $\pi$ bond has been replaced by two C–Br $\sigma$ bonds.
  - A common addition reaction is *hydrogenation*:

$$CH_3CH{=}CHCH_3 + H_2 \rightarrow CH_3CH_2CH_2CH_3$$

    - Hydrogenation requires high temperatures and pressures as well as the presence of a catalyst (e.g., Ni, Pt, Pd).
    - Note that the alkene is converted to an alkane.
  - Another common addition reaction involves the addition of hydrogen halides or water across the $\pi$ bond:

$$CH_2{=}CH_2 + HBr \rightarrow CH_3CH_2Br$$
$$CH_2{=}CH_2 + H_2O \rightarrow CH_3CH_2OH$$

- Alkynes are also capable of addition reactions.

## Mechanism of Addition Reactions[21]

- The *mechanism* involved in addition reactions is hypothesized to proceed in 2 steps.
- Consider the addition of HBr to 2-butene ($CH_3CH{=}CHCH_3$):
  - Step 1 (rate-determining) involves the transfer of a proton from HBr to one of the alkene carbons.
  - Step 2 involves addition of $Br^-$ to the positively charged carbon center generated in the first step.
- The energy profile for this reaction shows an energy minimum between the two steps.
  - This corresponds to the energies of the intermediate species.
- The electron shifts involved in such reactions are often shown with curved arrows.

## Aromatic Hydrocarbons[22,23]

---

[20] "Addition Reactions of Alkenes" Activity from MediaPortfolio

[21] Figure 25.12 from MediaPortfolio and Transparency Pack

[22] Figure 25.13 from MediaPortfolio

- Aromatic structures are formally related to benzene ($C_6H_6$).
  - Many aromatic compounds are given common names (e.g., naphthalene, toluene, anthracene).
- Benzene is a planar symmetrical molecule.
- The delocalized $\pi$ electrons are usually represented as a circle in the center of the ring.
- Benzene is not reactive because of the stability associated with the delocalized $\pi$ electrons.
- Even though they contain $\pi$ bonds, aromatic hydrocarbons undergo **substitution reactions** more readily than addition reactions.
  - In a substitution reaction, one atom of a molecule is removed and replaced or substituted by another atom or group of atoms.
  - Example: If benzene is treated with nitric acid in the presence of sulfuric acid (catalyst), nitrobenzene is produced.
    - Under some conditions, more than one nitro group may be added to the benzene.
    - If two nitro groups are added, three possible isomers may be formed: *-ortho*, *-meta*, and –*para-*dinitrobenzene.
  - Another type of substitution reaction is a *Friedel-Crafts reaction*, in which alkyl groups can be substituted onto an aromatic ring by reaction with an alkyl halide in the presence of aluminum chloride (catalyst).

## 25.5 Functional Groups: Alcohols and Ethers[24]

- Hydrocarbons are relatively unreactive.
- For an organic molecule to be reactive it needs something additional.
- A site of reactivity in an organic molecule is called a *functional group.* Functional groups determine the chemistry of a molecule.
- The simplest functional groups are $\pi$ electrons.
  - C=C double bonds and C≡C triple bonds are functional groups.
- Other functional groups contain elements other than C or H (heteroatoms).
- Chemists usually use R, R', R", etc., to represent alkyl groups.

### Alcohols (R-OH)[25,26]

- **Alcohols** are derived from hydrocarbons and contain –OH (*hydroxyl* or *alcohol*) groups.
- The names are derived from the hydrocarbon name with *-ol* replacing the *-ane* suffix.
  - Example: eth*ane* becomes ethan*ol*.
- Because the O–H bond is polar and can participate in hydrogen bonding, alcohols are more water soluble than alkanes.
- Consider the properties of some representative alcohols:
  - $CH_3OH$, methanol, is used as a gasoline additive and a fuel.
    - Methanol is produced by the reaction of CO with hydrogen under high pressure and high temperature:

$$CO(g) + 2H_2(g) \rightarrow CH_3OH(g)$$

  - Ethanol is produced by the fermentation of carbohydrates.
    - Ethanol is the alcohol found in alcoholic beverages.
  - Polyhydroxy alcohols (polyols) contain more than one –OH group per molecule (e.g., ethylene glycol used as antifreeze).
  - Aromatic alcohols can also be formed (e.g., phenol).
    - Note that aromatic alcohols are weak acids.

---

[23] "Chemistry in the Dyeing of Eggs" from Further Readings
[24] Table 25.4 from MediaPortfolio and Transparency Pack
[25] Figure 25.14 from MediaPortfolio and Transparency Pack
[26] "Oxidation of Alcohol by $Mn_2O_7$" from Live Demonstrations

- Cholesterol is a physiologically important alcohol.

### Ethers (R–O–R')

- Compounds in which two hydrocarbons are linked by an oxygen are called **ethers**.
- Ethers can be formed by a dehydration reaction:

$$CH_3CH_2\text{–}OH + H\text{–}OCH_2CH_3 \rightarrow CH_3CH_2\text{–}O\text{–}CH_2CH_3 + H_2O$$

  - This *condensation reaction* involves the removal of a water molecule from two molecules of alcohol.
- Ethers are commonly used as solvents.
  - Common examples are diethyl ether and tetrahydrofuran (a cyclic ether).

## 25.6 Compounds with a Carbonyl Group

- The **carbonyl group** is C=O.

### Aldehydes and Ketones[27]

- **Aldehydes** must have at least one H atom attached to the carbonyl C:

R–CHO

- **Ketones** must have two C atoms attached to the carbonyl C:

R–COR'

- Aldehydes and ketones are prepared by the oxidation of alcohols.
- Ketones are less reactive than aldehydes and are used as solvents.
  - A common example is acetone.
- Other examples of molecules that contain aldehydes or ketones are vanilla and cinnamon flavorings.

The ketones carvone and camphor are responsible for the flavors of spearmint and caraway, respectively.

### Carboxylic Acids[28]

- **Carboxylic acids** contain a carbonyl group with an –OH attached.
- The *carboxyl* functional group is –COOH:

R–COOH

- Common names of carboxylic acids reflect their origins (e.g., formic acid was first extracted from ants, the Latin *formica* means "ant").
- Carboxylic acids are generally weak acids.
  - Typical carboxylic acids are found in spinach (oxalic acid), vinegar (acetic acid), vitamin C (ascorbic acid), aspirin (acetylsalicylic acid), and citrus fruits (citric acid).
- Carboxylic acids can be prepared by oxidizing alcohols that contain a $–CH_2OH$ group.
  - Example: Oxidation of ethanol ($CH_3CH_2OH$) to acetic acid ($CH_3COOH$) is responsible for the souring of wines.
- Acetic acid can be prepared by reacting methanol with CO in the presence of a catalyst.
  - This kind of reaction is called *carbonylation*.

### Esters[29,30,31]

- **Esters** can be prepared by condensation reactions involving a carboxylic acid and an alcohol; the products are the ester and water.
- Esters contain –COOR groups:

R–COOR'

---

[27] The Disappearing Coffee Cup" from Live Demonstrations
[28] Figure 25.17 from MediaPortfolio and Transparency Pack
[29] "Ester, What's in My Food?" from Further Readings
[30] "Making Canned Heat" from Live Demonstrations
[31] "Trans Fatty Acids" from Further Readings

- Esters are named using the alcohol part first and then the acid part.
  - Example: The ester formed from ethanol and acetic acid is ethyl acetate.
- Esters tend to have very pleasant characteristic odors and are often used as food flavorings and scents.
  - Some common esters are: benzocaine (used in some sunburn lotions), ethyl acetate (a component of some nail polish removers), vegetable oils, polyester thread, and aspirin.
- In the presence of base, esters hydrolyze (the molecule splits into acid and alcohol).
  - **Saponification** is the hydrolysis of an ester in the presence of a base.
  - This process is used in the production of soaps from animal fats or vegetable oils.
    - Soap is made by heating fats or oils in a strong base (NaOH).
      - The long-chain carboxylic acid and alcohol components of the fats are released.
      - The soap made from this process consists of sodium salts of the long-chain carboxylic acids called fatty acids.

### Amines and Amides

- *Amines* are organic bases.
- Just as alcohols can be thought of as organic forms of water, amines can be thought of organic forms of ammonia.
  - They have the general formula $R_3N$ where R may be H or a hydrocarbon group.
    - Examples of organic amines are ethylamine ($CH_3CH_2NH_2$), triethylamine ($(CH_3)_3N$), and aniline ($C_6H_5\text{–}NH_2$).
- Amides are composites of carbonyl and amine functionalities.

## 25.7 Chirality in Organic Chemistry[32,33,34,35]

- Recall that molecules whose mirror images are nonsuperimposable are **chiral.**
  - Compounds containing carbon atoms with four different attached groups are inherently chiral.
- Chemists use the labels *R*– and *S*– to distinguish between these *enantiomers*.
  - The physical properties of enantiomers are generally identical.
  - Enantiomers have identical chemical properties if the molecules are reacting with reagents that are nonchiral.
    - Enantiomers exhibit different chemical properties in a chiral environment.
- A mixture of two enantiomers present in the same quantity is called a *racemic* mixture.
- Some molecules have more than one chiral center.
  - Examples include tartaric acid (found as crystalline deposits in wine) and some of the amino acids found in proteins.

## 25.8 Introduction of Biochemistry[36,37]

- The biosphere is the part of the Earth containing living organisms.
- Biochemical molecules tend to be very large and difficult to synthesize.
- Organisms build biochemical molecules from the smaller molecules available in the biosphere.
- Living organisms are highly ordered.
  - Therefore, living organisms have very low entropy.
  - Living systems must continually resist the tendency to become less ordered!
- Many biologically important molecules are polymers, called **biopolymers**.

---

[32] Figure 25.19 from MediaPortfolio and Transparency Pack
[33] Figure 25.20 from MediaPortfolio and Transparency Pack
[34] "Chirality" Animation from MediaPortfolio
[35] "Optical Activity" Animation from MediaPortfolio
[36] "Icie Macy Hoobler: Pioneer Woman Biochemist" from Further Readings
[37] "Why Teach Biochemistry" from Further Readings

- Biopolymers fall into three broad classes:
  - Proteins.
  - Polysaccharides (carbohydrates).
  - Nucleic acids.

## 25.9 Proteins

### Amino Acids[38,39,40,41]

- **Proteins** are macromolecules present in all cells.
- They are made up of building blocks called **α-amino acids**.
- At normal physiological pH, amino acids are present in aqueous solution as dipolar ions called zwitterions.
  - A zwitterion has both positive and negative charges in one molecule.
    - The carboxyl group is deprotonated ($-COO^-$) and the amino group is protonated ($-NH_3^+$).
- There are about 20 different amino acids that are used to synthesize proteins in biological systems.
  - These amino acids differ with respect to the nature of the R-group attached to their α-carbon.
  - Our bodies can synthesize about 10 of these amino acids in quantities sufficient to meet our needs.
  - The other 10 amino acids must be ingested; these are called *essential amino acids*.
- The α-carbon in all amino acids except glycine is chiral (has four different groups attached to it).
- The two enantiomeric forms of amino acids are often called *D*- and *L*-amino acids.
  - *L*-amino acids are used to synthesize proteins in living organisms.

### Polypeptides and Proteins

- Proteins are polyamides.
- When formed from amino acids, each amide group is called a **peptide bond**.
- Peptides are formed by condensation of the $-COOH$ group of one amino acid with the $-NH_2$ group of another amino acid.
- The acid involved in the peptide bond is named first.
  - Example: If a dipeptide is formed from alanine and glycine so that the $-COOH$ group of glycine reacts with the $-NH_2$ group of alanine, then the dipeptide is called *glycylalanine*.
  - Glycylalanine is abbreviated using a standard three-letter abbreviation for each amino acid, starting with the amino acid with the unreacted amino group.
    - Thus glycylalanine is abbreviated as gly-ala.
- **Polypeptides** are formed when a large number of amino acids are linked together by peptide bonds.
  - Proteins are polypeptides with molecular weights between 6000 and 50 million amu.

### Protein Structure[42,43]

- The arrangement or sequence of amino acids along a protein chain is called the protein's **primary structure** or primary sequence.
  - A change in one amino acid can alter the biochemical behavior of the protein.
    - An example of such a change is found in the disease sickle-cell anemia.
    - This disease results from a single amino acid substitution on two of the subunits of hemoglobin.

---

[38] Figure 25.21 from MediaPortfolio and Transparency Pack
[39] Figure 25.22 from MediaPortfolio and Transparency Pack
[40] "Proteins and Amino Acids" Animation from MediaPortfolio
[41] "Enantiomers of Alanine" 3-D Model from MediaPortfolio
[42] Figure 25.24 from MediaPortfolio and Transparency Pack
[43] "Reversible Oxygenation of Oxygen Transport Proteins" from Further Readings

- **Secondary structure** refers to the regular arrangement of segments of the protein chain.
  - One common secondary structure is the **α-helix**.
    - In an α-helix, hydrogen bonds between N–H groups and carbonyl groups hold the helix in place.
    - The pitch (distance between coils) and diameter ensure that no bond angles are strained and the N–H and carbonyl functional groups are optimized for H–bonding.
  - Another common secondary structure is the β-pleated sheet.
- **Tertiary structure** is the three-dimensional structure of the protein.
  - There are two broad categories of tertiary structure:
    - *Globular proteins*: proteins that fold into a compact, roughly spherical shape, are soluble in water and mobile in cells.
      - Globular proteins generally have nonstructural functions (e.g., enzymes).
    - *Fibrous proteins*: proteins that often feature long coils that align themselves in a fairly parallel fashion to give rise to water-insoluble fibers.
      - Fibrous proteins often play structural roles (e.g., components of hair, muscle, tendons).
  - The tertiary structure is stabilized by a variety of interactions.
    - In general, polar groups on the protein tend to be found on the surface of the protein while nonpolar groups tend to be tucked away within the molecule, away from the aqueous environment.
    - The polar groups interact with solvent and other polar molecules through ion-dipole, dipole-dipole or hydrogen bonding interactions.

## 25.10 Carbohydrates[44,45,46,47,48,49,50,51]

- **Carbohydrates** have the empirical formula $C_x(H_2O)_y$.
  - Carbohydrate means "hydrate of carbon".
  - The most abundant carbohydrate is **glucose**, $C_6H_{12}O_6$.
- Carbohydrates are polyhydroxy aldehydes and ketones.
  - Glucose is a six-carbon aldehyde sugar (aldose); *fructose* is a six-carbon ketone sugar (ketose).
  - One of the alcohol groups of glucose can react with the aldehyde group to form a six-membered ring.
  - Most glucose molecules are present in the ring form.
    - Note that the six-membered rings are not planar.
  - Depending on how the ring forms, we can have one of two different isomers.
    - Consider the groups on carbons 1 and 5:
      - If the $-CH_2OH$ group on carbon 5 and the –OH group on carbon 1 are on opposite sides of the ring, then we have the α form of glucose (α-anomer)
      - If they are on the same side of the ring, then we have β form of glucose (β-anomer).
  - The α- and β- forms of glucose are very different compounds.
    - Although these differences may seem trivial, they are not.

---

44 Figure 25.26 from MediaPortfolio
45 Figure 25.27 from MediaPortfolio and Transparency Pack
46 "The Use of Stick Figures to Visualize Fischer Projections" from Further Readings
47 "Carbohydrate Stereochemistry" from Further Readings
48 "A New Method to Convert the Fischer Projection of Monosaccharide to the Haworth Projection" from Further Readings
49 "'Absolutely' Simple Stereochemistry" from Further Readings
50 "The Biochemistry of Brewing" from Further Readings
51 "An Easy Way to convert a Fischer Projection into a Zigzag Representation" from Further Readings

- For example, the difference between these two forms is the key to the difference in the structures of starch and cellulose.

### Disaccharides[52,53]

- Glucose and fructose are **monosaccharides,** simple sugars that cannot be broken down by hydrolysis with aqueous acids.
- **Disaccharides** are sugars formed by the condensation of two monosaccharides.
  - Examples:
    - Sucrose (table sugar) is formed by the condensation of glucose and fructose.
    - Lactose (milk sugar) is formed by the condensation of galactose and glucose.
  - Sucrose is about six times sweeter than lactose, a little sweeter than glucose and about half as sweet as fructose.
- Disaccharides can be converted into monosaccharides by treatment with acid in aqueous solution.
  - For example, when sucrose is hydrolyzed it gives rise to a mixture of fructose and glucose, called *invert sugar*.

### Polysaccharides[54,55,56,57]

- **Polysaccharides** are formed by condensation of several monosaccharide units.
- There are many different types.
  - Examples of polysaccharides based on glucose: starch, glycogen, and cellulose.
- The term **starch** refers to a group of polysaccharides found in plants (e.g., corn, potatoes, wheat, rice).
  - Starch consists of many glucose units joined by linkages of the $\alpha$ form.
  - Humans are capable of digesting starch; it is enzymatically hydrolyzed to glucose during digestion.
- **Glycogen** is a starch-like polysaccharide synthesized by muscle and liver tissues.
  - In the muscle glycogen is an important source of quick energy.
  - In the liver glycogen represents a storage form of glucose for the body.
    - The liver is also maintains the body's blood glucose concentration.
- **Cellulose** is a polysaccharide that is the major structural unit of plants.
  - For example, wood is approximately 50% cellulose.
  - Cellulose consists of glucose units, however, unlike starch, the glucose units present are linked in the $\beta$ form.
    - Humans lack the enzymes required to hydrolyze cellulose.
    - Grazing animals such as cattle harbor bacteria in their digestive tract.
      - These bacteria have enzymes (cellulases) that hydrolyze cellulose.
      - The cattle are thus able to utilize the digested cellulose for food.

## 25.11 Nucleic Acids[58,5960,61,62,63,64,65,66]

---

52 "βrand the Name with the Linkage of the Same" from Further Readings
53 Figure 25.28 from MediaPortfolio
54 Figure 25.29 from MediaPortfolio
55 Figure 25.30 from MediaPortfolio
56 "A Variation of the Starch-Iodine Clock Reaction" from Live Demonstrations
57 Figure 25.31 from MediaPortfolio and Transparency Pack
58 "Rosalind Franklin: From Coal to DNA to Plant Viruses" from Further Readings
59 Figure 25.32 from MediaPortfolio and Transparency Pack
60 Figure 25.33 from MediaPortfolio and Transparency Pack
61 Figure 25.34 from MediaPortfolio and Transparency Pack
62 "DNAmonic" from Further Readings

- **Nucleic acids** carry genetic information.
  - **DNA (deoxyribonucleic acids)** have molecular weights around 6 – 16 x $10^6$ amu.
  - **RNA (ribonucleic acids)** have molecular weights around 20,000 to 40,000 amu.
- Nucleic acids are made up of monomers called **nucleotides.**
  - A nucleotides consist of three parts:
    - A five-carbon sugar.
      - DNA and RNA have different sugars (*deoxy*ribose vs. ribose).
    - A nitrogen-containing organic base.
      - Five bases are found in DNA and RNA:
        - Adenine (A),
        - Guanine (G),
        - Cytosine (C),
        - Thymine (T found in DNA only), and
        - Uracil (U found in RNA only).
    - A phosphoric acid unit.
- Nucleic acids form by the condensation of nucleotides (the phosphoric acid condenses with the O–H group of the sugar).
- DNA consists of two deoxyribonucleic acid strands wound together in a **double helix**.
  - The sugar-phosphate chains are wrapped around the outside of the DNA molecule.
  - Complementary base pairs are formed between bases on each chain.
    - The complementary base pairs are held together by London-dispersion interactions and hydrogen bonding.
      - The structures of T and A make them ideal hydrogen-bonding partners.
        - Two hydrogen bonds form between T and A.
      - The same is true for C and G.
        - Three hydrogen bonds form between C and G.
- During cell division the DNA double helix unwinds.
  - Each strand serves as a template for the replication of a new strand.
  - Optimized hydrogen bonding helps to ensure that the correct bases are used along the new strand.
  - The newly synthesized DNA contains a sequence identical to that of the original molecule.
  - This allows genetic information to be preserved during cell division.

---

[63] "A Simple Demonstration of How Intermolecular Forces Make DNA Helical" from Further Readings
[64] Figure 25.35 from MediaPortfolio and Transparency Pack
[65] Figure 25.36 from MediaPortfolio
[66] "DNA" 3-D Model from MediaPortfolio

## Further Readings:

1. Raymond B. Seymour, "Alkanes: Abundant, Pervasive, Important, and Essential," *J. Chem. Educ.*, Vol. 66, **1989**, 59–63.

2. A. Haudrechy, "A Simple Method of Drawing Stereoisomers from Complicated Symmetrical Structures," *J. Chem. Educ.*, Vol. 77, **2000, 864–866.**

3. Robert C. Mebane and Thomas R. Rybolt, "Chemistry in the Dyeing of Eggs," *J. Chem. Educ.*, Vol. 64, **1987**, 291–293.

4. Michele Clarke, Ann Brown, Dianne N. Epp, Mary Gallup, Jeffrey R. Wilson, and Judith A. Wuerthele, "Ester, What's in My Food?" *J. Chem. Educ.*, Vol. 63, **1986**, 1050–1051.

5. Ellin Doyle, "Trans Fatty Acids," *J. Chem. Educ.*, Vol. 74, **1997**, 1030–1032.

6. Sheldon J. Kopperl, "Icie Macy Hoobler: Pioneer Woman Biochemist," *J. Chem. Educ.*, Vol. **65, 1988**, 97–98.

7. Gil Downs, "Why Teach Biochemistry?" *J. Chem. Educ.*, Vol. 64, **1987**, 339-??

8. C. M. Drain and Barry B. Corden, "Reversible Oxygenation of Oxygen Transport Proteins," *J. Chem. Educ.*, Vol. 64, **1987**, 441–443.

9. Charles L. Bering, "The Biochemistry of Brewing," *J. Chem. Educ.*, Vol. 65, **1988**, 519–521.

10. Laurie S. Starkey, "The Use of Stick Figures to Visualize Fischer Projections," *J. Chem. Educ.*, Vol. 78, **2001**, 1486.

11. Qing-zhi Zhang and Shen-song Zhang, "A New Method to Convert the Fischer Projection of Monosaccharide to the Haworth Projection," *J. Chem. Educ.*, Vol. 76, **1999**, 799–801.

12. Robert S. Shallenberger and Wanda J. Wienen, "Carbohydrate Stereochemistry," *J. Chem. Educ.*, Vol. 66, **1989**, 67–73.

13. Philip S. Beauchamp, "'Absolutely' Simple Stereochemistry," *J. Chem. Educ.*, Vol. 61, **1984, 666–667.**

14. Sandra Signorella and Luis F. Sala, "An Easy Way to Convert a Fischer Projection into a Zigzag Representation," *J. Chem. Educ.*, Vol. 68, **1991**, 105–106.

15. James M. Garrett, "βrand the Name with the Linkage of the Same," *J. Chem. Educ.*, Vol. 61, **1984**, 665. A mnemonic for remembering the configuration of the glucosidic linkage in disaccharides.

16. Maureen M. Julian, "Rosalind Franklin: From Coal to DNA to Plant Viruses," *J. Chem. Educ.*, Vol. 60, **1983**, 660–662.

17. A. B. Wolbarst, "DNAmonic," *J. Chem. Educ.*, Vol. 56, **1979**, 733. A mnemonic device for base-pairing in DNA is suggested: Pure Silver Taxi (purine: Ag; T=A, G=C).

18. Michael F. Bruist, Wayne L. Smith and Galen Mell, "A Simple Demonstration of How Intermolecular Forces Make DNA Helical," *J. Chem. Educ.*, Vol. 75, **1998**, 53–55.

## Live Demonstrations:

1. Lee R. Summerlin and James L. Ealy, Jr., "Oxidation of Alcohol by $Mn_2O_7$," *Chemical Demonstrations, A Sourcebook for Teachers* (Washington: American Chemical Society, **1985**), pp. 103–104.

2. Lee. R. Summerlin,, Christie L. Borgford, and Julie B. Ealy, "The Disappearing Coffee Cup," *Chemical Demonstrations, A Sourcebook for Teachers, Volume 2* (Washington: American Chemical Society, **1988**), p. 96. A polystyrene coffee cup is "melted" in a pool of acetone.

3. Lee. R. Summerlin,, Christie L. Borgford, and Julie B. Ealy, "Making Canned Heat," *Chemical Demonstrations, A Sourcebook for Teachers, Volume 2* (Washington: American Chemical Society, **1988**), pp. 111–112. Saponification of stearic acid in the presence of alcohol is used to prepare a solid fuel--canned heat.

4. Lee R. Summerlin, Christie L. Borgford, and Julie B. Ealy, "A Variation of the Starch-Iodine Clock Reaction," *Chemical Demonstrations, A Sourcebook for Teachers, Volume 2* (Washington: American Chemical Society, **1987**), pp. 147–148.